GENERAL INTRODUCTION TO ETHICS

THE MACMILLAN COMPANY
NEW YORK · BOSTON · CHICAGO · DALLAS
ATLANTA · SAN FRANCISCO

MACMILLAN & CO., Limited
LONDON · BOMBAY · CALCUTTA
MELBOURNE

THE MACMILLAN COMPANY
OF CANADA, Limited
TORONTO

GENERAL INTRODUCTION TO ETHICS

BY

WILLIAM KELLEY WRIGHT, Ph.D.

PROFESSOR OF PHILOSOPHY IN DARTMOUTH COLLEGE

New York

THE MACMILLAN COMPANY

1931

SET UP, ELECTROTYPED, AND PRINTED BY T. MOREY & SON

IN THE UNITED STATES OF AMERICA

TO THE DARTMOUTH MEN

who have elected my courses in Ethics,
since I came to the College in 1916.

PREFACE

The aim of this book is to present a comprehensive view of the different fields of Ethics of most importance for the understanding of the moral outlook and problems of our own time. The volume accordingly begins with a Part entitled "Comparative Ethics", which contains an abstract outline of moral and social evolution in general, and a more concrete account of the sources of our modern occidental moral consciousness. Succeeding Parts discuss various phases of the psychology of ethics, systematic ethical theory, the ethics of the political state, the economic order and the family, and the significance of ethics in relation to metaphysics and religion.

While all this is a considerable journey to traverse in the ordinary college course of forty to forty-five class exercises, experience has proved that this can be accomplished if time is carefully planned. This text could be covered entire in such a course, or one Part could be left out in order to allow more time for supplementary reading. The book has been written so that any entire Part (or either Division of Part I) can be omitted or taken up independently. The ideal arrangement, when practicable, would be to teach ethics in a three hour course running throughout the year; or in two successive and complementary one-semester courses, which would ordinarily be taken by the same students, but neither of which would necessarily presuppose the other. Parts I and III of this volume could be used in one semester, supplemented by readings in classical writers like Bentham, Mill, Spencer and Kant; while Parts II, IV, and V with supplementary readings from writers of our own time would do for the other. Numerous references for supplementary reading are given in the lists at the ends of the chapters, most of which have been tried out for this purpose and found satisfactory. The Notes, primarily intended for teachers, advanced students, and general readers not in attendance upon classes, contain additional references and some pedagogical suggestions.

There is little place for originality in an elementary text which attempts to give a general view of ethics as a whole. Attention may be called, however, to some details in the correlation of moral and social evolution with the advance from customary to reflective morality in Part I; to the interpretation of the virtues in terms of sentiments in Chapter IX, especially to the virtues of economy and reverence; to the working compromise between Utilitarianism and Eudæmonism in Chapters XIII and XIV, which is empirically justified by the combined use of the two in Part IV; to the canon of distributive justice in Chapter XVI; and to various thoughts on metaphysics and religion in the last chapter. The temptation to expand the discussion of these topics had to be resisted, as the purpose of the volume is to give a general introduction to ethics as a whole, and not to defend personal theories.

I owe my first interest in ethics to undergraduate courses in the nineties with Dr. Warner Fite and Mr. Addison Webster Moore, then young instructors at the University of Chicago. My graduate work in ethics was taken with Professor James Hayden Tufts, under whose supervision I wrote my doctoral dissertation on an ethical subject, and in whose department I was later an instructor. I owe much to other senior colleagues among whom mention must be made of Professors George Herbert Mead, Edward Scribner Ames, Frank Thilly, Frank Chapman Sharp, Professor (now President) James Rowland Angell, Professor (later President) Sidney Edward Mezes, Professor (now Chancellor) Ernest H. Lindley, and Professor James Edwin Creighton now of beloved memory. My obligations to Professors William McDougall and Leonard T. Hobhouse can be noted in almost every chapter. Other obligations are made evident in the Notes, and by the lists of References at the ends of the chapters. My greatest debt, after all, is to my students in ethics, to whom this volume is dedicated. Their keen questions and criticisms have kept me awake, and their enthusiasm has been a constant inspiration and refreshment. Suggestions offered by the readers of the Macmillan Company have helped. Mrs. Adair Williams has typed the manuscript with meticulous accuracy. My wife has given much valuable assistance with manuscript and proof; if the book is now intelligible, it is chiefly due to her.

W. K. W.

HANOVER, NEW HAMPSHIRE,
May, 1929.

CONTENTS

INTRODUCTION

PART I

COMPARATIVE ETHICS

DIVISION A. SOCIAL AND MORAL EVOLUTION

xi

PART II

PSYCHOLOGY AND ETHICS

PART III

SYSTEMATIC ETHICS

PART IV

POLITICAL AND SOCIAL ETHICS

PART V

METAPHYSICS AND RELIGION

INTRODUCTION

CHAPTER I

THE SCOPE OF ETHICS

I. Moral Judgments

Throughout history, men have been keenly interested in moral issues. A discussion always waxes interesting when it raises questions of justice and fair play, of honor and loyalty, of the rights and duties of individuals, classes of society, or nations.

We are all constantly expressing judgments regarding our own conduct and that of others. Some acts and motives we judge praiseworthy and good; others we deem blameworthy and wrong. We admire the characters of some persons and wish that we were more like them; other persons we regard with aversion and disapproval. This man, this labor union, this church, or this nation we applaud for standing courageously for rights that ought to be maintained at whatever cost. That woman, that corporation, that secret society, that state, we condemn for distasteful or immodest demeanor, for unfair competition, for racial and religious intolerance, for bad faith in diplomatic relations. Such judgments, passed upon ourselves or other persons or groups, are *moral judgments*.

In the present generation, in America, there is less unanimity than in the past, respecting moral judgments. To be sure, every age has to some extent been one of transition. No generation have ever seen moral issues precisely as their fathers did. But in no previous period in American history have the moral judgments of the past been subjected to so extensive criticism and revision.

Let us glance at some illustrations. Alcoholic intemperance has received more sweeping condemnation than ever before,

3

and a large part, at least, of public opinion has sanctioned drastic legal steps for the prevention of such misconduct. On the other hand, the severe moral judgments of our ancestors regarding amusements, sabbath observance, and like conventions, have been modified. No generation in modern times have seen such changes in the conduct expected of women—what conventions they shall observe in public, what part they shall take in social, political, and economic activities. Never before in America have the rights and duties of the business man, the employer of labor, and the investor of capital been so keenly discussed and subjected to so much regulation by law and public opinion. In no previous age has the status of the laboring man become so greatly altered, and in few ages have farmers been so self-conscious as a class. During recent years we have passed through violent fluctuations in public opinion regarding our moral rights and obligations as a nation in relationship to the rest of the world. At first we thought we ought to remain neutral in the World War; later we decided that it was our duty to enter the war on the side of the Entente. We then found military conscription and regulation of discussion by the press and by public speakers justifiable in order to secure moral solidarity in the effort to win the war. Since peace has come again, the rights kept in abeyance during the conflict are asserted more vigorously than ever. Whether we can best serve humanity by adhering to our traditional policies, or whether we should enter into closer relations with other nations is still much in dispute. What respective positions shall be held by religion and science in our educational institutions is also a live moral issue. While preponderant American public opinion is still no doubt conservative, there probably has never been a time when the advocates of so many revolutionary changes in our economic structure, our form of government, our religious beliefs and practices, and even our family system, have succeeded in attracting attention and in organizing zealous groups of supporters.

At a time, therefore, when so many novel situations call

for moral decisions, a scientific study of moral judgments is of special importance. Whoever wishes to be an effective citizen of our age, and to make his life successful in service of self and society, will profit by it.

A precise definition of moral judgments is impracticable at the outset. Every one, however, can readily understand, from his own experience and observation, what is meant by them. Many experiences are easily recognizable, that cannot be defined in a popular way. This is true of elementary sense qualities. It would be difficult to define "red", "green", "sour", "sweet", "cold", or "pain"; but all know to what sensations these words refer. So it is with moral judgments. A moral judgment is never passed upon the processes of inanimate nature (unless they are personified and given human attributes, through savage superstition or poetic imagination). Moral judgments are not passed upon the behavior of animals. Such processes and behavior are not, properly speaking, human conduct, whereas moral judgments are confined to human conduct. Moral judgments are passed upon the actions of children, with allowance for their ages and mental capacities.

In the study of moral judgments, the adjective "moral" is used by ethical writers in two different ways. *In the wider sense, "moral"* is opposed to *"unmoral"* (of which *"nonmoral"* and *"amoral"* are synonyms). Most of our actions in the course of a day are unmoral. It was right to perform them, it would have been equally right not to have performed them, or to have performed them in a different way. No moral issue is involved. Under ordinary circumstances, as Herbert Spencer remarks, it would be ethically indifferent (*i.e.*, unmoral) whether one chose to walk, on a summer's afternoon, to the waterfall or along the seashore.[1] But choice between the alternatives would be moral, and not unmoral, if one were accompanied by a friend who had explored the seashore but had not seen the waterfall, or whose strength one walk might be liable to over-tax. *In the narrower sense, "moral"* is opposed to *"immoral"*, good and right choices being moral, while bad and wrong choices are immoral. The choice whether or not to take the friend on the walk that would most please him, however made, would be a moral choice, using "moral" in the wider sense, for it could not be an unmoral choice. If it were decided to take the friend on the walk best suited to him, the decision would also be moral, using "moral" in the narrower sense. But if a person selfishly and knowingly chose the walk that might overtax his friend's strength, his conduct would clearly be immoral. Human conduct can therefore be classified in accordance with the following table:

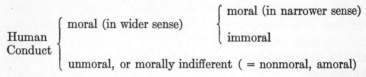

If the reader will keep in mind the two different senses in which the term "moral" is used in ethics, he will ordinarily have no trouble in determining in any given context which usage is employed. Since we all know, in a general way, what such terms as "good", "bad", "evil", "right," and "wrong" mean, it will be safe for the present to leave them undefined. Different schools in ethics attempt to define them in various ways, and some writers believe them to be ultimately indefinable. Such questions of ethical theory we shall consider in Part III.

II. Definition of Ethics

Ethics, or Moral Philosophy, may be defined in a provisional way, as *the scientific study of moral judgments.* There are various ways in which moral judgments can be studied, and so there are different divisions of ethics, as will be seen in the next section.

Ethics is here defined as a "scientific study", rather than as a "science". It cannot yet be claimed to have developed into a special science, in the sense of physics, biology, economics, and psychology. All the special sciences were branches of philosophy in the earlier stages of their development. Each became a separate science when a technique of some kind had been developed, by which investigation and reasoning could be practically tested, and conclusions could be regarded, at least for the time being, as established or refuted. Thus Galileo is credited with having made the new special science of physics possible, when he found a means of testing his theoretical reasoning regarding velocities by constructing an inclined plane at the tower of Pisa, rolling balls down it, and measuring the actual rate at which they fell. He had found a way of combining theoretical reasoning with practical experiment,—in other words, a technique. Each natural and social science has a more or less developed technique of its own, perhaps in no other instance so accurate as that of physics, but sufficient to enable investigators to test their hypotheses by direct observation, and so to accumulate considerable funds of generally accepted knowledge.

Until a technique has been developed in any particular field of human inquiry, the preliminary work has to be left to the philosophers. As "mother of the sciences", philosophy has venerable methods of her own, which enable her to make use of whatever information actually has been accumulated in any given field, and to illuminate this information with her own reflection on the nature of man and the universe. Philosophy in modern times has been glad to learn of her children, the special sciences. The methods, results, and general outlook achieved by each of them are carefully compared and correlated. A general picture of the nature of the universe, and the place of human activities in it, is thus achieved. Within this general setting a place is found for each of the separate disciplines still remaining within philosophy. Somewhat different general pictures of the world have been portrayed by philosophers of different contemporary schools—idealists, realists, pragmatists, and others. Accordingly, the setting of ethics within the picture has been variously conceived. All the interpretations are suggestive, as each contributes something that the others lack, and so enables us to understand better the significance of the moral life. But none has been entirely adequate or universally convincing. Rapid progress is now being made within the various divisions of ethics, and the time may come when ethics shall gain a technique of her own, and become a younger sister of political economy, political science, sociology, psychology, and education, all of which have become independent sciences within the last hundred years.

For the present, however, the words of Aristotle, prefatory to the first and greatest treatise that has ever borne the title of *Ethics*, still apply to works on the subject: "We must be content to indicate the truth roughly and in outline; and as our subjects are true generally, but not universally, we must be content to arrive at conclusions that are only generally true. It is right to receive the particular statements which are made in the same spirit; for an educated person will expect accuracy in each subject only so far as the nature of the subject allows." [2] So the beginner in Ethics must not expect too much. This subject cannot furnish him with a ready method for deciding all moral issues with mathematical exactness.

Nevertheless the serious student of Ethics will find his work both profitable and interesting to the highest degree. His understanding of moral problems will be widened, as he becomes acquainted with the thoughts of other men upon problems of good and evil, justice and injustice, virtue and vice, the rights and duties of the individual and of society. His critical faculties will be trained. He will know the reasons for his moral convictions, and also the reasons for the moral convictions of others. His reverence for duty will be deepened. On the whole, he will become more tolerant, but his moral judgments in becoming more discriminating will not become more lax. He will not confuse charity with condonation of vice and wrong. Far from finding that "to comprehend all is to forgive all", is a universal principle, he will learn that while sometimes to comprehend is to forgive, at other times it is to condemn with severity, though never with ignorance or injustice.

The study of Ethics will enable a person to understand better what his conscience is, how he acquired it, how far he is likely to be able to trust to its deliverances with safety, and how he can improve it and make it more intelligent. He will gain a clearer insight into his claims upon society, and the duties that he owes to society. He will learn to discriminate between the respects in which all individuals are mutually interdependent and those in which each is responsible for his own life, and ought to insist upon freedom of initiative. He will find that no essential moral principle depends upon the acceptance or rejection of any particular standpoint in religion or metaphysics. The same moral obligations toward society and self hold for theist and atheist, Jew and Christian, idealist and realist, absolutist and pragmatist, determinist and indeterminist. However, it will be seen that considerations based upon our moral judgments, in the author's opinion at least, favor faith in a moral world order, personal immortality, and a personal God. Finally, while a book on Ethics can by no means prescribe for anyone what should be his vocation in life, or his avocations, it can at least proffer some considerations, from the standpoints of self-realization, self-sacrifice, and service, that ought to help anyone in making such decisions.

III. Divisions of Ethics

The various divisions of Ethics rest upon no particular logical principle of division or classification. They represent, rather, the different fields in which, in view of the present state of human knowledge and interest, moral philosophers have undertaken studies of moral judgments. (The term "moral philosopher" is used in this volume for the specialist in ethics in preference to the more awkward term "ethicist".)

Comparative Ethics is *a study of the moral judgments of mankind in different periods of human history, and upon different levels of culture.* Now that human mental evolution is known to be an extension of animal behavior, there has been considerable interest in this side of ethics. We should like, if we could, to trace continuously the different stages in human moral evolution, from the first moral judgments of the most primitive men down to those of western civilized nations at the present time. This, of course, cannot be done with entire confidence. Too many chapters in the record are missing. Still, we know that the moral judgments of any age are closely connected with its social organization. And, in a broad way at least, the different stages in social evolution have been successfully outlined, and the characteristic moral judgments of each stage have been noted. In Part I, therefore, it will be the effort of this book to sketch the general course of human moral and social evolution, with emphasis upon those phases that have contributed most to the formation of the moral judgments generally accepted in occidental countries to-day. We shall be particularly concerned with the moral development of the ancient Hebrews, Greeks, and Romans, and the Christian church, inasmuch as our moral outlook still owes most to the contributions that have come down from these sources. On the other hand, we shall not discuss the developments in ethical theory and moral practice that have taken place in Egypt, Babylonia, Persia, Arabia, India, China, and Japan. While all these have high intrinsic merit and interest, and are useful for those who wish to study the Orient, they have had comparatively little influence on our western moral tradition.

The Psychology of Ethics is *a study of those phases of human consciousness and behavior that determine conduct and character, so far as these are moral or immoral.* The student of ethics is anxious to learn all he can from the psychologist about the ways in which impulses govern human conduct, how habits and sentiments are formed and broken, how virtues and vices go to make up human character, what selfhood and personality are, the part played by pleasure and emotion in human actions, the nature of conation and volition, and the relation of all these processes to reasoning. We obviously need to know how human conduct goes on psychologically before we can intelligently praise or condemn it, or consider how it can be made better. It is with these phases of psychology that Part II will accordingly be concerned.

Probably there is nothing in Psychology that is wholly without concern to the student of Ethics. It used to be said, that Psychology is concerned with a description of mental processes as such, while Ethics studies these processes in order to evaluate them, to determine whether they are right or wrong. Obviously it is impossible to evaluate any process without knowing how it actually goes on. However, much of the content of an ordinary text in Psychology is not of great moment to the moral philosopher. He gains little light on ethical problems, for instance, from a detailed study of the processes of sensation, or the various tests of intelligence, and not much more from meticulous analyses of the higher thought processes. The springs to human action are found rather in the affective and conative processes. Abnormal psychology has some significance for the advanced student of applied ethics, who is concerned with crime and punishment, with the determination of moral responsibility in doubtful cases, the moral education of persons of abnormally low intelligence, the reformation of moral degenerates, and like problems. In an introductory textbook, however, emphasis should be upon the conduct and moral judgments of ordinary human beings.

Systematic Ethics is the oldest branch of ethics, that to which the term was long exclusively applied. Ethics, as previously defined in this chapter, is the scientific study of moral judgments. The adjective "systematic" has a narrower connotation: it refers to *systems of philosophy*. The word Ethics in Greek is *tà ēthicá*, or *ēthicé*, or *ēthicè epistémē*, the study of *ēthŏs*, character. The latter word is connected with *ĕthos*, custom or habit. Morals, in the early stages of social evolution, are almost wholly customs regarded as obligatory. The Latin word *mores*, which sometimes means customs or habits and sometimes morals, illustrates the relationship. The singular of *mores* is *mos*, which refers to a habit of a person, or his general disposition, or his moral character. So moral philosophy (*philosophia moralis*) originally was the philosophical interpretation of custom and character.

Ever since the time of Plato, moral philosophers have sought to set forth an adequate philosophical interpretation of human conduct,—to formulate some all inclusive ideal for human endeavor, a *summum bonum* or highest good, which would serve as a criterion for right and wrong in all cases. Some have contended that the "good" is recognized intuitively, and that our moral sense or conscience enables us to recognize it without much effort. Others, the greatest of whom was Kant, have believed that some universal rule for moral judgments can be found, that will indicate what is right to do in all cases without exception. Still others deny that the "good" can be recognized by immediate intuition, or by deductive reasoning; we must carefully observe the consequences of actions, and judge right that which will in the long run further the best ends. Those of this last group who believe that the ultimate end or highest good is pleasure or happiness (conceived as a sum of pleasures) have been known as Utilitarians; while those of them who believe that the ultimate end is more inclusive, and comprehends character and other goods that cannot wholly be reduced to pleasure, have received various designations—the one adopted in this text is "Eudæmonism". The freedom of the will is another problem with which the great moral philosophers have been concerned: all have agreed that man is free in the sense that he is morally responsible; but determinists and indeterminists have advanced quite different theories as to the nature of freedom and moral responsibility. In Part III we shall study certain of the more important of these great classical systems, which throw light upon the nature of moral judgments, and the part that man can and should play in the world.

Political Ethics is the *study of moral judgments applied to the conduct of the state, including the rights and obligations of citizens and subjects.* The noun state and the adjective political in this definition are intended to apply to all governmental units,—precinct, town, city, county, "state" (in the American sense), national government,—and a world state, should one ever come into existence. Among the more important questions

of Political Ethics are those concerned with what rights and
duties the citizen holds with reference to the state, and the
state with reference to him. At the one extreme have been
those individualists who, like Spencer, thought of the state as
a kind of limited liability company, formed by the citizens to
perform a very restricted set of functions, like military and
naval defense, police protection, and the postal service. Individualists wish to afford each citizen as much freedom of
initiative as possible, and to limit state interference with
his activities to the minimum. At the other extreme have
been those who, like Plato, held the organic theory of the
state,—and believed individuals to be mutually interdependent
like the different organs of the human body. Those most disposed to this view at the present time favor more activities on
the part of the state for the promotion of the welfare of its
citizens than do the individualists—for instance, state regulation or ownership of railways and other means of transportation, of mines, forests, and other limited natural resources, and
even of factories and farms. Not all, or even the majority of
those who favor the organic theory go to such extremes, of
course. But most of them affirm that the close interdependence
of individuals upon one another and upon the state morally
justify a considerably larger amount of political control than is
exercised in this country at present. Probably the majority
of American thinkers are still individualists rather than believers in the organic theory of the state, but nearly all concede
the desirability of state interference in more instances than
did the individualists of earlier generations.

Another important set of problems of contemporary Political
Ethics deals with the basis of law and justice, with the reasons
why crimes are wrong, and why and how the state may rightfully punish those who commit them. Among the most serious
questions of our time are those dealing with the relations that
should prevail between national states, including the difficult
problems of how far a state, consisting of constantly changing
citizens and rulers, is accountable for treaties and other con-

duct in the sense in which an individual is, on what grounds it is
either its right or its duty to engage in war, the rules by which
warfare should be waged, the search for a moral equivalent of
war as a means for the development of character and the
settlement of international disputes, together with the moral
desirability of a world court, a federation or league of nations,
and a parliament of man. (Chapter XV.)

In relation to Political Science, the moral philosopher is concerned with the moral side of political issues. Ordinarily he
is not interested in the details of political structure or the mi-
nutiæ of law and government. He is, however, vitally concerned with the moral ideals of which a state is an institutional
expression, and with the morality of its undertakings. So, as
in the case of psychology, there is no detail of political science
or of law that might not sometime involve an important moral
issue, and so come within the domain of ethics. As a rule, the
author supposes, students of political ethics attach little importance to details of political machinery. The author, for instance, finds himself somewhat indifferent to agitation regarding the respective merits of short and long ballots, law making
by initiative and referendum or by legislatures, nomination of
candidates for office by caucuses or by primaries, and like issues.
Any fairly responsive form of machinery will achieve moral
ends in a community that is morally awake; none will do so in
one that is not.

Social Ethics is a rather vague term, hard to distinguish from
political ethics, which it overlaps. For that matter, all ethics
in a broad sense are social. When used in this book in distinction from political ethics, Social Ethics will mean *the study of
moral judgments regarding the relations of men in groups other
than the state.* Here enter the problems of distributive justice,
e.g., whether the correct solutions imply capitalism or collectivism. There is more wealth in existence to-day than ever
before and persons in every class are more prosperous in material goods and have more opportunities for education and culture than persons in the corresponding class ever knew in any

previous period of human history. However, the distribution of wealth and opportunity are quite unequal and in many respects hard to justify. We shall therefore have to consider the ethical basis of property rights, and how present injustices can best be corrected. Conservatives naturally are alarmed at any proposals to tamper with our present economic system; since the present condition of national wealth could easily be disturbed for the worse, it seems to them better to be very careful about making changes. A theoretically more just distribution of the total amount of wealth that could only be brought about by seriously reducing its bulk might actually benefit none, and be harmful to most. Radicals do not hesitate. They are eager to try experiments along the lines of state and guild socialism, coöperative societies, and other schemes in order to eliminate the "profit motive" in which they see the root of most social evils,—a motive which conservatives often regard as the source of all national and individual prosperity. (Chapter XVI.) In any event, whether we are radical or conservative, we are forced to recognize that the various professions and forms of business will, at least in the immediate future, continue to go on much as they do to-day. The Ethics applicable to each of them, as now organized, accordingly is of practical interest. (Chapter XVII.)

In considering such questions as these, Ethics is obviously dependent upon Economics. The economists can best determine what are the laws of the production, distribution, exchange, and consumption of wealth. In the light of this information, the moral philosopher tries to decide which of the different economic arrangements that these laws permit would be likely to produce the greatest amount of good.

Another topic in Social Ethics with which we shall be concerned is the Family, and the problems relating to it, such as marriage, the relations between the sexes, and the position of woman. Such questions need to be viewed historically. We must understand how and why monogamous marriage has superseded all other forms in the higher civilizations, before we can pass intelligent judgment upon proposals to alter our present laws and customs in any respects affecting the family. This is especially true regarding the rights and duties of husbands, wives, and children, the divorce problem, and our present standards of continence and chastity. Should women as a sex have the same or different rights and duties than men? What may women rightfully be expected to contribute to the solution of the problems of modern political, social, and domestic life? (Chapter XVIII.)

All problems of Political and Social Ethics are closely related to Sociology. So far as there is a difference between this part of Ethics and Sociology, it seems to be chiefly in two respects. First, Sociology is entirely concerned, according to some of its exponents, with social processes as they actually go on: it is purely descriptive and explanatory; it does not pass moral judgments. The student of ethics of course is concerned with moral judgments. But moral judgments are bound up with social processes, whether of the state, the economic order, the family, or other groups. It follows that the moral philosopher must study descriptive sociology in its general outlines. There are various details in this science, however, that do not concern him. Secondly, many sociologists are engaged in detailed surveys of social conditions in specific localities or industries. Such studies involve the passing of moral judgments. However, if the moral judgments are comparatively simple, and the work is mainly a matter of ascertaining facts, only a minimum of ethics may be involved. The moral philosopher is primarily a philosopher, concerned with the larger aspects of human life, and not with specific details. He of necessity must be a theorist rather than a reformer. He is confident that his knowledge of principles will be enlightening to reformers, he is appreciative of their efforts, and desirous to be of service to them. Many reformers are narrow and unintelligent, and so do more harm than good. This is often because of a lack of a thorough study of ethics. The chief task of the moral philosopher is to understand the human world. The reformer will do well to gain some of the understanding of the moral philosopher before he tries to effect sweeping changes.

The relation of Ethics to Religion is a question that demands consideration in the study of some, but not all, of the divisions of Ethics. In Comparative Ethics we are often confronted by a close relationship between moral and religious evolution, bound up, as both are, with social evolution. For while in primitive society there is sometimes little connection between judgments of right and wrong and notions of the supernatural, the relationship becomes closer in later stages of development. The possibility of moral progress appears at times to have been conditioned by the question whether human notions about the divine could be further moralized. This is notably true of certain periods in ancient Israel, Greece, and Rome. The moral history of the Occident during the past nineteen centuries is closely interwoven with the history of Christianity. Again, in the Psychology of Ethics, the nature of religious experience in relation to moral conduct, and of other virtues to the religious virtue of reverence, are important questions for the moral philosopher.

On the other hand, in the study of contemporary Systematic, Political, and Social Ethics the situation is somewhat reversed. The moral philosopher has little in these fields to learn from the theologian, while the latter has much to learn from him. Religion must sanction what is right, and forbid what is wrong. But to decide *what* is right and *what* is wrong must be the task of *Ethics*. Here Ethics must lead, and Religion must follow. At least, such has been the opinion of most writers on ethics during the past two centuries.

Religion must ultimately be taken into account if we are to gain a comprehensive view of ethics in relation to the whole of human experience. The student of ethics must appraise the function of religion in teaching moral judgments, prompting moral actions, and inspiring faith in the ultimate triumph of moral ideals. In considerations of ethics are to be found some of the strongest arguments in favor of certain postulates dear to religion. Among such are the beliefs that we are living in a world order capable of realizing moral ends, that our wills are really free, and that we are immortal. Ethical considerations, at least in the author's opinion, are favorable to belief in a personal God, who, among His other activities, has inspired men with a sense of the distinction between good and evil, who leads them to clearer understanding of this distinction, and to higher attainment of the good, and who reveals Himself to humanity in general through good men and sacred scriptures, and to individuals in their private devotions and participation in public worship. (Chapter XIX.)

Metaphysics is the "*study of the whole of things*", of "*first principles*", of the "*general nature of reality*". Besides the metaphysical arguments for the truth of religion, derived from ethics, alluded to in the preceding paragraph, there are several general metaphysical questions which ought not to be ignored, even in an introductory text. Are there absolute standards of good and evil implied in all our moral judgments? If so, what are they? How explain the fact of moral evolution, and the largely different ideas of good and evil manifest in every age? Will not any standards we may set up as absolute be outgrown in another age, just as we have outgrown those of our ancestors? On the other hand, if there are no absolute, eternal, unchanging standards of good and evil, does it not follow that morality is purely subjective, a matter of taste or caprice, just as, to borrow Rashdall's comparison, mustard is nice to one man and nasty to another? Are moral principles like those of mathematics, independent of human minds, as certain of the new realists have at times maintained? Or are moral principles to be tested by practical utilities, as pragmatists say; and if so, how define "practical" and "useful"? Or is morality an high order of "appearance", an important but not ultimate phase of reality, as certain Absolute Idealists have maintained? The beginner in Ethics deserves at least a glimpse into these and other profound as well as fascinating topics of metaphysical inquiry. (Such problems will be touched on incidentally throughout the volume, and more particularly in Chapters XIV and XIX.)

REFERENCES

* John Dewey and J. H. Tufts, *Ethics*, chap. I.
* Warner Fite, *Introductory Study of Ethics*, chap. I.
* W. G. Everett, *Moral Values*, chap. I.
* Frank Thilly, *Introduction to Ethics*, chap. I.
* S. E. Mezes, *Ethics*, chap. I.
* J. A. Leighton, *The Individual and the Social Order*, chaps. I–IV.
* F. C. Sharp, *Ethics*, chap. I.
* H. W. Dresser, *Ethics*, chap. I.
* H. W. Wright, *Self-Realization*, Part One, chaps. I, II.
* T. De Laguna, *Introduction to the Science of Ethics*, chaps. I, II.
  Friedrich Paulsen, *System of Ethics*, chap. I.
  J. S. Mackenzie, *Manual of Ethics*, Introduction.
  Aristotle, *Nicomachean Ethics*, Book I.
  James Seth, *A Study of Ethical Principles*, Introduction.

* Asterisks indicate references that are probably best suited to beginners. The others are more advanced, but not beyond the grip of some undergraduates. The references on this page deal with the definition and scope of Ethics. References to treatments of the different divisions of Ethics will be found appended to later chapters. More advanced references will be found in the Notes at the end of the volume.

PART I
COMPARATIVE ETHICS

DIVISION A
SOCIAL AND MORAL EVOLUTION

CHAPTER II

SOCIAL EVOLUTION

Comparative Ethics is as important for the moral philosopher as comparative anatomy is for the biologist. A knowledge of the different types of morality that mankind has recognized in theory and endeavored to observe in practice affords a richer understanding of human nature with its limitations and possibilities. In this chapter we shall consider the general types of social organization through which the race has passed, and in the following chapter we shall observe the corresponding steps in moral evolution. These chapters will necessarily have to be somewhat abstract, since they are intended to apply in a general way to all human history. Chapter IV, dealing with the ancient Hebrews, will be more specific, and afford an illustration of the moral evolution of a particular people in certain stages. Chapters II, III, and IV (constituting Division A of Part I) it is hoped, will afford some idea of social and moral evolution in general. In Chapters V–VII (Division B of Part I) will be sketched the phases of the ethical thought of Europe which are responsible for most of the moral judgments that constitute the conscience of the typical occidental man or woman of the twentieth century.

I. Introduction to the Outline of Social Evolution

It is safe to assume that the most simply organized and in other respects least advanced, of the savage tribes now in existence are fairly representative of the earlier stages of social evolution, which preceded the periods covered by recorded history.[1] Accordingly, the first of the three principal types of social organization here to be noticed, that of Kinship, is derived from the literature of anthropology. This is in part true

23

of the second type also, which is based upon Authority; but while this latter type had its beginnings in prehistoric ages, it has continued throughout most of the history of civilized nations. The third type, that based on Citizenship, holds only for the comparatively few civilized peoples, ancient and modern, who have progressed furthest in social evolution.

Many peoples are to be found in transitional stages between one type and another, or between two of the three subtypes into which the relation of Kinship is divided. Many, if not most present day savages in the kinship relation manifest phases of both mother right and father right in their institutions and customs. Moreover, when a succeeding type of social organization has become dominant, it never has obliterated the earlier types, whose rudiments and survivals persist even in the highest civilizations of the present time.

The reader needs to be warned that classifications of human societies, institutions, beliefs, and customs of every kind, are always more or less arbitrary. Such classifications inevitably overlook many interesting and important details. For instance, American Indians and Australian aborigines alike come under Kinship organization; Frenchmen and Americans alike enjoy Citizenship. Such classifications tell us nothing of innumerable significant details in which peoples of the same type differ.

Moreover, social progress never moves in a straight line; it moves by winding curves and zigzags, and experiences numberless setbacks and retreats. The outline of social evolution set forth in this chapter might be compared with a large scale wall map, on which the general course of a river is indicated, but the minuter twistings and turnings have been left out.

II. The Relation of Kinship

The most primitive form of social organization of which we have evidence in contemporary savage life is based upon the relation of *Kinship*. *The members of the social group are, or at least believe themselves to be, blood relatives; this explains their form of social organization.* The group, in the most primitive instances, is quite small, only a few families living in proximity. In more developed types, the Kinship groups sometimes have included larger populations scattered over wider areas. Most of the members of such a group are related in actual physical descent. But the group often includes other persons, captured in raids, subjugated in war, adopted, or for some other cause incorporated in it. In the course of time, myths and legends may arise, which attribute common ancestors to the whole group, and celebrate their exploits. Magical and religious ceremonials strengthen the consciousness of the Kinship relation. Whatever there may be of governmental or social control over individuals, means of ascertaining justice, methods of carrying on warfare, processes of an economic character (hunting, pastoral, agricultural, industrial) or magical rites and religious observances,—all imply the relation of Kinship. All the rights and duties that individuals have with relation to one another are bound up with this principle.

Under the relation of Kinship, we shall need to consider three different subtypes: the Primitive Horde, the Maternal System, and the Paternal System. These are believed to follow one another in time, in the order indicated. Many Kinship groups, it should again be pointed out, fall between these subtypes, in some respects resembling one, and in some another.[2]

III. THE PRIMITIVE HORDE

In the subtype of Kinship organization designated as the *Primitive Horde, all social organization is restricted to the single family* (husband, wife or wives, and children) *or to a group of a few such families living in the same vicinity.*

People with this form of Kinship organization are primitive indeed. They subsist upon what small game or fish they can capture with their bows and arrows, and what plant and animal food they can gather with their hands, or uproot with crudely sharpened sticks,—such as berries, roots, leaves, bark, wild honey, and insects. They live in caves, trees, or crude shelters of boughs and leaves that serve for little more than protection from the wind. Such are the Pygmies of the Congo, the Negritoes of the Philippines, the Senangs and Senoi of the Malay Peninsula, the natives of the Andaman Islands, the lowliest of the natives of Tierra del Fuego, and the Rock Veddahs of Ceylon.

Perhaps the most attractive of these peoples from a moral standpoint are the Rock Veddahs. These are a small folk in numbers, perhaps two thousand altogether. They cannot count, do not know the year, have no names for days or months, and, in general, manifest a very low order of intelligence. Each family lives by itself, upon its own hunting ground; but during the wet season two or three such families may inhabit a common cave. A dispute between members of different families may be fought out, or some of the leading men or women may act as peacemakers. There is no group organization to adjudicate disputes; and, of course, no ruler of any kind. Yet they recognize certain virtues and customs as morally obligatory. They are strictly monogamous, and have a saying that nothing but death parts a husband and wife. They are truthful, unaggressive, hospitable, sympathetic to strangers in need, grateful, plucky in fighting, and kind to animals. They respect the property of strangers as well as of one another. They have some fear of magic. They engage in a ceremonial dance about an arrow, which may be a rudimentary religion.[3]

IV. The Maternal System

A much more common form of social organization in the savage world is the *Maternal System* or *Mother Right* (*Mutterrecht:* formerly but erroneously called the "matriarchate", for the women do not rule the group). In this system, *social organization is built about maternal relationships.* Children and their mothers live with, or under the protection of, their mother's brothers or her maternal uncles. When a man marries, his wife is still regarded as belonging to her own people. In a few extreme cases he stays for the most part with his own mother and sisters, and merely visits his wife and children from time to time, feeling more closely bound to his mother and sisters and his sisters' children. Whatever hereditary possessions or titles he may have, pass from him at death to his brothers, or to his sisters' sons. His own children are reckoned as members of their mother's family, and inherit from her brothers.

A phenomenon that usually accompanies the maternal system is *Totemism*. *Members of a particular totem believe that there is some kind of close affinity between them and an "emblem"* (a specific kind of animal, plant, or material object). This emblem gives its name to the totem. Members of the same totem feel strong ties of loyalty to one another. Fine distinctions of grammar do not exist in primitive tongues, and a man says that he "is" a Fox, a Leopard, or an Emu. He of course knows that he is not really an animal, and that no animal is a man. His rational and linguistic powers are not sufficient to enable him to make more precise the close relationship that he firmly though rather mystically feels with the nonhuman members of the totem. As men become more reflective, and seek reasons for things, some explanation is likely to appear; *e.g.*, myths may arise, narrating how the living human and non-human members of the totem have been descended from an original ancestor.[4]

Their totemic relationship is thought to give the men of each totem peculiar powers. The animals give important information to the men of their totem. The men of a totem are supposed to be more able than other men to snare the animals of the totem. Some of the Australian aborigines believe that the men of each totem through elaborate ceremonies imitative in dress and behavior of the totemic animal or plant, can increase its fertility, and so better the food supply of human beings. The totemic ceremonies are a kind of primitive co-operative undertaking in which the men of each totem profit by the work done by men of other totems. To eat of the food of one's own totem, except on special ceremonial occasions, is regarded by the native Australian with something of our horror of cannibalism. It would be sure to work great harm on mankind, so close is the tie between the human and nonhuman members of the totem.

The close relationship between members of a totem is further illustrated by the fact that all over the world except where totemism shows signs of decay, members of the same totem must not intermarry. The relationship between the men and women of a totem seems so close that sexual relations between them arouse a horror similar to that which we feel at incest. So such offenses meet with death inflicted by the concerted action of the group. This holds true of tribes who leave the punishment of ordinary adultery to the initiative of the injured husband as an affair of private and not of general concern.

The maternal system and totemism mark a decided advance beyond the isolation of the primitive horde. Families are allied in marriage with others living at a distance. Coöperation over larger areas is made possible, and more progress can be made in all human activities. This is evident, even in Australia, where the general industrial and economic condition remains very low, where during winter the unclad natives shiver in caves or under trees, behind lean-tos of boughs, and subsist on what food they can gather with their hands or bring down with their boomerangs. For these natives have developed elaborate initiation and totemic ceremonies, which gather together people living at great distances, preserve and pass on to another generation traditions that they deem sacred, and so strengthen common social consciousness and good will.

In other parts of the world, more substantial advances have usually been made under mother right and totemism. Permanent dwellings have been erected, clothing manufactured from skins, and beginnings made in tilling the soil as well as in herding sheep and cattle. Festal occasions, both in times of peace and war, give rise to song and dance, commemorative of the exploits of their ancestors. The fine arts thus have their beginning. Ceremonies are conducted by old men, or specially trained medicine men, having for their aim the securing of approved social and personal ends through supernatural assistance. Thus religion begins.

The most successful development under the maternal system and totemism known in history is the case of the famous League of the Iroquois, a federation of American Indians which came into existence about 1570, and continued to function successfully until after the American Revolution. The League originally consisted of five tribes or so-called "nations",—the Mohawks, Onondagas, Senecas, Oneidas, and Cayugas; to which a sixth, the Tuscaroras, later was added. This federation brought under a common government a total population of at least fifteen thousand persons, belonging to five or six separate and warlike tribes. The League was remarkably successful in maintaining internal peace and security from external attack. It was able to hold an area which usually extended in all directions somewhat beyond the boundaries of the present state of New York, and even at one time spread from the west of New England to the Mississippi river, and from the St. Lawrence to the Tennessee river.

Each of the Iroquois tribes originally seems to have consisted of eight totems—Wolf, Bear, Beaver, Turtle; Deer, Snipe, Heron, and Hawk. The first four mentioned constituted one moiety, and the latter four a second moiety. An individual originally had to marry outside of his own totem and moiety. Later on, some of the tribes lost part of their totems, and the distinction between the moieties disappeared; but marriage between two persons of the same totem was always forbidden. Each totem of each tribe had one or more sachems who represented it in the Council of the League. A sachem was ordinarily elected for life, and at his death the members of his tribe and totem elected a successor, usually one of his brothers, or a son of one of his sisters. Membership in the totem followed the mother, so that a child belonged to the same totem as his or her mother. The Council of the League had full power to declare war and to make peace, to send and receive embassies, make treaties, and govern other Indian tribes that had come under their rule through conquest. It ordinarily exercised its influence to maintain peace among the member tribes and with the external world. The office of sachem had high prestige, and was surrounded by impressive ceremonial.

Lewis H. Morgan, the historian of the League of the Iroquois, gives it too much praise when he says that it was "the means of effecting the most perfect union of separate nations ever devised by the wit of man."[5]   However, it seems evident that the Iroquois could rightly claim that "the great object of their confederacy was peace—to break up the spirit of perpetual warfare, which had wasted the red race from age to age."[6]   The Iroquois recommended to our forefathers a union similar to their own, as early as 1775. Morgan says that Benjamin Franklin's plan for American union was directly inspired by observation of the Iroquois constitution. Morgan's editor adds that for twelve years, under the Articles of Confederation, the government of the United States (called by the Iroquois "The Thirteen Fires") was similar to the Iroquois plan.[7]

The strength of the League was due to the totemic tie. The Mohawk of the Wolf totem recognized the Seneca of the Wolf totem as his brother; in fact, every member of the same totem, in whatever tribe, was as much his brother or sister as if children of the same mother. This held the tribes together, made them reluctant to fight one another, and quick to come to one another's support when a common danger threatened.[8]

While the maternal system and totemism were decided advances beyond the primitive horde, their powers of expansion and coherence were limited. There is no other case on record, so far as the author knows, where so large a number of persons were held together in any coherent social organization under the maternal system as the League of the Iroquois, and the number in this case was certainly not over twenty-five thousand.[9] A local community composed of members of different totems lacked complete coherence; each person was subject to two loyalties—one to his local group or tribe, and one to his totem—and these might conflict. The individual family lacked sufficient stability; a woman was not always permanently tied to her husband in a system where she and her children had closer interests in common with her brother. There was no great stimulus to personal initiative in an economic order where a man was not responsible for his own wife and children. This economic system was a close approximation to a communism.[10] It, to be sure, guaranteed that all had a share in whatever the men brought in from the chase, or the women were able to raise in their little fields. No one was famished when others had plenty. But for all to be on the verge of starvation was not unusual. Early communism was an equality in poverty. Serfs and slaves under civilization have rarely not been better off than the members of a savage commune. For these and other reasons, the Maternal system was sooner or later replaced everywhere that society made a substantial advance, by the Paternal system.[11]

V. The Paternal System

Under the *Paternal System (Father Right, Vaterrecht) social organization rests upon the relation between a father and his children.* The father governs his wife and children, but in turn obeys his own father, oldest brother, or other head of the larger family group. So this system may properly be called the *Patriarchate.* Husband, wife (or wives) and children live together, children inherit their father's name, status, titles, possessions. So long as a man lives, his sons and sons' sons and their families (with the exception of married daughters and grand-daughters who belong to their husband's families) constitute a "greater family". After his death, the greater family in some cases tends to dissolve, but in others continues to hold together as a clan, under the headship of a surviving brother or son of the deceased patriarch. Under this system, the wife tends to be regarded as the property of her husband. His title to her has been established by the payment to the head of the family of sheep or cattle, by service in case he is too poor to buy her (as in the Biblical story of Jacob serving for Rachel), by exchange of one of his sisters for her, or by capture in war or upon a raid.

Economic advance as a rule is more rapid under the paternal system than under earlier forms of social organization. In the most primitive stages of father right all the descendants of a common paternal ancestor may live together or in close proximity as a clan, owning land and cattle in common. Communisms of this kind have been found in connection with the paternal system in India, China, Russia, ancient Greece and Rome, and Wales. The general tendency has been, however, for communism to yield gradually to private ownership, so that a man becomes economically responsible for his own wife, children, aged parents, and unmarried sisters, and for them alone. The paternal system stimulates economic progress because men feel more incentive to work to support their own wives and children, rather than their married sisters and their sisters' children. So men are less disposed to make hunting and fishing their sole peaceful occupations, and devote themselves to more productive agricultural and pastoral activities.

Under the paternal system the administration of justice by the head of the family marks an advance. Internal order is better secured. The family stands solidly together against the outside world. If one of its members commits an offense, his relatives are in a measure responsible with him. If vengeance cannot be had upon an offender, his kinsmen may be punished in his place by the kin of the injured man. This notion of *collective responsibility* is wholesome at the stage in which it first appears; then it indicates moral progress; only at a higher point of development does it give way to individual responsibility as we know it to-day.

The paternal system does not so unequivocally make a forward step in the position of women. Under the maternal system women are not the chattels of their husbands; women probably have more to say in choosing husbands and divorcing them, and they certainly enjoy more freedom in their daily life in many ways. Sometimes, as in certain of the American Indians, women have a little to say in the government of the tribe. On the other hand, under the paternal system a woman is the property of her father (or her brother, if her father is dead) before she is married, and of her husband after her marriage. Yet there are compensations, even for women, under the paternal system. The very fact that she has been bought with a price leads her husband to regard her as of some value. He appreciates her industry, for in the earlier stages of father right she continues to do much of the work. He assures himself of his wife's chastity, which he could not do so easily under the maternal system; and he sees that his daughters are continent, so that they may bring him a higher bride price when they marry. Warmer affection springs up in the breast of the savage man for a family who are his property, and so belong to him and are in his power. Women respect themselves more, as the men set higher prices upon them, and esteem them for their industry and chastity. They share in the greater economic prosperity. On the whole, then, it is a question whether the position of women is not improved under father right.

Survivals of the paternal system are observable in modern laws and customs. A wife and children bear the name of the husband and father. They ordinarily live with him, and he is responsible for their economic support. They inherit his property. Until within a very few generations he exercised much authority in the home, and was in far more than a titular sense, the "head of the house".

VI. The Relation of Authority

This type of social organization follows that of Kinship, which it partly supplants, and on which it partly superimposes itself. The essential principle of the relation of Authority is, that *social and political obligations rest upon the commands of a ruler or ruling class.* It is the duty of all to obey the ruler implicitly. Distinctions of right and wrong rest largely upon his will. To be sure, he may not be able to alter immemorial customs and written laws.[12] But his is the power, and perhaps the duty, to enforce laws and customs, and to interpret their significance in doubtful cases. This form of social organization began before man had risen above the level of savagery, and it has prevailed among most civilized peoples until recent centuries. Among savages, such despotisms as Dahomey, Ashanti, and Uganda (prior to European control) are good illustrations. The early empires of antiquity, like Egypt, Assyria, Babylonia, and Persia, are illustrations from civilized peoples, as are also the feudal kingdoms of medieval Europe and modern Japan (prior to 1871). The "benevolent despotisms" of the seventeenth and eighteenth centuries in Europe, especially those of France, Prussia, Austria, and Russia, manifest this principle at its highest level.

How Kinship groups passed into this very different form of social relationship is not difficult to understand. Conflicts between Kinship groups in a locality became frequent and severe. More discipline and better military organization were needed than councils of patriarchal chiefs and temporarily chosen commanders could afford. A successful military leader in a time of emergency assumed absolute control with general approval. When victory ensued, and the enemy were defeated, he became a popular hero, able to retain his military authority, especially if the general security might again be threatened. Such a hero could become a king. The defeated enemy might not all be massacred. Some might be spared, but reduced to servitude or serfdom, and obliged to contribute to the economic support of the victorious group or its rulers.

As contrasted with Kinship, in which there are no marked social distinctions, at least four classes appear early in the development of Authority: the king and *royal family;* the military and other favorites on whom the king relies and who with their families constitute the *nobility;* the ordinary members of the conquering people, now the *common people;* and the conquered peoples who occupy a decidedly inferior position as *serfs, slaves, low castes* or *outcastes.* A *priestly* class is often recognized, and given special distinctions and privileges.

Prior to the invention of writing, there were limits to the area and population that could be successfully governed within a single kingdom. Once this invention was made, civilization, in distinction from savagery, may be said to have begun. Rulers could send messages to generals in the field and governors in distant provinces. Precedents could be recorded, and the experience of the past could be more fully and accurately preserved. The production of literature was stimulated. Recorded history had its beginning.

With the expansion that writing and the beginning of civilization made possible, a further development in social organization sometimes followed. Considerable areas were conquered, and generals subordinate to the king were made governors of these districts. Being at considerable distances from the seat of royal authority, however, the generals ruled their provinces in partial independence. They sent in tribute and recruits to the army, and obeyed general instructions, and that was about all. Thus the original king became a "great king", or "king of kings", with enhanced wealth, dignity, and power.

In such a vast kingdom or empire, the conquered peoples often were left comparatively unmolested in the forms of local Kinship organization that they had known before their conquest. The central government protected them from external invasion, in return for levies of taxes and recruits. Otherwise it interfered little with their customs and institutions. The Assyrian, Babylonian, Persian, Greek, Roman, and successive Moslem empires in the Near East are said to have left local patriarchal village organizations comparatively intact during the past three thousand years.

The authority of the king originally rested upon his popularity and prestige with reference to the conquering people whom he led to victory, and upon force in the case of conquered folk. Partly to maintain his power, and partly to serve his people, the king endeavored to keep order within his domains. Quarrels among his subjects, he decreed, should no longer issue in prolonged fights among quarreling Kinship groups often resulting in blood feuds with great loss of life and economic disturbance. All were commanded to keep the king's peace, and bring their disputes to his courts. It often took many generations before the kings could establish the full authority of their own courts of law, but ultimately they succeeded. While this evolution was going on, the royal authority became strengthened by the sanctions of religion. In ancient Egypt the king became a god; in Japan he still is believed to be a descendant from the gods; in ancient Israel and medieval Europe he was the Lord's anointed, and ruled by divine right.

As laws and justice came to be increasingly associated with royal administration, a further evolution took place. It became the duty of subjects to obey the king because he stood for justice and right. Instead of mere popularity and prestige, or brute force, or superstitions about his divine nature and authority, the chief sanction for obedience became moral. Such an evolution in the attitude of subjects toward their king implied a corresponding change in his attitude toward them. He now saw it to be his duty to exercise his authority in the interests of right; he had obligations to his subjects; in a sense he was their servant. Thus the classical sages were constantly instructing the rulers of China regarding their duties. Nor did the Church allow the rulers of medieval Europe to be ignorant of their responsibilities. Gradually the laws assumed in some measure an authority superior to the will of the king himself. At first this was largely due to religious sanctions, the law code supposed to have been given by a god to an earlier king or lawgiver. In civilized times, after jurists had evolved principles of law and developed them rationally, a prince would hesitate to set them aside by arbitrary decrees. Only when conditions had changed, or some real emergency had arisen, could he find moral and popular support for sweeping changes in legislation.

In its last stages, kings ruling by Authority came to believe it their primary duty to promote the welfare of their subjects. Their authority had finally come to rest morally and physically upon the consent of their people. So long as their rule (or that of their ministers) was efficient, the royal authority remained undisturbed, and even became strengthened. Such was the condition in England under the Tudors, in France under Louis XIII and Louis XIV, in Prussia under the abler Hohenzollerns like Frederick the Great, in Russia under Peter the Great and Catherine the Great. However, when the relation of Authority had come to owe its sanctions chiefly to moral service, mankind was almost ready to pass into a new form of social organization. When the royal administration became inefficient and unjust, as in England under the Stuarts, or in France under Louis XVI, a revolution was inevitable. Under such conditions the people came to believe that they could best decide questions of their own welfare. They deposed their king or curtailed his authority. The people made many mistakes, and for a time their condition was probably worse than before. But ultimately they learned in some measure to govern themselves, and the relation of Authority was successfully replaced by that of Citizenship.

The disadvantages of the principle of Authority over that of Kinship which it replaced were numerous. The rule of the early despot was always arbitrary and often cruel. The rulers of Dahomey and Ashanti capriciously killed and enslaved their subjects, seized their wives and daughters and confiscated their goods. Instead of the comparative equality of all people under Kinship, social classes appeared. If there were large conquests, like those of the early empires of antiquity, the mass of the population consisted of tributary peoples who had lost their independence and become subjugated to an alien rule that at best did not wholly understand them, and was more than likely to exploit them cruelly. The Pharaohs forced their subject peoples under the lash to build the pyramids. The great monuments of Nineveh and Babylon were built in the same way. The lot of the masses—villeins and serfs—in medieval Europe was wretched in the extreme.

Under civilization, the system of Authority develops traits

characteristic of its military nature. In a time of actual or threatened warfare, all other considerations give way to the public security. Every one must cheerfully bear his part of a crushing burden of taxation; or, at the government's call, leave his family to shift as well as it can for itself, while he serves in the army. Military officers constitute a superior caste, to whom deference must be shown at all times, and to whose domineering ways submission must be complete and respectful. A despotic government must always be on its guard against intrigue and revolt. Everything and everybody must therefore be regulated. There can be only such freedom in religion as the state thinks expedient. Nothing can be published in the press or spoken in public gatherings that the officials deem prejudicial to the interest of the state. Educational institutions must be carefully supervised to assure that they are teaching nothing seditious. Industry, trade, and agriculture are all regulated by the bureaucracy, so that freedom of initiative is hampered, while privileges and monopolies are granted to royal favorites. Voluntary associations even for the most harmless purposes are regarded with governmental suspicion, and it may be dangerous to belong to them. Fearful of treason, the government may rely on an elaborate system of espionage; it may be unsafe to express a mild criticism of existing institutions to one's neighbor, who may prove to be a paid governmental spy. Minute details of living are subjected to law, and the slightest infractions are punished with pitiless severity. But of course, a strong and efficient despotic government will not usually be at war on an extensive scale, and if its rule is just and its people prosperous, it can with safety allow more individual liberty. It is only while carrying on war, or when in decay and fearful of being overthrown, that authoritarian governments carry oppressive measures close to the limit of human endurance.

On the whole, the relation of Authority was a decided advance upon that of Kinship. Without it, civilization could not have arisen. And without civilization, free institutions such as we know to-day under Citizenship could never have come into existence. As we have seen, under Authority larger areas and populations were brought together under a firm common rule, than could have occurred under Kinship. Order was usually maintained within conquered areas, and in the long run wars became fewer. Over large areas homes were safer from devastation than ever before. In place of frequent raids and plunderings, with blood feuds and other family quarrels, firm rulers afforded more lasting security. This more than offset heavy taxation and the destructiveness of the extensive wars that were occasionally fought with rival kingdoms and empires.

Under these circumstances a larger economic development became possible. Men cultivated their farms more thoroughly as they felt sure that they would enjoy the fruits of their labor. Trade routes were opened and exchange of commodities over vast distances was effected by ships and caravans. Progress in the industrial arts became more rapid. With trade and industry developed, more wealth came into existence, and a leisure class emerged,—a class that did not have to devote all its energies to warfare and making a living. This class had time to further the fine arts, partly by their own efforts, but more by patronage of those with talent. Thus, in Greece, the Homeric bards developed epic poetry. Travelers visited distant lands to observe other civilizations, and learned to criticize their own beliefs regarding nature and human institutions. So Greek philosophy and science were born under the principle of Authority, and the foundations were then laid for the brilliant developments that came after the Greeks had entered the relation of Citizenship. While Greece is the best illustration, the rise of economic prosperity, the emergence of a leisure class, and the beginnings of the fine arts took place to some extent under Authority in all of the early empires—Egypt, Babylonia, Phœnicia, Persia, and little Israel.

The economic development that preceded the rise of civilization and made it possible, was based to a very large extent on forced labor. Civilization could have come in no other way.

Before the invention of large machines not enough wealth could be produced to maintain a cultivated class except by the toil of the masses, who only shared to a limited extent in the higher standards of living which their work made possible. Men just emerging from savagery would not of their own initiative have been willing to work continuously enough to maintain a high standard of living, even if they had shared more fully in it. Civilization is made possible only by continuous work at monotonous tasks. So the principle of Authority gave men discipline in economic production, and a cruel but necessary training in obedience.

In the political sphere the rôle of Authority in evolution is equally, and for our purposes, even more significant. The king, his courts and army, learned to make and enforce laws, and the rest of the people learned to obey them. It is easier to lay down laws for other people to obey, than it is to obey them oneself; and it is easier to obey rules that another imposes upon one than it is to obey the commands that one lays down upon oneself. So the relation of Authority had to precede that of Citizenship. However, the time came when men learned to legislate for themselves, and to revere and obey their own laws. Then the era of freedom under Citizenship began.

VII. The Relation of Citizenship

The relation of Citizenship is not necessarily based upon ties of kinship, nor upon obedience to the will of a ruler or of a ruling class; although a state with free citizenship is more likely to prosper if its population is homogeneous in race, and if it is well trained in obedience and respect for legal authority. The essential thing about the relation of Citizenship is, that *the members of a free state* directly or through their representatives, *make and administer the laws that they obey.* It is a government in some sense "of the people, by the people, and for the people". The people are more nearly upon a plane of *political and social equality* than in the relation of Authority, although class and race distinctions may survive to a limited extent, especially if they are thought to serve a useful purpose, and to be morally justified. There is *larger recognition of the individual* than in the relations of Kinship and Authority. Statesmen realize that individual citizens have diverse interests and talents; effort is made to respect their rights, and to give them freedom of opportunity. Such individualism implies that *the individual is free to think, speak, and act for himself.* He may freely criticize existing institutions, and advocate their modification by lawful means.

On the other hand, the individual citizen *must obey and respect the laws* which he and his fellow citizens have made. He may emigrate, and transfer his allegiance to another state. But so long as he remains within the domain of a state of which he is a citizen, he is *morally and legally bound to be loyal in times of peace and war* and *to seek to promote the common good.* The "common good" consists first, of those interests of individual citizens that can best be secured by the state for all—defense from foreign invasion, law and order within the state itself, security of life, liberty, and property, and the like. It may also include whatever other undertakings for the public welfare may be agreed upon: the maintenance of temples and public worship for the welfare of the state, and of great public dramatic, literary, musical and athletic festivals (as in ancient Athens); or a great educational system including elementary, secondary, and higher liberal and technical schools of every description, and various public utilities; whatever the citizens believe should be undertaken by the state for the promotion of their intellectual, spiritual, or physical welfare. It will be convenient to employ the term "free" to designate states and citizens living in the relation of Citizenship. From what has been said, it will readily be seen that they are free in many respects not characteristic of other forms of social organization.

The best examples of the relation of Citizenship are the city-states of ancient Greece, the "free cities" of the middle ages, and the city-states of the Italian Renaissance, on the one hand; and, on the other, the self-governing national states of the modern world. The city-state of antiquity was limited in area— a city or town, the surrounding country, possibly colonies at a distance. The citizens were only a minority of the population. A more numerous inferior class engaged in manual labor and shared little in the "common good" afforded to the citizens. Such city-states gave their citizens larger freedom and opportunity for self-expression than had ever before been possible; while Athens made the greatest original contributions to literature, art, architecture, and philosophy of any one state in all history. The ancient city-states did not endure permanently because they were incapable of growth beyond a limited extent. Lacking our modern means of communication and transportation over vast distances, and our devices for government through representatives, they proved ineffective when they became too large for a considerable proportion of the citizens to be able to come together in a single public meeting and deliberate upon the public interest. So the Greek city-states weakened one another in wars due to lack of understanding, and ultimately became incorporated in the Macedonian and subsequent empires at the cost of most of the ideals of Citizenship and reversion to Authority.

Rome was a city-state that through successive conquests ultimately gained dominion over the entire western civilized world. This expansion saved the Romans from conquest by a foreign state; but they were unable to govern their vast empire in such a manner as to conserve their own freedom as citizens. They had to revert largely to an authoritarian system, and hand over the rule to the Cæsars. However, the ancient ideals of Citizenship were not wholly forgotten even under these circumstances. Creative genius in most fields disappeared with the loss of civic freedom, but the culture of the past was appreciated and conserved. On the whole the Roman imperial rule was beneficent, protecting its subjects, affording them a better administration of law than they had previously known, and in time extending to them what remnants of the rights of citizenship the Romans themselves still enjoyed. With the fall of the empire, a complete reversion to Authority was inevitable; the feudal system presently developed. The Church, however, survived; a little of civic freedom remained in the organization of her clergy, and her monasteries at least preserved in ancient manuscripts the classical literature of the ancient city-states.

Thus the modern revival of the ideals of Citizenship, beginning with the Renaissance, was rendered possible. In modern times civic ideals have developed within larger political units than the ancient city-states. Our national states are therefore stronger to resist attack from without, and they are not so greatly threatened with faction from within. Our higher civilization is the consequence of modern science and mechanical inventions. Since the invention of the printing press, books have become more plentiful, making it possible to give an elementary education to the entire population, and a higher education to larger numbers than was ever possible in the past. Machinery makes it no longer necessary that a large servile population should do all the heavy work and live in poverty to maintain a comparative few in the privileges of Citizenship. The device of representative government makes it possible for a nation to enjoy self-government without a convocation of all its citizens in a single public assembly. Better means of communication allow all the citizens to gain some appreciation of issues and of the personalities of leading candidates for office. Notwithstanding all the evils of modern propagandism, it is probably safe to say that the average American citizen, casting his ballot on a national election day with his fellow citizens spread over a vast continent, votes as intelligently as did the average Athenian citizen who attended the civic assembly in person.

Two serious problems confront national states under Citizenship to-day. The first arises from the fact that not all the world at the present time is as yet capable of self-government under Citizenship. Most of the population of the earth is still living in less advanced forms of social organization, extending clear back to the crudest and earliest of all, the Primitive Horde. Whether all men are capable through a long process of education of finally arriving at the level of Citizenship, or whether many peoples are too limited in natural mental capacities ever to advance far beyond their present condition is a question to which anthropologists and psychologists are as yet unable to give a definite answer. At any rate, for a long time to come, many peoples will have to remain subject to Authority, whether exercised by native rulers, or by administrators sent out to them by modern national states now under Citizenship. In the latter case, it is now generally recognized as the duty, and notwithstanding many abuses it is in the main the practice, of a modern national state to govern subject races for their own good. The natural resources of a subject country should be, and now often are, exploited so as to benefit the native population. To the natives should be given as many opportunities of education in schools and participation in the political administration and economic development of their country as their experience and real capacities make practicable.

The second serious problem that confronts modern national states under Citizenship is that of international relations. Can our modern free states reach some form of mutual understanding and coöperation? Can they learn to settle their disputes by agreement, and to harmonize their national, cultural, and economic aspirations, so that they can all progress peaceably? Or are our modern national states destined to destroy one another in wars, as did the free city-states of ancient Greece? Should the latter occur, a partial or complete reversion to the relation of Authority would be inevitable. But the hope is that some form of Internationalism will be evolved that will conserve the freedom and integrity of the national states now in the relation of Citizenship, eliminate destructive economic and military competitions, afford civic rights to all races and nations capable of using them, and teach to all men of all races loyalty to a common, universal, and harmonious Humanity.

REFERENCES

(to Chapters II and III)

L. T. Hobhouse, *Morals in Evolution*, Part I, chaps. I, II. *Social Evolution and Political Theory*. *Social Development*.

F. Müller-Lyer, *History of Social Development*.

* Robert H. Lowie, *Primitive Society*.

* E. C. Hayes, *Introduction to the Study of Sociology*, Part III.

W. Wundt, *Elements of Folk Psychology*, chaps. I, II.

F. H. Giddings, *Principles of Sociology*, Book III.

* Lewis H. Morgan, *The League of the Iroquois*.

B. Spencer and F. J. Gillen, *The Natives of Central Australia*.

F. G. Frazer, *Totemism and Exogamy*.

Edward Westermarck, *Origin and Development of Moral Ideas*, vol. II, chap. XXXIV.

R. M. MacIver, *The Modern State*, Book One.

* J. Dewey and J. H. Tufts, *Ethics*, chaps. II–V.

* H. W. Dresser, *Ethics*, chap. VI.

* Paul Radin, *Primitive Man as Philosopher*, chaps. IV–VII.

CHAPTER III

MORAL EVOLUTION

I. INTRODUCTORY

Moral Evolution cannot be traced as an independent thread in the tangled skein of social evolution. Moral judgments often change from one age to another as a result of circumstances—economic, political, and religious—that are unmoral (using "unmoral" as defined on pages 5, 6 above). Not until we reach the higher stages of social evolution—the later periods of Authority and Citizenship—are moral judgments likely to be as powerful in affecting other conditions of life as they are liable to be themselves modified by external causes. However, there is always some interaction, and moral considerations influence human conduct to a constantly increasing extent as man advances. Moral progress has not been consistent and continuous. There have been frequent reverses. Advance has never been uniform in all respects in any given period. Progress has been slower in the moral field than in others,—for instance, in the field of the applied sciences, during the past few centuries. But mankind in the higher civilizations is to-day, both in ideals and actual conduct, measurably in advance of preceding epochs.

Evidence for the statements of the preceding paragraph will be proffered in this, and in the following chapters of Part I. The present chapter will furnish an abstract model of the general course of moral evolution. In the case of any particular people or period, characteristic details, peculiar to it, would need to be added. Such details will be sketched in certain Hebrew, Greek, Roman, and Christian developments contributary to the moral outlook of the present time, in Chapters IV–VI.[1]

II. The Primitive Horde

The Primitive Horde, at the lowest level of the Kinship relation, of which an account was given in the preceding chapter, shows that moral judgments and customs antedate the appearance of a much more extensive social organization than the family. A little reflection will lead us to see why this is the case.

In the common life of husband, wife, and children, all the essential moral relations and problems are bound to arise, and lead to moral judgments.[2] Father and mother care for their children; from their instinctive affection emerge the simpler moral judgments regarding the conduct of parents. Children learn to obey their parents, and so to recognize authority. They learn to play and work together, to respect one another's rights to toys and other small personal possessions, to defend themselves against aggression, to protect still smaller children against the attacks of older ones, to exercise self-control in fits of temper, self-assertion, and greed.[3]

To be sure, savage parents and children do not act upon a family moral code as well, even, as we do. Their conduct is crude and rough. They are often indifferent to filth and squalor. Some of them engage in cannibalism and head-hunting. They certainly lack the refined sentiments and cultivated manners of civilized people. Such words as "duty" and "obligation" perhaps never appear in their vocabularies unless they have come into contact with civilized races. Yet, in their own fashion, they practice the elements of family affection, loyalty, obedience, coöperation, truth telling, chastity, benevolence, respect for property rights, courage, justice, self-defense, self-control, and thoughtfulness. They cultivate these virtues in a very different social organization from ours, and their conduct naturally differs in many details. Let us cite an illustration. To kill one's parents when they are old and feeble, or to leave them to starve, is not exactly our idea of filial affection. Under the conditions of life among some savage tribes, however, where it is necessary to move rapidly over wild country in pursuit of food and flight from enemies, such treatment of the aged who are no longer able to keep up with the rest is not only customary, but kind and just.[4] It also needs to be pointed out that the lower savages maintain a higher level of morals in their relations to fellow members of their little groups than they do to the outside world, with which they only slightly come into contact. Yet they usually show hospitality to strangers, and are rarely hostile or treacherous unless they have previously been mistreated.[5]

III. Group Morality and the Higher Subtypes of Kinship

As we ascend the path of social evolution to Mother Right and to Father Right, we find that moral conduct assumes several distinctive aspects. Two of these are particularly important, "Group Morality" and "Custom Morality." These are not names of distinct moral codes, but merely convenient terms to designate certain features of morality that had their origin in the maternal and paternal subtypes of Kinship. They have persisted, though in a modified way, in the relations of Authority and Citizenship.

Group Morality consists of moral judgments conceived in terms of the relations of men to one another in groups, with comparatively slight consideration of individuals as such, apart from their group relationships.

Under either the maternal or the paternal systems, the most important facts about a man are the groups to which he belongs. He has a strong sentiment of loyalty toward each of these groups. He is always the member of a *local* or *village* group, composed of a few families living together or in close proximity (the family organization within the group being different in the maternal and paternal systems). Under Mother Right, and in the earlier stages of Father Right, as well as in societies in the stages of transition between the two, he belongs also to a *totemic group* which is not local, but consists of individuals in different localities. In all cases, he belongs to a larger group, composed of all (or most) of the families occupying a considerable region, and known as a *tribe*. Perhaps, as in the case of early Israel, recounted in the book of Judges, a number of different tribes may recognize a common kinship, and think of themselves as a *nation*, before they have any permanent and well articulated national political organization. Or kinship tribes may form a federation, as we saw in the case of the League of the Iroquois, in the preceding chapter. National organization, however, is not usually very effective until the principle of Kinship has given place to that of Authority.

So, either under Mother Right or Father Right, the groups into which a man is born—local, tribal, perhaps totemic, possibly national—determine his status, rights, and obligations. He remains, his life long, identified with these groups. They prescribe into what groups he may and into what groups he must not marry. His economic condition and activities are those of his group. He must go on the chase with the other men, at least when large game is sought, and the captured game is divided on communistic principles. When women engage in "hoe culture", the grain and vegetables that they raise are likely to be shared communistically. So an individual prospers when his group prosper, and he suffers from hunger, cold, and other ills when they suffer. There is a little more individualism after the point is reached when men begin to till the soil themselves, instead of leaving this wholly to the women. Individual allotments of land are then frequently made, yet the ownership of the soil remains with the group, reapportionments being made from time to time. Often a "common" or pasture land is left undivided, open to the animals of all the members of the group.

Every member has to serve his part in an offensive raid, as well as in a defensive fight to protect the land or persons of the group. Conscription is a matter of course, and "conscientious objectors" are unknown. Every one is friendly or hostile to those to whom his group is friendly or hostile. The group determines the acts and sentiments of its members toward the outside world. The group protects each of its members from injuries by the rest, and inflicts suitable punishments upon offenders. If a man under the paternal system commits a crime, the immediate members of his family may be thought to participate in his guilt to some extent; his parents for not having brought him up properly, his own wife and children and slaves because they are his property and so bound up in some way with his personality. If an injury is done to a member of a group by some one in another group, the injured man's group calls upon the other group for the punishment of the offender. If his own group thinks the accused man guilty, they deliver him over for punishment. If they take his part, a struggle may break out between the two groups. The members of the group of the injured man capture the man they believe guilty if they can; but if they cannot, they avenge themselves upon any man of his group.[6] Thus blood feuds often arise. It is the duty of every member of a group to assist in revenging the injury of any brother member; and every member of the wrongdoer's group may suffer vengeance for the wrong that anyone of them has committed, or is believed by a hostile group to have committed. The aspects of Group Morality described in this paragraph are known as Collective Responsibility.

It should be observed that in such a system the individual, as such, is kept more in abeyance than with us. He has comparatively little freedom of initiative in marriage and war, as well as in hunting, farming, cattle raising, and other economic activities. There is little differentiation of occupations except on the basis of sex: all men hunt and go on raids together; all women engage in the same tasks in and about the huts and tepees. Every member of the group participates equally in its prosperity and adversity, and shares in responsibility to the outside world for the misconduct of any of its members.

The psychological explanation of the strength of group morality is to be found in the strong sentiments of "group spirit" or *esprit du corps* which groups are able to inculcate in all their members. This combined spirit of love, pride, and loyalty binds the members of the group together and makes possible their common activities.[7]

Religion is one of the important activities that fosters sentiments of loyalty to the group, and so strengthens group morality. Religion among the lower peoples consists chiefly of ceremonies connected with the life of the home and family, the local, tribal, or totemic group. The ceremonies are believed to conserve or increase some value recognized as important by family or group. Australian ceremonies are thought to effect a magical transformation in boys and girls so as to assure their growth into manhood and womanhood, to transmit the lore and traditions of the group to a succeeding generation in an impressive manner, and to increase the food supply. Higher savages in different parts of the world employ religious ceremonials to conserve values dear to them. The values are material and utilitarian as a rule: food; water; success in a hunt or raid; counsel regarding future policies; security from pestilence, earthquake, and flood; fertility of the soil, of animals, or women; propitiation of unfriendly spirits and gods; love, sympathy, and assistance from ancestral ghosts, nature spirits, and gods. Such ceremonies always strengthen consciousness of group relationships, and build up powerful sentiments and emotions, whether of fear and awe, joy and ecstacy, or good will to one's kinsmen and hatred of hostile groups. Religion at this level does much to teach the individual to think, feel and act, to love, fear and hate with his group.

Whatever the character of a religious ceremony, on whatever level of human culture, it always induces in those who participate, the feeling of the presence of some power other than their individual selves. It is the presence of this power that gives men courage in battle and strength to overcome obstacles in every emergency, that relieves fears and comforts the sorrowful, that heightens joy and brings ecstacy on festal occasions like harvests and victory in war. This experience is explained psychologically as the release of subconscious and reserve powers in the human organism induced by the stimulus of group action.[8] Metaphysically, it may be attributed to God, or a world soul, immanent in human social evolution, and revealing Himself to men at different levels of civilization to whatever extent they are capable of knowing Him.[9] At any rate, men in the Kinship relation feel these experiences and explain them as best they can. There is some strange force in things—*mana, manitou, wakonda*—that is made available in these ways.[10] The force is believed to be common to the animal and human members of a totem, and to be strengthened by the ceremony. It may be personified as an ancestral ghost or a nature spirit or god; or it may be regarded as a manifestation of such a being. Whatever the explanation, religion in the Kinship stage is a group affair, engaged in by the members of the group collectively, or by the head of the family or the priest as their representative. The ends of religion are group ends. Religion fortifies and intensifies group spirit.

The beginnings of art, whether employed in the service of religion or independently, also serve to strengthen group sentiment. Dancing, singing, the recitation of sagas and ballads, drawings on rocks and the walls of caves, designs of pottery, crude sculpture,—all are frequently employed to celebrate in some way legendary, historical, or contemporary events felt to be important in the collective life of the group.

IV. Custom Morality

Custom Morality is a convenient term to designate a prominent feature of most moral judgments made in the relation of Kinship. *A custom is a way of acting which has been followed by the members of a group in the past, and which furnishes a rule that all are under moral obligation to obey.* Among civilized people to-day under the relation of Citizenship we have customs in the sense of this definition. But, to a large extent, at least, individuals among us are free to reflect upon the reasons for our customs, and to advocate changes in them. On the contrary, under the relation of Kinship, the reasons for customs are seldom asked; and when asked, the answer is probably found in some absurd myth, or other religious or magical superstition, even in cases where the custom is in reality a very good one. Very rarely are a Kinship group willing to consider a change in their customs. Every one is obliged to accept a custom and to act upon it. Provided he does this, it matters less whether he knows or believes in the traditional explanation of its origin. *Custom Morality*, therefore, is *the moral system*, prevalent in the relation of Kinship and earlier stages of Authority, *under which moral judgments are based on customs accepted unreflectively and unconditionally*. Since customs develop in the life of the group, are maintained by it, and can only be altered through its consent, Custom Morality is largely co-extensive with Group Morality. The two expressions are sometimes used interchangeably.

vogue Morality

Customs are often compared with the habits of an individual. An individual's habits are usually said by psychologists to be due to coördinations in the nerve cells of the brain. A stimulation follows the line of least resistance through these nerve cells, the pathway that has previously been followed by similar stimulations. Instinctively a child is frightened when it hears a strange and loud noise, like thunder. Such sounds arouse a nervous reaction following inherited pathways of discharge. The instinctive response of fear to the sound of thunder may become a confirmed habit in an individual. But, fortunately for most of us, as the sound of thunder was heard on repeated occasions in childhood, and became familiar it ceased to evoke the reaction of fear; and a habit of indifference or even enjoyment was formed in connection with it.

Habits formed by the "trial and error" method are of a different type, not so obviously connected with instincts. They are formed originally with the aid of attention, but the attention is uncritical, indiscriminating. A door opens with difficulty. The housemaid jerks it various ways, and finally gets it open. Each successive time she goes through, she unreflectively jerks the door again. In the course of time, however, without ever

knowing why, she raises the door a little by the knob as soon
as she takes hold of it, and passes through without delay or
annoyance. A more discriminating person would have studied
the mechanism of the door; and finding that it sagged a little
on its hinges, such a person would have adopted the device of
pulling upward a little upon the knob when opening the door.
So habits can be formed by trial and error, or by discriminating
observation and reflection; and sometimes the habit, after it
has been formed, will not be different in one case than in the
other. But, as a rule, reflectively formed habits are better
adapted to the needs of a situation.

The *habits of a group* may be conveniently called *folkways.*[11]
A group of persons does not possess a single brain and nervous
system. Obviously, therefore, a folkway is not precisely the
same as the habit of an individual. Perhaps a folkway could
best be described as a habit that each new individual growing
up in a group forms in conscious or subconscious imitation of
the others. Some folkways appear to be unmoral, or to involve moral considerations only to a slight extent, like languages
and dialects, use of knives and forks or chopsticks in eating,
turning to the right to pass, etc. Such folkways persist in a
group because they are convenient. It is perhaps a duty to
conform to them; it certainly would be awkward not to do so;
and one does feel a certain social pressure toward conformity.
In view of the fact that social pressure is felt to some extent,
perhaps all folkways may be said to be at least quasi-moral.

On the other hand, some folkways involve a much more
decided moral element, and are therefore to be distinguished
from the rest as *mores* or *customs*. It is morally obligatory to
accept these ways of conduct. The welfare of the group is
thought to depend in some measure upon observance of the
mores, and any violation meets with strong disapproval, and
probably with severe punishment. Marriage inside of the totem,
murder and theft within the group, and treachery to a guest
are commonly regarded as grave violations of mores. Such
serious violations are punished by the group (except in the

case of the Primitive Horde) while milder violations are still
left for redress by the injured individuals and their friends,
supported by public opinion. [12]

V. How Customs Originate and Change

Folkways and mores seem to have originated in various
ways. (1) Sometimes as expressions of *instinctive needs* they
have sprung up spontaneously under the conditions of the
environment. The obligation of every man to go on the hunt
or raid is probably an illustration. (2) Other customs grew
accidentally by the *trial and error method,* like prescribed ways
of making bows and arrows, canoes, and huts among people in
the Kinship relation. (3) Still other customs originated as *expressions of emotions,* felt collectively. Everybody likes to see
a bully whipped, and to see a fearless man perform daring exploits. Most people like to "show off" a little at times and
gain admiration. Much fighting and dueling, and perhaps the
first wearing of clothing, arose and became customary because
of such emotional appeals. (4) The savage, untrained in the
observation of causes and effects and the uniformity of nature,
has numerous *crude ways of thinking* that can hardly be called
reflective. Something happened fortunately once; it will do
so again. So he wears charms, seeks to make his fields fertile
by planting *mana* stones in them, consults omens before engaging in serious undertakings, and goes through endless performances that to our minds are ridiculous, in order to bring
"good luck" and to avert "bad luck". Such ways of thinking
perhaps should not be called prelogical, but they certainly are
not rational or logical according to our standards.[13] (5) To a
certain extent, usually to an extremely limited extent, even
savages have been known to change their customs as a result of
deliberate *reasoning.* The old men of Australian tribes have
made changes thus; and modifications of customs have been decided upon in the councils of American Indians and palavers of
Africans. Only to a slight extent, though, is Custom Morality
under the control of conscious reasoning.

The changes in customs among peoples in the relation of Kinship are very slow. They are gradual growths seldom effected in one generation, and probably never by a single individual. The causes of change are more often unmoral than moral, although moral influences are at times operative. It will be worth while to devote a few pages to a discussion of this last statement, illustrated by marriage, which is of special ethical significance in the relation of Kinship.

How did the maternal system, with its different customs, replace the primitive horde? To-day the temporary appearance of an abundance of food in any locality brings together lower savages in vast numbers, who remain until it is consumed.[14] Where the primitive horde had given place to the earliest forms of mother right, probably a permanent improvement in the food supply drew together a larger number of families than could remain peaceably in the same neighborhood without some more definite form of social organization.

The new form of organization that sprang up under these circumstances had the women as its nucleus. Women do not move about so much as men, and the men always returned after their wanderings to the women and children. The relation of the mother to offspring is obvious and impressive. Certain lower savage tribes, notably in Australia, are reported not to realize the function played by males in reproduction.[15] Perhaps the significance of this function is never fully felt in the maternal system. Not only does the fact of birth call attention to the relation between mother and child, but her continued care of the child during infancy strengthens the tie. So emotions develop into lasting sentiments, and bind together the children of the same mother. That a man should feel attached to his mother, his brothers, and sisters, and to the children of his sisters, was inevitable.

With the close tie between brothers and sisters thus recognized, marriages between them have almost universally been regarded with horror. It was probably an extension of this horror of incest that led to *Exogamy, i.e., the prohibition of marriage be-*

tween members of specified groups (like totems) *who were felt to be in some peculiarly intimate relationship.* On the other hand, the ties of Kinship not only forbid marriages within a considerable circle; they also enjoin that marriages must take place within a somewhat larger circle. Marriages with persons of totally different races were felt to be repulsive, and so arose the customs of *Endogamy, which prescribe groups within which one must marry.*

Thus unmoral causes, like the food supply, probably brought about the transition to the maternal system, while the development within the latter of the customs of exogamy and endogamy seem to have arisen from feelings that could be classified, though perhaps only vaguely, as moral.

The transition from mother right to father right seems to have been largely due to unmoral causes. The relation of the father to the child had become understood and appreciated. Men were giving up hunting, and settling down to pastoral and agricultural pursuits which kept them more in one place, and made them more important in the economic processes than women. The labor of the women, as well as their greater physical attractiveness under more prosperous economic conditions with better food, shelter, and clothing, made them desirable assets for a man to have and to hold. So men bought or traded for their wives if they were affluent, captured them on raids if they were poor but bold and warlike, and worked for them if they were poor and inaggressive.

Where the sexes are equal in numbers, marriages are usually between a single pair. But where a hardy and warlike or rich and prosperous Kinship tribe lives in the vicinity of weak, poor, less intelligent and less aggressive peoples, the latter are forced or bribed to part with many of their daughters to the former. Hence there is *polygamy* (the marriage of several women to one man) in the stronger tribe. Extreme poverty may (but more rarely) force weak and backward tribes into *polyandry* (the marriage of several men to one woman). These causes are unmoral. Though custom morality under father right has often permitted polygamy, it has only rarely enjoined it as a duty. Where polygamy has been regarded as a duty, the reasons have usually been religious rather than strictly moral. For instance, a religion may teach that descendants must be left to continue the worship of the ancestral ghosts, and preserve the family name. So, when a wife is barren it may be thought a duty to take an additional wife. Among the Hebrews, long after the disappearance of ancestral worship, it remained the law that if a man died without issue, it became his brother's duty to marry the widow, regardless of whether he were already married, and children born of the union were regarded as descendants of the deceased man.[16]

Most marriages in nearly all stages of moral evolution have for practical reasons been *pair marriages*, *i.e.*, the marriage of one man to one woman. The sexes are usually approximately equal in numbers. It is too costly and troublesome for most men to maintain more than one wife and her children. So, even in countries where polygamy is permitted and regarded with favor, pair marriages have been the usual practice. A social system in which most marriages are pair marriages but in which polygamy is not forbidden, is not, strictly speaking, monogamous. *Monogamy, in ethics, is the moral system that forbids all marriages except those between one man and one woman as wrong, and not merely impracticable.* Monogamy in this sense is comparatively rare in savage life. When ethical monogamy appears at a low level (and not merely the practice of pair marriage for unmoral reasons) we must suppose that the sexes are approximately equal in numbers, that there are no marked social or economic classes, and for other reasons that there is little inclination toward polygamy.

At higher levels the reasons for insistence on monogamy are partly moral and partly unmoral. (1) The moral worth of woman has become appreciated. In conditions of greater economic comfort, she no longer loses her physical attractiveness at an early age, and she is appreciated more for mental qualities. Husbands no longer think of her chiefly as an economic asset—so that the more wives a man has, the more wealthy he is judged to be, either because (at a less advanced stage) the women do most of the work and so increase their husband's wealth; or because (at a higher stage) they are all supported by him in ease and probably seclusion, and to have a large number of wives is a mark of prestige. On the other hand, men have learned that in permanent devotion to a single wife the greatest happiness in home and children is to be found, for themselves as well as for women and children. Such considerations as these are moral. They may be felt rather than reasoned; but the reflective element would seem to be more in evidence than is ordinarily true of custom morality. (2) The unmoral factor enters in this way. A monogamous family holds together more loyally, being free from the rivalries and jealousies of the harem. Peoples who maintain a strictly monogamous family system have a stronger and more durable social organization. They have therefore won out in the struggle for existence, as a matter of selection.[17] Few nations at the present time are to be found among high civilizations that are not strictly monogamous in their customs. The chief exceptions are Turkey and China, in each of which there is now a strong movement in favor of monogamy.

It will be understood that monogamy more often appears under Authority than Kinship, but since it does occasionally appear under the latter, it has been convenient to mention it in connection with other forms of marriage, to illustrate the combined influence of moral and unmoral causes in the production of customs.

VI. The Relation of Authority

The immediate effect of the rise of the primitive despot was to strengthen the hold of custom in most respects. He wished order within his domain, forced disputes to be brought to him for settlement, and decided them most often in accordance with the customs of the group. In the expansion of kingdoms and building up of empires, rulers usually recognized the local customs of subject populations. With more power to enforce compliance with their decisions, the sway of custom was on the whole rather strengthened, in comparison with the earlier era of the relation of Kinship.

However, the spread of a kingdom or empire could not leave customs wholly undisturbed. The rise of social classes developed new customs. A slave was less important than an ordinary citizen, still less than a nobleman. Punishments for murder and other crimes varied therefore in accordance with the social status of the offender and his victim. With commercial expansion over wider areas and with advances in the arts and industries, laws had to be formulated to cover a larger variety of situations than simpler ages had known. Precedents could not always be found; and, if found, they often conflicted as larger areas and more diverse populations were brought within the domain. It became necessary more frequently for decisions of king and courts to be based upon some fundamental principle thought to underlie earlier law and custom, though never formulated theretofore.

Thus, not only in the case of the common law of England, which is the best example, but to a less extent in the evolution of law under an authoritarian government everywhere, there was a gradual evolution of reasoned principles thought to apply universally. Courts and rulers could only interpret these principles; decisions must not be made at the caprice of the judge, but in accordance with the law. As the development continued, and laws became more rational, systematic, and comprehensive, judges became bolder. When they could, they asserted that the laws were supreme even above the exercise of arbitrary power by the king himself. Above all was law.

But such a development of the conception of law took it beyond the boundaries of Custom Morality into those of Reflective Morality. When one generation begins to seek for the principles that underlie customs, and to formulate them, it is preparing the way for a later generation to criticize these principles, and discard those that do not appear to suit present conditions.

While, therefore, the immediate effect of the inauguration of Authority was to strengthen custom, yet ultimately the régime of Authority stimulated reflection. We have seen the influence of the development of law and justice in this respect. Other circumstances that contributed to the same result were the industrial expansion and foreign trade which empires made possible, the development of literature and the fine arts, improved methods of carrying on warfare, the multiplication of diverse myths, rituals, and dogmas, and the rivalry between different religious cults within the empire. All such advances stimulated the exchange of ideas, and criticism of existing customs. And criticism implies reflection. And as a final consequence, the régime of Authority was undermined. As a people learned to think for themselves legally, politically, socially, religiously, and morally, they became ready for the era of Citizenship.

VII. Citizenship and Reflective Morality

When citizens overthrow the system of Authority, and in the relation of Citizenship undertake self-government, they assume the responsibility of reasoning out what will be for their own good, and of obeying the laws that they have decided upon. Just as the customs of a group may be compared in some respects with the habits of an individual, the collective decisions of a self-governing state may be compared with the voluntary acts of an individual. An individual may act upon a sudden impulse, an irrational suggestion, or a hasty generalization based on superficial impressions. Such an act is his own, and he is responsible for it; but such an act is not truly rational. On the other hand, a decision carefully made after long deliberation, in which all of a man's interests and impulses have had time to come into consciousness, and all facts and probable consequences have been taken into account, is rational. It is a correct expression of a man's self, character, and will. Few human acts probably come up to this ideal entirely; the nearer all a man's more important decisions approximate to it, the stronger character and personality he has.

Now a state has no single mind or brain like an individual; a state is a group of individual minds and wills organized for political purposes. The decisions of a state are the decisions which the majority (or the controlling members) of the state have made. If these decisions have been carefully weighed by the leaders of the state, after long consultation and deliberation, in which all conflicting interests and impulses have been taken into account, the decisions are rational. They express the common will. Probably they will promote the common good, since rational decisions are usually farsighted, and not likely to be mistaken. A free state in which important decisions were always made in this manner would realize the ideal of Citizenship. No state ever has realized this ideal, of course; but the ancient city-states and the modern national states have endeavored to come as near to it as possible.

Representative government, with a system of checks and balances, a written constitution, and an independent judiciary, is believed by conservatives to be more likely to result in rational decisions for the common good than a pure democracy in which laws would be passed by direct popular initiative and referendum, in which all officials, including judges, could be recalled at any time of popular excitement, and in which a complete reversal of local and national precedents and policies could be effected as a result of a popular vote at a single election. On the other hand, radicals point out that if there are too many checks and balances, if a written constitution is too difficult to amend, and if courts are out of touch with popular opinion and contemporary conditions of living, work, and business, there will be few rational decisions for the common good. The problem is, to secure a proper balance between radicalism and conservatism.

The problems of a people in an era of Citizenship are by no means wholly political. Similar difficulties exist in every phase of modern life—religion, marriage, industry, commerce, education, art, science. Everywhere the question is, how to secure real progress through collective deliberation. Moral judgments enter into the situation at every hand. Conservatives in all these fields are keenly appreciative of the attainments of the past, by which we have reached our present level. They sometimes are more scholarly than the radicals. Not being in a hurry to change things overnight, they have time to study history, philosophy, science, and theology thoroughly. Radicals, though usually sincere and well meaning, are liable to be impulsive and excitable, to jump at wide generalizations on the basis of scant and misunderstood evidence, and to identify change of any kind with progress. But the radicals do not monopolize ignorance and passionate prejudice. Some men are conservatives, simply because they retain throughout life the conceptions that they learned in childhood, especially in fields lying outside of their own specialties, and refuse to read, observe, or reflect upon what has been going on about them since they left school.

One thing is clear. It is impossible to reason about everything at once. An individual has to make most of his decisions day by day as matters of habit or routine. He can reason carefully only about the more momentous questions that face him. So it is with public affairs under Citizenship. During any year, even during any generation, most of the customs, beliefs, and institutions of the past must remain little disturbed. Changes can only be considered when serious crises have arisen, making readjustment imperative, and where practical knowledge can be drawn upon to meet the situation.

By Reflective Morality is meant, therefore, the moral order that has its beginnings under the relation of Authority, and comes to fuller development under Citizenship, in which *endeavor is made to formulate moral judgments in new and serious situations on the basis of thoughtful criticism of principles as well as careful and dispassionate observation of facts.* This endeavor is often unsuccessful. Conservatives have sometimes been too devoted to customs sacred because of historical associations, and have prevented revisions that critical reflection would have favored. Radicals have sometimes been blind and passionate in their indignation at real or fancied wrongs, and have forced hasty adoption of impracticable measures for reform that left matters in the end worse than ever. It has been hardest to secure truly reflective moral judgments in situations involving deep-seated sentiments and loyalties, related to religion, the family, races, classes of society, and national interests. But on the whole, in each generation since the Renaissance progress toward the ideal of Reflective Morality has been made. Increasing toleration for differences of opinion on debatable subjects, increased respect for scholarly research and expert opinion, and indifference to conservative and radical prejudices mark every field of present day discussion. This assertion may seem optimistic. But no one will be unduly discouraged at the considerable amount of irrationality of our own age, if he will compare it with the much greater extent of irrationality in earlier periods.

In an age of Reflective Morality and Citizenship, custom morality is not and should not be superseded. Most of our moral judgments are and should be based on customs. These customs are handed down by tradition, and children learn them uncritically and unreflectively, just as they learn to speak, to dress themselves, and to use their knives and forks. Nearly all of us believe in monogamy, democracy, and the abolition of human slavery, as convictions that have come down to us in the moral tradition. The ordinary citizen could hardly advance arguments in favor of any of these offhand, should he fall into an unexpected argument with, say, an educated Arab who believed in polygamy, aristocracy, and slavery. This is not to be regretted. The point is, that these questions were all seriously and reflectively considered and decided upon by our cultural ancestors, and in our generation there has been no need to question the wisdom of their decisions. The student of comparative ethics and other historical subjects may profitably trace the history of such moral judgments, and learn their rational foundations. But most citizens should devote to the issues of our own time and country all the time they can afford to give to moral deliberation on public questions. It is our duty, as free citizens, to help solve these right, and to enrich further the moral tradition which we have inherited, and should in an improved form pass in our turn to the generation that succeeds us.

The difference, then, between custom morality in our age, and custom morality prior to the appearance of reflective morality is, that when necessary we can examine critically the reasons for customs, and alter them in the light of experience. We still act chiefly by customs, and hold the moral judgments of the groups to which we belong. But neither customs nor groups are so rigid that they cannot be criticized. Nothing can claim immunity from reflective criticism. On the other hand, no institution or custom should be seriously attacked unless there is time and will to make a thorough and scholarly study of all its aspects. Reflective morality no more connotes frenzied attack upon tradition than blind conformity to it.

VIII. Three General Characteristics of Moral Evolution

In concluding this chapter, attention is called to three characteristic tendencies in moral evolution that have been implied in the foregoing account. There is a *socializing*, an *individualizing*, and a *rationalizing* tendency. The three tendencies have not always been equally marked, and progress in one has occasionally been more rapid than in the others. Each tendency has usually, but not invariably, furthered the others.

A socializing tendency (or a tendency to socialization) *effects increased capacity on the part of human beings to enter with one another into relations implying increased sympathy and coöperation.* This tendency and its goal are not necessarily to be identified with the aims of "socialists", with "socialism", or with anything "socialistic". All moral philosophers believe in "socialization". Only the comparative few who are socialists believe that this socializing tendency ever will or should lead to a social order of a type that could be called a form of socialism.

The primitive horde, the maternal system, the paternal

system, and the relation of Authority each in turn enabled larger numbers of mankind to become organized in groups, which inspired in them sentiments of loyalty and common interest, and afforded them security under a common government extending over a wider area. This quantitative increase in socialization made qualitative increases possible also. The latter included economic progress, *i.e.*, a higher standard of living for every one, in comparison with that previously available to persons of the same class and status. Men became capable of mutual sympathy and coöperation within larger groups. This in turn made possible advances in cultural activities of every kind—architecture, literature, religion, and the fine arts. Political and economic progress opened the way for higher spiritual achievements.

Has the relation of Citizenship effected further progress in socialization? The ancient city-states could not carry the extensive side of socialization beyond a limited area and population, without in some measure relapsing into the relation of Authority. Modern national states have done better. However, they have not yet wholly succeeded in effecting sympathetic relations with one another. Patriotism—the group spirit of a nation—is a powerful socializing factor when at its best. Can it be combined with a still more inclusive group spirit, with a love of humanity that will serve as a solid basis for more socialization in international relations? On the whole, perhaps, we can venture an affirmative answer, and prophesy that the relation of Citizenship shall in the end prove a lasting advance in both quantitative and qualitative socialization. The realization of this hope should prove to be one of the greatest achievements of this century.

An individualizing tendency affords increased opportunity for each person of his own free choice to pursue interests in accordance with his tastes and capacities. "Individualization" and "individualizing" will be used throughout this volume in this sense. They do not necessarily imply "individualism", nor is the advocate of them necessarily an "individualist" or a believer in "capitalism" in the technical sense in which such terms are opposed in controversy to "socialism" and "collectivism",—a controversy which will receive due notice in Chapter XVI. Everybody, of all schools in ethics and social philosophy, probably believes that social progress connotes increased individualization in the sense of the above italicized statement.

The general course of social evolution has manifested this tendency toward increased individualization. Progress in economic activities, warfare, and the arts, even during the successive stages of Kinship, gave wider scope to the individual to express himself. Increased division of labor and greater diversity of occupations afforded the individual more of a chance to choose what he most liked to do. Under the relation of Authority the great development of warfare afforded military careers with honor, power, and wealth for the courageous. The gradual recognition of individual ownership of land and other forms of property made it possible for the talented, thrifty, and industrious to carry on a wide variety of occupations, and to acquire wealth and pass it down to their descendants. The breakdown of endogamous and exogamous restrictions left the individual greater freedom in marriage. Kings and courts of law as a rule afforded the individual more real security in life, liberty, and possessions than Kinship groups had been able to give him. With the abolition of collective responsibility, the individual was no longer necessarily involved in the quarrels of his kinsmen, and so liable to suffer vengeance for misdeeds in which he personally had no part. During Citizenship, the individual has enjoyed freedom in religion, speech, publication, and association. Compulsory military service has been less frequent, as wars have become fewer, and usually less destructive in proportion to the size of the nations involved. Educational institutions of all kinds have multiplied, elementary schooling has become open to all, and secondary and higher education, both cultural and technical, is accessible to a larger proportion of individuals.

As a rule, increased socialization and increased individualization have progressed together. As individuals have had freer opportunity to develop their tastes and talents, they have been able to sympathize and coöperate with one another more effectively. However, there have been exceptions. Some of these have been more apparent than real. For instance, a revolutionary age has sometimes sought to increase individualization by overthrowing all restraints such as those afforded by religion, the family, and property. The resulting chaos, however, including economic distress, not to say famine and pestilence, lack of security in family ties, universal suspicion of fellow men, and the breakdown of educational institutions has not only been anti-socializing, but has been anti-individualizing as well, since the individual has had little free choice to express or develop himself in any way. The real exceptions are less pronounced. They are merely cases in which an increase in individual rights is not attended at once by a like increase in public spirit and service; and conversely. To some extent the age of Socrates and the Sophists was more individualized than socialized; while the thirteenth century A.D. in western Europe was more socialized and institutionalized than individualized.

A rationalizing tendency leads men to display more intelligence in their conduct, and to seek new and higher personal and social ends and values. Before the development of reflective morality this tendency was present, but men were hardly conscious of it. Men spoke intelligently, and in accordance with rules, long before these rules were consciously and reflectively discovered and set forth in grammar. So, during Kinship and the early stages of Authority, customs developed that on the whole were intelligent and promoted the common good, before they were codified as laws. Even the first codifications were not fully reflective. Only later, out of changed political or economic conditions, new situations arose which law and custom had not anticipated. Then for the first time customs had to be thoroughly criticized. Morality became rational, in the sense that reasons for customs were carefully and critically estimated. First attempts to explain the reasons for customs were often only partly successful. Bad reasons were given for good conduct; and conduct was sustained that better reasoning would have condemned.

So far as reasoning is used illogically to support conduct by individuals or groups it may be called *pseudo-rationalization.* Freud and other contemporary psychologists often employ the term "rationalization" to describe any reasoned explanation of conduct, whether logically correct or not; and they usually give as illustrations cases where the reasoning is illogical. In the present volume, however, "reason", "rationalizing", and "rationalization" will not be used in this broad sense, but will be confined to logical processes. "Reasoning" and "reasoned", however, will be used broadly, to include both good and bad ratiocination. All *reasoned* conduct thus is either *rational* (logical rationalization) or is *irrational* (illogical reasoning or pseudo-rationalization).

Under Kinship, the development of the maternal system and totemism may be regarded as the expression of a rationalizing tendency. As compared with the primitive horde, the relations between men were better thought out and defined. The organization on the whole made for the common good. Moreover, men learned to appreciate new ends and values, such as loyalty to one's kin, and coöperation with them in defense and in retaliation for injuries. Under the paternal system, the organization of family life was still more intelligent. New values, including a fuller appreciation of fatherhood, and love and respect for parents and remoter ancestors developed. During these periods, intelligence was also appearing in the improvement of tools and weapons, in singing, dancing, the making of textiles and pottery, in the practical and fine arts generally. In the early eras of Authority, before conduct became reflective, men manifested increased intelligence in the evolution of law and justice, in the advances in commerce and industry, the invention of writing and the beginnings of literature, in submission to the king and respect for his moral and religious functions and responsibilities. Whatever reasons were given for customs in these prereflective ages were likely to be irrational—myths and superstitions, magic and mistaken science.

The dawn of reflective morality and the changes that it makes in moral evolution, as rationalizations take the place of blind customs and pseudo-rationalizations, will be indicated in subsequent chapters, with specific reference to the Hebrews, the Greeks, and the modern Renaissance and Enlightenment. Suffice it to say here, that conduct, as it has become more intelligent and reflective, has succeeded better in attaining ends already known, and has learned to seek higher values that had not previously been appreciated. Respect for the worth and dignity of every human being is one outstanding instance of a higher value that was first appreciated in the relation of Citizenship and its reflective morality. This has led to the abolition of slavery, the emancipation of women, the spread of popular education, and attempts to make it possible for every one to share in all the goods of modern civilization, provided he does his part.

REFERENCES

See References to Chapter II.

CHAPTER IV

THE MORAL DEVELOPMENT OF THE ANCIENT HEBREWS

I. INTRODUCTORY. HISTORICAL OUTLINE

A study of the moral development of the ancient Hebrews is of special interest to the student of comparative ethics for two general reasons. First, many principles of social and moral evolution are well illustrated. This is particularly true of the transitions from the paternal system of Kinship organization to the relation of Authority, from group and custom morality to reflective morality, and from collective responsibility to personal responsibility. The socializing, individualizing, and rationalizing tendencies are all in evidence. The unique features of the Hebrew moral development, such as the rôle of religion and the conception of a covenant between the people and their God, are also significant. Secondly, the Hebrew Scriptures, accepted by both Christians and Jews as divinely inspired, have been read and studied in every age, and continue to exercise a profound influence on the modern moral consciousness. Many moral judgments widely current to-day could hardly be understood without reference to the contributions made to our moral tradition by the ancient Hebrews.[1]

It will be necessary to begin with an outline of a few facts in ancient Hebrew history. From perhaps the thirteenth to the tenth centuries before Christ (dates in this chapter are often rough approximations) the land of Palestine (or Canaan) was gradually invaded by bands of nomads coming northward from the Arabian desert. The nomads lived in tents and raised sheep and cattle. They did not practice agriculture. Their social organization was the paternal form of Kinship, and they were grouped in patriarchal families, clans, and tribes.

Some authorities believe that they retained rudiments of an earlier maternal system, including totemism; but this is uncertain.[2] There was no intertribal organization, but they had a dim national feeling that their tribes were by blood related. Perhaps the tradition already existed that each of the tribes was descended from a different son or grandson of a single man called Jacob or Israel. They gradually conquered the "Canaanites", the agricultural peoples whom they found in Palestine, partly exterminating them, and in time intermarrying with the descendants of the survivors. The nomads believed that they had a covenant with Yahweh, their national war god, who aided them in their battles, and in turn expected them to express their loyal devotion by offering sacrifices to him, and by obeying the customs ordained by him. On their entrance into Palestine, the former nomads settled down to agriculture. Following the example of the Canaanites, they supplemented their worship of Yahweh with that of various local nature gods (Baals or Baalim) believed to produce fertility in the soil and to safeguard its products—grain, fruits, wine, honey, and the like.[3]

By the tenth century, the Israelitish tribes had sufficiently conquered and fused with the Canaanites to develop a national consciousness. They became sensible of their lack of unity in their relations with one another, and their need of a more united front against the strong and often hostile nations surrounding them. So the transition to the relation of Authority by the institution of a king to lead them in war and govern them in peace came about naturally. The kings, supported by the sanction of Yahweh, enforced group and custom morality. At first the country was under the rule of a single king (Saul, David, Solomon). Subsequently it became divided into two kingdoms—the northern, sometimes called "Israel", and the southern, called "Judah". During this period unwritten customs gradually became formulated into written laws.[4]

The transition to reflective morality largely began in the eighth century with the "writing prophets" of whom Amos was the first in time. These prophets in the name of Yahweh commanded extensive reforms in customs and conduct, to correct the evils of the times. They threatened that Yahweh would punish disobedience to these commands by the loss of national independence. The morality of these prophets, critical as it was of the practices of the times, may rightly be called reflective. It was, however, nationalistic, with little appreciation of the moral worth of other peoples. However, these prophets made some moral impression on the national consciousness, and achieved a temporary political success when King Josiah attempted to carry out their reforms in the southern kingdom. The original code of Deuteronomy embodied their ideas in its legislation.[5]

The northern kingdom came to an end with the Assyrian conquest of 722 B.C. The southern kingdom was subdued in 586 B.C. by Nebuchadnezzar, king of Babylon, who destroyed the temple of Yahweh in Jerusalem and took many of the leading families away into captivity in Babylon, leaving the remainder of the population in a wretched condition. This period of enforced captivity in Babylon, known as the "exile", came to an end shortly after 538 B.C., when the Babylonian domain, including Palestine, became incorporated in the empire of Persia. Those of the Jewish exiles in Babylon who desired to do so were then permitted to return to Palestine. A movement, in which Ezra and Nehemiah played important parts, effected a thorough revival of the study of the Law, and the promulgation of new legislation. Presently synagogues arose throughout all the Jewish communities in the world, where the Law was studied, and Yahweh was worshiped without animal sacrifices, as the latter were permitted only in the temple at Jerusalem. In 332 B.C., Palestine was conquered by Alexander the Great, after whose death it passed into the empire of his Greek successors in Egypt, the Ptolemies. Jews migrated freely to other countries, and large numbers of them settled in Alexandria, which became an important center of Jewish culture.

The experiences of the exile had profound effects on Hebrew

reflective morality. The exile itself naturally broke down
whatever survivals of the primitive Kinship organization had
persisted in family, clan, and tribal systems. So collective
responsibility gave place to personal responsibility. Increasing
contact with the outside world under Persian, and still more
under Greek rule, broke down much of the narrower nationalistic outlook. A more universalistic note is manifested in
such writings as Isaiah II, Ruth, and Jonah. The writers of
the "Wisdom" literature—perhaps under the more or less conscious influence of Greek philosophy—were able to state moral
principles in detachment from nationalistic theology, though
they remained faithful to Yahweh. Other writers, however,
remained more narrowly nationalistic, and Hebrew morality on
the whole assumed a legalistic and ritualistic form, closely
bound up with the Jewish religion. The real Hebrew contributions to morality have therefore been closely associated with
the religion. By means of this, the Hebrew moral judgments
enlist emotions and sentiments in a lofty and spiritual way, and
become effective in conduct. The ancient Hebrews never
passed beyond the relation of Authority in their political and
social system, although the synagogue was always democrati-
cally organized, and is suggestive of the spirit of Citizenship.
Perhaps the failure to attain Citizenship in their political
structure partly explains why the differentiation of ethics from
religion, and the keener discernment of moral principles thereby
afforded was not the contribution of the ancient Hebrews, but
only of the ancient Greeks, to the modern moral tradition.[6]

II. The Kinship Period

The conquest and occupation of Palestine by the nomadic
tribes of Israel, as has been said, was a gradual process which
was only completed in three or four centuries. During the
earlier portion of this period, each tribe fought largely by
themselves, and the territories captured and successfully held
were often separated by land still occupied by unconquered
Canaanites. Sometimes, prompted by their common Kinship

and their Yahweh religion, two or more Israelitish tribes would temporarily combine forces in a campaign.[7] A successful leader in war won prestige, and continued to exercise some authority in his own locality as a "judge". He maintained order and settled disputes, probably in accordance with customs handed down in oral tradition.

In that era of group morality, defeated enemies had no rights. So the vanquished Canaanites were massacred, expelled, enslaved, made tributary, or assimilated by intermarriages—whichever at the time seemed to their victors most expedient (Judges I–III). It was a man's duty to avenge the slaughter of his relatives and near kinsmen (Judges VIII. 18–21). Under ordinary conditions of peace, hospitality was shown to strangers, even at personal risk and sacrifice (Judges XIX. 15–24). However, the custom of hospitality did not prevent Jael's treacherous murder of a guest and trusting ally from making her "most blessed among women", since she did it in the national interest (Judges IV. 17–22, V. 24–27).

Toward the close of the period, after the tribes had developed a stronger sense of their common kinship, an outrageous violation of customs of hospitality, involving rape and murder, aroused general indignation. The common comment was that "there was no such deed done nor seen from the day that the children of Israel came up out of the land of Egypt unto this day: consider it, take counsel and speak". The tribe of Benjamin, of whom the offenders were members, were called upon to deliver them over for punishment, but the closer blood tie led the Benjamites to protect their guilty fellow tribesmen. In consequence the other tribes united in a common attack, and the Benjamites were nearly exterminated. There was then a reversion of sympathy in favor of the Benjamites, who were doubtless thought to have been sufficiently punished, and ought not to perish as a tribe. The whole incident well illustrates the good and bad features of group and custom morality, blood revenge, and collective responsibility, in a period when "there was no king in Israel" (*i.e.*, no authoritative interpreter and enforcer of custom and law) and "every man did that which was right in his own eyes" (*i.e.*, the tribes by informal group action gave expression to their collective sentiments in almost moblike fashion. (Judges XIX–XXI.)

Yahweh, the war god of all the Israelites, was believed to inspire the leaders with his "spirit" (*mana* ?) when acting in their military and judicial functions. Yahweh could be consulted by the casting of lots and the use of ephods. He revealed himself in dreams, and he or his representative appeared in human form to give instructions (Judges II. 1–5; VI. 11–22; XIII; I Samuel III). In his personal characteristics, Yahweh was an idealization of the heads of their paternal families and clans. Vows made to him must be kept at any cost, even to the sacrifice of an only daughter (Judges XI. 30–40). A curse in his name would frighten a son to restore property that he had stolen from his mother (Judges XVII. 2). Yahweh was believed to enforce group and custom morality, *e.g.*, in revenging the murder of brothers (Judges IX. 5, 56, 57), and sending lying spirits to mislead the guilty to their ruin (Judges IX. 23). He was thought to have sent an assassin in time of peace to kill a foreign ruler who received him in good faith (Judges III. 15–23). During this period Yahweh was probably thought not to object to the worship of Canaanite Baals for success in agricultural activities, then supposed not to fall within his domain; although such practices were denounced by the Deuteronomic editor of Judges in the comments he inserted into the book at a later date. Yahweh was believed to be vindictive in war, and to demand severe treatment of the conquered. Yahweh, it was thought, would send defeat upon the whole people for the guilt of one of their number, in accordance with the principles of group morality. In such cases Yahweh could only be appeased by the burning of the guilty man together with his children, cattle, and all his possessions (Joshua VII).

Though such a moral outlook and the religion that gave it sanction were savage, the Israelites at this time were a virile people, with ideals and conduct for the most part normal for the Kinship stage. They were brave in war, loyal to kinsmen, frugal in living, and generally hospitable to strangers. The position of woman, as is common in the paternal system, was not exalted. Her chastity, however, was usually protected. She received some consideration as the property of her father or husband. Deborah, a woman with marked powers of leadership, even became one of the "judges" (Judges IV, V). The story of Hannah, who lived toward the close of the period, reveals a high appreciation of motherhood. (I Samuel I, II.) In a later age a story writer with verisimilitude could place Ruth, one of the most attractive women in the Bible, in this period. Polygamy and concubinage were permitted, and were practiced by the prosperous in this, as in all periods down to the exile.

This was a period of increasing socialization, individualization, and rationalization. The necessity for common action in wars, both of conquest and defense, must have been an important socializing influence. The cultivation of land, which passed into private ownership, was a cause of individualization. The rule of the judges, who had to interpret old customs under changing conditions, made for rationalization. The worship of Yahweh, the strongest force in all Hebrew history, furthered these three tendencies, each of which in many respects strengthened the others.

III. THE KINGDOM PRIOR TO AMOS

The rule of the kings reinforced the earlier moral traditions. The historical books relate further incidents of group responsibility and blood revenge, like the hanging up before Yahweh of two of Saul's sons and five of his grandsons in retribution for Saul's slaying the Gibeonites years before (II Samuel XXI. 1–14): and the pestilence sent upon the people of Israel for David's sin in taking a national census (II Samuel XXIV).[8] Those defeated in wars—whether foreign or civil—are treated with ruthlessness. Blood is shed freely upon mere suspicion and jealousy (II Samuel XX. 9, 10; I Kings II. 36–46; XII. 18). There is the same fear of violating an oath (I Kings I.

50–53; II. 5–9, 19–25) or even unwittingly incurring the curse of Yahweh (I Samuel XIV. 36 ff.); otherwise moral restraints upon treachery are not very powerful (II Samuel XI; I Kings XXI. 10–13). Kings and other prosperous men are polygamous, the former largely to strengthen the kingdom by marriages with foreign princesses. On the other hand, the better aspects of group morality—courage, loyalty, friendship, generosity, gratitude, hospitality, and rough justice are also in evidence. (I Samuel XI. 12, 13; XIV. 6 ff.; XVII. 32 ff.; XVIII. 1; XXIII. 15 ff.; XXVI. 6 ff.; XXXI. 11 f.; II Samuel I. 25 ff.; VIII. 15; XVII. 27–29; XXIII. 8 ff.; I Kings II. 7; III. 16 ff.)

If we can regard the "Covenant Code" (Exodus XX. 23–XXIII. 33; XXXIV) as containing the customs that became written law during this period, further light is thrown upon the moral consciousness. Codes and laws are conservative; they represent what have become matters of general agreement, rather than the forward look of moral leaders and reformers. Still, unlike the Hebrew historical books and our modern newspapers, they do not relate unusual and startling incidents that are more lurid than typical. The codes show recognition of the simpler rights of property, forbid theft and abuse of trusteeships and assess damages for injuries. Women and Hebrew slaves are protected in various ways, though from the point of view of the paternal system which puts them more or less in the category of property. Personal rights are also recognized: murder, laying a curse on one's parents, sacrificing to other gods than Yahweh, manstealing, sorcery, and keeping an ox that kills a freeman are all capital offenses. Certain other personal injuries are punished by damages. There is some conception of social justice: protection is afforded the poor and weak, including the fatherless, the widow, and the concubine; slaves are not to be overworked, but allowed to rest on the Sabbath; no interest is to be charged on a loan to a poor Hebrew. The laws seek to assure administration of justice by penalizing false witness, trickery, slander, libel, and judges who bend to the pressure of popular clamor.[9]

This period, therefore, was one of increasing socialization, illustrated by the consolidation of the tribes into the kingdoms, and by the centralization of the worship. Increasing individualization is shown by the development of agriculture and commerce. Both rationalization and individualization attended the development of custom into written laws that recognized personal, property and social rights and obligations. Morality, however, remained in the prereflective stage of custom and group morality.

IV. THE PREËXILIC PROPHETS AND THE BOOK OF DEUTERONOMY

The chief credit for effecting the transition to reflective morality among the ancient Hebrews is due to Amos and the other "writing prophets"—men who reflected upon the political, social, and moral problems of the times, and in the firm conviction that they were speaking under the guidance and inspiration of Yahweh, publicly proclaimed what ought to be done. Their chief work was preaching moral and religious reforms; they occasionally professed to predict future events, but this was more or less incidental. They are called "writing prophets" because they left some of their discourses in written form—in contrast to the earlier prophets like Nathan, Elijah, and Elisha—an indication of more profound and systematic thought and more constructive contributions in a period of greater culture.

The rapid agricultural and commercial development beginning with the brilliant reigns of David and Solomon had been attended by some of the abuses characteristic of such periods. Like all radical reformers of every age, the prophets before the exile probably exaggerated these evils. However, economic prosperity had not come to all; the successful were often ostentatious in the display of their wealth, and sometimes unscrupulous in the ways in which they acquired it. The poor were exploited by usurers, and were even sometimes sold into slavery for the collection of trifling debts. Merchants sometimes used false weights and measures. Kings and queens were sometimes unjust and oppressive. While these wrongs were all forbidden in the laws, it was difficult to get justice under judges who took bribes. Personal morality was low; there was much drunkenness and sexual misconduct, which the worship of Canaanite Baals and imported foreign deities encouraged.

Amos vehemently called attention to these wrongs, and urged reformation in the name of the religion of Yahweh. At that time there was a current tradition that a "Day of Yahweh" was coming in which the national enemies would all be overthrown, and Israel would reign supreme over all the earth, and enjoy abundant prosperity. Amos, on the contrary, proclaimed that unless the people repented, and thoroughly reformed in their personal and social conduct, this "Day of Yahweh" would prove to be a day of doom in which Israel would be punished by foreign conquest. Merely faithful compliance with ritualistic sacrifices will not satisfy Yahweh; he demands personal righteousness and social justice. The messages of the other prophets before the exile were similar in their general tenor.

These prophets made Hebrew morality reflective. They built upon the moral and religious tradition of their times, but gave it a new interpretation. According to the tradition, the relation between Yahweh and the Israelites was based upon a covenant. Yahweh was to lead them in war, assist them to conquer Canaan, and maintain them there free and prosperous. The Israelites, as their part of the covenant, were to keep up the ritualistic worship of Yahweh, and obey the customary moral judgments which they supposed to be the commands of Yahweh. Ritualistic worship had probably seemed the more important part of the obligation to Yahweh, and in this period of prosperity sacrifices to Yahweh were more lavish than ever before. As king and father of his people, Yahweh would never forsake the Israelites, and allow their enemies to conquer them. Such was the tradition.

The prophets, however, pointed out that there was much social injustice and personal immorality in the land, in clear violation of unwritten customs and written laws commanded by Yahweh. Elaborate performance of ritual could not atone for unrepented wrongs. Yahweh demanded justice more than sacrifices. If the Israelites kept failing to keep their part of the covenant, Yahweh would repudiate them. This new conception of Yahweh held by the prophets is in marked advance of earlier periods. For the prophets, Yahweh is sublime, powerful, loving, and wise, but sternly just and capable of righteous indignation and uncompromising anger against wrong-doers. All his rewards and punishments are thought to be material; but the distinctions between right and wrong conduct are firmly and definitely drawn. What these prophets did, therefore, was to fix attention upon the difference between good and evil actions, to insist that their god stood absolutely for the good and against the evil, and to interpret the national outlook accordingly. No other god but Yahweh should be worshiped by the Israelite.

In other words, the preëxilic prophets detached moral judgments from mere customs and from ritual, and made a direct appeal. They correspondingly rationalized and moralized the conception of Yahweh. In this sense they made morality reflective. But the reflective character of their morality had limitations. They saw moral obligations between different individuals and classes within the nation much more clearly than they recognized moral obligations to other nations. And they still thought in some respects in terms of group morality and collective responsibility. The nation as a whole might be punished for the sins of earlier generations. Their relation to Yahweh in many respects was that of a group, rather than of separate individuals. Yahweh, while supreme in all the earth above other gods, is concerned only for the good of Israel; he is indifferent to the welfare of other peoples as ends in themselves. So the morality and religion of these prophets were only partly reflective after all.

The partially reflective character of morality and religion in this period is illustrated in the book of Deuteronomy. The good features of the earlier code are retained, and there are some advances. The covenant relation is brought into prominence. Yahweh has chosen Israel because he loved them, and he expects them to keep his laws, as set forth in this code, on pain of punishment. His appeal is both to fear and to love. He forbids them to worship any other god than himself. He enforces collective responsibility through successive generations. The social legislation of the code seeks to protect Israelites who are poor, fatherless, widows, slaves, concubines, or in other ways unfortunate and defenseless. Debts of Israelites are to be canceled every seven years, interest on loans is not to be charged to Israelites, and they are not to be sold the meat of animals which have died a natural death. There is much less protection afforded foreigners. In war a foreign nation living in the vicinity of Israel should be utterly exterminated. The arbitrary power of the father over children in the paternal system is restricted so that it does not extend to taking their lives without the consent of their mother and of the elders. The *lex talionis* holds in punishment of wrongs: an eye for an eye, a tooth for a tooth, a life for a life. However, distinction is made between accidental and intentional homicide. Kindness to animals is commanded.

V. THE EXILE AND AFTER

The bitter experiences of the exile promoted the development of Hebrew reflective religion and morality. It forced a new and more spiritual interpretation of the relation between Israel, other nations, and Yahweh, and also the recognition of profounder moral values. It broke down whatever had persisted of the old paternal, family, and tribal organization, and placed a larger emphasis on the rights and responsibilities of the individual. It ultimately resulted in a deeper appreciation of the importance of human motives, and in a recognition of righteousness as good in itself, apart from worldly prosperity.[10]

The capture of Jerusalem and the temple of Yahweh by the Babylonians was a severe shock to those who still held to the traditional views in religion. Could it be true that Marduk, god of Babylon, had so overcome Yahweh, god of Israel, in battle that the latter's holy temple, his peculiar habitat, had been destroyed? They were loath to believe this; they preferred to accept the interpretation of the prophets from Amos to Jeremiah who had been insisting that Yahweh would punish Israel by a foreign conquest. The more reflective view of religion thus became generally accepted by the Jews, and was now given a further extension.

The second Isaiah urges that Yahweh is all powerful. He is in fact, the only God of the whole earth; heathen gods are mere idols made by human hands. (Isaiah XL, XLIV. After the exile the Jews worshiped Yahweh exclusively, without the use of images of any kind; they became strictly monotheistic.) Moreover, Yahweh cannot have forsaken Israel, any more than a mother would forsake her suckling child (Isaiah XLIX. 14, 15). The severe punishment in Babylon has been sufficient, and Yahweh has blotted out her sins from His memory (Isaiah XLII. 25). Yahweh, who is supreme over all the earth, has called the heathen Cyrus, king of Persia, to deliver Israel from the Babylonian yoke, and to permit the exiles to return to Jerusalem to rebuild the temple there, and to revive his worship, for the sake, not of Israel only, but of all nations. (Isaiah XLV.) Why has Yahweh punished Israel so much more severely than other nations, although, notwithstanding her sins, she has not been so wicked as they? It is in order that Israel may become "a light of the nations", so that the deliverance of Yahweh "may be unto the end of the earth". In other words, Israel has borne the sins of the world, and the other nations have regarded Israel as smitten of God and afflicted, whereas this chastisement of Israel was in punishment for the sins of all nations. (The "servant songs"—Isaiah XLII. 1–4; XLIX. 1–6; L. 4–9; LII. 13–LIII. 12—are now agreed to refer to Israel, who is the "suffering servant" afflicted by Yahweh for the sins of the world.) In a certain sense, this is a movement toward an international view in ethics.

The second Isaiah gave a new and more spiritual interpretation of group morality. Before the exile it was the belief that one generation of Israelites might be punished by Yahweh for the sins of earlier generations, or the whole nation for the sin of one of its members. In other words, there was a moral solidarity in the nation that made it a collective personality. This idea is now extended to include all humanity. Israel as a nation may be punished for the sins of humanity, so that through her suffering all nations may repent and be led to accept Yahweh as their God. So the exile was interpreted to signify the moral solidarity of mankind, and their redemption through the mediation and sacrifice of Israel.

Apart from any religious considerations, every ethical student will concede that we have here a discovery of profound moral truth. Individuals and nations are constantly suffering not only for their own wrongdoing, but for that of others; and sometimes it is possible for those who thus suffer not only to gain greater strength and sweetness of character for themselves, but also to impart a richer moral insight to those on whose account they have suffered. The doctrines of group solidarity and collective responsibility, thus rationalized and socialized, reveal deep ethical significance. To those of us who believe in religion, the second Isaiah was right in associating this ethical truth with a theistic interpretation; Jews and Christians are right in affirming that through the sufferings of the ancient Hebrews God was revealing Himself to mankind for all time.

In other respects, reflective morality means the breakdown of group morality, and the sole responsibility of every individual for his own conduct, and not for that of his ancestors, nor for that of his adult children. Jeremiah, probably, and Ezekiel with unmistakable emphasis, proclaimed that Yahweh does not punish children for the sins of their fathers nor fathers for the sins of their children, but every one for his own sin. (Jeremiah XXXI. 27–34; Ezekiel XVIII.) The legislation of the postexilic period recognizes the principle of individual responsibility before the law (Deuteronomy XXIV. 16). Jeremiah is preëminent for his intimate discourses with God, which show how individualistic and personal was his religious experience (e.g., Jeremiah XIV, XV).[11] Ezekiel feels a personal responsibility, like that of a modern pastor, to serve the individuals committed to his care (Ezekiel XXXIII).

With the affirmation of the worth of the individual, reflective morality advanced to the formulation of precepts for guidance in the personal conduct of life. These, as ultimately collected in the books of Proverbs and Ecclesiasticus, set forth fundamental moral principles applicable to all subsequent ages. A man should honor his father and mother and have regard for the aged. He should be loyal to his friends and generous to the poor. He should be frugal and industrious. He should love his wife and be faithful to her. He should avoid greed, covetousness, envy, lying, hypocrisy, slothfulness, and drunkenness. A simple and contented life is better than one of luxury and ostentation. A good name is rather to be chosen than great riches. In all his life a man should cultivate wisdom and understanding; to think clearly and discern intelligently is the foundation of all welfare. And to do this best one should worship God. The fear of the Lord is the beginning of wisdom. A man who follows such precepts will usually prosper in a material sense. In any event, his is the kind of life that is really most worth while. Similar virtues are recognized and commended in women.

These books contain, we are sometimes told, merely worldly wisdom. It might be replied that it is wisdom upon which too few men have ever earnestly endeavored to act. If the majority of mankind would sincerely follow these precepts, the earth would soon be a far better place than it has ever yet become, or shows much prospect of becoming in our time. The sages who talk to us in these books are free from bigotry and fanaticism. They know better than to fancy that visionary schemes for social regeneration will ever work so long as most men continue to be weak and foolish in the conduct of their individual lives. They seek to build a better age on the solid foundation of individual integrity. However, the outlook of the sages would have been impossible except in a well ordered civilization. No one could have conceived the morality of the "Wisdom" literature in the time of the Judges. Men of wisdom and integrity are the products of an advanced society; if we are to have them we must study how to maintain good social institutions; we cannot take the latter for granted, as did the writers of these books.

Again, wise and good men are not always happy. They usually are, but there are exceptions. How, if we believe in the providence of God, are we to explain the exceptions? Such problems as these are confronted in different ways in the books of Job and Ecclesiastes. The conclusion of the former is, that while we cannot discern the providence of God in the afflictions of the righteous and the prosperity of the wicked, we should none the less in view of our ignorance and finitude firmly trust His omniscience and omnipotence. Goodness is an end in itself, regardless of whether it brings worldly prosperity. The original book of Ecclesiastes, before it was amended by a later editor who made pious additions in the interests of orthodoxy, seems to have taught that the world order proceeds in accordance with fixed mechanical laws, and that the ultimate reasons for things cannot be known by man. The best thing for us to do is to be virtuous and cheerful, benevolent and prudent, and to enjoy life while we are young. If we do this we shall probably be happy. At any rate, we should not fret at what we cannot understand, but smile and make the best of things.

Hebrew ethics were bound up with Hebrew religion. The books of Job and Ecclesiastes, in their doubt as to the religious foundations of ethics, are not typical. More characteristic are the Psalms, whose confidence in the goodness, justice, mercy, and forgiveness of Yahweh is constant and sublime. If in the imprecatory Psalms this is combined with an immoral desire for fierce and cruel vengeance on the national enemies, it can at least be said that this was only human in view of the miseries suffered by the Israelites during foreign oppression.

A delight in the Law of Yahweh—ultimately compiled in the Torah or Pentateuch, the first five books of our Bibles—with close attention to ritual and love of personal and social justice became and has remained the characteristic mark of Judaism as a religion, and of the ethics that this religion has supported. To be sure, this has at times degenerated into formal ceremonialism in ritual, and finely spun casuistry in ethics. At times, harassed by persecution, Judaism has degenerated into a narrow nationalism "convicted of hatred against all mankind", and inspired by the hope that Yahweh would inflict wholesale retribution upon the Gentiles, and subjugate the whole of humanity to the physical and spiritual domination of the chosen people and their Messiah. But as a rule, the love of the Lord and of His Law has been spiritual and sublime. It has often induced the Jew to love his Gentile neighbors even while they persecuted him. It has taught him to seek purity of heart and inner motives, and patiently to bear his burdens. He has faithfully studied the Torah in the synagogues and preserved traditions of morality and pure religion when the rest of the world was ignorant or forgetful of them. On the whole, Judaism has been heroically true to the sublime universalism and the priestly service to mankind proclaimed by the second Isaiah.

REFERENCES

* Dewey and Tufts, *Ethics*, chap. VI.
* L. T. Hobhouse, *Morals in Evolution*, Part II, chap. IV.
* J. B. Pratt, *Psychology of Religious Belief*, chap. V.
* J. M. Powis Smith, *The Moral Life of the Hebrews. The Prophets of Israel.*
* W. B. Bizzell, *The Social Teachings of the Hebrew Prophets.*
* G. F. Moore, *History of Religions*, vol. II, chaps. I–IV.
* W. K. Wright, *A Student's Philosophy of Religion*, chap. X.
 Karl Budde, *Religion of Israel to the Exile.*
 C. G. Montefiore, *Lectures on the Origin and Growth of the Hebrew Religion. Outlines of Liberal Judaism.*
 W. Robertson Smith, *The Religion of the Semites. The Prophets of Israel.*

H. P. Smith, *The Religion of Israel.*

S. R. Driver, *An Introduction to the Literature of the Old Testament.*

H. G. Mitchell, *The Ethics of the Old Testament.*

L. H. Paton in *The Evolution of Ethics*, edited by E. Hershey Sneath.

Morris Joseph, *Judaism as Creed and Life.*

Kaufman Kohler, *Jewish Theology.*

Solomon Schechter, *Studies in Judaism. Aspects of Rabbinical Theology.*

The New-Century Bible. The International Critical Commentary.

The Jewish Cyclopædia. Encyclopædia of Religion and Ethics (edited by Hastings).

The following Biblical passages are sufficient to illustrate the various points in Hebrew moral development mentioned in the chapter: *Kinship and Group Morality*, Judges I; II 16–23; IV; V (1, 24–27); VIII (22–35); IX; XI 24; XVII 6; XIX–XXI; Joshua VII. *Respective Advantages and Disadvantages of the Principle of Authority:* I Samuel VIII; Psalm LXXII. *Prophets before the Exile:* Amos II 6–8; V 4–15, 21–24. Micah II 1, 2, 8, 9; III 11, 12; VI 6–8. *Reforms in the Deuteronomic code:* Deuteronomy XV 1–15; XVI 18–20; XXIV 7, 14–16; XXV 13–16. *Exilic and Post-exilic:* Jeremiah XXII; XXIV; XXIX 1–14. Lamentation V. Ezekiel XVIII; XXXIII 10–16; XXXVI 22–38. Psalms LXXIX; CXXXVII. Ezra I 1–4. Nehemiah VIII 1–3. Isaiah XL 1, 2; XLIV 9–17; XLV 1–7; XLIX 3–7; LIII; LVI 3–7. Jonah III; IV 6–11. Proverbs II; VI; VIII; XV; XXII; XXXI. Ecclesiastes I, II; IV; V 8–19; VII 1–3, 13–20, 23–28; VIII 6–10, 14–17; IX; XI 9, 10. Job I, II, IX, XXXVIII–XLII 6. Wisdom of Solomon, I–III.

PART I
COMPARATIVE ETHICS

DIVISION B
OCCIDENTAL ETHICAL EVOLUTION

CHAPTER V

THE MORAL DEVELOPMENT OF ANCIENT GREECE AND ROME

In the three preceding chapters, which constitute Division A of our discussion of Comparative Ethics, the general course of moral evolution was outlined in correlation with social evolution, and given specific illustration in the case of the ancient Hebrews. The purpose of this chapter and the two which follow it and constitute Division B of Comparative Ethics as here discussed, will be to disclose the more important strata (besides the contributions of the ancient Hebrews discussed in the preceding chapter) that underlie the moral consciousness and determine the moral judgments of people in the free states of the Occident at the present time. These strata are chiefly the contributions of ancient Greece and Rome (this chapter), the Christian Church (Chapter VI) and the great modern cultural movements beginning with the Renaissance (Chapter VII). Ethics as a part of philosophy since the time of Socrates has played an important rôle in European moral evolution, although sociological, political, religious, and economic factors have also been influential. Our attention in these chapters will largely be directed to the great ethical systems, considered chiefly from an historical standpoint. A more critical evaluation of the merits of ethical systems will be undertaken in Part III.

I. Greek Political and Social Evolution

The general course of Greek political and social evolution may be sketched briefly.[1] In Homeric times (about 1000 B.C.) the Greeks were passing from the relation of Kinship to that of Authority. Each village with the land about it was occupied by a paternal clan (*genos*), a group of families supposed to have a

91

common ancestor. The clan held the land in common, and thought it sacred because it contained the graves of their ancestors, whom they worshiped. A group of clans constituted a tribe (*phyle*), and had a common head or "king" (*basileus*). The king led in war and council, directed religious ceremonies, and acted as judge or arbiter in disputes between members of different clans. In all important matters, he had to call a council of elders (heads of the more important clans). From time to time the king summoned all freemen of the tribe into an informal assembly (*agora*) to "hear and acclaim" what he and the council proposed to do. Inferior to the free men were slaves and serfs, who had been captured in war, or were descendants from the earlier inhabitants whom the original Greeks had spared when they first invaded and subjugated the country. While all Greeks had some sense of their common racial relationship, as yet no organization united the different tribes. The moral outlook was in most respects that of Kinship organization. Group and custom morality and collective responsibility prevailed; but the blood feud was held in check by the tribal organization, the king usually being able to prevent disputes from disrupting or seriously weakening the tribe, whose organization was firmer and stronger than that in Israel under the Judges.

The subsequent evolution was different in various parts of the Greek world, consisting as it did of a region broken up geographically into the mainland peninsula (open everywhere to the sea but with land communication made difficult by mountain ranges), many islands, and numerous settlements in Asia Minor and southern Italy. Everywhere, however, the original tribes became organized into somewhat larger groups. In some instances, as that of the Eleans, clans continued to live in separate villages, and the larger grouping was informal and loosely held together. In Macedon the power of the king increased, and the relation of Authority supplanted that of Kinship. In most cases, however, a city-state (*polis*) developed. The villagers in a plain or valley or island came together in the vicinity of the royal fortress, probably for greater security.

So a city grew, consisting of members of different tribes and clans. In this city the life of the whole region centered. Temples were built for the worship of protecting deities. A market facilitated exchange of goods and furthered economic development. Courts adjudicated disputes. The clan and tribal organizations sank in importance. In these cases loyalty to country, native city, and religion were identical with loyalty to the city-state. The citizen believed that the ghosts of his ancestors, inhabiting the tombs near by, were loyal members of this city-state as well as he.

As these city-states evolved, the powers of the king diminished. The council of elders gained control, and the government ceased to be a monarchy and became an *aristocracy*, ruled by a group of old and influential families. Land usually passed from clan or family to private ownership; commerce and industry arose and made great advances. With a few exceptions like Sparta, private ownership of property prevailed and individual economic initiative was stimulated. To the traditions of the aristocracy the Greeks owed some of their best moral traits. The noblemen felt a keen sense of civic loyalty and responsibility; they must lead in peace and war and further the common good. "It was the Greek nobles, then, who first recognized the true nature of the State, and of its infinite capacity for ennobling man; they realized 'the good life' (*tò eû zén*) of the citizen in contrast to the mere life (*tó zén*) of the village community. With them begins the development of art and poetry, of education and discipline, of law and public order, in immediate and healthy relation to the State and its needs." [2] They gave to Greece and to the world the ideal of manly virtue (*aretē*) as valor, wisdom, honor and self-respect, symmetry and moderation in all things, and many sidedness of interest leading to true culture,—marks of the nobleman everywhere when at his best. In some portions of Greece, notably Sparta and her allies, the social and political organization remained aristocratic down to the Macedonian conquest, in the fourth century B.C.

In certain of the city-states, notably in Athens, a further evolution took place. The government of the city-state ceased to be an *aristocracy* (a rule of the best families in disinterested service for the common good) and became an *oligarchy* (a rule of the few for their own selfish interests). The "people" (*demos*, the free citizens, but not the slaves and other subject population at least as numerous[3]) gradually learned some of the virtues of government and began to assert themselves. They first secured a written codification of the laws, in which their duties and privileges were definitely stated, together with some concessions that improved their status. (In Athens this was done by Solon in 546 B.C.) Rulers and courts thereafter had to be guided by the written laws. Gradually the "people" gained control of the government and made of it a *democracy*. (This holds of Athens after the reforms of Cleisthenes in 508 B.C.) The free citizens had by this time acquired some of the ideals of the old aristocracy. They had a feeling of civic loyalty and responsibility. They respected the laws, which they now had the power to make. They esteemed education and culture, and sought to acquire them. As in our modern democracies, every man wished to possess the virtues and manners of a gentleman (to be *kalokagathos*).

The Athenian democracy in the fifth century B.C. is the finest illustration of Citizenship in the ancient world. Virtually every free citizen became familiar with the problems of government by occasionally holding office himself.[4] The general Assembly (*ecclesia*) of all the citizens met at least forty times a year, and had the final decision on all matters of moment. The Council of Five Hundred, a large committee of the whole people, elected every year, prepared the business to be presented at the meetings of the Assembly. All political administration passed through its hands. The excellence of the Athenian democracy at its best, during the Age of Pericles (461–431 B.C.) is hardly exaggerated in the famous funeral oration which the historian Thucydides put into the mouth of Pericles:

"Our form of government does not enter into rivalry with

the institutions of others. We do not copy our neighbors, but are an example to them. It is true that we are called a democracy, for the administration is in the hands of the many and not of the few. But while the law secures equal justice to all alike in their private disputes, the claim of excellence [as a qualification for office] is also recognized; and when a citizen is in any way distinguished, he is preferred to the public service, not as a matter of privilege, but as the reward of merit. Neither is poverty a bar, but a man may benefit his country whatever be the obscurity of his position. . . . A spirit of reverence pervades our public acts; we are prevented from doing wrong by respect for authority and for the laws. . . .

"And we have not forgotten to provide for our weary spirits many relaxations from toil; we have regular games and sacrifices throughout the year; at home the style of our life is refined. . . . Because of the greatness of our city the fruits of the whole earth flow in upon us; so that we enjoy the goods of other countries as freely as of our own. . . .

"For we are lovers of the beautiful, yet simple in our tastes, and we cultivate the mind without loss of manliness. Wealth we employ, not for talk and ostentation, but when there is a real use for it. To avow poverty with us is no disgrace; the true disgrace is in doing nothing to avoid it. An Athenian citizen does not neglect the state because he takes care of his own household; and even those of us who are engaged in business have a very fair idea of politics. We alone regard a man who takes no interest in public affairs, not as a harmless, but as a useless character; and if few of us are originators, we are all sound judges of a policy. . . .

"We alone do good to our neighbors not upon a calculation of interest, but in the confidence of freedom and in a frank and fearless spirit. To sum up; I say that Athens is the school of Hellas. . . . And we shall assuredly not be without witnesses; there are mighty monuments of our power which will make us the wonder of this and of succeeding ages. . . . For we have compelled every land and every sea to open a path for our valor, and have everywhere planted eternal memorials of our friendship and of our enmity." [5]

In the period described by this speech the Athenian democracy was the head of a vast confederation of over two hundred city-states situated on the mainland of Greece, the islands, and the mainland of Asia Minor. This maintained a large and powerful navy to afford common security against Persia. The leadership of Athens had become an almost authoritarian control of the other members of the confederacy. In many respects this Athenian imperialism was beneficent. The rule was mainly just, and all were secure from attack. Democratic constitutions along Athenian models were generally introduced, and free citizens came into political control, with larger economic and educational opportunities than ordinary citizens had ever known before. On the other hand, the Athenian allies lost part of their civic independence. Though Greeks themselves, they were not permitted to have an equal voice with Athenians in the government of the empire. Tribute raised from them was frequently used for purposes chiefly of benefit to Athens herself.

Athenian imperialism made great contributions to culture. On the Acropolis were erected some of the finest monuments of architecture and sculpture that the world has ever known. Great dramatists, poets, historians, painters, and philosophers arose among the Athenians, and talented men from all over the world flocked to Athens to secure recognition and to benefit by the intellectual atmosphere of the place. Never has a city so small in population been distinguished for so many names that have continued great in history. Æschylus, Sophocles, Euripides, Aristophanes, Thucydides, Lysias, Phidias, Anaxagoras, Socrates, and Plato are a few who in this period or shortly after contributed to the eternal renown of Athens. It was the dream of Pericles and other imperialists to extend Athenian dominion throughout and beyond the Greek world, diffusing everywhere the political, cultural, and economic benefits of democracy along Athenian lines.

The fatal political disease that made impossible an enduring union of enlightened city-states under the democratic imperialism of Athens was factionalism (*stasis*). Within Athens itself were the old nobility, common citizens, slaves, and unnaturalized foreigners. Each class became hostile to the others. The poor were jealous of the rich. Statesmen defeated in an important vote were often permanently exiled, and the benefit of further services by them was lost. A defeated faction would sometimes ally themselves with a hostile city-state with whose help they hoped to regain power. Such factionalism was probably inevitable from the very nature of the city-state; for, as area and population increased, it became impossible for the citizens to assemble and decide momentous questions intelligently. The immense popular assembly often fell victim to demagogic orators and crowd psychology. The Athenians did not sufficiently develop representative government. They relied too much on "pure democracy", *i.e.*, to the direct action of voters themselves at meetings and elections. A small city-state could be governed like a New England country township; a vast empire could not.

External causes also hastened the end. Subject city-states resented what seemed to them to be the tyranny of Athens. Under the leadership of Sparta, a rival league of the more conservative city-states with aristocratic constitutions fought and defeated the democratic Athenian empire. Thebes formed another league that fought the other two. Each of the three at different times sought the aid of barbarian Persia against the others. Students of eugenics think that the best blood of Greece perished in the wars that Greeks fought among themselves, and that subsequent generations were descended from inferior stocks ineligible for military service. Notwithstanding some manifestations of a national consciousness, like the great Panhellenic games in which representatives from all Greece met in friendly athletic and artistic contests, the Greeks were never able to unite in a free national state. They were too particularistic in their loyalties to their hundreds of separate city-states. The unification of all Greece in the relation of Citizenship was impossible.

A consolidation finally came through the conquest of Greece by Philip, king of Macedon. Alexander the Great, son and successor of Philip, dreamed of spreading the civilization of the Greek city-states throughout his vast empire, which extended from the Danube to the upper Nile, and eastward to the Indus. During the twelve years before his death in 323 B.C., he founded cities on Greek models everywhere in the foreign lands he had conquered. He hoped that his whole domain would presently consist of city-states, each with its own assembly and council, choosing its own magistrates and making its own laws, speaking Greek, and participating in Greek art, literature, and science. Under the overlordship and protection of the Macedonian kings, order would prevail throughout the domain, there would be free interchange of commerce by ships and caravans, and East and West would be united in a common free civilization. His untimely death put an end to these projects. Even if he had lived, it seems improbable that city-states subject to a monarch in their external affairs could internally have preserved free institutions.

The Macedonian generals who succeeded to the different portions of Alexander's empire lacked much of his vision and statesmanship. However, the domain that Alexander conquered became to a large extent *Hellenistic* (speaking Greek, imitative of Greek culture) if not *Hellenic* (really Greek) in language, spirit, and institutions. This remained true down to the Mohammedan conquests. Athens, Alexandria, Rhodes, and Tarsus became great university centers in which philosophical and scientific research and instruction continued for many centuries.

This social and moral evolution from the early era of mixed Kinship and Authority, in which group traditions were enforced by king and head of clan, down to free citizenship in the Athenian democracy, was a process of increased *socialization*, *individualization*, and *rationalization*. Men learned to live in mutual adjustment and coöperation; larger opportunity for self-expression was afforded to the individual citizen; the principles of law and government were thought out and given expression in institutions. But the process stopped with the evolution of the city-state. A larger expansion, by which the city-states could have entered into a federal union on terms of equality, mutual coöperation and good will, was impossible. The best substitute was imperialism, the overlordship of many peoples by one. But Athenian imperialism, the leadership of the lesser groups by the most progressive and democratic of them all, also failed. Only the harsher and more autocratic Macedonian imperialism, the arbitrary control of the city-states by a monarch, met with any enduring success. This was a partial reversion to Authority, but nevertheless the Hellenic culture produced by the city-states was to some extent propagated and handed down to later ages. While free Greek citizenship proved incapable of expansion in area and endurance in time, not only its ideals but some of its achievements proved capable of transmission under authoritarian imperialism. To which do we owe the more? To Athenian democratic citizenship, or to Macedonian imperialism? Each rendered a service.

II. Roman Political and Social Evolution

The Roman political and social evolution must be sketched even more briefly.[6] Perhaps as early as a thousand years before Christ, central Italy was already fully occupied by Indo-European invaders from the north—Latins (including the ancestors of the Romans), Sabines, Samnites, Umbrians, etc. These peoples were organized in paternal clans (*gentes*), and the clans were loosely combined in tribes, and perhaps larger confederations like the "Latin League". There was no very strong organization more extensive than the small villages (*pagi*) where the people lived, going out by day to farm the tillable land, probably already under private ownership, while the pasture land was still held in common.

In the sixth century B.C., Rome (an Etruscan name) was a

small fortified city-state, comprising a considerable number of clans under the rule of the Etruscans.[7] The king (*rex*) had the three functions of commander in war, priest in state religious ceremonies, and judge in the settlement of private disputes. It was an instance of an authoritarian system built upon earlier Kinship organization, in which the power (*imperium*) of the king, though absolute in theory, was in practice limited by the fact that he was supposed to consult the council (heads of the more important clans) on matters of importance, and to convoke the assembly of the people (*comitium*) to hear, and if they chose, approve the most important decisions made by king and council. Attempts of the Etruscan kings to rule in an arbitrary way, more independent of council and assembly (in which the Romans were probably in the majority) brought on a revolution in 509 B.C. This resulted in the expulsion of the kings and the establishment of the rule of the aristocracy.

The *imperium* was thereafter held by two consuls, each elected annually. Though the power of each consul was in theory absolute, his exercise of it was limited by the presence of the other, and the shortness of his term of office. So in fact the general direction of policies and determination of matters of consequence was in control of the council (senate). This came to consist of a body of former magistrates, chosen for life, all members of the aristocracy (patricians), and mostly men of wide experience and seasoned judgment. They long passed upon all important questions, usually with masterly statesmanship. The transition from aristocracy to democracy in Rome was a slow process, marked by much political struggle but little actual bloodshed. First, the people (plebeians) obtained the reduction of the customs to written laws and their codification in the Twelve Tables (451 B.C.).[8] In time they gained numerous other concessions, and by 287 B.C. they were on a level of practical parity with the patricians. The senate and consuls could do nothing to which the people objected in their popular assemblies or through their representatives, the tribunes. However, the ordinary conduct of affairs long continued to remain in the hands of consuls and other magistrates under the supervision of the senate, because of their experience, moral prestige, and hold upon popular confidence. This comparatively peaceful evolution is in sharp contrast to the Greek city-states, rent by factionalism. It was the result of the general Roman sense of fairness, and willingness to make practical compromises.

External expansion was carried on by the Romans with extraordinary success. As one portion of Italy after another was added to the Roman domain, the conquered populations were successfully assimilated. They were gradually granted the full rights of Roman citizenship on a parity with the people of the city of Rome itself, and ultimately came to think of themselves as Romans. Most of Italy, though not yet assimilated, was firmly united under Roman rule during the wars with Carthage, which ended in 146 B.C. with Rome supreme in the West. This remarkable expansion of Roman citizenship furnishes a contrast to Athens, which failed to include subject states in full citizenship. One reason for Roman success was because the routine of government was not carried on in popular assemblies, subject to crowd psychology and devoid of continuous political traditions. The Roman assemblies met chiefly to elect officials—consuls and other magistrates—who performed their duties under the supervision of the long experienced and aristocratic senate.

When Rome conquered the world, however, the popular assemblies and the magistrates of their choice, even with the aid of the senate, no longer proved to be either sufficiently representative or sufficiently cognizant of world problems. After a century of internal wars, proscriptions and dictatorships, the solution was found in a considerable reversion to the principle of Authority. Octavius—later known as Augustus Cæsar —an experienced general and statesman, won universal confidence, and in the years following 29 B.C. became "first citizen" (*princeps*) and "commander-in-chief" (*imperator*)—terms which later came to mean "prince" and "emperor". Augustus and his successors, notwithstanding personal faults and occasional oppression of the wealthy in Rome, down at least to the death of Marcus Aurelius in 180 A.D., usually exercised with ability and statesmanship the wide powers which, in theory, had been delegated to them by the senate and the Roman people. The civilized world enjoyed comparative peace. At least for the first century or two of the empire economic conditions were in many respects good. Provinces, especially after they had passed from the administration of proconsuls chosen by the senate to that of personal representatives of the emperor, in most cases enjoyed more just and orderly government than they had ever known before, as well as more intimate cultural and commercial relations with the outside world.[9] Provincials in increasing numbers obtained more and more of the rights of Roman citizenship. Many emperors and other leading men after the first century A.D. came from the provinces; and after the famous edict of Caracalla (212 A.D.) all free citizens of the provinces became Romans in every political and legal sense.[10] Latin was the common language of the western provinces. In the East, the Greek language and traditions were allowed to remain dominant. Except for Judaism and Christianity there were no religions in conflict with the imperial administration.

In some respects Roman imperialism has been the most successful in the history of the world.[11] The splendid morale of the Romans enabled them to conquer the world by force. Their equitable civil and judicial administration gave them moral prestige and enabled them to hold it. The deification of the emperors and of the city of Rome gave the imperial government an effective religious sanction among the pagans. Even Christians regarded the emperor and other rulers as in some sense clothed with divine authority.[12] Provincials were completely assimilated, and armies for the defense of the empire were largely recruited from them. The vast barbarian hordes were prevented for centuries from overwhelming the empire; after its fall, the fiction of the Holy Roman Empire had a tremendous hold on thought and life throughout the middle ages.[13] Traditions of Roman law to-day remain basic in modern codes, particularly in continental Europe.

In no period did Rome realize such ideals of free citizenship as Athens knew in her best days; nor were Roman achievements in art, literature, philosophy, and science comparable with those of Greece. On the other hand, the Romans were hard-headed and practical. They held together, and did not destroy themselves in factional struggles. The administration of their city-state, though less democratic, was for a longer time just and efficient. With the loss of political liberty, and increasing dependence upon the personal authority of the emperor and his bureaucracy, decadence manifested itself in art, literature, philosophy, science, and most other forms of creative genius. However, the world was held together, and civilization saved for many centuries from downfall. Will our modern national states prove as long successful in preserving civilization from destructive wars? Rome succeeded, better than any modern empire has yet done, in assimilating conquered provinces.[14] And, in one important domain, the Roman creative genius never failed in ancient times. The evolution of Roman law, as interpreted by some of the greatest jurists the world has ever known, continued, clear down until its codification in the reign of the emperor Justinian (527–565 A.D.).

The Roman evolution was thus one of *socialization*, in which the various peoples and classes of society of the ancient world learned to coöperate. There was increased *individualization*, with economic progress and wide diffusion of Greek and Roman civilization, made accessible in some measure to all free men within the empire. There was increased *rationalization*, notably in the development of the law and government by which so vast a domain was held together. None of these processes was complete. Liberty and creative genius disappeared. Economic burdens in the later empire became oppressive. The empire ultimately fell, and social and political evolution had to start over again with its barbarian conquerors.[15]

III. Greek and Roman Moral Consciousness

Before discussing the moral philosophers, let us notice certain traits of the ancient popular morality which they interpreted.[16] The moral evolution of the Greeks was unique in several respects. The advance in morality was not accompanied by a corresponding advance in religion, but was largely an independent development. The Greeks, as we have seen, did not achieve a national government prior to the Macedonian conquest, but only federations of city-states. Since each city-state retained its own traditional cults, there was really no national religion. To be sure, the Homeric poems were studied everywhere; thus the splendid Olympian gods and goddesses with their beautiful forms and sublimated human personalities, became universally fixed in the popular imagination. These deities, however, practiced the morals of the early age in which the Homeric poems took their form. As men became more civilized and recognized higher moral standards, they outgrew the popular religion, and thought out their moral problems without reference to it.[17] Probably the ordinary Greek never fully realized this. But he, unlike the Hebrew, did not think of right and wrong as righteous obedience and sinful violations of divine commands, but rather as success and failure to act *like a natural human being.*

To-day most of us probably think of the Greeks as famous especially for their artistic genius, their athletic sports, and their contributions to science and philosophy. Their remarkable talents in these fields throw light upon their moral consciousness. To the Greek, at least prior to the rise of Stoicism, goodness and beauty were almost identical. A good life was a beautiful life,—well rounded, symmetrical, and well proportioned. The emphasis was upon virtues, upon character and personality, which make a man what he is, rather than upon the performance of duties and obligations. They admired the all-around athlete with a well proportioned body. The Greeks— at least before the rise of neo-Platonism and Catholic Christianity—were not ascetics; they did not seek to mortify their bodies and were not ashamed of them. Their ideal was a beautiful soul in a beautiful body—such was part of what they meant by the perfection of man as a natural being.

Prior to the Macedonian conquest, a man could best realize his nature by making the most of his citizenship in a free state. For a man to be *natural* was to be a good citizen, faithful in loyalty and service to the city-state; to fulfill his part as son, husband, and father to ancestors, wife and children; in peace and war to perform the functions of his rank and status. After the Macedonian conquest, life as a *natural human being* was conceived in terms at once more individualistic and more universal. Each must primarily seek his own good as an individual man, now that the abject condition of his city-state threw him upon his own initiative. Unlike his ancestors, he could not remain aloof to men of other cities, and contemptuous of non-Greeks as "barbarians". Closer contact with outsiders under the universal rule of Alexander, his successors, and the Romans, in a world in which there was much travel and commerce and interchange of ideas, taught him to recognize that all men are much alike in moral and intellectual attainments, and have similar rights and obligations.

The moral character of the Romans in some respects differed from that of the Greeks. This is especially true of the earlier republican periods, before the Romans came under the influence of Greek civilization. The early Romans were a simple agricultural people, with strong social organization and moral traditions in which the authority of the father of the family was almost absolute. Frugality, industry, obedience, and a strong hold on the practical values of life were marked traits. Successive wars of the republican period strengthened these traits. Military successes of that age were not so much the result of superior wealth and mechanical equipment as of firm discipline, and patriotic devotion. Warfare made the best men of the republic heroes, who performed brave acts regardless of material interest, mindful only of personal honor and the welfare of the state. They had an unconquerable respect for themselves and reverence for Rome. Down to the first century B.C., the best Romans of the older school held to these traditions. Their vices were often the defects of these qualities. They were frequently cruel to slaves, debtors, and defeated foes. They were likely to be unappreciative of the refinements of civilization, indifferent to art, literature, and philosophy, lacking in kindness and sympathy, and blind to the merits of other peoples. Though they respected their women, they gave them few legal rights, and subjected them in most respects to the authority of their fathers and husbands.

During the last century of the republic and the establishment of the empire the national character gradually altered. Some of the changes were for the worse. Frugality and simplicity were succeeded by manifestations of luxury and sensuous indulgence that were unwholesome. There was much ostentatious display of wealth. As agriculture declined in Italy, the descendants of industrious farmers migrated to the cities and became an idle proletariat, supported by gratuitous distributions of food, and amused by public games and spectacles. An earlier age had admired heroes and imitated them upon the battlefield. The Roman of the empire often indulged his admiration for bravery vicariously; he watched gladiators fight, while provincials and barbarians took his place in the legions and defended the empire. Idle people, rich and poor alike, fell into debauchery in drink and sex. On the other hand, the empire in some ways marked moral progress. The Romans emulated the more refined manners of the Greeks whom they had conquered. They studied art, literature, and philosophy, and learned to appreciate them, although they developed little creative ability. First as a matter of expediency, and later from a sense of right, the provinces from the time of Augustus on were governed with increasing justice and equity. To some extent the common equality of mankind was affirmed; gradually the rights left to Romans under the empire were extended to all subjects. The condition of slaves was mitigated, although bad economic conditions due partly to excessive and ill-distributed taxation reduced many peasants to serfdom. Clemency had become a recognized virtue, and no longer was thought to be a mark of weakness. During the early empire married women gained more legal rights than ever before in Europe.[18]

Greek and Roman morals are one aspect of that which is often called *"paganism"*. The classical pagan view of life had its limitations, as Christian and Jewish moralists are constantly reminding us. Its ideals were not sufficiently high, its sense of sin and duty not poignant enough. It did not feel the pangs of conscience with bitterness, and long ardently for moral regeneration (except to some extent in the case of Stoics). It fell short of Hebraism in deep emotion and sympathy. It lacked charity and altruism, if compared with the best periods of Christianity. It kept too close to the level of ordinary life, and did not yearn enough for the transcendent.[19] Perhaps it never occurred to the average classical pagan that he ought to love any God with all his heart, his mind, his soul, and his strength, or that he ought to love his neighbor as himself. He recked little of "the high that proved too high, the heroic for earth too hard", and did not think of binding himself "by such vows, as is a shame a man should not be bound by, yet the which no man can keep".

On the other hand, the classical pagan had many fine moral qualities. He appreciated devotion to home and parents, husband and wife, children and ancestors.[20] He displayed loyalty and patriotism.[21] He excelled in love of beauty in mind and body. He was no ascetic, but usually practiced moderation in food and drink, speech and personal demeanor.[22] He knew the joy of life. Pagan culture stood for clear thinking, for the light of reason that expels darkness and superstition. Knowing that moral issues are better understood by clear and intelligent minds, free from disturbing emotions, the pagan acted accordingly. He was freer on the average from bigotry, prejudice, and fanaticism than the Christian who succeeded him became until the eighteenth century.[23] His favorite mottoes were "know thyself", "nothing in excess", and "follow nature". Wisdom, courage, temperance, and justice, the four virtues in which Plato summed up morality, were the moral traits most commended in the pagan mores.[24]

IV. SOCRATES AND THE EMERGENCE OF ETHICS

Although moral maxims were earlier enunciated in China, India, and Persia, and although anticipations of a systematic point of view in ethics may be discovered a generation or two earlier in other parts of the Greek world, to Socrates of Athens († 399 B.C.) may be given the credit for effecting *the emergence of ethics or moral philosophy in the strict sense of the scientific study of moral judgments.*[25]

General conditions in Athens in the latter portion of the fifth century B.C. were favorable for the rise of Ethics. Under the recently acquired democratic constitution, laws had been enacted which favored the masses at the expense of the old aristocracy. Such laws did not have behind them in the popular mind sanctions of immemorial tradition and divine institution. So it was inevitable that thoughtful men asked on what grounds a person should obey laws and customs. Is it purely a matter of coercion and physical necessity? Is justice merely what has been decreed by the party temporarily in power, is it simply "the interest of the stronger"? Has a person the moral right to do whatever he considers to be to his own interest, obeying the laws when he must, and evading them when he considers it practicable and profitable? Are right and wrong only matters of private and public opinion? Or, on the other hand, is there an absolute moral obligation to obey laws and generally accepted moral judgments? Are there rational standards for human conduct, to which all, if they are honest, will have to assent, once they understand them? The teachers of higher education, the Sophists, brought such questions to the attention of the young men whom they taught, and sometimes attempted to answer them constructively. Under their influence Athenian thought broke with the unreflective morality of custom and tradition.   No Sophist, however, really succeeded in advancing a constructive solution of ethical problems.[26]

Socrates was the first to discover a systematic *method* for the analysis of moral judgments that was at once thorough, critical, and constructive.   By its use he established the broad *principles* of all subsequent European ethical systems.   We can only briefly note his method of investigation, his mode of teaching, his main ethical principles, and his personality.

His method of investigating moral problems may be called "inductive" and "empirical" in the freer ancient sense, although it lacked the precision of a Bacon or a Darwin, or a moral philosopher of our own times.   For instance, he would write down under "Justice" all actions under that head, which occurred to him or others, and contrast them with all actions that come under "Injustice".   Lying ordinarily is unjust, but it is sometimes just to deceive sick children, or disheartened troops in a campaign.   In general, misrepresentations performed with the intention of injuring the persons affected by them are unjust.[27]   On one occasion Socrates is described as criticizing successively various popular definitions of justice current at the time, such as "giving to every one his due", "doing good to our friends and evil to our enemies", "helping our friends if they are good men, and injuring our enemies if they are bad men", and "the interest of the stronger".   Instances are pointed out by him in which each definition will not apply.[28]   In such ways he succeeded in making the general sphere of justice better understood, though he probably never arrived at a formal definition of justice.   His illustrations reveal constant and keen observation of human life.   His method implies that formal definitions exist in the field of ethics, and that these can be approximately ascertained by comparing different moral judgments and actions, and by testing hypothetical definitions in every possible way.

His mode of teaching was, or seemed to be, completely informal.   He frequented public places, and started discussions among those who were interested.[29]   He would begin such a discussion by asking some one's opinion on a moral question, assuming ignorance on his own part, and a desire to be instructed. A pretentious Sophist would thus be trapped into assertions that on critical examination were shown to be inconsistent. He was more kindly in his treatment of young men who were honest seekers after truth. With all, however, his method of instruction began with *irony*, a process of showing the learner by questioning him, his ignorance of the subject. Only he that knows that he does not know is in a position to learn anything. The second phase of the method Socrates called *maieutic* ("mental midwifery"). By leading questions the learner is assisted to give birth to ideas—a process hardly less painful than that endured by a woman in travail—but attended with joy when the new principle has been born in the mind.[30]

Socrates believed that every one acts, and ought to act, in the line of his own interest, provided he really understands what his interest is. And his interest is to lead a happy life; and that, for Socrates, probably meant a life containing the greatest pleasure in the long run. One's highest interest and greatest happiness are to be found in a simple and abstemious life of personal integrity and service to others. "Since justice is the health of the soul, it is better to suffer wrong than to do injustice to another." In the former case one's own character is uninjured. One should return good for evil, and never harm anyone. We expect justice and good faith from others; we cannot refuse to render the same to them. Since virtue is always the supreme good for every one, to know what is right necessarily implies that a person will act accordingly; wrongdoing is the result of ignorance. Such virtues as wisdom, courage, temperance, justice, reverence, and love are carefully analyzed and described. Strong as is Socrates' emphasis on individualism in teaching that each should follow his own interest, the Socratic conception of where the true interests of a person really lie makes the doctrine profoundly social. In laying the foundations of ethics, Socrates makes morality markedly individual, social, and rational in its constitution.

"last is erroneous" JHJ.

The feature of Socratic ethics most open to criticism is the contention that virtue can be identified with knowledge and vice with ignorance.   It is true that this contention was more plausible in the generation of Socrates than at any subsequent time in history.   Ethics was then only having its beginning; the student of Socrates could not derive his moral conceptions from the reflective thought of earlier ages.   He had to think them out for himself through the painful method of irony and maieutic; in so doing he understood their concrete and practical applications to his own life and that of the city.   Such knowledge gripped one's soul and refashioned one's sentiments and character.   The situation is quite different to-day.   Our moral judgments have come down to us from diverse traditions— Hebrew, Greek, Roman, Christian inheritances from remote ages—traditions often inconsistent with one another, and not obviously applicable to our own circumstances.   The adolescent acquires them by hearing older persons talk, and by reading books.   So we only half understand or believe our moral intuitions; and we cannot always trust our consciences to guide us to right decisions.   Socrates would say of us, that when we do wrongly or judge wrongly it is because of our ignorance; we do not understand because we have never really thought out and made part of our own life experience the moral codes and conceptions that we profess.   But Socrates was not wholly right, even for his own day.   Few of his pupils went into active public service in a time when Athens sadly needed the loyal support and moral leadership of her best trained men; and two of those who did go into politics, Alcibiades and Critias, proved bad men in their public as well as private careers.   The evil records of a few of his pupils prejudiced many against Socrates at the time of his trial; the creditable though not politically active careers of the majority of his pupils were overlooked.

The personality of Socrates has left a vivid impression upon the ages.   With homely features and bald head, simply clad in a single garment, crude and grotesque in outward appearance like a mask of Silenus, inwardly his character was of pure gold.[31] His life was devoted to the search for moral truth and the endeavor to teach it to others. Prompted by an inward impulse or sense of duty which he perhaps thought of as a guiding spirit (*daimonion*), he sought to carry out what he believed to be a divine commission.[32] Pronounced by the oracle at Delphi to be the wisest man in Athens, he humbly concluded that this could only be true because he appreciated his own ignorance and limitations; so he ever sought to learn from all whatever he could, and he unhesitatingly exposed sham and false pretense whenever he found them. When put to the test, he stood resolutely by his own convictions at whatever peril. Unmindful of the commands of tyrants and of popular clamor, at the risk of personal safety he steadfastly refused to commit or sanction wrong.[33] When brought on trial for his life, to face the false charges of rejecting the gods acknowledged by the state, of bringing in strange deities, and of corrupting the youth, at a time when he and his friends were unpopular in Athens, he refused to leave the city to escape prosecution. He faced his accusers fearlessly in the court, declining to make an emotional appeal to the jury of five hundred citizens. After a slight majority had pronounced him guilty, he would not seek to avert the death sentence, asked by his prosecutors, by proposing banishment as an alternative, or by promising to refrain from teaching in the future. After he had been condemned to die, he rejected an opportunity to escape from prison because he believed it to be his duty to Athens, of which he was a native citizen, to submit to the lawful authority of the court that had sentenced him. He spent the hours preceding his execution in cheerful conversation with his pupils and friends, and he died peacefully. His life and death supplied a model for moral emulation throughout antiquity. The lives and deaths of only two other men in all history—Buddha and Jesus—have made comparable impressions upon subsequent generations of mankind.[34]

V. Hellenic Ethical Systems

Socrates taught the world that it is possible to think out ethical principles in the light of observation and experience. No system builder himself, he marked the way for ethical systems to be formulated in succeeding generations. Diverse as were the different ethical systems of ancient Greece and Rome, they all show in some way spiritual descent from Socrates.

Two famous ethical systems founded by pupils of Socrates carried certain of his teachings to conclusions at once extreme and absurd. Antisthenes in Athens at the gymnasium of Cynosarges (which gave the school the name of Cynics) developed the Socratic emphasis on simplicity of living and absence from unnecessary wants, to a life of ostentatious poverty and almost savage simplicity that was not Hellenic in spirit. Aristippus after the death of Socrates returned to his native city of Cyrene, and there established the Cyrenaic school, which lasted several generations. This school understood Socrates' teaching that one should act in accordance with his own interests and seek a life of pleasure, to mean the cultivation of personal pleasure as the highest good (*egoistic hedonism*). They put chief emphasis on the most enduring sensuous pleasures. They lost sight of the social spirit and higher idealism of Socrates.

One of the youngest, but altogether the greatest of Socrates' pupils was Plato of Athens († 347 B.C.). He was descended from one of the old noble families whose influence had waned with the advance of democracy. He lived in an age when the blunders of the Athenian assembly and law courts had facilitated the decline of Athens from her old position of culture, power, and glory. Above all, he suffered the shock of the condemnation of his beloved teacher, Socrates. For these reasons Plato was no lover of democracy. He established his school, the Academy near the grove of Academus, a public park in the suburbs of Athens, where it might be possible for him and his pupils to study philosophy unannoyed by the traffic of the streets and the agitation of popular gatherings. The Academy remained little disturbed by the outside world and carried on scholarly investigations for nearly nine hundred years.

Plato sought to develop moral principles by reasoning rather than by observation of the Socratic type. To do this more effectively, in his greatest book, the *Republic,* he describes an ideal city-state. All citizens of a state should be *temperate,* in the double sense of self-control of personal habits and of obedience to the laws and customs of the state; the military and police must be *courageous* as well as temperate, and the governing class must possess *wisdom* in addition to the other virtues mentioned. Wisdom implies thorough theoretical training in ultimate scientific principles as well as practical administrative experience. *Justice,* the cement that holds society together, can only exist in a city-state where all classes coöperate, where laws and public policies are decided upon with wisdom, where external security and internal order are maintained with courage, and all are loyal and obedient.

The psychology of the individual man is to be understood in the light of that of the state. In each man are reason, spirited emotions, and animal appetites. So his good as a whole is a kind of justice or harmony of character, in which conduct is directed by reason (wisdom), which implies right direction of his emotions (courage) and control of appetites (temperance). Such a character would be possible for all in a perfectly just and well ordered society. For everybody can at least be temperate and law-abiding, and the ordinary citizen would learn to act courageously and wisely in a society where those who excel in these more difficult virtues determine political policies and direct public opinion. Plato agreed with Socrates that virtue is knowledge and vice is ignorance, that justice is the health of the soul, that it is better to suffer injustice oneself than to do injustice to others, that it is a primary duty to be loyal to the state, and that right conduct is in accordance with a person's selfish interests provided one realizes what the interests of his true self really are. How far the good of man may ultimately be identified with pleasure or happiness, and how far the perfection of the soul implies other and higher goods impossible to state in terms of pleasure, are questions on which Plato gave somewhat different answers in dialogues written at different periods in his long life.[35] However, he is always confident that only the philosopher (*i.e.*, the liberally educated man who knows all goods, and has been trained to reason) is in a position to pass upon the ultimate values of life.

Among the more doubtful points in Plato's moral philosophy are his emphasis upon the organic theory of the state and his partial advocacy of communistic socialism. He was confident that first consideration must always be for the good of the city-state as a whole, and that if this is assured, the good of each class of society and of each individual citizen will follow as a matter of course. He thought of citizens as closely interdependent like the different organs of the human body. To assure wisdom in government he vests supreme power in a ruling class, whose members have been selected in competitive examinations. These rulers or "guardians" are to have no private property of their own, live in barracks, and eat at common tables. Their marriages are to be regulated in accordance with eugenics. Their children are to be separated at an early age, so that children and parents will not know one another in after years. Under such conditions, the disinterested devotion of the guardians to the common good will be assured; they will conserve the property of the city-state unselfishly, and love all the children of the succeeding generation impartially, as if the property and children were their own. Few believers in the organic theory of the state, or socialism, or sex equality, or eugenics, in later times have so consistently and courageously thought out these doctrines to their ultimate logical consequences and proclaimed them so unreservedly.

Plato was not contented with a formulation of ethical principles in the setting of a model city-state. To demonstrate that justice is not a merely human conception but an ultimate principle grounded in the very nature of the universe, he carried his ethical studies into the field of metaphysics. By keen logical reasoning, as well as by sublime flights of poetic imagination, he maintained that general principles are more real than particular facts which can only be applications of them, that all is dependent in the last analysis on one universal and all embracing truth—the ultimate source of all justice, truth, and beauty—the Idea of the Good. The eternal justice of the universe implies human immortality, so the *Republic* closes with a consideration of this theme, intended to show that the good life will bring ultimate rewards and the evil life ultimate punishments, retributive and purgatorial, in the life beyond the grave.[36]

Plato's extreme rationalism and his fondness for absolute and unchanging principles prevented him from grasping the laws of moral progress. He could only outline the course of moral and social dissolution in the state and in the individual. His contributions, therefore, consist in the delineation of absolute and abstract ideals with great fertility of imagination and literary charm. Even more than other great classical moral philosophers, Plato must be studied for suggestiveness and inspiration rather than for accurate conclusions. The modern reader of Plato, by being impelled to think out the reasons for the philosopher's mistakes and refuting him, gains a firmer grasp upon ethical principles than he would obtain from a more orthodox but less stimulating writer.

Aristotle († 322 B.C.), who had studied in the Academy during the last twenty years of Plato's life, afterwards established at the Lyceum the "peripatetic school". Under the patronage of Alexander the Great, who in his youth had studied under Aristotle, the Lyceum became a great institution of research and instruction. As its head, Aristotle combined vast learning with practical knowledge of men. His method in ethics reminds us in some ways more of Socrates than of Plato. His reasoning is strictly empirical, starting with facts gathered from observation and research, and making generalizations

with caution.   Moral principles disclose themselves in life and
conduct; they do not exist off by themselves in a world of abstract ideas.

Ethics ascertains the true good of mankind.   And man is a
social or political animal (*zóön politikon*) whose true nature is
realized after social organization has progressed beyond the
family and village to the city-state (*polis*).   "For man as in
his condition of complete development [*i.e.*, in the city-state]
is the noblest of all animals, so apart from law and justice he is
vilest of all". [37]   So Ethics is really a part of Politics (political
science and political philosophy).   Like Socrates and Plato,
Aristotle conceived ethical problems in terms of citizenship in
a free state.

The supreme good of man is *eudaimonía*, which really includes what we mean by "happiness", "well being", "welfare",
"perfection", and "self-realization".   (For convenience, in this
volume, *eudaimonía* and its adjective *eudaimon* will be referred to as "happiness" and "happy", but it must be understood that these words have a special significance as used with
reference to Aristotle, that is quite different from use in other
connections.)   Happiness for Aristotle is found in fulfilling one's
real nature as a man.   For pleasure attends the proper exercise
of functions, and is not successfully sought as an end in itself.
The characteristic function of a man, that which indicates his
true nature and differentiates him from other animals, is his
reason.   So in the right exercise of reason is happiness to be
found.   A life of reason implies a settled character, *i.e.*, the
possession of virtue.   Virtue alone does not guarantee happiness,
but without it happiness is impossible.   The ideally happy man
is he who leads a life of perfect virtue, and is adequately furnished with external goods, and is otherwise prosperous.   Solon
was right that it is impossible to judge whether a man has been
thus happy until after he is dead, and it is possible to review
his life as a whole.

Virtues are not innate; they are the reward of training and
experience.   Highest are the *intellectual* (dianoëtic) virtues, *e.g.*,

the life of a scholar passed in disinterested study (*theoria*); the cultivation of these virtues is best and happiest and most like that of the gods.[38] The *moral* virtues are also indispensable. The possession of a moral virtue implies that a person has acquired a settled habit (*hexis*) of deliberate purpose, by which his impulses, desires and appetites are subjected to his reason. A virtue implies self-knowledge and self-control, an understanding of the world, and responsiveness to personal and social demands. Many of the virtues stand midway between two extremes (vices), one of which is an excess and the other a deficiency in the proper trait. The virtue of courage is thus a "golden mean" between rashness and cowardice; truthfulness (about one's talents) between boastfulness and self-depreciation; liberality between prodigality and illiberality. The mean will lie at different points for different individuals; the courage of a soldier is more inclined toward rashness than cowardice, and different on occasion from that of a civilian; what constitutes liberality in expenditures depends upon one's resources. In general, Aristotle gives the sensible advice to endeavor to pull one's self in the direction opposite to one's inclinations, just as if one were to try to pull a crooked stick straight.

A celebrated passage in the Ethics describes the virtue of "highmindedness". Many modern students of ethics admire this ideal, and many do not. This passage taken alone would not give a fair impression of Aristotle's ideal of the good life. However, it is a thoroughly characteristic presentation of some phases of the ideal held in the Hellenic period of what a man of high rank should be.

"A highminded person seems to be one who regards himself as worthy of high things and who is worthy of them. . . . He estimates his own deserts aright, while others rate their deserts too high or too low. . . . It needs no proof that highminded people are concerned with honor; for it is honor more than anything else of which the great regard themselves, and deservedly regard themselves, as worthy. . . . The highminded man, as being worthy of the highest things, will be in the highest degree good, for the better man is always worthy of the highest things. . . . It is difficult to be truly highminded, as it is impossible without the perfection of good breeding. . . .

"He [*i.e.* the highminded man] will take a moderate view of wealth, political power, and good or ill fortune of all kinds, however it may occur. . . . [He] is not fond of encountering small dangers, nor is he fond of encountering dangers at all, as there are few things which he values [enough to endanger himself for them]. But he is ready to encounter great dangers, and in the hour of danger is reckless of his life, because he feels that life is not worth living without honor. He is capable of conferring benefits but ashamed of receiving them, as in the one case he feels his superiority, and in the other his inferiority. . . . He will try to return a benefit which has been conferred upon him with interest, as then the original benefactor will actually become his debtor, and will have been the recipient of a benefit. . . .

"It is characteristic, too, of the highminded man that he never, or hardly ever, asks a favor, that he is ready to do anybody a service, and that, though his bearing is stately toward persons of dignity and affluence, it is unassuming toward the middle class; for . . . while a dignified demeanor in dealing with the former is a mark of nobility, it is a mark of vulgarity in dealing with the latter, as it is like a display of strength at the expense of an invalid. . . . His performances will be rare, but they will be great and will win him a great name. He will, of course, be open in his hatreds and his friendships, as secrecy is an indication of fear. He will care for reality more than for reputation, he will be open in word and deed. . . . Nor will he bear grudges; for no one who is highminded will dwell upon the past, least of all upon past injuries; he will prefer to overlook them. He will not be a gossip, he will not talk much about himself or about anybody else; for he does not care to be praised himself or to get other people censured. On the other hand he will not be fond of praising other people. And not being a gossip, he will not speak evil of others, even of his enemies, except for the express purpose of insulting them. . . .

"It seems too that the highminded man will be slow in his movements, his voice will be deep and his manner of speaking sedate; for it is not likely that a man will be in a hurry, if there are not many things that he cares for, or that he will be emphatic, if he does not regard anything as important, and these are the causes which make people speak in shrill tones and use rapid movements".[39]

Aristotle distinguishes two kinds of Justice,—Distributive, which has to do with the proper apportionment of wealth, honors, and other goods in a well ordered state, and Corrective Justice. The latter is subdivided into Voluntary, dealing with contracts and similar civil relations into which one enters of his own accord, and Involuntary, dealing with the punishment of crimes and torts. He distinguishes between law and equity; between what is legally and morally right; and between crimes that are premeditated, those prompted by passion, and injuries caused by accident. Many of the broad features of law and social ethics were laid down by him for all time. He relies mainly upon individual initiative to effect justice in the economic order, and thinks, like Adam Smith, that prices are likely to be rightly determined by demand and supply in an open competitive market. His criticism, in the *Politics*, of the socialistic and communistic doctrines of Plato's *Republic* anticipates many of the arguments advanced by modern individualists in refutation of similar doctrines to-day.

Two delightfully written chapters on Friendship or Love (*Philia*) contain a masterly analysis of a virtue which he says is indispensable in all ages and circumstances of life. It is instinctive between the members of a family, and is social as the bond that holds states together. The motives that lead to friendship are diverse; friendships based on mutual interest and utility and those based on pleasure and hospitality are legitimate in their place; but perfect friendship or love is based on virtue, on the desire of the friend's good for the friend's sake, and such friendships alone are permanent.   The various aspects of friendship and love in the relations of husband, wife, children, masters, servants, rulers, subjects, and fellow citizens are thoughtfully drawn, and leave little for later ethics to add, except for the more religious phases of Love and Benevolence that have been distinctively a Christian contribution to modern ethics.

Aristotle's empiricism is shown in his discussion of the merits of different political constitutions.   Any government, whether by a king, an aristocracy, or the people, is normal if actuated by a regard for the community, and a perversion if the class in power favor itself at the cost of the common welfare.   He hesitates as to which form of government is absolutely the best, but inclines—in some passages at least—toward a government by all the citizens in states in which the general average of intelligence and virtue is high, since a large group is more likely to be wise collectively and less liable to passion and prejudice than a small group.   Control is safer in the hands of the middle class, than of either the very rich or the poor.   Mechanics and artisans are deficient in virtue, and not to be trusted with political control.

In states where only a small group has high civic ideals and capacities an aristocracy is best; where a state is attached to a capable royal family, a monarchy may be best.   Education is indispensable to make any kind of state successful, and educational aims and methods are discussed at length.   Aristotle is confident that natural inequalities exist among mankind. Some people are naturally incapable of free Citizenship.   Some races of mankind, barbarians, are naturally unable to care for themselves properly; therefore it is right for the Greeks to enslave them.   Women and children are naturally inferior to men in intelligence and virtue.   A man should rule his wife like a magistrate in a free state, his children like a king, and his slaves like a benevolent despot.   However, Aristotle concedes that all individuals should have as much freedom as they are capable of using intelligently.   His statements are evidently based on extensive and discriminating observation and study of condi-

tions in the Greek world of his time. For it they were justified.
From a modern point of view his chief error is the failure to
realize that those who were in inferior conditions about him—
barbarians, mechanics, artisans, women, slaves—could have
acquired intelligence and character in a more favorable social
environment. He charged to differences in natural capacities
much that we now know was the consequence of differences of
opportunity.

As compared with Plato, Aristotle gives larger recognition
to individuals, and so makes more room for individualization;
the state exists to afford a good life for its citizens, and not vice
versa. He does not make the Socratic and Platonic mistake of
identifying virtue with knowledge alone; virtue is a rational
habit in control of impulses. His ethics emphasizes socialization; the full good of the individual is only possible in a free
state. His ethics is in the best sense a profoundly rationalizing
interpretation of the life and experience of the Greek civilization which he knew.

VI. HELLENISTIC AND ROMAN ETHICS

The *Hellenic* (or purely Greek) period ends with Aristotle.
The *Hellenistic* period follows, in which philosophers were not
necessarily strictly Greek in blood and culture. They were
sometimes crude in expression and outlook; but all spoke and
wrote Greek of a kind, and all had a more cosmopolitan vision
than the thinkers of earlier periods. The Macedonian conquest
broke down invidious distinctions between Greeks and barbarians, and between citizens of different Greek states. In this
way its effect on moral philosophy was good. On the other
hand, in the partial reversion to Authority, it no longer remained possible to define the moral life in terms of citizenship
in a free city-state; some other standpoint must be found, and
until this was done satisfactorily, ethical systems appeared
that were less well rounded than that of Aristotle, and over-
emphasized some aspect of life at the cost of other aspects. For
all schools, the necessity of a reflective standpoint was appre-

ciated; and for all, the problem was, *How should a wise man,* since he can no longer identify his good with citizenship in a free state, but must rely upon himself, *so act as to secure for himself the most satisfactory life?*

Epicurus († 270 B.C.) a native of Samos, but of Athenian descent, came to Athens fifteen years after the death of Aristotle and opened a new school in his private Garden.[40]   He is said to have suffered great sorrows in early life, and later to have arrived at a moral philosophy in which he found peace.   This he was ready to impart to others.   An amiable friend, of spotless character, who attracted many followers, both men and women, as well as a diligent scholar who wrote many treatises, he so thoroughly developed his system and indoctrinated his pupils with it, that it remained the teaching of the school practically without modification for centuries.   A wise man should find his happiness in his own inward peace of mind.   He can then survey external events over which he has no control with imperturbability (*ataraxia*).   This is a somewhat unusual form of hedonism, for while happiness is identified with pleasure, the active pursuit of pleasures is not commended so much as inward calmness.   It is in this respect different from the Cyrenaic school.   A temperate and frugal life is best, with necessities provided and enjoyed, but without the cares of wealth.   Such a life is free from desires and passions, pains and disappointments.   Friends should be cultivated, for in friendship is greatest happiness found.   Marriage and the bringing up of children, although not forbidden, were regarded with some disfavor because of the anxieties and responsibilities involved.   For similar reasons, the Epicurean was not disposed to engage in political activities.   Even intellectual pursuits, except so far as they were of practical value in relation to the moral life, were regarded as irksome and of little consequence.

The ethical outlook of Epicureanism was supported by a mechanistic metaphysics which taught that all things, including the soul of man, are combinations of material atoms.   Man is therefore mortal, and need fear none of the hells described by

Plato and the popular religious cults. The gods are unconcerned with men; they lead a sheltered and happy life; the Epicurean need only take them into account so far as contemplation of them affords him delight in literature and art. Man's will is free; he is no slave of circumstance, but may, if he is wise, choose the serene and truly pleasurable life of the Epicurean.

Such a moral philosophy had merits. It taught men in an age of despotic repression contentment in the cultivation of friendship and æsthetic pleasures. It liberated men from the superstitious fears that increasingly weighed upon them in an age of religious decay. It was kindly and tolerant, free from fanaticism and bigotry. The Roman poets Lucretius and Horace present the Epicurean view with great attractiveness. However, at best, Epicureanism tended toward social irresponsibility; and often, especially among the Romans of the last century of the republic and during the empire, its hedonistic teachings were misunderstood. Many who were led by it to believe that the best life is that which contains most pleasure and least pain, failed to realize that only such a life as that of Epicurus himself can meet this requirement. And as the philosophy knew of no rational way to evaluate pleasures except by appeal to the individual's own experience, it had no means by which to show a man of narrow sensual outlook the falseness of his standard of happiness. So many of the Roman Epicureans led lives that brought the school into bad repute.

A very different moral philosophy was presented by the school opened in 294 B.C. at Athens in the Stoa (a famous painted Porch) and so known as the Stoics.[41] The founder and two succeeding heads of the school were Zeno († 264 B.C.), Cleanthes († 232 B.C.) and Chrysippus († 204 B.C.). Zeno was probably of Hebrew descent, with a temperament like the sterner prophets of Israel.[42] All three were Hellenists with little of the old Hellenic culture and love of moderation and symmetry, notwithstanding the fact that Cleanthes' *Hymn to Zeus* is one of the world's sublimest religious poems.

The wise man, according to Stoicism, will live in accordance with nature, and lead a life of absolute virtue for its own sake. Thus alone can happiness be found. The wise man, according to the early Stoics (in opposition to Aristotle) will render himself absolutely free from all desires and emotions; a state of apathy (*apatheia*) so that no outward circumstances that may come to him—health, riches, honor, poverty, sickness, disgrace, approaching death—will greatly concern him; for none of these things can affect his character. In contrast to the Epicureans, the early Stoics insisted that the wise man will seek no pleasures, not even the pleasure of moral excellence; for the pursuit of pleasure is no proper object of moral effort. The early Stoics advised men not to marry nor engage in politics, and in general to keep aloof from any social contacts that might interfere with concentration upon a life of absolute integrity. This last alone gives true contentment; no misfortune can take it away. So it is best not to care too much for anybody or anything external to one's self and not completely within one's own power. The wise man is absolutely without fault, he alone is beautiful, rich and happy, since he has virtue, and that alone is of worth and can afford contentment. The wise man, during his life time, in no way falls short of the happiness of Zeus. And all are either wise men or fools: there can be no middle ground, and most men are fools, ignorant, wicked, unhappy, cowardly, impious, mad. Socrates, Diogenes, Antisthenes, and (in Roman times) Cato were exemplars of wise men. The actual passage from folly to the state of wisdom is instantaneous, a kind of conversion. Stern and pitiless in discipline of himself, the earlier Stoic sometimes was cruel in treatment of others.[43]

In an age of moral laxity, when the old mores of the city-state were breaking down under imperialism and cosmopolitanism, we can see that such a standpoint in some ways had excellence. But its harsh self-righteousness is repellent. Moreover, it bred bigots and fanatics, as is inevitable in an ethics that regards only motives, is heedless of consequences, and insists that a man should carry out his inflexible duty and enforce rigorous justice, though the heavens fall. However, it enabled men to lead lives of dogged endurance in an age when endurance was often called for. If a Stoic's life became absolutely intolerable through the weakness of age, incurable disease, dire poverty, the decay of mental powers, the tyranny of a despot, or other extreme circumstances, he believed it his moral right to bring it to a voluntary end.[44]

In its later evolution, especially in Roman imperial times, Stoicism became greatly mollified in its harsher features. Stoics came to realize that there is a large region of goods that one may seek and enjoy without hurt to one's conscience, even if they do not directly contribute to the cultivation of virtue. All pleasures are not wrong. Moreover, we are in a social world; no one can live wholly to himself. Men ought to marry, be good neighbors and citizens, and help carry on the tasks of government which require the efforts of honest men even in an empire. Mercy and kindness, even to wrongdoers, became a virtue. So Stoicism, thus softened and sweetened, produced men like Seneca, an emperor's minister, and the emperors Antoninus Pius and Marcus Aurelius Antoninus, great administrators who governed earnestly, mercifully, and faithfully, and found that the Stoic ideal of virtue and duty could best be realized in lives of service. No moral system has excelled Stoicism in its absolute separation of virtue and duty from inclination and selfish interests.

Stoicism, though primarily an ethic, made moral philosophy rest upon metaphysical and religious foundations. The Stoics knew enough science to believe that in some sense everything is composed of matter and moves in space. But this did not lead them to a materialism of a mechanistic kind like that of Epicurus. The whole world, though material like our own bodies, is knit together into a harmonious organic whole, and has a soul (*pneuma*) of its own,—God. All of us are expressions of the universal Reason (*Logos*); there is a divine spark in each of us, all are brothers, children of a common Father. We should think of ourselves as fellow citizens, not of Athens or

Sparta, but of the universe. The world is one city of gods and men. So, at least in theory, the cosmopolitanism of the world empire for the Stoic broke down invidious distinctions between races, bond and free, men and women. All is willed by God; but we have freedom of assent; we can commit our wills to Him, and in carrying out His purposes we can realize our own. The earlier aloofness to other persons and events became, in the later Stoicism, simply a heroic resolution to bear misfortunes cheerfully, and to carry on one's work manfully.

Stoicism was a form of pantheism. God is identified with the material universe, or at most distinguished as its soul. He has ordered the world as a whole for the best, and men ought to commit themselves to Him. But there is no room to think of God as a particular Providence, personally accessible to each individual in prayer; and the Stoic was hesitant about continued personal existence after death. Believing in the absolute goodness of God and the universe, the Stoics had to account for the presence of evil. They advanced most of the philosophical explanations since adopted by Christian and Jewish theology. Physical evils like tempests and human diseases cannot affect character, and so they are really not evil at all; they are due to natural causes framed by God for purposes that on the whole are good; many things are evil only because they are misused; others that at first appear evil prove to be of the greatest value. Moral evils must exist because of the free will of men; they are necessary to make possible the development of human character; without evil there could be no good; all evil will ultimately be turned by God to good; and so on.

The moral advance made by later Stoicism in its ideal of a good life, illustrated by the case of a man of commanding eminence, may well be seen in the contrast between Aristotle's description of the high-minded man and Marcus Aurelius' delineation of the character of his distinguished predecessor and adopted father, the emperor Antoninus Pius:

"From my father I learned gentleness, and unshaken adherence to judgments deliberately formed; indifference to outward show and compliment; industry and assiduity; an ear open to all suggestions for the public weal; recognition inflexibly proportioned to desert; the tact that knew when to insist and when to relax; chaste habits and disinterested aims. His friends had free leave to forego the imperial table, or miss attendance in his suite, and he took no umbrage at those who were detained on various calls. At the council-board he pushed inquiries pertinaciously, where others would have held their hand, content with first impressions. His loyalty to friends was free from fickleness or extravagance. He rose to the occasion, always, with a smile. . . . Vigilant in providing for imperial needs, he husbanded his resources, and put up with the inevitable grumbling. In his relations with the gods he was not superstitious; while with men, he neither courted popularity nor pandered to the mob, but was in all points sober and safe, distrusting flash or novelty. . . . He did honor to all true philosophers; to the rest he was civil, but he kept his distance all the same. His manner was friendly; gracious, but not excessive. In attention to the body he hit the happy mean; . . . his wise self-management made him almost independent of doctoring, medicines or salves. He was forward and generous in recognizing talent, in rhetoric for instance or jurisprudence or history, or any other subject; and eager to assist any to shine in the sphere of their choice. Sound Roman through and through, he never studied appearances. Free from caprice or humors, he kept constant to the same places and the same things. After paroxysms of headache, he was back fresh and vigorous at his usual tasks. His official secrets were few, the rare and occasional exceptions being solely matters of state. . . . There was nothing fractious about him, no black looks or fits; he never forced things, as one says, 'past sweating point'; but was invariably rational and discriminating —giving judgments leisurely, calm, suitable, vigorous and consistent. One might fairly adapt to him what is recorded of Socrates, that he could either enjoy or leave things which most people find themselves too weak to abstain from, and too self-indulgent to enjoy." [45]

In most respects the Romans added little to the Hellenic and Hellenistic systems of moral philosophy. Their genius was practical and administrative, and writers like Cicero († 43 B.C.) and Seneca († 65 A.D.) merely took from Greek philosophy what they found suggestive and helpful, and applied it in a popular and untechnical way to the topics in which their contemporaries were interested. A philosophical point of view is helpful in every problem of life: how to appreciate friendship and reconcile one's self to the infirmities of old age, how to worship the gods avoiding superstition, the value of clemency especially on the part of a prince, how to enjoy leisure and control anger, and the like. Through such contributions Greek ethics not only proved helpful to the Romans of those times, but became firmly planted in the western moral tradition that has come down to us.

The most important original contribution of the Romans to the moral development of Europe was in the field of law and jurisprudence. An account of this cannot be attempted here, since it was largely a movement within the law itself—decisions of courts, opinions of jurists, legislation by the senate and other deliberative bodies, and edicts of princes. However, Stoic philosophy exercised an important though external influence on it that must be briefly noticed.

Cicero affirmed many Stoic conceptions and gave them a juristic tone. In his *Republic* and *Laws* he says that the origin of justice is to be sought in the divine or *natural law* of eternal and immutable morality, known to man because he participates in the divine reason. All races of mankind share in the same reason and the same senses, and make the same moral judgments, approving kindness, benignity and gratitude and detesting arrogance, malice, and cruelty. "There is a true law, a right reason, conformable to nature, universal, unchangeable, eternal, whose commands urge us to duty, and whose prohibitions restrain us from evil. . . . This law cannot be contradicted by any other law, and is not liable either to derogation or abrogation. . . . It needs no other expositor and interpreter than our own conscience. It is not one thing at Rome and another at Athens; one thing today and another tomorrow; but in all times and nations this universal law must forever reign, eternal and imperishable. It is the sovereign master and emperor of all beings. God himself is its author,—its promulgator,—its enforcer." [46]

Seneca does not use the phrase "natural law", but he affirms the natural equality of mankind, and the general Stoic conceptions on the subject. He teaches that the slave is of the same nature as his master, and the difference in their positions is due to fortune and not to inequality in natural capacities. Slaves can be just, brave, and magnanimous; the institution of slavery has no justification in nature, and is hateful to all men. [47]

The Roman jurists of the empire were confronted by a practical problem. The Civil Law of the city of Rome (*ius civile*) had slowly developed from time immemorial, and retained all kinds of anomalies and anachronisms, including distinctions in rights and status that no longer were in accordance with moral sentiments and practical convenience. On the other hand, the prætors had gradually been developing another body of law (*ius gentium*) for foreigners resident or doing business in Rome, and for the administration of the provinces. At first the *ius gentium* had been looked down upon as inferior law for those not entitled to the full privilege of Roman citizenship. But since the prætors had had a freer hand in developing the *ius gentium*, making use of precedents from all over the world, including the older and more experienced cities of the East, this had become in many respects the more rational law of the two. Under these circumstances it became desirable for the citizens of Rome to have the benefit of the better features of the *ius gentium*, and for this and the *ius civile* to be assimilated to one another. In consequence, therefore, there arose a tendency to identify the *ius gentium* with the Stoic conception of a natural law (*ius naturale*) universal in its applications, and revealed to some extent in the laws of all nations. At times in the history of legal progress some broadly unifying philosophical conception has done much to hasten advance, setting up a distinct object to aim at in improvement. Just as Bentham's principle that the good of the community must take precedence over every other object gave a clear rule of reform in England and elsewhere in the first half of the nineteenth century, this conception of a law of nature did much to reform Roman law under the empire.[48]

The Stoic conception of the equality of mankind in natural law must, in combination with other influences, have done much to further the reforms under the empire by which the condition of the slave was mitigated and he was given some legal rights; by which women came upon a more nearly equal plane with men regarding marriage, divorce, property, and personal rights; and those by which free men of all nations came to enjoy the rights of Roman citizens. The Stoic doctrines, too, helped no doubt to strengthen the tradition of the Roman jurists that all the powers of government, even those of the emperor himself, were ultimately derived from the consent of the people.

Nor was it a benefit to the ancient world only that such moral conceptions became embodied in Roman law and tradition. In modern times, the doctrine that all men are by nature free and equal has received new applications in the fields of political, religious, and economic liberty of which the Roman jurists never dreamed. The modern bills of rights in our constitutions, and the more recent movements for conferring equal rights and opportunities upon slaves, women, and workingmen may be said in some measure to have their roots in Stoic philosophy. Movements for the development of international law, the prevention and mitigation of warfare, and a better spirit in the relations between nations, greatly modified though they now are, can be traced back to the revival in the seventeenth century by Grotius of ancient ideals and practices.[49]

VII. Ethics and Religion

Stoicism, as we have seen, attempted to ground ethics in a religious and metaphysical view of the world. In some respects, the later Stoics did attempt to establish a religion. Their philosophers, dressed in a distinctive costume, conducted services, delivered sermons, wrote tracts and epistles. Socrates and other saintly men of the past were praised as models whom men ought to follow. But the appeal of such a philosophy was too coldly intellectual to grip the masses. It could only reach a limited few.

Other philosophical and religious movements appearing from time to time sought to enlist religion more adequately as a sanction for the moral life. Among the more philosophical movements was that at Alexandria with Philo Judæus († 50 A.D.) as its most renowned leader. This sought to reconcile Judaism with Greek philosophy. The Neoplatonism of Plotinus († 269 A.D.) sought a higher moral life through mystical absorption in the Deity. These movements were also too intellectual to reach the masses, while their ethical merits on the whole were inferior to later Stoicism. The various mystery religions, notable among which were the mysteries of Cybele, Isis, and Mithra, made a more vivid emotional appeal through ritual, with sacraments in which water, bread, and wine were employed; and the assurance of personal immortality was given to those who dedicated themselves to the service of the god. But such religions contained gross and superstitious rites and doctrines that offended the refinement and intelligence of the cultivated man.

All these movements, however, prepared the pagan mind for the acceptance of a new religion, and help to explain its rapid growth. Christianity taught whole-hearted consecration to duty as emphatically as Stoicism, and like it, recognized that all men are children of a common heavenly Father. It was able to add a tender emotional appeal, in which love, a virtue scarcely noticed by the Stoics, played a dominant part. As a model for all men to follow, it had the blameless Jesus, whom the Gospel of John proclaimed to be the Logos (or Word) incarnate in the form of a man who had lived in recent times. So the Logos became concrete, human, personal, and was brought down from Heaven to earth. Instead of citizenship in a universal city-state of gods and men that at best was only a shadowy ideal, the Christian had a highly organized holy catholic church, to which he was devotedly loyal, and which he believed to be the bride of Christ. Instead of wandering philosophers, he had a zealous and well-disciplined clergy. Instead of miscellaneous and somewhat contradictory philosophical treatises written at various times during many centuries, he had in the New Testament a canon of sacred books all written within three quarters of a century of one another, and presenting a more harmonious point of view. He had a more inclusive and more humanly appealing moral system. He believed in personal prayer to a personal God. He was so confident of personal immortality that he was willing to undergo martyrdom rather than renounce his religion. Christianity had more to offer its converts than any of its rivals. In the course of three centuries it spread through the known civilized world, and became the established religion of the empire.

REFERENCES

* J. Dewey and J. H. Tufts, *Ethics*, chap. VII.
* F. Paulsen, *Ethics*, Part I, chaps. I, III.
* L. T. Hobhouse, *Morals in Evolution*, Part II, chap. VI.
* T. De Laguna, *Introduction to the Science of Ethics*, chaps. VI–IX.
* J. A. Leighton, *Field of Philosophy*, chaps. VI–IX.
* G. P. Conger, *A Course in Philosophy*, chaps. IX–XII.
* W. K. Wright, *A Student's Philosophy of Religion*, chap. IX.
* G. Lowes Dickinson, *The Greek View of Life*.
* W. Warde Fowler, *The City-State of the Greeks and Romans*, esp. chap. VI.
* W. S. Ferguson, *Greek Imperialism*, pp. 38–78, 116–148. *Hellenistic Athens.*

* A. K. Rogers, *A Student's History of Philosophy.*
* F. Thilly, *A History of Philosophy.*
* H. E. Cushman, *A History of Ancient Philosophy.*

Walter Pater, *Plato and Platonism. Marius the Epicurean.*

Matthew Arnold, *Essays in Criticism. Culture and Anarchy.*

R. W. Livingstone, *The Greek Genius and its Meaning to Us.*

Fustel de Coulanges, *The Ancient City.*

Th. Gomperz, *Greek Thinkers.*

A. E. Zimmern, *The Greek Commonwealth.*

Samuel Dill, *Roman Society from Nero to Marcus Aurelius.*

W. E. H. Lecky, *History of European Morals.*

J. B. Bury, *History of Greece.*

L. V. Schmidt, *Ethik der alten Griechen.*

W. H. S. Jones, *Greek Morality.*

CHAPTER VI

CHRISTIANITY

I. Introductory

Christianity, the dominant religion in the occident for sixteen centuries, has exercised a profound influence upon moral evolution. It will be impossible to outline here the long course of ethical development within the Christian church, closely allied as it has been with political and social history, and the succession of theological systems. However, a few outstanding contributions that Christianity has made to our moral tradition can be indicated.[1]

Two preliminary comments need to be made. First, it should be noted that Christianity is not an ethical system with religious sanctions like those of Plato and the Stoics; on the contrary, it is an *ethical religion*, something quite different. As a *religion*, its first concern has been to bring men in some way into proper relations with God through Jesus Christ—the precise manner has varied in different periods and theological systems. As an *ethical* religion, it has taught many ideals that have grown with the moral development of western civilization, without losing the characteristic stamp that they received in New Testament times under the influence of Jesus. In its best periods, the moral ideals of Christianity have shone clearly and enlightened mankind; there have been other periods when the subordination of ethics to theology proved less favorable to moral progress. Since the Reformation, ethics has gradually escaped from its subordinate position, and reflection on the moral life has come to be regarded, at least in philosophical circles, as properly a cause rather than a consequence of belief in religion.

135

The second preliminary observation is, that *there is no one ethical system that can exclusively claim the designation of Christian Ethics.* Every moral philosopher who has professed and called himself a Christian has believed his to be *a* (if not *the*) true system of Christian ethics. Moreover, no moral principle loses its place as a part of Christian ethics because it has originated independently of Christianity, or is held by some who are not Christians. Every teacher of Christian morality, beginning with Jesus himself, has taken for granted most of the moral tradition of his time, only criticizing and correcting it in order to meet pressing personal and social problems. Christianity in every age has assimilated moral teachings that had independent origin, made them part of its moral tradition, and so handed them down to later ages. All true ethics is Christian ethics; and Christianity teaches no moral principles that are contrary to the best reasoning and observation of moral philosophers generally. (Statements similar to those of this paragraph can rightly be made by the modern Jew with respect to Jewish ethics.)

II. Moral Teachings of the New Testament

The outstanding feature of New Testament morals is *love of God and men, and discipleship of Jesus Christ.* The whole of the Law, Jesus taught, is summed up in the commandment to love God with all one's heart, mind, soul, and strength, and one's neighbor as oneself. In the synoptic gospels (Matthew, Mark, Luke), Jesus speaks with authority, and his teachings are lovingly accepted as morally obligatory. The burning desire of Paul, throughout all his letters, is that he may lead as many as possible to a life in union with God through the acceptance of Jesus as Lord and Saviour. The Fourth Gospel (John) proclaims Jesus to be the Stoic Logos (Word) become flesh, and puts first emphasis on complete union with God through him.

The personality of Jesus in the simple grandeur and pathos of his life and death has profoundly impressed the western moral consciousness. There is something tender and compelling about all that he says and does, that has gripped the hearts of mankind. Moral precepts conceived in terms of loyalty to him, and through him to God, are warm and vital; they make a profound and personal appeal to human emotions and desires, and transform sentiments and character, as the teachings of no mere philosopher—not even Socrates—ever has been able to do. Perhaps this is the most important contribution of Christianity to the moral tradition,—*the personalization of the moral appeal* through its identification with Jesus, and through him, with God.

An individual makes moral progress through *self-renunciation* in the service of God and Christ, and *identification with the "kingdom" or "church"*. Jesus says, according to Matthew, "If any man would come after me, let him deny himself, and take up his cross and follow me. For whosoever would save his life shall lose it, and whosoever shall lose his life for my sake shall find it." (Matthew XVI. 24, 25.) In such self-renunciation, even at the cost of suffering and death, the early Christian thought that he gained perfect *freedom* (Galatians V; *cf.* James I. 25). A person's will is free when he is expressing his true desires and finding self-realization; only in the higher life in peace with God, attained through discipleship of Christ, could this be won and a person's true vocation found.

The individual could believe that through complete submission to God and Christ he would gain real freedom because of *the inestimable worth of the individual soul to God*, beautifully expressed, for instance, in the parable of the "lost sheep", the "lost coin", and the "prodigal son" (Luke XV). As an individual child can turn in confident petition to a loving parent, so Jesus teaches his followers to pray to a personal God who loves and cares for them as individuals. Since it is the dwelling place of his soul, the body of the individual is also sacred and holy—a "temple of the holy Ghost" (I Corinthians VI. 19); and his glorified body is assured physical resurrection (I Corinthians XV; Philippians III. 21). The individual, both body and soul, redeemed, and glorified, will be saved to a life of *blessed immortality* if he is faithful in acceptance of the grace of Christ. Thus we see that Christianity has been a potent *individualizing* influence in moral evolution.

This individualizing tendency makes morality assume a form of *ethical inwardness*. This conception of inwardness, by no means unknown to Jew and Stoic, is given a new and tender emphasis in Christian teaching. It is blessed to be humble, meek, merciful, pure in heart, peaceable, to hunger and thirst after righteousness. Such motives must be strictly inward, basic in one's character. Wrongdoing is the consequence of wrong inner motives; it is thoughts and feelings of anger that lead to murder, of lust to adultery, of boastfulness to profanity and perjury. One should love all men, including one's enemies, praying for them and forgiving them, in accordance with the Golden Rule. In all things a person must endeavor to be perfect, as God is perfect. Thus he will feel in unity with God. He will be able to trust in His protecting care, knowing that if he seeks first His kingdom and His righteousness, all needful things will be provided.

This strongly individualized moral attitude of the New Testament, unlike Hellenic ethics, is not the perfection of man as a natural being. Unregenerated human nature is essentially evil; it can only be corrected by a *complete rebirth or religious awakening* (Ephesians II. 1–3; Romans VII. 5, VIII. 5–8; John III. 1–7). To a certain extent this rebirth reminds one of Stoicism; but the differences are, that for the Christian this is not to be effected by his own efforts, but by trust in divine grace, and it is a reconstitution rather than a suppression of his emotional nature. It assumes a deep and genuine *contrition* for his sins. The value of thus frankly facing the evil in one's life and with the help of religion making a complete break with it, is manifest. The harm that sometimes has attended modern revivalism, with its insistence that the conversion must be a spectacular emotional upheaval, has been due to a misinterpretation of New Testament teaching that was made during the eighteenth century.

Faith equals = Knowledge + belief + confidence.

Three Christian virtues conspicuous in the New Testament that are not mentioned in Greek ethics are *faith*—trust in the guidance of God and hence resolution to carry out His will; *hope*—confidence in the victory through God of the good; and *charity* (or "love", *agapé*) a distinctively Christian virtue different in many ways from what Plato meant by love (*éros*) or Aristotle (*philía*). Charity is an indispensable virtue; without it other virtues are worthless. Charity positively implies kindness, patience, and endurance, as well as freedom from envy, jealousy, anger, spitefulness, boastfulness, self-display, and malice (I Corinthians XIII). It requires helpfulness to all those in need, given with loving interest and sympathy, as in the parable of the Good Samaritan (Luke X. 25–37). Combined with personal integrity it constitutes pure religion in the worship of God the Father (James I. 27). It is the earlier Hebrew virtue of love of neighbor, applied more intensely and whole-heartedly, not to fellow countrymen alone, but to all men. It enjoins many of the same actions to which a later Stoic would have felt impelled from a sense of duty; but charity requires that the service rendered should be done with a spirit of tenderness and sympathy quite in contrast to Stoic apathy. The teaching of charity has led Christians in all ages to the establishment of hospitals, schools, orphanages, and philanthropic institutions of every kind, and much private benevolence. The latter in ancient and medieval times led to open-handed almsgiving that was well intended, though not in accordance with sound economics.

The doctrine of the universal mission of the religion is an assumption by Christianity of what the second Isaiah conceived to be the mission of Israel.[2] In the sight of God all have *spiritual equality*, regardless of race, sex, social, or economic status. Gentiles, as Paul established, might become Christians without conforming to Jewish ritual. This conception of the spiritual equality of all mankind had important consequences in subsequent moral evolution. Paul taught Philemon, the Christian master of a runaway slave named Onesimus, to regard his slave as a brother in Christ (Philemon: *cf.* Colossians IV. 9).

Christians treated their slaves kindly, and often emancipated them. After Christians came into imperial power they strengthened the earlier legislation of Roman jurists under the influence of Stoicism for the protection of slaves. When abolition of slavery and serfdom at last in modern times became economically feasible, the Christian tradition operated to awaken the conscience of Christendom. Belief in the personal equality of mankind has, moreover, strengthened demands for human equality in other respects,—for political, religious, cultural, and industrial freedom and opportunity, as well as for the emancipation of women.

The New Testament is everywhere emphatic that *home life must be pure*, that the *"single standard"* in sexual conduct applies to men and women alike, that abortion and infanticide and all forms of sex perversions are to be absolutely forbidden, that men and women should be pure in thought and words as well as in outward conduct. In all aspects of sexual purity Christianity has immeasurably improved the mores of Europe, which were extremely low in these matters at the time of its advent.

Thus far all that has been said of New Testament moral teaching is probably quite generally agreed upon. It is now necessary to touch upon some important but disputed points in which diverse interpretations of the New Testament have greatly influenced subsequent moral evolution.

Roman Catholics interpret the New Testament to forbid divorce absolutely, and to brand the remarriage of divorced persons as adultery. Eastern Catholics and most Protestants believe that the New Testament permits divorce because of adultery; and many of them add that at least by implication it allows divorce on all grounds so grave that continuance in the marriage relation would be morally unwholesome for spouses and children; in other words, on the grounds provided in the legislation of most modern Christian countries. As a result of New Testament teaching Christian mores on the subject of divorce have become more restrictive than was law and custom in the Roman empire, the extent to which restriction has gone depending on which interpretation of the New Testament prevailed in any given place and time. Catholics, both Roman and Eastern, believe that Jesus and Paul taught that celibacy is a higher moral state than marriage, and to be recommended to those able to observe continence who have a vocation for a religious life. Protestants, on the other hand, believe that the New Testament regards marriage no less highly than celibacy, and that the contrary Catholic teaching has put a premium on an unnatural manner of life often attended by bad physical and moral effects upon the celibates, which has deteriorated the stock of Europe by inducing spiritually gifted people to go into convents and leave others to become the sole ancestors of future generations.[3] So the New Testament has contributed to two different traditions regarding divorce and celibacy.

There are passages in the New Testament that can be interpreted as teaching nonresistance to evil. One should turn the other cheek, no matter how great the injury. It is wrong even to seek one's rights in a court of law (I Corinthians VI. 1–8). Christians during the first few centuries often thought military service wrong, and when conscribed preferred martyrdom to enlistment in the army.[4] The New Testament has sometimes been interpreted to commend poverty, and to look with disfavor upon the possession of wealth. The church at Jerusalem temporarily at least tried the experiment of communism.[5] Fasting and other forms of asceticism are occasionally mentioned in the New Testament.[6] A life of nonresistance, poverty, communism, and ascetic practices was obviously impossible for every one; but it was long believed by nearly all Christians that for those with a vocation to it such is a higher life, more meritorious in the sight of God. This is still the belief of Roman and Eastern Catholics, constituting perhaps three-fourths of all Christians at the present time.

While women are everywhere respected in the New Testament, it has sometimes been thought that in the writings of Paul, at least, the Oriental view of the subjection of women to

Women are not subjugated by sheltering them from the business world. They are lifted above it; such work is left to the stronger men to worry about.

men is taught.[7] It is certain that such views came to prevail in the world after the triumph of Christianity and the downfall of the Roman empire. Women lost most of the personal and property rights that Roman law had granted them They only regained these rights in the nineteenth century, in face of the opposition of many ecclesiastics, who quoted the New Testament in favor of the subjection of women. However, it is open to question how far interpretations of the New Testament were originally responsible for the loss of feminine rights. The later Roman empire was flooded by Oriental ideas and customs of every kind quite apart from Christianity, and the northern barbarians gave their women few rights.

It has been charged that the New Testament is inferior in its moral outlook to the best Greek philosophers in that it never conceives moral problems in terms of citizenship in a free political state. Political rights and duties are never discussed. Law and justice are ignored. Meek submission to governmental authority is enjoined on the erroneous theory that rulers derive their power from divine right,[8] and not, as Roman law taught, from the consent of the people. So the church in later times taught a false political philosophy, and the struggle for liberty in modern times was rendered more difficult. On the other hand it has been contended that the doctrine of the divine right of kings in its extreme form is a modern invention that hardly antedates the Stuarts; patristic views on the subject were much more regardful of the rights and welfare of the people.[9]

The New Testament has been accused of putting a low premium on all intellectual undertakings. We find in it nothing like the Hebrew and Greek praise of wisdom and learning. The wisdom of this world is contemptuously dismissed as "foolishness with God". (I Corinthians III. 19–21). The result was, so it has been claimed, that in later generations Christians became indifferent to liberal education, and thought it at best a serious handicap to the Christian life, if not a positive danger to one's salvation. It is true that the later ancient

fathers advised against pagan classical studies on the part
of the young; but conditions at the time rather than misinterpretations of the New Testament were probably responsible.

Bitter indignation at heretics is occasionally expressed in the
New Testament; that is, at Christians with other convictions
than those of the writers themselves.[10] This, it is charged,
laid the foundation for later persecutions after Christians were
in power. On the other hand it is replied that the "heretics"
of the New Testament were former pagans, only recently
converted, who were bent on introducing immoral and superstitious practices that would have been utterly contrary
to the Christian life; they had to be withstood, and this was
done firmly, and with great though loving and kindly moral
indignation. There was no thought of persecuting them in any
way, except to prevent their introducing pagan beliefs and
practices into the churches.

In regard to all these disputed points of interpretation of
the New Testament, several observations can be made as a result of the historical study of the Bible in our own time. Had
earlier ages known the sacred books from the modern point of
view, many misinterpretations which have had unfortunate
effects on moral evolution would not have occurred. It is evident, for one thing, that most of the New Testament writers,
including Paul and the authors of the synoptic gospels, supposed
that the end of the world and the second coming of Christ
would shortly occur.[11] To a certain extent, therefore, they
interpreted the teaching of Jesus as an "interim ethic" applicable to a small group of believers preparing for life in another
world. Under such conditions, it well might be best neither
to marry nor carry on other new undertakings of an extensive
character. Furthermore it must be remembered that in the first
century, the Christian congregations were small and persecuted.
They believed that they had a message of supreme importance
to all mankind. Their chief duty and privilege was to impart
this "good news" to all to whom they could. Under such circumstances we can well see that it might have seemed imprudent

for a believer to carry a lawsuit into the courts. That would in any event take time, trouble and expense, and divert attention from his chief duty as a Christian, and it might call the notice of the civil authorities to the presence of Christians in the community, and cause many to lose their lives.

Devoid of political influence, questions of government and citizenship and justice did not enter into the living problems of the Christian communities of the first century, and so were not discussed. Most of them were provincials upon whom the rights and privileges of Roman citizenship had not yet been conferred. They knew nothing of the philosophy that underlay Roman law. Their ancestors had been forcibly conquered by the Romans, evidently by the will of God. It was their duty to obey the rulers as ordained by God; except when their orders conflicted with the Christian conscience, in which case they must obey God rather than men.

The first century Christians in most cases had little education. Even the learned Paul could not write good literary Greek. There was neither time nor opportunity to cultivate the intellect and acquire "wisdom". What little time these poor hard working people could spare from the toil of earning a living, they felt it their duty to spend in religious activities, preparing themselves and as many others as possible for the day of the Lord.

So we see that the circumstances under which the New Testament books were written precluded the development of a complete system of morality to be handed down for the literal observance of all Christians of all future ages. Nowhere do the writers of the New Testament attempt to formulate a moral code like the Mosaic Law. Their attitude in this respect is in marked contrast to that of the Old Testament. Jesus had left no code or detailed ethical instructions; in fact, he left nothing in writing at all. His sayings seem only to have been treasured in oral tradition for some years, perhaps a generation, after his death. In the form that they have been gathered together in the synoptic gospels, and so come down to us, they consist chiefly of trenchant aphorisms and parables, profound in meaning, but obviously not designed to be obeyed as literally as if they were statutes. The necessary applications and qualifications to make them workable under specific circumstances, especially those of remote lands and centuries, are left by Jesus to the judgment of his followers. What is true of the synoptic gospels is even more true of the rest of the New Testament. Paul was writing to local congregations with their special problems in mind; he was not consciously laying down laws for all time. Only so far as his advice to a local church can be seen to apply to conditions of our own times does it have value or authority for the modern liberal Christian. The general epistles and the Johannine literature are colored by the conditions of the particular Christians for whose benefit these books were originally written: *viz.*, times of unusually severe persecution; times when heresies were especially rife; the problem of preserving the original Jewish tradition and yet accommodating it to Hellenistic philosophy; and other peculiar circumstances in the primitive churches.[12]

The lofty ideals of the New Testament upon which there is general agreement in interpretation have been of immense value to the moral tradition. The disputed interpretations have also greatly influenced European moral development, but not always favorably. The New Testament books, beginning with the second century, were for ages accepted in their present form as verbally inspired, infallible, and authoritative, and attempts were made to carry out their teachings literally. Only in the course of the nineteenth century did modern critical scholarship disclose the conditions under which they were written. Misinterpretations were inevitable under the circumstances. This was obviously not the fault of the sacred writers themselves, much less of Jesus.

III. CATHOLICISM

All of the books now included within the New Testament were written well within a century after the death of Jesus (30 A.D., or a few years later). During this period the church was an informal grouping of different congregations somewhat like the Jewish synagogues, with no central administration, authoritarian liturgy or creeds. The spirit of Jesus and his message was preserved through the personal influence of the apostles (including evangelists like Paul as well as the original twelve), and of those converted by them and working under their supervision. However, the churches were rapidly growing. Numerical estimates are speculative, but it is not unlikely that by the end of the first century A.D. the membership of the churches had increased from the five hundred in the early church mentioned by Paul (I Corinthians XV. 6) to half a million or more. The accessions were mostly Gentiles—converts from Hellenistic philosophy, the various mystery religions, and other pagan cults—persons who had had little or no previous contact with Judaism, and whose moral and religious outlook in consequence was quite different from that of the first followers of Jesus. During the following two centuries new converts kept streaming in, so that by the time Christianity became officially recognized by the emperor Constantine in 312 A.D. the religion may have numbered thirty million adherents.[13] Under these circumstances the leaders of the churches were confronted by a formidable problem. How could the spirit of Jesus be preserved? How could Christianity be saved from submergence in Gentile beliefs and practices?

The problem was met by various authoritarian measures. Local church officers (presbyters and deacons) kept assuming more initiative and authority over the members of the churches, becoming clearly differentiated as clergy, while the head of the leading church in a region came to be obeyed as bishop. A *hierarchy* thus came to govern the church, somewhat similar to the efficient administrative system of the Roman empire. The writings of the first century leaders of the churches were carefully studied, and in course of time our New Testament *canon* of twenty-seven books came to be generally regarded as authoritative and divinely inspired. Impressive *liturgies* developed. A system of *sacraments*, ultimately fixed in the West

Sacramentarianism

as seven in number, became enforced upon believers. These sacraments are miraculous ceremonies in which benefits through divine grace are conferred upon the believer; *viz.: baptism*, a mark of dedication to Christ attended by forgiveness of sins; the *Church was fully sacrament* *eucharist*, the bloodless sacrifice of bread and wine in which Christ is really present; *confirmation*, in which the bishop receives the believer into the fellowship of the Church; *penance*, in which a person honestly calls to mind his sins, has whole-hearted contrition for them, including the honest resolution to commit them no more, confesses them to a priest, accepts such punishment as he imposes, and receives absolution from him; *matrimony*, made a sacred relation by the blessing of the Church; *holy orders*, the sacred ceremony by which clergy are ordained; and *extreme unction*, in which the priest anoints with oil the believer in danger of death, fortifying him with divine aid in the crisis. These developments, according to the Catholic contention, came about through the guidance of the Holy Ghost, and they were all either explicitly or implicitly instituted in the first place by Christ. By them the Catholic communicant is sustained and guided by Holy Church through supernatural means in all the important crises of his life.

Deep reverence was felt for the Blessed Virgin Mary, the *Mary-Worship* mother of Christ. Through the honors paid to her, and in less degree to other saints, men and women felt themselves able to come into closer personal relationship to God through Christ, to *Saint-worship* make more vivid what the Christian life should mean to them, to receive the intercession of Virgin and saints in their own behalf, and so to grow in grace themselves. People previously accustomed to Polytheism thus were enabled to worship one God, without God seeming to them to be an abstraction. Christianity remained a personal and human religion, and the ancient Catholic could feel himself under the protection of his guardian angel and patron saint. Holy men and women followed a higher vocation than was obligatory upon the layman. They forsook the world and sought a more perfect life of solitude in the desert, spending their days in meditation and prayer, fasting and scourging themselves, and seeing celestial visions. Later, life in a religious community was found to be better, and orders of monks and nuns in convents observed vows of poverty, continence, and strict obedience to ecclesiastical superiors.

After Christianity became the official religion of the empire, new moral problems entered its horizon. Christian laymen had to defend the empire against barbarian invasion, police the cities, punish criminals, and protect society generally. It became right, and even a duty to do these things. The further interpretation of Roman law was continued by the Christians, and important juristic conceptions enriched Christian ethics. Riches were seen not necessarily to be an evil. They are a gift of God, of which the owner should regard himself as a responsible steward; he must not squander them wastefully, but give of his superfluity to the Church and to the poor. In general, the Christian layman had to undertake the duties of a citizen of this world; the clergy gave him counsel, and kept before his vision the higher ideals that should be realized as far as possible in this life, with the expectation of their full attainment in Heaven.

A less pleasant feature of Christian mores must be mentioned. We have already seen that the New Testament writers sternly rebuked those of the newly converted pagans who wished to introduce beliefs and practices that would have been morally debasing. When orthodox Christians gained control of the empire they were not content to rebuke pagans and heretics. By laws they made it uncomfortable for them, and in mobs they proceeded to massacre and exterminate them. Later, with full authority of the law, the Inquisition in the middle ages and counter Reformation disposed of heretics. We must remember that back of most of the technical controversies in which the Church was engaged in ancient and medieval times there were moral issues of importance. If ancient orthodox Christians had not been bitterly intolerant of all influences threatening to undermine their moral and spiritual outlook,

Christianity would first have become corrupted and then completely submerged in the welter of cults and superstitions with which it was in conflict. This helps to explain, but not to justify, the brutal intolerance toward all nonbelievers that became imbedded in Christian tradition. Salvation, it was thought, could only be had by those who accepted Christ in the precise manner taught in the orthodox creeds; all other persons must burn in hell. So it was really merciful to torture, burn, and kill numerous unbelievers in the hope that a greater number might be saved from everlasting fire.

With the fall of the Roman empire, a further revision in the Christian moral outlook became necessary. The pagans of the Roman empire—at least in the earlier centuries—had become Christians from personal moral conviction and at great sacrifice, often at the cost of martyrdom. On the contrary, the northern barbarians were baptized wholesale at the behest of their rulers. Their savage minds, although impressed by the high moral and religious opportunities that the Church had to offer, were more dazed at the brilliance of the ceremonial, and frightened at the awfulness of hell, from which the Church alone could save them. Nor were they unconscious of political advantages to be gained by an alliance with the Roman Church. Catholic Christianity was something externally adopted by the northern barbarians from an alien civilization; it was not an outgrowth of their own experiences, nor accepted as a matter of deep inner conviction.

In its immediate impact with the northern races Catholic Christianity did not undergo great modifications in ecclesiastical organization, doctrine, or ritual. The previous developments were rather strengthened and extended. The sacraments were regarded with greater awe, and in them men found great comfort; to be deprived of them temporarily would speedily bring individual sinners and rebellious governments to submission. The discipline of penance brought people to a realization of the sinfulness of wrongdoing and hence to genuine contrition, as mere preaching could never have done.

In some ways the Church became more practical in its morality. Monastic orders ceased to be merely retreats for a contemplative life; monks and nuns devoted much of their time to active service,—caring for the poor, conducting hospitals, orphanages, and schools, preaching to the people and hearing their confessions, copying manuscripts, and so preserving ancient learning. Convents were havens of refuge in troublesome times, when all the rest of the world was in warfare and confusion. There the wronged and helpless could find protection and some one to plead their causes.

The barbarians already had high respect for women, before their conversion. The Church in time persuaded chiefs to abandon polygamous practices that occasionally occurred among them. After a long struggle she succeeded in establishing for all time in the mores of Christendom the principle that the free consent of a man and woman to their marriage is necessary and sufficient—that in this supreme relation of life parents, feudal lords, and kings may not dictate. The ancient crimes of abortion and infanticide were forbidden. Men were taught the single standard in sex morality. The purer conception of sex led to the idealization of women in romantic poetry and song. In some respects this last, no doubt, was extravagant. But it had an enduring effect on the mores of Christian lands. Romantic love on its more spiritual side has ever since held a prominence in literature and life unknown before.

The barbarians were not disposed to limit warfare to the defensive. But the Church at least succeeded in putting warfare within bounds that made it less horrible and destructive than it had been in the times depicted in the sagas. In parts of Europe the "Truce of God" restricted fighting to certain days of the week and seasons of the year. Popes often succeeded in mediating between conflicting princes, sometimes averting wars, and at other times bringing them to an end. The life of the warrior was idealized in the institution of Chivalry; his investiture as a knight assumed a religious character, and he vowed to defend women, orphans, clergy, and pilgrims, always *no need to develop ethics if take ethics of N.T. Deeds flow out of a heart of love.*

to fight for worthy causes and to attack injustice and oppression of every kind.

While comments on ethical topics are frequent in ancient Christian literature, the center of interest is always theological, and no serious attempt to develop an ethical system is discoverable; although tendencies in that direction can be found occasionally, notably in the writings of St. Augustine of Hippo († 430).[14] During the middle ages, elaborate ethical systems were developed, in subordination to Catholic theology. The main requisite of the moral life is acceptance of God and submission to Him in the manner prescribed by the Church. The principles of ancient ethics were assimilated, and further extended and applied. It will only be possible here to notice briefly the greatest and most influential of the medieval ethical systems, that of St. Thomas Aquinas († 1274).[15]

Following Aristotle, St. Thomas maintains that the end of man is to be found in the realization of the function peculiar to him,—the reason, and in the achievement of this end happiness is attained. Every human act is motivated by personal ends; but in their pursuit consideration of others is necessarily involved, since man is a social being. (In modern terminology it might be said that St. Thomas' moral philosophy is in the first place egoistic, and that from egoism he deduces altruism.) In human experience we find some ends subordinated to others; can a supreme end or highest good be found to which all others are subordinated, and in which all others are included? (In answering this, St. Thomas supplements the deficiencies of Aristotle.) Yes, objectively this supreme end is God; subjectively it is the highest happiness which attends intellectual contemplation of God,—knowing Him and loving Him. This cannot be completely attained in this life, but will be the reward of the redeemed in Heaven.[16] In this life all human goods, cultural, emotional, physical, are given recognition,—since all are included within the supreme good, when judged rightly. Thus Thomistic moral philosophy is neither ascetic, nor, in the main, other worldly. The distinction between moral good and evil is objective, and follows from the very nature of things. Ultimate moral principles rest on *Eternal Law,* they are known to God intellectually; and even His will could not change them.[17] Eternal Law with reference to a specific creature becomes *Natural Law;* and for man, a rational creature, natural laws are rational. In accordance with natural law men are obliged "to preserve their own life and to ward off its obstacles . . . to know the truth about God and to live in Society".[18]

By means of a special natural faculty (*synderesis*) we know the ultimate moral principles, which are universal and immutable. The act by which our reason applies these principles to particular cases is an act of *conscience.* That you must be honest in business and give to each his due is a universal principle; that you must return to a particular person a sum of money paid in excess of the price agreed upon is an act of conscience. The application of universal principles to the peculiar circumstances of men living in space and time can be effected by means of precepts that hold in the majority of cases, but not in all. For instance, it is a good precept that we ought to restore goods held in trust; yet we should not do so if claimed for the purpose of fighting against one's country. The fact that precepts concerned with the affairs of daily life are often not of universal application puts great responsibility on the individual conscience. A person must always act in accordance with the promptings of his conscience, which is his best guide, although it may err. It is his duty to enlighten his conscience by instructing himself concerning his moral obligations, studying doubtful points, and weighing probabilities; since error, doubt, and hesitation are blameworthy if they are voluntary. However, moral responsibility is lessened by unavoidable prejudices due to heredity, education, emotions, and passions.[19]

The deficiencies of human reason are largely corrected by *Divine Law, i.e.,* the revelations made by God to men, especially in the laws of the Old and New Testaments. And the individual believer, of course, always has his spiritual adviser to assist him in solving the problems of conscience. The moral virtues are summarized in accordance with the Platonic classification: prudence, fortitude, temperance, and justice; but they are conceived in Aristotelian fashion as rational habits, and to them the principle of the golden mean applies. It is to be observed that while the system of St. Thomas is rationalistic and formal in its affirmation of ultimate moral principles that are eternal and immutable, it is largely empirical in the concrete application of these principles to human conduct. How to live and act in the affairs of daily life is for St. Thomas almost as much a matter of applying practical experience and common sense as it is for Aristotle. His system is to be classed with that of Aristotle, rather than with those of the Stoics and Kant which profess to lay down absolute principles capable of infallibly deciding every question of conduct.

Besides eternal, natural, and divine law, St. Thomas discusses *Human Law*. Human laws are deductions or applications of natural law made by rulers for the common good. Human enactments not in accordance with natural law are unjust; they are perversions of law. In a manner similar to Aristotle, distinction is made between forms of government (monarchical, aristocratic, and democratic) that aim at the good of all, and the unjust forms that aim at the good of rulers alone. St. Thomas is inclined on the whole to favor monarchy as most likely to be free from dissension and to promote peace. The danger in both monarchy and democracy is degeneration into tyranny, and this must be guarded against. Living in a later age than Aristotle, St. Thomas sees superior advantages in a medieval kingdom, in bringing larger areas and populations together, and affording greater strength and security, as compared with the smaller city-state, at least in its medieval forms.[20]

In recent times Roman Catholic moral philosophers have adhered in general to the basic features of Thomistic ethics, with detailed additions, modifications, and applications in the manner of the Jesuit and other schools. They have accepted such features of modern non-Catholic systems as seemed meritorious to them, and not in conflict with orthodox Catholic ethics. While the conversion of heretics is still thought desirable, the futility of employing persecution for the purpose is generally recognized. The more kindly side of the teaching of the Church has been brought into emphasis; there is hope, in the next world as in this, for those invincibly ignorant of the true faith, if they act according to the best light their consciences afford them. Since in Catholic systems of ethics all conduct should be subordinated to the supreme end of knowledge and love of God, and only by this means can ethical principles be brought into coherence and unity, it follows that all really adequate moral teaching must be based on Catholic theology. So Catholic writers repudiate all attempts in modern times to make ethics a discipline independent of theology, whether based on reason, perfection, duty, self-realization, pleasure, happiness, utility, the social contract, evolution, or what not. This explains the Catholic insistence that schools ought to be under ecclesiastical control; unless based on Catholic religious teaching moral training cannot adequately be given to the young. Contemporary Catholic writers are keenly alive to the political and economic problems that have arisen since the industrial revolution, and they offer constructive programs for the betterment of social conditions.[21]

Catholic morality has rendered an incalculable service to the modern world by preserving the best elements of Christian teaching from ancient pagan and medieval barbarian corruption. The outstanding merit of Catholic moral teaching is on the disciplinary side. Penance and confession insure that the individual will frankly face his own sins and shortcomings and receive the counsel and sympathy of an experienced spiritual adviser; the ignorant are thus afforded guidance, and all are more likely to experience true contrition, for without true contrition absolution does not avail. Catholicism teaches respect for authority, and for the experience of the past. The Catholic is disposed to yield to the expert in all fields that do not conflict with dogmatic theology. His influence in the modern world is a helpful corrective of the common tendency of democracies to become "cults of incompetence" through indifference to real talent and training. He uses his influence to safeguard individuals and society from moral shipwreck as a result of hasty and thoughtless radical doctrines advanced by well-meaning but inexperienced reformers. At the same time no one is more interested than he in the support of most movements for really constructive social reform at the present time. Our own country is immeasurably richer and saner in its moral outlook because of his presence among us.

Catholicism in its moral influence has made for individualization in its doctrine that Church, state, and all other institutions exist to serve individuals as such, and in its close attention to individual rights, needs, and capacities. It has been a strongly socializing influence in its emphasis on the need by the individual of institutions; he gains salvation through the Church; he becomes a man through his social relations in the family, state, etc.; his ultimate end is to share an immortal life in the celestial society of the redeemed. It has been rationalizing in its development of the Thomistic and other great ethical systems which coördinate ethics with theology.

What has been said above regarding Catholic ethics has had Roman Catholicism chiefly in mind. Much but not all of it would hold for the Catholic party in the Church of England and in the American Protestant Episcopal Church. Anglo-Catholics have been insistent on submission to authority, and the dependence of the individual upon the sacramental system of the Church. They manifest more latitude than Roman Catholics in the expression of individual differences of opinion. They deserve high praise for their efforts to make religion more personal, spiritual, and beautiful, and to make it an agency for personal and social reformation, and for their active missionary and charitable work among the poor.[22]

IV. PROTESTANTISM

The Protestant Reformation was at bottom a moral movement, notwithstanding many nonmoral causes that were contributory,—national, racial, political, economic, cultural, and others. The deeply moral and religious spirit of St. Thomas Aquinas and his contemporaries of the thirteenth century did not dominate the life of the Church at the beginning of the sixteenth century. The circumstances under which the northern barbarians had been converted necessitated some ecclesiastical guidance of princes as well as laymen throughout the dark ages, and brought organized Christianity into politics. Inevitable as this was, by the close of the middle ages the effect had proved unwholesome.[23] Many ecclesiastics had become more interested in exercising political power than in the promotion of the spiritual life. The state necessarily treats wrongdoing externally; it inflicts punishments, and commutes them with fines when offenses are not too serious; it overlooks wrongs that are either minor, or, though grave, are intangible and can only be corrected by public opinion; it can rarely appeal to the principles of ethical inwardness which religion should inculcate. The later medieval church, immersed in politics, imitated the state in its methods of administering the sacrament of penance. Punishments and indulgences were mechanically allotted; penitents were liable to feel little inward contrition. Many of the higher clergy became fond of luxury, and passed their lives in magnificent churches and palaces maintained with money extorted under false representations by lower ecclesiastics from the poorer and more ignorant of the laity. These last were induced to pay sums that they could not afford for indulgences to save the souls of their deceased relatives from the tortures of purgatory, and enable themselves with divine impunity to engage in whatever sins they wished.[24] The clergy of all ranks, including even a few popes, often took their vows lightly, and led scandalously immoral lives. Princes and people in the northern countries patriotically resented the ecclesiastical bullying to which they frequently had to submit in the conduct of their affairs, as well as the economic impoverishment from which they suffered as a result of the heavy contributions exacted from them by Rome.

Moreover Catholicism had never been an indigenous growth among the peoples of northern Europe. It had been accepted by them in their infancy, but had never really expressed their own genius and satisfied their moral and temperamental needs. By the sixteenth century these peoples had in a measure grown up intellectually, and were ready for churches that would better satisfy their characteristic wants and be under their own control. The northern peoples are comparatively self-reliant, individualistic, and self-assertive. They do not readily submit to authority, especially if it is externally imposed upon them, and not of their own making. They have a keen sense of justice, and talent for self-government both in their private lives and in their institutions. In literature and art their tastes and talents are romantic and unconventional rather than classical and restrained. Such peoples were bound to chafe at control of their churches by a clergy not of their own choosing; as individuals they were certain to find more inward peace from prayer and confession of their sins to God in private than through the mediation of a sacramental system. The printing press had been invented. In accordance with their own dispositions, they preferred public worship of an intellectual rather than æsthetic nature.[25]

While, therefore, the immediate causes of the Protestant Reformation were existing abuses in the medieval Catholic system, back of these as ultimate causes were profound differences in mental characteristics as well as consequent moral and spiritual needs. The Protestant reformers all stoutly maintained the rights of "Christian liberty", as they conceived them. Inner religious peace they found in their own experience as a result of simple faith in God and personal repentance ("justification by faith"). Confession to a priest, performance of works of penance imposed by him, reception of physically miraculous sacraments, and the interposition of church and saints in their behalf they found superfluous, and believed to be a detriment rather than a help in the spiritual life. Thus when the old abuses in the Catholic Church were corrected as a result of the reforms initiated by the Council of Trent (1545–1563), and discipline was again made pure, Protestants in populations where northern stocks prevailed felt little inclination to return to the old Church.

To convince the public of the rightfulness of the changes that they demanded, the Protestant reformers called upon the public to read the New Testament. In doing this, the Protestant argument was in a sense authoritarian,—it was an appeal to the authority of Scripture; but it implied that readers would exercise their private judgment in accepting the Protestant interpretation of the New Testament, and rejecting the Catholic interpretation that had been generally accepted for ages, and had given rise to existing doctrines, liturgy, and church government. At first, the Protestants recognized no authority except the Bible, which all were free to interpret for themselves. But new sects kept multiplying, some of which were quite fantastic in their interpretation of scripture, thinking that they found sanctions for free love, communism, and the overthrow of existing social and political institutions generally. It proved impossible to leave scripture a matter of private interpretation devoid of all control. As in the ancient church, authoritarian measures had to be introduced. The more conservative reformers, like Luther and Calvin, found it necessary to develop ecclesiastical organizations, formulate creeds, and regulate the private conduct of church members rigorously, even in smaller matters like dress and amusements. They were also forced to go into politics.[26]

As the churches were unable to convince everybody peaceably they resorted to force. In Catholic countries heretics were made to recant on pain of death or banishment. In Protestant countries the sects struggled with one another for political control, and whichever gained it persecuted dissenters in various ways, often making it so unpleasant for them that many migrated from the country. Catholic and Protestant nations fought one another with unparalleled ruthlessness and disregard for all humane observances, until in the course of the

Thirty Years' War (ending in 1648) considerable portions of Europe were totally devastated, and the major portion of the population exterminated.

Horrified at the excesses of religious warfare, and convinced of the impossibility of bringing every one to agreement in matters of religion, a more tolerant spirit prevailed after the middle of the seventeenth century. Private citizens everywhere slowly gained the right to practice their own religions, provided they did not violate ordinary standards of moral decency, and did not incite to civil rebellion. The assumption was ultimately abandoned that all morality rests logically on a system of religious doctrine, which it is necessary to force all the inhabitants of a country to accept on pain of severe persecution.

Other influences led to religious toleration. From the fifteenth century onward, the revival of classical studies by laymen had informed the cultured that high moral standards had been maintained by ancient Greeks and Romans on philosophical grounds largely independent of religion, and wholly uninfluenced by distinctively Christian dogmas. In some respects pagan morality was even thought by many to be broader and more humane than the Christian morality of their own times.

The rapid growth of astronomy and physics refuted many ecclesiastical beliefs and rendered others doubtful: the earth is round, and it moves about the sun, no matter what scriptures and church fathers say; the universe has no specific center and circumference; if God is anywhere He must be everywhere, His throne cannot be spatially located at a fixed point in the heavens perpendicular to the temple at Jerusalem. Uniform physical laws prevail everywhere; if miracles happen at all they are very rare, else they could be scientifically observed and reported. Witchcraft, demoniac possession, black magic, the evil eye, alchemy, astrology, and other superstitions and pseudo sciences were discredited by the intelligent, and the theological writers and systems that had taught them were seen not to be infallible, at least in matters of science.[27]

The development of commerce, especially in great trading

countries like Holland and England, favored religious tolerance at home and abroad. It does not pay to quarrel with one's customers about religion. Practical experience showed that men of diverse religious beliefs as well as downright "infidels" (atheists, skeptics, deists) often are men of high integrity in business and personal obligations, while the most rigorous religious orthodoxy is not an absolute guarantee of moral rectitude.

All these tendencies became strengthened in the course of the cultural and philosophical movement known as the modern Enlightenment (1690–1781), of which further mention will be made in the following chapter. As a result, complete religious toleration, except for ephemeral controversies, has long since been won in all Christian countries, Catholic as well as Protestant. If conservatives still believe that the best moral outlook can only be gained by acceptance of their particular creeds, they have ceased to seek by physical force to bring dissenters into agreement with them, and they admit that for the affairs of ordinary life sufficiently common moral standards are recognized without legal requirements of religious uniformity.

The chief contributions of Protestantism to the moral tradition have tended toward individualization and rationalization. It has insisted on individual initiative and self-reliance in moral conduct. A person cannot commit the guidance of his conscience to another. He is personally responsible to God alone, speaking in religious terms. However, he must be open-minded, look for light from all sources on doubtful points, and seek the counsel of others. He cannot rightly do anything just because he pleases to do so. He is personally accountable to God for all his thoughts, words, and deeds. Protestantism has done much to promote individual conscientiousness and thoughtfulness, and to make the moral life a matter of deep personal experience. Its influence on political institutions in consequence of its individualism has been in favor of democracy as a form of government. Popular government was first won in Protestant countries. Until comparatively recently, Protestants were nearly always emphatic individualists on economic questions.

Since the industrial revolution the problems of a just distribution have led many of them to favor measures of social amelioration; so Protestantism in this respect is an influence for socialization, though not usually for socialism.

Protestants were slower than Roman Catholics to become interested in foreign missions; but during the past century, especially in America, they have been very active in such work. This has had the result of making them somewhat acquainted with the needs of backward races, and has led them to use their influence in favor of greater consideration of such peoples by the foreign and colonial administrations of their governments. Contact through missions with non-Christian peoples of high culture has also broadened the outlook of Protestant churches in recent years, and taught tolerance and respect for other religions.[28]

There have been no really brilliant ethical systems based on Protestant theology. As a rule the early reformers merely discussed moral problems in connection with exposition of theological doctrines. Rarely has a Protestant theologian of more recent times attempted to formulate an ethical system based primarily on religious conceptions, that would be comprehensive enough to cover the whole field of ethics. On the contrary, the conviction has spread that since all true ethics is Christian ethics, ethical problems can be studied independently.[29] Those ethical conclusions which bear the tests of sound reasoning and careful observation must be accepted. Such conclusions will be sure to agree with true religion. If they do not agree with any theological beliefs, this is an indication that the latter are erroneous and must be revised. Sound theology cannot be in contradiction with the moral consciousness of our age. (Modern Jews have come to similar conclusions regarding the relationship between ethics and their religion.)

So, without further reference to religion in subsequent chapters until we come to Part V, the reader will understand that the author believes that the conclusions advanced by him are in the spirit of true religion, and in accordance with the best Christian and Jewish ethics.

In conclusion, it may be said that the influence of Christianity in modern moral evolution has been beneficial in intensifying ethical inwardness, and in making morality more personal by associating it with love and loyalty to a personal God. The individual through prayer and other religious activities gains a firmer grip upon himself, and is more faithful to calls of duty. Association with his fellows in a church broadens his moral outlook. The churches promote social reforms, and also help to conserve the best in the present moral tradition. They, and the homes and other institutions which they influence, are the chief agencies by which moral teaching is given to the young. Without them it is hard to see how the moral tradition could effectively be passed from one generation to another. Any individual will be a better and happier person himself, and his life will be of more service to others, if he identifies himself with the church or synagogue of his choice, and in the endeavor to be true to his higher moral ideals engages in public and private worship of God.

REFERENCES

General:

* F. Paulsen, *System of Ethics*, Book I, chaps. II–VI.

* L. T. Hobhouse, *Morals in Evolution*, Part II, chap. IV.

* Dewey and Tufts, *Ethics*, pp. 108, f., 142–169, 195–198.

* G. B. Smith, et al., *A Guide to the Study of the Christian Religion*, esp. chaps. IX and XI.

* W. K. Wright, *A Student's Philosophy of Religion*, chaps. XI–XIII.

T. C. Hall, *A History of Ethics within Organized Christianity*.

Williston Walker, *A History of the Christian Church*.

H. Sidgwick, *History of Ethics*, chap. III.

The New Testament:

* Matthew V–VII; Luke VI, XI, XV; Romans XII–XIV; James I–V; I Peter II–IV; John XIV–XVII.

* W. L. Davidson, *Christian Ethics*.

* E. F. Scott, *The Ethical Teachings of Jesus*.

C. F. Kent, *The Social Teachings of the Prophets and Jesus.*

Shailer Mathews, *The Social Teachings of Jesus.*

* E. J. Goodspeed, *The Story of the New Testament.*

B. W. Bacon, *The Making of the New Testament.*

A. J. Carlyle, *History of Medieval Political Theory in the West* vol. I, chap. VIII.

H. Rashdall, *Conscience and Christ.*

C. A. Briggs, *The Ethical Teachings of Jesus.*

H. C. King, *The Ethics of Jesus.*

A. Bayet, *Les morales de l'évangile.*

E. F. Scott and C. H. Dodd in *The Evolution of Ethics*, edited by E. Hershey Sneath.

Catholicism:

* St. Thomas Aquinas, *Summa Theologica* (Trans. by English Dominican Fathers), Part I of Part II (Prima Secundæ), especially questions 90–100.

Jos. Rickaby, *Aquinas Ethicus.*

H. C. O'Neill, *New Things and Old in St. Thomas Aquinas.*

* Maurice De Wulf, *Medieval Philosophy Illustrated from the System of Thomas Aquinas*, chaps. I–XV.

* J. H. Ryan, *Introduction to Philosophy*, pp. 273–277, 295–303.

Joseph Rickaby, *Moral Philosophy.*

Cardinal Mercier, et al., *Manual of Modern Scholastic Philosophy*, vol. II, pp. 209–338.

W. E. H. Lecky, *History of European Morals.*

J. M. Robertson, *A Short History of Morals*, Part IV, chap. I.

Article on "Ethics" in the *Catholic Cyclopædia.*

J. A. Ryan and Jos. Husslein, *The Church and Labor.*

J. A. Ryan, *Distributive Justice.*

Jos. Husslein, *Evolution and Social Progress.*

Bishop Gore, et al. (Anglo-Catholic Socialists), *The Return of Christendom.*

Protestantism:

* Luther's Primary Works, trans. by Wace and Buckheim, esp. "Concerning Christian Liberty" and "To the Christian Nobility, etc."

John Calvin, *Institutes of the Christian Religion*, especially Book III, chaps. 6–11, 15, 19.

(General texts, mostly theological:)

T. von Häring (trans. by Hill), *Ethics of the Christian Life.*

Newman Smyth, *Christian Ethics.*

J. C. Murray, *Handbook of Christian Ethics.*

A. B. D. Alexander, *Christianity and Ethics.*

(General discussions, more philosophical:)

James Martineau, *Types of Ethical Theory.*

* George Harris, *Moral Evolution.*

H. Rashdall, *Theory of Good and Evil.*

(Contemporary Social Ethics:)

* G. B. Smith, *The Principles of Christian Living.*

* F. G. Peabody, *Jesus Christ and the Social Question.*

* Walter Rauschenbusch, *Christianity and the Social Crisis. Christianizing the Social Order.*

* C. A. Ellwood, *Reconstruction of Religion. Christianity and Social Science.*

B. H. Streeter, et al., *Property, its Rights and Duties.*

CHAPTER VII

MODERN MORAL DEVELOPMENT

I. Introductory

The rise of nations struggling for territorial independence, and their advance from authoritarian feudal systems to free Citizenship, have been two outstanding features in modern political history. This evolution has been accompanied by a corresponding development of the moral tradition, and has been interpreted in many ethical systems.[1]

Modern social development in almost every direction began as a process in which groups contended for social control in order to assure their own rights. Such a group, whether a nation, a class, a religious sect, or what not, originally had little regard for the rights of other groups. If in power, it would endeavor to force every one into conformity and submission. This phase of the process was wholly one of individualization. But in due course claimants of rights began to seek for underlying principles by which to justify their claims,—a process of rationalization. Such investigations sometimes led to the study of ancient doctrines of natural rights in Roman law and Stoic philosophy. It proved impossible on rational grounds to claim rights for one's self or one's group without conceding like rights to others. Thus came to be recognized the general principles of Citizenship—equal rights for all, and maintenance of the common good. This is socialization. Modern moral evolution, then, has been mainly a process in which ever increasing individualization has led to rationalization, and this, in turn, to socialization. Each tendency has interacted upon the others, strengthening them and accelerating them. Abstract as this description is, and impossible as it is here to follow the lines of this evolution in detail, it includes in a broad characterization the rise of national self-consciousness and the struggles for independence and self-determination, religious freedom, civil and political rights, and industrial democracy.

Different as our spirit has since become, the sources of our moral traditions can be found in the middle ages. Our debt is greatest to the medieval Church, for the transmission of ancient Christian and pagan moral teachings, together with further development and application of them. The Church taught the Christian doctrine of the inestimable worth of every human being in the eyes of God. This implied spiritual equality. She accordingly carried on educational and benevolent activities. She sought to promote internal and international peace, and to mitigate the inhumanities of war and strife. She taught the moral value of labor, the duty of every one to make a conscientious use of the talents and opportunities which God has given him. In the modern world these teachings have become secularized; the institutions that do most to carry them out are the state and nonreligious voluntary associations—schools, universities, hospitals, social settlements, charitable organizations of divers kinds, and societies for the promotion of social reforms. The Church has taught many lessons to the world so thoroughly, that they are now acted upon in ways independent of her control and supervision.

Besides the contributions of the Church, we owe to the medieval social system four group or class ideals, corresponding to the four principal types of laymen. To the medieval knight, we owe the ideals of the nobleman or gentleman,—refinement, courtesy, chivalry, courage, honor, and respect for culture. The medieval burgher or merchant class has taught us thrift, respect for property rights, good faith in keeping contracts and paying debts, honesty and fair play in business transactions of all kinds. The medieval guilds handed down traditions regarding the rights of workingmen, and their duties to one another, their employers, and the public,—such as solidarity for mutual protection and betterment, industry, and honest workmanship. The agricultural classes of the middle ages were in a wretched condition—

largely villeins and serfs—yet they are the ancestors (functionally speaking) of modern peasants and farmers, a class noteworthy for self-reliance, honesty, frugality, assertion of rights, industry, and desire for personal ownership of the land they cultivate. With the growth of democracy, the ideals of each class are becoming the ideals of all. Every man now wishes to be thought a gentleman, with manners and intelligence. He desires to be honest and responsible in business transactions. He feels it dishonorable not to be a worker, engaged in useful activity of some kind. He admires those who are successful in honest undertakings and have become owners of property. He feels it disgraceful not to stand up for his rights in a reasonable way, or to be afraid on suitable occasions to express his opinions freely.

Following the usage of histories of modern philosophy we may distinguish the following epochs in modern moral development and ethical interpretation: the Renaissance, from 1453, the year of the fall of Constantinople, to 1690, the year of the publication of Locke's *Essay on Human Understanding;* the Enlightenment, from 1690 to 1781, when Kant's *Critique of Pure Reason* appeared; and the subsequent period, which for want of a better name, may simply be called the Nineteenth and Twentieth Centuries. For those who prefer political dates, it will be sufficiently accurate to remember that the middle period, the Enlightenment, followed and was largely a consequence of the English Revolution of 1688, and that it terminated early in the decade preceding the French Revolution of 1789, of which it was one important cause.

II. The Renaissance

Although it is customary to date the Renaissance from the fall of Constantinople in 1453, when the exiled scholars brought ancient manuscripts in large quantities to the West, the new spirit had begun to manifest itself a century earlier in such men as Petrarch († 1374) who has been called "the first modern man". He studied ancient classical literature and art from a desire for personal pleasure and a wider outlook upon life. His classical reading taught him to appreciate natural scenery, and it is recorded that he (absurdly, if not wickedly, from a medieval standpoint) climbed a mountain in order to enjoy the view. His full and free inward experiences found expression in poetry in his mother tongue. He protested against blind traditionalism in the arts and sciences, and called for experimental methods in medicine and law. In such activities Petrarch was introducing *Humanism,* the enrichment of personality on all sides, and its free expression in art and life, results to be achieved by the study of the ancient classics from the standpoint of the original writers themselves. This attitude is in sharp contrast to the middle ages: when the classics were studied for practical purposes, such as the light they threw on theology, law, medicine, and astrology; when few but clergymen had learning, and study for the mere sake of culture and enjoyment would have been deemed sinful; and when few ventured to challenge the accuracy of the standard authorities on any subject or to conduct independent observations.

In succeeding centuries Humanism had a brilliant growth in Italy, and spread to other countries. For the first time since Christianity had become dominant in Europe, the attractive features of classical paganism and the cultural possibilities of a secular education for laymen became appreciated. This attitude was not necessarily hostile to religion. The artists, literary men, scientists, and philosophers of the Renaissance were usually professing Christians, either Catholic or Protestant. They simply insisted that art, literature, science, and philosophy should be employed by laymen to express secular interests and satisfy secular needs. Thus began the movement by which nonreligious activities have multiplied, while many, like education and philanthropy, that once were carried on by the Church, have passed in large measure to secular control.

The men of the Renaissance observed that a few mechanical inventions, that had luckily been discovered without much technical knowledge, were changing the whole life of Europe.

The mariner's compass had made possible the discovery of America and the new route to India, and the subsequent voyages of exploration, conquest, and settlement. Gunpowder had revolutionized warfare, and placed the citizen of the town more nearly upon terms of equality with the armored knight living in a castle. The printing press had made the Bible widely accessible, and so brought the controversy over its interpretation to general attention and forced the Reformation. The telescope had multiplied celestial observations hard to explain in terms of the old astronomy, and led to the discovery and acceptance of the Copernican system. Thus a few mechanical inventions had changed the whole outlook on life. The social system, the prevailing religion, the dimensions of the earth and of the heavens had all become transformed. What, then, might it not be possible to accomplish if scientific research could be carried on extensively and methodically?

If the men of the Renaissance could by some miracle return to earth to-day, they would not be surprised at the great advances in natural science and its applications. Francis Bacon († 1626), for instance, predicted the improvement of telescopes and microscopes, the invention of telephones and microphones, flying machines, submarine vessels, the transmutation of metals, and great progress in chemistry and embryology. He laid the foundations of inductive logic and empirical scientific methods. René Descartes († 1650) showed the importance of mathematical and deductive methods in scientific investigation. Besides becoming the father of modern metaphysics, he made important contributions to mathematics and physiology, including analytic geometry and the mechanistic conception of life. The most brilliant scientific progress, however, was made in astronomy and physics, in which a succession of great minds—Copernicus, Galileo, Kepler, Newton, and others—combined deductive development of hypotheses with experimental observations. They established that the physical world is everywhere subject to uniform processes, open to empirical observation and mathematical statement. The great achievements of the natural scientists inspired a spirit of emulation in moral philosophers. Could the laws by which human conduct does and those by which it ought to proceed be discovered by careful reasoning and observation in a manner imitative of science?

The problems that provoked ethical reflection were partly social and partly individual. Constant conflicts between the petty states into which Italy was divided led Niccolo Macchiavelli († 1527) to study and describe objectively the methods by which princes actually carried on government, war, and intrigue. He was thus the first empirical political scientist. His chief errors, which met with condemnation immediately, resulted from his failure to take account of the effectiveness of constructive moral ideals in public affairs, leading him to suppose that the unification and freedom of Italy, which he ardently desired, could only come by unscrupulous means. Lack of principle and inhuman cruelty manifested by all sides in the Thirty Years' War—in an age when the rule of princes was absolute—led Hugo de Groot († 1645, generally known by his Latin name of Grotius) to derive from Roman law and its underlying philosophy ultimate moral principles that should govern princes and nations in their relations with one another. The Natural Law that is the basis of these principles does not owe its validity to the decrees of political rulers, nor to religious dogmas on which Catholics, Protestants, Jews, atheists, and Mohammedans differ. It is as eternal and absolute as God Himself; even He cannot change it any more than the laws of mathematics. Much less can any earthly prince alter it; all ought to obey it. The appeal which Grotius made to human reason and conscience aroused thinking men all over Europe, and initiated subsequent movements in the development of international law.

Thomas Hobbes († 1679), shocked by the violence and intolerance of the internal conflicts in England in the age of the Puritan Rebellion, concluded that all men are naturally like selfish and greedy wolves in their dispositions toward one another (*homo homini lupus*). In the natural state of "war", each has a right to all that he can take and hold—this is deduced from the natural law of self-preservation. The same law, however, leads men to realize that peace and security in their own lives and possessions are worth a sacrifice. Each, therefore, has agreed to keep his hands off others, with the understanding that they similarly leave him alone. To enforce the consequent relation of "peace", as well as to develop and interpret the law, men have agreed to obey unqualifiedly a common sovereign. In Hobbes' version of this *social contract*, the agreement is between the different members of society with one another; the sovereign is not a party to it. The sovereign can do as he chooses and cannot be held responsible; the king can do no wrong. To rebel against him would bring society back into its original condition of anarchy. All ought to have a right to believe privately whatever religion they choose; but only the church of which the King is head may hold public services; this restriction is necessary to prevent conflicts. It is doubtful whether Hobbes really supposed that the "social contract" was an actual historic event. The question whether the doctrine is valid does not depend on its historicity, but on whether human political and social relations can most effectively be stated and understood by means of this fiction. Are the relations between members of society analogous to those between persons who have entered into a mutual contract for specified purposes?

Benedict Spinoza († 1677), though a lonely excommunicated Jew, regarded unfavorably by the adherents of all religions, found personal peace and happiness in his own system of ethics. All events are part of the uniform and mechanical processes of nature; but nature is also God, and can be loved with an intellectual love. Such love of God will free a person from "bondage" to disturbing emotions, and afford him "freedom" and inward serenity. It will be possible for him to live in peaceable and kindly relations with his neighbors, to love those that hate him, and to return good for evil. This ethical philosophy is interesting as an attempt to combine the mechanical necessity of physical science with religious pantheism in a manner affording moral support to the individual in his personal life. Spinoza made some advances beyond Descartes and Hobbes in the psychology of ethics,—notably in his analysis of the fundamental instinct of self-preservation, and derivation from it of the various emotions and passions, including sympathy. His political philosophy is more modern in spirit than Hobbes. He maintains, for instance, that subjects are not obliged to obey a ruler if he is unable to afford them security; they then have the right to institute another form of government. A democracy is the best form of government, recognizing the principle that all powers come from the people. Spinoza was perhaps the first to point out the gradual development of moral and religious conceptions in the Hebrew Bible; to this extent he was a forerunner of modern comparative ethics.

Brief mention can only be made of a few other important ethical systems of the Renaissance. Herbert of Cherbury († 1648) sought to find fundamental moral principles on which adherents of all religions might agree. He revived and applied in his own way the Stoic doctrine that there are innate moral principles common to men of all nations and ages; these *innate ideas* have been implanted by God in the human mind, and are recognized intuitively. The Cambridge Platonists, Ralph Cudworth († 1688) and Henry More († 1687) in refutation of Hobbes affirmed that moral principles, including benevolence, are as rational and eternal as those of mathematics, and not human conventions resulting from a social contract. Their method is highly abstract and formal; they could not make practical applications of their eternal principles to everyday experience. Richard Cumberland († 1718) was broader in his outlook. The fundamental moral laws of nature are rational and absolute, and come under the supreme law of benevolence, "the common good of all." However, we have to learn the laws of nature and their practical applications inductively, through experience, rather than by formal deduction. Thus he sensibly tried to combine rationalism and empiricism in ethics, although he did not succeed in formulating a moral philosophy that was either coherent or easily understood.

III. The Enlightenment

The Revolution of 1688 gave the control of the British government to the people as represented in Parliament. The new dynasty and their ministers were conciliatory in their policies, and succeeded in winning the loyal support of nearly all of the various factions that had been contending for domination throughout the seventeenth century. This was done by persuading all to live and let live; by affording wide religious toleration, freedom of speech, publication and association, and removing excessive governmental regulations of trade and of colonization. Great Britain became the leading commercial and financial nation of Europe, and acquired a vast empire beyond the seas. The only large nation whose citizens were really free, the British led Europe in the philosophical interpretation of what freedom means. The intellectual classes in the other nations admired and emulated them.

The British have always been a practical nation, more interested in results than abstract theories. The rival theological and metaphysical systems of the preceding century had in a sense refuted one another; if any had been able to prove itself right, everybody would have come to accept it, just as everybody did the conclusions of Copernicus, Galileo, and Newton. It is better not to trouble ourselves about questions that cannot be solved by human experience. We should, as Pope expressed it, know ourselves, and not attempt to speculate about the nature and attributes of God, for "the proper study of mankind is man". Everything must be judged from the standpoint of human reason and experience.

John Locke († 1704) was the philosophical interpreter of the new period, and all subsequent developments in its thought can be traced to his influence. His works were widely read in all countries throughout the eighteenth century. With his first philosophical book, *An Essay on Human Understanding*, the

Enlightenment begins. The first thing to determine is the limits and character of human understanding. All our knowledge has its origin in sense perceptions and their interpretation by the mind. There are no innate moral principles; for no moral maxims are universally recognized by all races, as would be the case if any were innate. He does little to set forth a system of individual ethics, although he makes a few suggestions: (1) All conduct is and should be motived by the desire for pleasure and the avoidance of pain; (2) God has so ordained events that, in the long run at least, when the next world as well as this is taken into account, righteous acts will afford most pleasure and evil acts most pain; (3) moral principles can be deduced and demonstrated like those of mathematics. The first of these suggestions makes Locke a forerunner of the Utilitarians; the second is a continuation of theological ethics that influenced later theological writers like Paley; the third is prophetic of ethical realism, which still has adherents.

In his subsequent books Locke made important contributions to political and social ethics. His polemical *Treatises on Government* are a philosophical defense of the Revolution of 1688. In refutation of Hobbes, Locke pointed out that men in a state of nature, according to the reports of explorers, frequently observe good faith and keep agreements. They often manifest good will toward one another. So Locke concludes that life, liberty, and property are natural rights that are morally binding logically and historically prior to a social contract and formation of a state. The social contract is between the citizens and the ruler; they have the right to depose him if he proves an unsatisfactory agent, and to choose another in his place. Locke thinks of revolution—"the appeal to Heaven" and the arbitrament of war—as an expedient to which resort should only be made when all other efforts to secure redress of grievous wrongs have failed. In opposition to Hobbes and to contemporary defenders of the Stuarts, Locke maintains that there is a moral right to revolution in such cases. (The American Declaration of Independence is in the spirit of Locke's philosophy. It affirms the natural rights of mankind, which the ruler has disregarded, and recounts the wrongs suffered in consequence. It refers to unavailing efforts of subjects to secure redress, in order to show that they are now justified in an appeal to Heaven and the judgment of a candid world.) A government, according to Locke, should be a balance of powers between executive and legislature, with primary control in the latter.

Locke believed that property originated by the accumulation and saving of the fruits of labor; it is a natural right that antedates the formation of states whose duty is to protect it—a doctrine that has influenced both individualistic and socialistic thinkers down to our own times. It is a natural right to follow the religion of one's own choice; so Locke in his *Letters on Toleration* defended the right to religious toleration.[2] He was a devout and kind-hearted Christian. As its title indicates, one of his books is a defense of *The Reasonableness of Christianity*; simple trust in Christ is of chief consequence, and relatively slight importance is to be attached to theological doctrines like the Trinity. His two essays dealing with education (*Thoughts on Education* and *Conduct of the Understanding*) were a great advance upon the theory and practice of the times: teaching should appeal to the interests of the pupils and learning be made pleasurable; education is chiefly concerned with the formation of right habits of study, and, above all, of moral conduct. He emphasizes—some would say exaggerates—the value of mathematics, logic, and other formal subjects for the sake of mental discipline. On these sides of educational theory Locke can hardly be improved upon to-day; his chief defects are a failure to take account of instinctive tendencies in the child, and to allow him sufficient freedom of initiative.[3]

The third earl of Shaftesbury (Anthony Ashley Cooper, † 1713) applied the empirical standpoint to systematic ethics, in its individual aspects. In many respects he deserves to be called the father of modern ethics. He saw the importance of instincts in human conduct and put ethics on a psychological foundation. Man has certain "affections"—instincts as we would now say:—the "self-affections", which lead him to seek his own welfare; the "natural affections" that lead him to seek the welfare of others; and the "unnatural affections" that are detrimental to both. The natural and self-affections when properly balanced are found to coincide in their promptings: man is a social animal, he can find no happiness except as he shares his pleasures with others, undue self-sacrifice is both contrary to self-affection and to social welfare. This thesis is defended at length, with empirical arguments. The ideal life is therefore one with a symmetrical development of natural and self-affections, and with unnatural affections eliminated. The general conception is largely Hellenic and æsthetic in spirit, a modern adaptation of the Aristotelian golden mean. Man has a moral sense that affords him pleasure at rightful actions and displeasure at cruelty and injustice. The promptings of this sense help to assure the proper balance of the affections.[4]

It will only be possible to review rapidly a few of the many ways in which the brilliant conceptions of Locke and Shaftesbury were developed in the ethical thought of the Enlightenment. Bernard Mandeville († 1733) in the *Fable of the Bees* (a clever satirical poem followed by a dry commentary) attacked the benevolent optimism of Shaftesbury's interpretation of human nature, and disclosed the frequent selfishness of human beings which he argues leads them to actions of public benefit. Francis Hutcheson († 1747) developed constructively the æsthetic side of morality, and the doctrine of a moral sense, making the latter more cognitive and rational in his posthumous book, *Moral Philosophy*. Joseph Butler († 1752) advanced with great penetration arguments to show that self interest and conscience ultimately coincide in their promptings, but that conscience is the safer guide. David Hartley († 1757) and Joseph Priestley († 1804) developed Locke's ethical standpoint along lines prophetic of modern physiological psychology. David Hume († 1776) described with great acuteness the rôle of sympathy in moral conduct, and the moral approval and pleasure that utility (in the sense of what promotes happiness) affords. Adam Smith († 1790), a close friend and largely a disciple of Hume, improved several of his conceptions. He is now probably best known for his *Wealth of Nations*, in which are set forth the foundations of the science of political economy. In his hardly less important *Theory of the Moral Sentiments* he foreshadowed the important modern sociological doctrine of "consciousness of kind". [5] Smith rationalized the doctrine of sympathy in ethics: the sympathy we most desire in moral conduct is that of one whom we might conceive as a wise and impartial spectator of all that we think and do. In this manner he coördinated the rôles of sympathy and conscience. Of all the moral philosophers of the Enlightenment, he best understood the nature and importance of sentiments, which we shall find in Part II to be basic for the psychology of ethics.

Early in the eighteenth century Voltaire († 1778) brought the spirit of the Enlightenment into France, where under his leadership and that of Denis Diderot († 1784) and the other Encyclopedists, it permeated the literature and life of the intellectual classes. There church and state were still autocratic, and the men of the Enlightenment with some personal peril fought bigotry and intolerance, and won a moral victory for principles of freedom of scholarly investigation, speech, and publication. Bitter because of repression, they attacked dogmatic theology vehemently, vindicating the independence of ethics, psychology, and the natural sciences. Montesquieu († 1755) imported and further developed Locke's political philosophy, setting forth the doctrine of the parity and coordination of executive, legislative and judicial functions (which became a fundamental principle in the Constitution of the United States).

In the early years of its existence in both England and France the Enlightenment had been largely intellectual. It had deprecated the emotions, and taken little account of the needs and rights of the common people. John and Charles Wesley, George Whitefield, and other leaders in the "evangelical movement" appealed to the emotions and sympathies of the common people and intensified their religious life. Among British philosophers Hume and Adam Smith in their interpretation of sympathy recognized the place of feeling and emotion in the moral life. In France, Jean Jacques Rousseau († 1778) asserted still more fully the worth of the feelings. He did much to initiate the Romantic movement in literature, in which feelings and sentiments were given free expression in poetry, autobiography, fiction, and descriptions of natural scenery. In contrast to Locke, Rousseau in his views on education of the young takes larger account of the training of the feelings and the encouragement of natural spontaneity. His influence strengthened the desire in France for free political institutions, and for the abolition of the unjust privileges of the upper classes and the economic oppression of the poor. All men have natural rights of liberty and equality. A true state would be the expression of the common will (*volonté générale*) of the entire people. By being a citizen a person should at once be maker and obeyer of the laws. The Enlightenment in this later phase, under the influence of Rousseau, did much to bring about the French Revolution, which asserted the rights of man, and ultimately, not only in France, but elsewhere in continental Europe, abolished serfdom, freed the peasants from oppressive taxation, gave them a voice in the government, and to some extent ownership of the land.

The faults of the Enlightenment were many. It proved impossible—or at least premature—to ignore metaphysics altogether in the study of ethics, and to base everything on empirical observation. Experimental methods in psychology were as yet unknown, and there was little understanding of evolution. Human nature in consequence was analyzed superficially. In reaction against bigotry the real merits of religion were underestimated, especially in France, where some wished to do away with it altogether and championed skepticism and materialism. In gaining rights for themselves, victorious factions in the French Revolution did not bring about equal justice for all elements in the nation. Triumphant democracy—if such it was—became violently oppressive, and order was only restored through a reversion to authoritarianism under Napoleon. Only gradually, as the hastily liberated lower classes acquired education and political experience, could each of the continental nations of the nineteenth century learn how to avert the injustices of political, religious, and economic oppression by a victorious party, and counter oppression by previously subjected parties when they in turn came into power. Ultimately, however, free national states under Citizenship realized in some measure the ideals implanted by the Enlightenment.

On the more theoretical side of ethics, a firmer and more rational basis for moral conduct had to be sought than was afforded by eighteenth century systems based on affections, sympathy, the moral sense, and subjective though generous sentiments. The theoretical weakness of these systems was that they had no rational principles to which to appeal in order to convince those deficient in kindly emotions that it was their duty as well as their interest to observe the dictates of reason and conscience. So in the following period, a more objective basis for ethics was everywhere sought.

When all the faults of the Enlightenment have been taken into account, the fact remains that with it the spirit of freedom first became dominant in modern thought and life. To the Enlightenment modern ethics owes its present position as an independent discipline, and many of its most important conceptions. We are living in a richer world, intellectually, socially, and morally, because of the great movement which Locke and Shaftesbury did much to initiate.

IV. THE NINETEENTH AND TWENTIETH CENTURIES

Modern moral development in this period manifests three notable characteristics. First, on the social side, the Romantic movement in literature and the life which it interpreted, the new spirit that Rousseau, Kant, and other philosophers brought into modern thought, the political and social tendencies manifested in the American and French revolutions,—all combined with the traditional teachings of religion to effect on every side an unparalleled increase in *humanitarianism*. Never before in the Occident had motives of kindness and sympathy for all classes and conditions of men become so powerful. Constant improvement in the conduct of prisons and treatment of criminals, debtors, paupers, the insane, and the poor and unfortunate of every type has been made in every generation in this period; although, of course, there is still abundant need for further progress. The emancipation of serfs and slaves throughout the entire civilized world took place in the course of the nineteenth century. Foreign missionary efforts, especially in America, have been carried on with the gifts of millions of people of moderate means, and immense sums have been raised to relieve sufferers from wars, famines, earthquakes, and pestilences in all parts of the earth. Women and children have been cherished and safeguarded by law and public opinion as never before. Both married and unmarried women have received equal protection with men in civil and property rights such as they had not known before, even in Roman imperial times. The mother has been legally placed in an equal position with the father with respect to their children. Educational and economic opportunities have been afforded to women on equal terms with men. Since the opening of the present century women have received the suffrage and the right to hold office in the majority of civilized countries.[6] Free public schools and compulsory educational laws are found everywhere, and movements to prohibit or restrict the labor of children are becoming successful. A more humane theology has supplanted the harsher conceptions of previous times.[7]

Secondly, on the economic side, the opening decades of the nineteenth century witnessed the *industrial revolution*. With the employment of steam in industrial processes, and with other inventions, large scale production became economically advantageous. Commodities were produced in large quantities at smaller cost. Laborers flocked to the cities for employment and were forced to live and work under wretched conditions. Their work became monotonous and uninspiring, with little chance for personal craftmanship. Their nerves were exhausted in the effort to keep up with steam impelled machinery running at excessive speed. With production concentrated in large manufactories, personal contact between employers and men became rare. For workingmen to combine in unions or to strike in order to obtain better wages and working conditions was at first a criminal offense. There was little protection to women and children, and their labor was cruelly exploited. Conditions were probably worst in England during the decade of the "terrible thirties". The state of agricultural laborers and small farmers was not much better. As a result, notwithstanding the great advances in cheapness of production, the mass of workingmen and farmers were little if at all benefited by the industrial revolution. They had no equitable share in the increased wealth that it had brought into existence.

Such injustice could not remain unchallenged in so humanitarian an age. The struggle has been long and is by no means ended, but the worst conditions began to be corrected by the middle of the last century. Workingmen were legally permitted to organize. They received the suffrage. Partly by their own efforts, and partly by the aid of sympathetic members of other classes, they have been constantly gaining a larger proportion of the earnings effected by their labor. Their condition has become immeasurably better than it was before the industrial revolution. It has even become debatable whether, at the present time, American workers in some of the skilled trades are not receiving more rather than less than their just share of the products of industry. The moral consciousness of the period has become increasingly in sympathy with farmers. It is now recognized that social justice will never really be attained until men of all classes and conditions receive *equality of consideration* in the distribution of wealth, culture, and opportunity, taking into account their efforts and talents and the requirements of the common good.[8]

Thirdly, on the scientific side, the moral tradition in this period has probably been most profoundly affected by the rise of the doctrine of *evolution*. The German idealistic philosophers of the early nineteenth century already had the notion; but with them it was speculative, lacking scientific confirmation. Their contemporary, Laplace († 1827), however, advanced the nebular hypothesis in astronomy; and subsequent observations, strengthened by spectroscopic analysis, have established the fact of some kind of celestial evolution. Charles Lyell's epoch making *Principles of Geology*, published in the early thirties, established the fact that the earth's crust has passed through successive alterations in accordance with the same laws and processes that we now see in operation upon it; catastrophes and miracles have since been banished from this science. Since 1859, when Charles Darwin's *Origin of Species* appeared, the descent of all plants and animals from a common ancestry has been generally regarded as established in biology; although the precise method of this evolution is still partly in controversy. Recent discoveries indicate the evolution of all chemical elements from energy in a less organized state. Comparative psychology has been able to indicate the probable course of the development of animal consciousness and behavior. Beginning with Herbert Spencer's early work in the sixties, sociologists and moral philosophers have been busily tracing the successive steps in social and moral evolution.

The man of to-day therefore realizes that he is in a world of constant change and growth. He is seeking to understand the laws of this evolution, and wherever possible, to control them. Such an outlook is in marked contrast with the static world view of the Renaissance and Enlightenment, when matter, animals, and men were supposed to be fixed quantities, capable of only slight modification and improvement. In those epochs men were likely to be either optimistic, like Leibnitz and Pope— this is "the best of possible worlds", "whatever is, is right"; or else, like Calvin, to be rather pessimistic,—mankind is by nature totally depraved since the fall, although a few may be made better by miraculous acts of divine grace. Men to-day are as painfully aware of their shortcomings as before. But, by study of the laws of social and moral evolution, we are learning how to improve our own social and personal environment, and to hand down to the coming generation a better world and a finer moral tradition. The rise of the doctrine of evolution has made mankind wiser, more hopeful, and courageous. Nor is it necessarily making people less religious. Those religiously disposed can discover their God operating in the evolutionary processes of the physical world, gradually revealing Himself to mankind in the development of religions, and coming to the aid of individuals in their personal worship of Him.

Immanuel Kant († 1804) with whom it is customary in the history of philosophy to date the beginning of this period, desired a more objective basis for ethics than can be found in feeling and emotion. Influenced by the great accuracy of mathematics and physics, he sought moral laws that would be equally exact and universal. Rousseau had inspired him with the humanitarian spirit, and he recognized the moral value of every human being. He sympathized with the movements toward free institutions in America and France, until he became horrified by the excesses of the French Revolution. One of Kant's formulations of the moral law, considerably paraphrased, is that every person should always act on principles that he would be willing to see become universal laws of nature governing the actions of all mankind. Another formulation is, that every human being should act with respect for his own moral worth as a human being, and the similar worth of every other person. Kant's theoretical philosophy asserted the dignity of humanity; it taught that the whole physical world in the form in which we experience it is the construction of our minds, so we have no way of knowing its ultimate nature. On moral grounds he advanced arguments in favor of faith in the existence of God, the freedom of the human will, and immortality. In reaction against the materialistic and skeptical tendencies of the Enlightenment, Kant's philosophy was welcomed with great enthusiasm by the more spiritually and idealistically minded.

It exerted great influence throughout the nineteenth century. The merits of Kant's ethics will be appraised in Part III.

An objective basis for ethics was sought in a simpler manner by the Scottish or Intuitionist school. While some of the chief contentions of this school were previously stated by Richard Price († 1791), who revived the general standpoint of Cambridge Platonism, Thomas Reid († 1796) is regarded as its real founder. The general position rests on *ethical realism*: "good," "right," and similar ultimate moral notions are intrinsically valid, independent of human knowledge and feelings about them; they cannot be reduced to pleasure, happiness, perfection, sympathy, social welfare, or anything else. To ethical realism this school added its distinctive doctrine of *intuitionism*: the rightfulness and wrongfulness of actions in the course of our lives is directly perceived by us through the common sense and conscience that God has given to us. Of course the moral faculty of each individual is not infallible; it needs education, training, exercise in social relations, and habit formation. But introspection and experience disclose the fundamental values. Emphasis is put on character and right motives; opportunism and undue concern about consequences are deprecated. Dugald Stewart († 1828), Thomas Brown († 1820), William Whewell († 1866), and James Martineau († 1900) developed the principles of Intuitionism, the latter two with modifications and concessions to other schools. Intuitionism was long the prevailing philosophy in America, where Presidents James McCosh of Princeton († 1894), and Noah Porter of Yale († 1892) were two of its last and most eminent representatives.

The Intuitionists carefully described the motives to human conduct and so contributed to the psychology of ethics. They wrote wisely from their observation of human life. They exercised the sound common sense which they professed to be the foundation of their philosophy. They escaped absurdities into which logical consistency sometimes forced the more doctrinaire philosophers of rival schools. On the other hand they lacked system and coherence; their moral maxims were often vague and superficial. With the advance of comparative ethics, which has disclosed the gradual evolution and modification of the dictates of common sense and conscience, intuitionism has become untenable. Ethical realism, however, has recently been revived as an independent doctrine, and has supporters at the present time.

The Utilitarian school sought an objective basis for ethics in hedonism. Pleasure and pain are definite; we all know what they are. "The greatest good to the greatest number" becomes a working standard, once we know that the "good" can be identified with the "pleasant". Happiness is a summation of pleasures. Virtues are traits of character, and duties are principles of conduct, that bring happiness in the long run; that is precisely why they are such. Jeremy Bentham († 1832) believed that pleasures and pains can be measured *quantitatively*: those pleasures are most valuable which are most intense, certain, lasting, unalloyed, and productive of other pleasures; the pains with corresponding quantitative characteristics are to be avoided. John Stuart Mill († 1873) admitted that pleasures differ in *quality*; intellectual and sensuous pleasures cannot be reduced to the same denominator, the former are absolutely preferable. Henry Sidgwick († 1900), while adhering in the main to Utilitarianism, corrected many of the crudities of the earlier doctrine, and tried to do justice to the contributions of other schools. The earlier Utilitarians affirmed *egoistic* or *psychological* hedonism: every man as a matter of fact actually does and should seek his own pleasure. With egoistic hedonism as their point of departure, they advanced arguments to show that men in promoting their own interests will further the general happiness of mankind. All social measures should be adopted that will promote the greatest happiness of the greatest number of people.

The Utilitarians were enthusiastic and successful advocates of social justice. Bentham started movements that led to sweeping improvements in the civil and criminal laws of England and many other lands. J. S. Mill developed the principles of political economy, and interpreted the significance of civil and political liberty, representative government, and the emancipation of women. All the humanitarian movements in England during the first half of the century were greatly assisted by the Utilitarian movement. To attack obsolete laws and bad social conditions and to contend for better treatment of workingmen and women on the ground of intuitive rights or the Kantian philosophy was indeed possible, but it was simpler and more convincing to show that proposed reforms would be sure to add to the bulk of human happiness and to diminish human misery. The Utilitarians were emphatic individualists in their social and political philosophy. Regarded as radicals in their own times, Bentham and J. S. Mill are now more often quoted by conservatives. Critics of Utilitarianism have found the philosophy too opportunistic in its consideration of practical consequences and not sufficiently idealistic in its exaltation of character; they have also pointed out various logical and psychological difficulties in hedonism. The extreme individualism of their social philosophy would not to-day be thought to allow sufficiently for public control of private interests, and governmental activities for the common good; perhaps this cannot be said of Sidgwick. The merits of Utilitarianism will be evaluated in Part III. Suffice it to say here that although it was one of the most fruitful moral philosophies of the last century, few think that it can be retained to-day without considerable modifications in the light of recent social psychology, comparative ethics, and political experience.

Beginning with the German philosophers succeeding Kant in the first half of last century, many different ethical systems have been based on *metaphysical idealism: the world order is, or in some sense is governed by, spiritual and not material principles; it is therefore to be understood in terms of Mind.* Johann Gottlieb Fichte († 1814) believed that the whole universe has been willed into existence to carry out an ethical purpose. The vocation of any individual or nation is to make some unique contribution to this purpose. To realize one's vocation is to be free; such freedom implies coöperation with others in society and identification with the Infinite Ego (a pantheistic God) whose will is revealed to one's conscience. Progress is due to men in whom the Infinite Ego expresses itself in marked degree; they arouse the rest of us to shake off our inertia and slothfulness and set about fulfilling our own vocations. Human history reveals the progressive advances of the Infinite Ego,—a kind of philosophy of history that is at least evolutionary and not static in its interpretation. The Fichtean type of idealism is lofty and inspiring in many ways, though Fichte himself and some of those influenced by him have appeared to the rest of the world at times rather visionary and at others egotistical. Of the later philosophers who in some way or other show the influence of Fichte may be mentioned: Thomas Carlyle († 1881), Ralph Waldo Emerson († 1882), Hugo Münsterberg († 1916), Wilhelm Windelband († 1915), and Rudolph Eucken († 1926).

Georg W. F. Hegel († 1831) was probably the most influential German idealist of the nineteenth century. The universe is an organic and spiritual whole, every part of which can be understood only in relation to the rest in accordance with rational principles. While the inorganic world, life, logic, and history are full of apparent paradoxes and contradictions, all these when understood philosophically are parts of this symmetrical whole, —"the truth is the whole", "the real is the rational". The absolute or universal Mind or Spirit (this conception is usually interpreted by students of Hegel as a pantheistic God) passes through stages of evolution in human history, law, custom morality, and ethical institutions like the family, civil society, and the state. The individual finds his freedom by identifying himself with the life and institutions of his time. The perfect State is the goal of history; progress is the development of freedom embodied in institutions. Though Hegel's philosophy contained many fantastic and absurd features, its admirers in time eliminated most of them, and developed the workable features into *Neo-Hegelianism*. This last became the dominant philosophy in Great Britain and America during the generation ending about 1900, and still has numerous supporters; few philosophers of the present time have not been influenced by it to some extent, especially in ethics.

Among the fruitful ethical conceptions advanced by the Neo-Hegelians, the following are important. Individuals are organically dependent upon one another, so that each can only achieve his personal good through contributing to the common good. Ethical ideals are embodied in institutions like the family, voluntary associations, and the state; so institutions should be appraised in the light of their moral purposes. Such institutions are not mechanical combinations formed by an arbitrary social contract; on the contrary, they have grown out of human needs and interests, as expressions of our natural organic relationship to one another. There is a progressive moral and social evolution of ideas and institutions, in which man becomes more rational and free. Like Plato and Aristotle, emphasis is put upon the social and rational nature of the individual, and the interdependence of individuals upon one another. Like the Stoics, men are conceived as somehow participating in a common Mind or Reason; to be social, rational, and free implies identification with the universal Mind or Will. With some of the school, the universal Mind or "Absolute" has been prominent, and there has been some tendency toward a mystical pantheism; with others, there is little reference to the Absolute, and attention has chiefly been put upon the social nature of rational thinking and conduct, and in general upon human personal and social problems and relationships.

The Neo-Hegelians have done valuable work in ethical theory, political and social philosophy, and the philosophy of religion, although their prime attention has usually been directed to logic and metaphysics. Their chief faults have been a tendency to read their own logical schemes into facts better interpreted otherwise, and to prefer metaphysical speculation to the empirical methods of modern social psychology and comparative ethics. Their influence on the general public has probably been less than that of either Intuitionists or Utilitarians because few of them have been able to state their somewhat subtle and elusive ethics, dependent in their estimation on logic and metaphysics, in a manner comprehensible to those who are not specialists in philosophy. Perhaps Robert Browning has been most successful in popularizing the position in poetry.[9] The Neo-Hegelians have sometimes been accused of a quiescent attitude toward social problems; since all is harmonious in the universal mind of the Absolute, we need not disturb ourselves about the evils in this world. This charge is unjust. Many of the greatest of them have been very active in carrying on social reforms, as well as in formulating social philosophy. The belief that all is harmonious in the Absolute, instead of making them quiescent, has stimulated them into active effort to make more of this harmony effective in human life and society.[10] Among the famous Neo-Hegelians in Great Britain who have contributed to ethics may be mentioned: Thomas Hill Green († 1882), Francis Herbert Bradley († 1924), James Seth († 1924), and Bernard Bosanquet († 1923). Hastings Rashdall († 1924) was influenced both by the idealism of T. H. Green and the utilitarianism of Henry Sidgwick. Among eminent American Neo-Hegelians interested in ethics may be mentioned Josiah Royce († 1916), James Edwin Creighton († 1924), and Professor George Herbert Palmer. Professor John Dewey's earliest contributions to ethics were Neo-Hegelian in tone. Professors James Hayden Tufts and Frank Thilly have to some extent been influenced by Neo-Hegelianism.

Arthur Schopenhauer († 1860), in contrast to Hegel, gave a pessimistic turn to German metaphysical idealism. The world order, though at bottom spiritual, is the expression of an endlessly frustrated "will to live" instead of a successful deity; finite existence is selfish, and doomed to perpetual pain and disappointment. It is not much use to strive after anything; probably one will fail to attain it, and even if one does succeed, he will not be contented, but will want something else. The wisest thing to do is to "deny the will to live" by eliminating all personal desires and ambitions, leading a life of self-renunciation, practicing an ethics of sympathy, becoming absorbed in æsthetic contemplation, performing works of asceticism like the saints of old, and steadily regarding life from the standpoint of this philosophy. Some critics credit this philosophy with important ethical contributions that can be separated from its pessimism: *e.g.*, its analysis of the will is a corrective of the over-intellectual tendencies in Hegel; to some extent the conceptions of the recent psychology of the subconscious have been anticipated; the import of sympathy in the moral life is developed in detail; the interpretation of art is illuminating. Schopenhauer long had a great influence in Germany which was not altogether wholesome. Probably this was mostly due to his charming literary style. Perhaps those who in their youth have become converts of an over optimistic idealism (like that of Hegel) and later become disillusioned by the hard facts of life, are disposed to pessimism. It is said that many of the disappointed young patriots, after the failure of the Revolution of 1848 in Germany, sought comfort in this philosophy. For some reason it became popular about that time. E. von Hartmann († 1906) developed ethical pessimism more systematically, and moderated its harshness considerably.

German idealism went through another surprising mutation in the philosophy of Friedrich Nietzsche († 1900), for whom the "will to live" becomes the "will to power". One should affirm this vital impulse vigorously, "all good is instinct", and banish the maudlin sympathy for the weak and incompetent which Christianity, Utilitarianism, and democracy have inspired. Pity, sympathy, and the pursuit of happiness are all bad; one should "be hard". A return should be made to the noble, aristocratic, and self-assertive morality of pre-Christian Greece, Rome, and Germany. Thus a finer and more virile race of super-men (of whom Napoleon was a prototype) will replace the decadent man of the nineteenth century. The ethics of Nietzsche, partly on account of the brilliant literary style in which his pungent and striking aphorisms and poems are written, had a tremendous vogue in Germany in the generation before the Great War, and also made some impression in France. It has been claimed that this influence did much to create in Germany a militaristic spirit, especially when combined with the jingoism of the political philosopher Treitschke. This is quite possible, as it would be natural to interpret many of Nietzsche's expressions, to favor brute force and ruthlessness. However this does not seem to have been what Nietzsche really intended. In many ways an extremely kind-hearted and sympathetic man himself, he only meant to glorify spiritual force. He despised Darwin and Spencer, and the sources of his evolutionary views are not to be found in British biology but in German and Greek classical and romantic literature and philosophy.

More constructive idealistic moral philosophers in Germany during the second half of last century were Friedrich Paulsen († 1908), who assimilated in a consistent system many of the best developments of modern theoretical ethics, and Wilhelm Wundt († 1921), who made important contributions to the comparative and psychological sides of ethics.

Auguste Comte († 1857), and the philosophers and sociologists in France who have been influenced by the latter—Jean M. Guyau († 1888), Émile Durkheim († 1917), and many others—have conceived of social and moral evolution as closely connected. Rights and duties imply social relationships. In the family, the nation, and humanity, man has been learning to control the conditions of his growth, mastering physical conditions through natural sciences and learning in sociology and ethics to bring about a better social order. Like the Utilitarians, they make ethics an objective study of facts and values in the spirit of a social science, independent of theology and metaphysics. Like the Neo-Hegelians, they conceive of moral progress as the evolution of humanity become self-conscious and intelligent, and they emphasize the organic side of human relationships. Man should seek and love the good for its own sake, as an expression of his social nature, and not from a feeling of coercion by obligations and sanctions forced upon him from without. The French moral philosophers have been alive to the humanitarian, scientific, and industrial tendencies and problems of the period, and have made substantial contributions to comparative, psychological, and social ethics.

Herbert Spencer († 1903) was the first philosopher to grasp and work out on a comprehensive scale an interpretation of social and moral evolution after Darwin had put biological evolution on a truly scientific basis. Making free use of analogies suggested by physics, biology, psychology, and sociology, he showed that the egoistic and altruistic tendencies that Shaftesbury had found instinctive in man, are in the course of evolution tending to converge. External sanctions, like fear of the wrath of ghosts, deities, and human rulers, which in the earlier stages coerce men into moral conduct, are gradually being replaced by regard for good because of its natural results in increasing human happiness. As men become more perfectly adjusted to the physical environment, and to one another in society, their desires are becoming more harmonious, and warfare is giving place to peaceful commerce and industry. Spencer believed that eventually men will find it so completely in accordance with their interests and desires to act justly and generously with one another that they will do so spontaneously, and the feeling of duty and obligation will no longer be needed to overcome perverse inclinations. Moral conduct will have become natural conduct. Spencer was a Utilitarian in defining good in terms of pleasure and happiness, though he improved Utilitarianism by giving it an evolutionary form of statement. He was also a Utilitarian in his attitude toward social justice: the general good can best be served if individuals of their free initiative look out for their own interests. State interference with individuals should be kept at a minimum, and state activities confined chiefly to maintaining national defense from external invasion, and preserving internal order. While in some respects society is like an organism, the state is more like a joint stock company with limited liabilities, charged merely with the functions for which it has been brought into existence.

Experience has shown that the state should undertake more activities for the common welfare than Spencer supposed. Few to-day would be optimistic enough to hope that altruism and egoism will ever be completely reconciled. Nevertheless (in the opinion of the author at least) Spencer in his evolutionary standpoint took the most important forward step in ethics of any philosopher of the nineteenth century.

Among contemporary writers in English who have recently made important contributions to the study of moral development from an evolutionary standpoint, mention may be made of Professors A. Sutherland, Edward Westermarck, L. T. Hobhouse, William McDougall, John Dewey, and James H. Tufts.[11] All of these writers have progressed beyond Spencer, yet the work of none of them would have been possible except for the foundations laid by him. Further discussion of moral evolution is unnecessary at this point, as the whole of this Part (especially Chapters II and III) has been intended to set forth an interpretation of it in connection with social development, while Part II will treat moral evolution from a psychological point of approach.

One very important characteristic of the moral development of this period has been the intensification of self-consciousness in one national group after another, attended by the virtue of patriotism and the vice of chauvinism or jingoism. A good result has been the independence and unification of many oppressed peoples. A bad result has been the fierce national, industrial, and commercial rivalries that led to the Great War of 1914. Philosophers have considered how the morally good in national self-consciousness can be combined with the love of humanity and international good will. Problems coming under this head will be discussed in Chapter XV.

REFERENCES

* Dewey and Tufts, *Ethics*, chap. VIII.
* L. T. Hobhouse, *Morals in Evolution*, Book II, chap. VII.
* F. Paulsen, *System of Ethics*, Book I, chaps. V, VI.

* Th. De Laguna, *Introduction to the Science of Ethics*, chaps. X–XII.
F. Thilly, *History of Philosophy*.
H. Höffding, *History of Modern Philosophy*.
W. Windelband, *History of Philosophy*.
H. Sidgwick, *History of Ethics*.
R. A. P. Rogers, *Short History of Ethics*.
W. A. Dunning, *A History of Political Theories*.
J. G. Hibben, *The Philosophy of the Enlightenment*.
E. A. Albee, *A History of English Utilitarianism*.
A. K. Rogers, *Morals in Review*.

PART II
PSYCHOLOGY AND ETHICS

CHAPTER VIII

SENTIMENTS

In the approach of ethics from the side of psychology the most important principle for study is the *sentiment*. Moral conduct, when considered from the side of the agent, largely consists of the formation and execution of moral sentiments (*virtues*); while immoral sentiments (*vices*) are responsible for much conduct that is wrong. A man's sentiments, taken together, constitute his character, or personality, that is, his *self*. His *moral consciousness*, consisting of the moral judgments that he accepts, arises in opposition to conflicting impulses as the voice of *conscience*, and he feels it his *duty* to obey it. Whether the judgments that his moral consciousness passes upon his own conduct and that of others are correct, depends upon the capacity of his self (*i.e.*, his organized sentiments) for *reason*, in the ethical sense of the word. An action that is the expression of a hasty impulse, or of a single sentiment that is not wholly inclusive, is not rational; nor is it a *free* act of the *will*. An action that expresses the desires of the *whole* self—the sentiments in their organic unity—is an act of will or volition, and in some sense is free. But before analyzing sentiments themselves, it will be necessary to notice more elementary processes that contribute to their formation.[1]

I. REFLEXES AND HABITS

The nervous system, as every one knows, consists of (1) afferent or sensory cells (neurones) leading from sense organs to the central system (spinal cord and brain) and the sympathetic system (ganglia in the viscera); (2) connecting cells; and (3) motor cells leading to the muscles. If a sense organ is stimulated, a nervous current at once runs from it to some point in the central system; an adjustment is there made, and energy is released; then an impulse passes down motor nerves to muscles. This may occur automatically. The pupils of a person's eyes contract and expand to the stimulation of light without his being aware of it; his hand is involuntarily withdrawn from a hot stove which he has accidentally touched before he is actually conscious of pain. Such coördinations of afferent, central, and efferent nerve cells are called *reflexes*. They are mechanistic in operation. Given stimulation a over some sensory pathway to the central system, the central reaction c ensues, and evokes the motor impulse m; the process as a whole effects some adjustment of the organism to the stimulus. Consciousness need not attend the operation at all; such reflexes do not appear to be under our guidance or control, even if we happen to be aware of them. All reflexes are *innate*; if not present at birth, they make their appearance early in life, when nerve cells have sufficiently developed.

Many modes of behavior are combinations of reflexes. The reflexes are inherited, but the combinations are acquired. Walking is an illustration. A baby learns to coördinate the necessary reflexes when nerve cells and muscles are sufficiently developed, and he takes his first steps. More conscious effort is necessary to control the reflexes of the vocal cords and other organs involved, and to learn to talk. Such coördinations of reflexes might in a sense be classified as habits, since the coördinations have to be learned, although the constituent reflexes are inherited, and the infant has strong and possibly innate impulses to coördinate them. Riding horses and bicycles, operating typewriters, driving automobiles, and playing pianos are indisputably habits; for in such cases there can be no hereditary impulse to acquire the form of behavior.

A *habit* is a coördination of reflexes that has been *acquired*, as a result of activities of the organism prompted by a *conscious impulse*. In the process of the formation of a habit, more or less attention and direction are necessary. After the habit has been well established it will go on somewhat automatically, with much less attention than was requisite while it was being learned. The different movements involved in buttoning our clothes and tying our shoes go on so automatically that as adults we are hardly aware of them; so we find it difficult to discriminate between them in order to point them out in succession to a little child who is trying to learn them. However, a conscious (or subconscious) impulse is always requisite to initiate any habitual action, to direct its general course, and to terminate it. Habits like dressing and writing are different from reflexes like breathing and sneezing. Though combinations of reflexes, habits are always subject to at least a minimum of conscious guidance and control, and are employed to carry out conscious purposes.[2]

II. IMPULSES AND INSTINCTS

An *impulse*, as the term will be here employed, may be defined as an *enduring disposition* of the human organism, imbedded in the structure of the brain and nervous system, which is sometimes *quiescent* and sometimes *active*. (This usage is arbitrary on the part of the author, but convenient.) The impulse is aroused into action through stimulation by an object of some general type. It then includes a *desire* or *appetite* impelling exertion in order to effect a more favorable change in the situation in which the person is placed. Attending the awakened impulse is a characteristic *emotion* which is intimately connected with (perhaps consists of) various organic processes, largely in the viscera, and the sensations and feelings that accompany them.[3] The emotion serves to reinforce the drive in various ways, mental, and physiological. If the impulse is checked in its operation by external obstacles, or by the competition of other impulses, further organic disturbances occur, and the emotion becomes more intense. Sometimes an emotion becomes blended with other emotions and modified in various ways. If an impulse is successful in its operation, and the simultaneous mental and organic processes are unimpeded, *pleasure* will be experienced; if it is seriously thwarted but remains intense, the feeling tone will be *unpleasant*. Impulses are more complicated than the kinds of reflexes and habits mentioned in the preceding section. They are more vehement and persistent in efforts to achieve their goals. They are more adaptable in modifying behavior to changing conditions in the external situation. Consciousness (or the subconscious) is conspicuous in them.

As an illustration, the primary impulse of *flight* or *escape* is an enduring disposition of the human organism. It may be aroused into action through stimulation by various objects. The stimulating objects may be physical, and perceived through the senses; or they may be the outcome of processes of imagination or reasoning that render an individual apprehensive, either for himself or for other persons or interests which concern him. In any event, he experiences the *emotion* of *fear* and an *appetite* or *desire* to escape from the impending danger. When confronted by a physical object of danger, the motor mechanism of escape may be the reflexes and habits involved in running on the ground, dodging, climbing a tree, hiding behind a wall, or calling a police officer; the successive employment of each may occur in any order, depending upon the changing circumstances. When confronted by a danger imagined or conceived, motor mechanisms may be chosen to effect the person's entrance into the office of an insurance agent, a banker, a lawyer, a physician, or a clergyman, in search of appropriate counsel and assistance.

In all cases, whether the object of danger is physical or ideational, the emotion of fear has certain characteristics; at the least, slight irregularities in respiration and heart action that a close observer could detect, and a peculiar mental state hard to describe, but which every reader will recall. The organic disturbances of fear increase as danger appears more imminent, and means of escape prove unavailing; in extreme cases fright has been known to eventuate in paralysis and death. If measures of escape prove successful, there is little awareness of organic disturbances, attention being concentrated on the

external situation. While success is being achieved, the activity
is felt to be pleasurable, and thrills of satisfaction are experienced. Those who are hardy and athletic often seek physical
dangers, and keenly enjoy escaping from them; the weak and
timid find efforts to escape difficult and intensely unpleasant,
so they avoid such situations at every cost. Those fond of
dangers of an ideational sort delight in financial speculation,
law suits, flirtations, and other perilous adventures.[4] Prudence
is a moral and virtuous exercise of this impulse; acts of cowardice are immoral expressions of it, while phobias are nonmoral
because pathological and hence irresponsible manifestations
of fear. This impulse of escape or flight includes all attempts
at self-preservation through the avoidance of danger; its attendant emotion of *fear* includes all feelings of fright, alarm, and
trepidation.

The other *principal primary impulses* of most importance
for ethics will be reviewed more briefly. The impulse of *combat*
or *pugnacity* (including aggression and resentment) is attended
by the emotion of *anger* (including rage, fury, annoyance, and
irritation). This impulse is peculiar, in that what evokes it is
an obstacle to the satisfaction of some *other* impulse. Animals
and men fight for objects of hunger and sex, and for the protection of self and offspring; they probably do not fight from the
sheer desire for combat for its own sake.[5] This is an ethically
important fact, which explains why law courts have supplanted
private vengeance in social evolution, and affords hope that international law may sometime entirely displace wars. The
impulse of *repulsion* and the emotion of *disgust* (nausea, loathing,
repugnance) are aroused by physical objects that are slimy to
touch or emit bad odors, as well as by those morally slippery
and repulsive persons to whom such epithets as "skunk",
"reptile", and "copperhead" seem appropriate. There is less
chance for a person who has become an object of disgust to
overcome the unfavorable sentiments of those who dislike him,
than for a person who is only the object of hatred evolved from
the pugnacious impulse. We may respect enemies with whom

we are habitually angry, and ultimately become reconciled with them; this is hardly possible in the case of enemies whom we loathe.

The *parental* or *protective* impulse, in evolution first applied instinctively by female animals to their young, often becomes extended in the case of human beings to small children, to animals, and even to delicate works of art and other inanimate objects. The impulse is strong in most men toward women, especially if they are young, beautiful, helpless, or confiding. It is attended by *tender emotion*, a feeling of kindliness, tenderness, and protection. This emotion often manifests itself in connection with sympathy; it is also a constituent of the complex emotion of pity, and the sentiment of love. With none of these, however, should it be confused, for it is the primary basis of movements for the welfare of children and animals, and plays an important part in acts of altruism of many kinds. The impulse of *sex*, the specific attraction of each sex for the other, is extremely important for ethics. Its attendant emotion has no very satisfactory name. *Lust* will answer, if it is possible to restore the word to its original significance, as a normal emotional state in proper circumstances. It is only one of the impulses constituent of the sentiment of sexual love. *Curiosity*, the will to know, and its emotion of *wonder*, a desire for acquaintance with the unknown, is a constituent impulse of all inquiry and discovery, from foolish gossip to serious scientific research.

Self-abasement or *submission* (with the emotion of *subjection*, including inferiority, humility, submission, and negative self-feeling) normally manifests itself in shy modesty and proper regard for superiors. It is immoral in chronic lack of self-reliance, and habitual understatement of one's capacities, and it is pathological in "inferiority complexes". *Self-assertion*, with the emotional accompaniment of *elation* (or positive self-feeling, including masterfulness, domination) is moral when it appears as a demand for recognition of one's deserts, but is often immoral in manifestations of arrogance, undue pride, vanity, and conceit, and becomes pathological in paranoia and megalomania. The *social* or *gregarious* impulse causes men to seek the society of their fellows, and, when this is impossible, to feel the emotion of loneliness, isolation, or nostalgia. This impulse may simply lead persons to flock to towns and crowds, in which it is more like the herding instinct of animals. In its higher forms it prompts to associated life in larger groups than the family.

The *food-seeking* impulse with the emotion of *hunger*, the *acquisitive* impulse with the emotion of *ownership* or possession, and the *constructive* impulse with the emotion of *creativeness* or workmanship, are sufficiently obvious. All three are extremely important for the moral philosopher.

All the impulses that have been named are present in all human beings. Each of them plays an invaluable part in the moral life of the individual as well as in society, and to each we owe some of the highest achievements of man. None of them ought to be suppressed; attempts to exclude any primary impulse from consciousness are liable to work havoc in the subconsciousness, and to lead to grave mental and moral disturbances, which have been disclosed by psychiatrists in recent years.[6] The moral problem is how to afford each impulse normal expression in a way that will unify it with the others in the development of character.

These principal primary impulses do not appear with the same degree of strength in all individuals, races, and nations. Pugnacity, self-assertion, sex, and fear appear in many individuals and races with too great vehemence for the demands of modern civilized life, and so give rise to many contemporary moral difficulties. Acquisitiveness (as thrift and industry in the accumulation of property) and curiosity (in the sense of keen desire for learning) are too weak in the majority of people to-day, while they are extremely potent in the case of a talented few: a condition that partly accounts for the unequal distribution of wealth and culture. For an individual to possess an unusually vehement impulse—especially if it is pugnacity, sex, or self-assertion—may well prove to be his moral ruin; but if he can learn neither to give it free rein, nor yet to suppress it or dissociate it from his other impulses, but to coördinate it with other interests and activities in individually and socially beneficial channels, such an impulse may enable him to be an effective and perhaps a great man in his generation. Pugnacity and self-assertion, rightly directed, may make a man a great constructive leader in all righteous conflicts. Sex energy diverted—the technical term is *sublimated*—into other than its spontaneous channel of expression, may make a person a successful poet, musician, religious leader, social worker, or athlete. Strong primary impulses furnish the driving power for great talents. The nations that have contributed most to human progress have had for their leaders men with strong primary impulses.

Since individuals vary in the relative strength of their principal primary impulses, they may be said to have different "dispositions" in the popular sense of the word (not in the technical sense of disposition used at the beginning of this section in the definition of impulse). In this popular sense we speak of a person's "disposition" as "pugnacious", "curious", "cautious", "thrifty", "sociable", "meek", or "ambitious" according to the ruling impulse in his character and conduct. Many men of each kind of "disposition" are valuable members of society, and it is well that there is such a diversity. On the other hand, there are men whose undisciplined "dispositions" are hurtful to themselves and others. Further ways in which impulses vary in individuals are in their *persistency*, and in the degree of their *affectability* by pleasant and unpleasant feelings.[7] The problem of moral education might well be stated as that of the right education of impulses.

Are these principal primary impulses instincts or are they habits, or are they partly one and partly the other? An *instinct* is an *inherited* impulse, not so mechanistic as a reflex, but adaptable to different situations and subject to training. We have seen that a *habit* is *acquired* in the course of one's life, and that such activities as operating a typewriter and driving an automobile are habits. Much attention is necessary to acquire habits; but once they have been acquired, little attention is needed to direct them, although they never go on so automatically as reflexes. If the principal primary impulses are habits, they are certainly habits of a very different nature, for they are attended usually by powerful emotions and desires. They appear early in life, most of them in the first few months of infancy.[8] All human conduct is found on analysis to contain them. They are present in all individuals of all races of mankind, and vary only in degree, persistency, affectability, and perhaps a few other traits.

The question whether and to what extent these primary impulses are inherited instincts or acquired habits is now widely debated among the psychologists, and there is no general agreement. The opinion of the author is that each of them at least has its foundation in an instinct. This instinct and its peculiar emotion, together with its traits of intensity, persistence, and affectability, remain unaltered through life except with the modifications natural to youth, middle life, and old age.[9] However, the causes that evoke an instinct, and the modes of behavior by which it is expressed are mostly modifiable, and so may be classified as habits. What particular objects make a man angry, afraid, acquisitive, and curious, and in what ways he will seek to gratify these impulses depend on his experience and training, and what these later may be depends upon the moral tradition of the group; all this is habit and custom. On the other hand, the emotions attending these instincts—the characteristic feelings of anger, fear, ownership, wonder, and the rest—remain unaltered throughout life, except for their combination into complex emotions. Primary impulses may be organized into sentiments that are virtues and so constitute a good character or personality; or they may be organized into individually and socially harmful sentiments that are vices.

The question whether the primary impulses are instincts or habits is momentous in its ethical importance. On the hypothesis that they are habits, infants are born into the world with little or no native psychological equipment except their reflexes. Present differences in the character and attainments of adults are owing to habits or "conditioned reflexes" acquired during infancy and early childhood, when, as certain psychologists from John Locke to Professor John B. Watson have affirmed, they are like putty in the hands of their parents and teachers.[10] The moral problem for the educator is simply to select the mental and moral traits which he wishes a child to have when he is grown, and he can "condition" him accordingly. The statesman needs only to determine what kind of a social order is desirable, and to persuade society accordingly; this done, human nature in a few generations at most can be made over completely, so that it will assume the form of the social order decided upon. The present century may see man alter his own nature through the instrumentality of applied psychology as radically as he changed the conditions of his physical environment in the nineteenth century by application of the physical sciences.

On the hypothesis that the principal primary impulses are habits, it would be entirely practicable, should it be deemed desirable, for children in the future to be so educated that they would grow up entirely lacking our acquisitive, self-assertive, and parental impulses. As substitutes they would have impulses of an entirely different order. Every individual would be totally devoid of all desires for the ownership of private property, or for recognition of his own achievements by special honors or privileges of any kind. Instead, he would have a passionate desire to accumulate wealth to be owned by society collectively, without the least credit of any kind being given him for his services. He would impartially love all children as much or even more than parents now love their own children. The pugnacious impulse, too, would no longer exist, even in its modified form of competition, and an unhampered impulse to coöperative effort would take its place. This done, conflicts between individuals, groups, and nations would be psychologically impossible. Personal fights and law suits, strikes, lockouts, civil and international wars, would all be unknown. Every action of every one would be inspired by the intense but totally disinterested desire to serve humanity.

In accordance with this hypothesis it seems to follow that men of all races and nations are equal, so far as native inheritance goes. Present differences are the result of varying traditions, customs, and physical environments,—in a word, of differences in opportunity. Since men of all countries are equal by nature, the only justification upon the part of any state for restricting immigration is to prevent newcomers from entering so rapidly that their children could not be taught the national tradition. Children of every race can in time be as completely assimilated in American culture as if they were lineal descendants of the Pilgrim Fathers.[11]

The author personally rejects the hypothesis that the principal primary impulses are habits. He favors the contrary hypothesis, that the principal primary impulses are instincts, fixed in prehistoric and largely in prehuman ages, and now subject to Mendelian laws of heredity. It follows (in his opinion) that these instincts can now be modified only by slow processes of natural selection. The descendants of highly gifted stocks should be encouraged to leave a large posterity. The feeble-minded should be segregated or sterilized. More sweeping measures to improve the native qualities of future generations should be taken, as soon as eugenics shall become a more mature and reliable science, with definite recommendations to make. Immigration laws should be carefully administered, so as to admit into a country only those whose native talents are at least equal to those of the present inhabitants. No future social or economic program should receive consideration, if it fails to take into account any of the principal primary instincts. Human nature can never be so transformed by social arrangements that men will have different passions from ourselves.

However, even on the hypothesis that the principal primary impulses are not habits but instincts, much opportunity and responsibility are afforded parents and teachers. What objects provoke instincts, how the person acts when they are aroused, whether he forms virtuous or vicious sentiments, all are largely a matter of training. Advances in social evolution can be effected by statesmen and reformers through improvement of the moral traditions. For instincts, on the hypothesis now under consideration, are modifiable in at least three important respects. (1) Men can be trained so that new objects will evoke the instinct. This has happened frequently in past moral and social evolution. New objects, for instance, have aroused general resentment, and come to be classified as injustice, *e.g.*, religious intolerance, feudal economic privileges, slavery, the subjection of women. (2) An instinct may no longer be stimulated by objects that once provoked it. Americans no longer feel anger at every individual German because of the Great War of 1914. (3) Instincts can be organized into sentiments and virtues, in ways to be later described in this and the following chapter. Three illustrations may be mentioned here. (a) Just as individuals have long since learned to satisfy their pugnacious instincts by peaceful litigation in the courts, so nations are now learning to bring their disputes before international law courts. (b) During the past few years, while workingmen have been receiving larger incomes, they are beginning to accumulate savings, and have even gone into banking on a considerable scale. Present economic opportunities are releasing their acquisitive instincts which had long been suppressed. It begins to look as if there may not be so much difference between the relative strength of the acquisitive instinct in different individuals as has been supposed; and that all, if given the opportunity, may be stimulated toward the accumulation of wealth. If this should prove to be true, a more nearly even distribution of wealth can be expected to come about on an individualistic basis.[12] (c) Persons who are now instinctively and sentimentally attached to their children, neighbors, and friends, can be taught to extend their good will more widely and deeply than they now do to humanity in general.[13]

III. Nonspecific Impulsive Tendencies

Man as a gregarious animal is disposed to experience the same impulses as his fellows, particularly those in his own group. Impulses of flight, pugnacity, curiosity, and their attendant emotions spread rapidly through groups when conditions are favorable. During a financial panic every one is liable to become fearful, during a boom to become overconfident, during a religious revival to have the superficial emotions of conversion (though not the real experience itself) and during a time of national indignation toward a foreign country to become pugnacious and clamorous for war. To adopt a certain form of *conduct* uncritically through the influence of others is unreflective *Imitation;* similarly to hold emotions is *Sympathy* (in the technical sense); while to adopt *beliefs* under the influence of others without careful examination is *Suggestion*. The three are closely related and similar in principle. They usually occur together, and in such cases they are to be regarded as phases of the same process.

This human susceptibility is the cause of the evils of crowd psychology. Yet on the whole, it is a valuable human trait, whose service in moral evolution has been pointed out in previous chapters.[14] It has made possible the transmission of the moral tradition. Enabled in the main to adopt the beliefs and customs of the past, each generation has leisure to attack reflectively the new problems that it must solve for itself. Furthermore, since man is peculiarly apt in these ways to follow the leadership of those in each generation who have *prestige* (and usually deserve to have it), progress is furthered. People in general adopt the beliefs, practices, and sentiments of the experts of their groups. From this principle it follows that society should be differentiated to the extent that there will always be a superior group to assume leadership, while class lines should not be so sharply defined as to prevent the general population from following their leadership. Neither a communistic democracy, with every one upon a dead level of mutual equality, nor a rigid caste system is favorable to social and moral progress.

Sympathy (in the technical sense) calls for special notice. It enables us to put ourselves in the place of others, to understand how they feel, and hence to coöperate with them. Such sympathy does not necessarily guarantee kindly action. It enables a vindictive person to enjoy the sufferings of his defeated enemy. A selfish person who feels sickened by sympathetic suffering hastens away from scenes of misery and makes himself speedily forget them. For physicians and nurses to feel the emotions of patients excessively would handicap them in their service. Clergymen and undertakers who felt as much suffering as the bereaved whom they serve would soon break down under the burden. However, all who aid others in times of emotional crisis must to some extent sympathize; else they would be too cold blooded to be really helpful. *Pity* is a composite of sympathetic suffering and tender emotion. While first drawn to such work by pity including much sympathetic suffering, those who constantly serve the unfortunate gradually learn to feel tender emotion without being inundated by the full flood of sympathetic suffering. Sympathy is also a contributing element to all movements of benevolence and social justice. Mutual toleration and good will among rival religious, economic, national, and other conflicting groups would become complete if it were possible to induce the members of each group to share the emotions and sentiments of the others.

Play differs from other expressions of impulses through the fact that in it activity is engaged for its own sake, without ulterior motives. Children are serious in play; adults engage in games and sports as recreation, as a mode of relief from serious undertakings. The plays of children are often imitative of the activities of adults; by enacting the rôles of policeman, fireman, mother, or nurse, they come into better though still imperfect understanding of these activities and so enrich their own personalities and outlook upon life. Many games give expression to the pugnacious or competitive impulse in a peaceful manner, affording an outlet to energy that might otherwise be expended in actual fighting. Baseball has been said to divert American boys and Filipino savages from actual fighting, and so to promote peace and good will. All the other principal primary impulses are also occasionally expressed in play—self-assertion on the part of leaders, submission on the part of the led, curiosity in games of guessing, both curiosity and escape in games of hiding and seeking, and so on.

The value of athletic sports for moral education has often been pointed out, and sometimes exaggerated. Athletics foster self-control. They unify the competitive, self-assertive, submissive, and gregarious impulses of different individuals in interest and effort for a common cause. They teach contestants—and sometimes spectators—respect for fair play and good sportsmanship,—ideals allied in principle to the virtues of justice and loyalty. The evils in athletic sports come chiefly under two heads. (1) Athletics, as Theodore Roosevelt pointed out to his children, tend to absorb a person's interest to the exclusion of matters of more importance.[15] (2) The majority of those interested in athletics are spectators and not participants, and so fail to get the full moral benefit of the contest. Some spectators, with over excited impulses which have not been afforded a normal outlet in playing in the game itself, find relief only in immoral diversions—gambling, drinking, and sexual misconduct.

Æsthetic activities are in some ways psychologically allied to those of play. In them, too, the interest is in activities for their own sake, regardless of ulterior consequences. In literature, music, and all the fine arts, expression is given to impulses in a way that purges emotions of excess and grossness, as Aristotle knew.[16] Violent impulses of pugnacity and sex, particularly, are diverted from immediate expression in harmful ways, and manifest themselves in sublimated forms that are beautiful, and either unmoral or morally uplifting. Symmetry and proportion are essential in virtuous, well balanced conduct. A beautiful life is a morally good life, viewed from the Hellenic standpoint, as well as from that of such modern moral philosophers as Shaftesbury and Hutcheson. The value of art in the expression of character and the teaching of morality has sometimes been exaggerated. To identify the beautiful with the good would be to narrow both art and morality unduly. Yet there is undoubtedly some connection. Reference was made to the function of art as a socializing and moralizing agency in Chapters II and III.

IV. Sentiments

A sentiment is an organization, with reference to some object, of the most powerful and persistent human impulses. Sentiments become organized with reference to all kinds of objects: oneself and other persons, animals, inanimate objects; classes of objects and activities of all kinds imaginable—*e.g.*, rare coins, miniatures, hunting, golf, genealogical research, dogs in general, soldiers, fundamentalists, scientists; institutions, abstract qualities and ideals—*e.g.*, alma mater, the Christian Church, the Republican party, higher mathematics, liberty, internationalism, justice, truth. The term "complex" is sometimes used by psychiatrists in a manner almost synonymous with "sentiment" as here defined. However, psychiatrists are chiefly concerned with mental abnormalities of different kinds, and the complexes which they discuss are usually pathological. Consequently it is preferable to reserve "complex" for morbid and pathological sentiments. The term "sentiment" has had a long history in ethics and is preferable for the moral philosopher, who is chiefly concerned with the judgments and actions of normal human beings who are morally responsible.[17]

Let us consider illustrations of sentiments. A stray kitten attracts a woman's attention. Being small and helpless, and needing assistance, it evokes the protective impulse for the moment, is petted, and given food. The kitten reappears at the next meal, and the acts are repeated. Before the woman realizes it, she has formed the habit of giving the kitten food and shelter, and it has established itself in her affection as a household pet. Other impulses are soon evoked by the kitten in its mistress. She is curious to discover its tastes and activities, she is angry if a dog chases it, she feels elation at its prowess when it catches mice and brings them in to be commended. She feels shame and self-abasement if she discovers the kitten devouring a song bird which it has caught. She enjoys the kitten's companionship when lonely (gratification of the gregarious impulse), and is fearful when the kitten has been hurt and seems liable to die. Thus a whole system of impulses may become organized about a forlorn little kitten. This is an illustration of a sentiment of *love* (or friendship), having its origin in unthinking expressions of the protective impulse which become habitual, and gradually organize other emotions into a system with reference to the same object. A dog is capable of arousing a finer sentiment of love, as is shown in an eloquent description by Professor McDougall.[18]

More highly developed friendships, of course, are formed for human beings. A friendship for a person of the same sex might arise as an expression of the gregarious impulse, and the desire for the sympathy of a person with similar tastes and interests. Perhaps a little self-feeling is involved in such friendships:—either in the form of admiration for a person who has, or is thought to have, superior accomplishments; or of self-assertion and gratification afforded a person by an admirer; or perhaps the simple desire for comradeship among equals, neither of whom looks up to or down upon the other. As Aristotle pointed out, in his incomparable discussion of the subject, those friendships based on common character and virtues alone are likely to prove permanent; those based on utility and love of enjoyments are more transient.[19] Romantic love between the sexes may, as romances and dramas show, begin and develop in innumerable ways. This sentiment, as Professor McDougall points out,[20] sometimes originates with the social and protective impulses, before the sex impulse itself adds its immense energy to the system. All the important impulses in due course become centered about the beloved, who becomes the chief object of interest and concern. If marriage ensues, a home is established and children come, husband and wife find most of their impulses for the rest of their lives organized in sentiments about a common object, their family.

Sentiments of *hatred* have pugnacity or disgust as their nuclei. The same object repeatedly evokes one of these; it becomes habitual to be angry or disgusted at a certain person. Other impulses become organized in this sentiment of hatred. Fear is felt if an enemy prospers, curiosity is aroused to know what he is doing, self-assertion is strengthened by his defeats and subjection by his successes; and, in general, impulses are evoked in a contrary manner than toward objects of love and friendship.

Still another group of sentiments are associated with the *self*. The self is ever with us, when we attend to it; we praise, condemn, criticize, and pity ourselves. We try to preserve a proper balance between the impulses of self-assertion and self-abasement in our estimates of ourselves: if we succeed, we attain the moral sentiment or virtue of *self-respect;* if we fail, we have some morally defective sentiment or vice,—egotism, vanity, conceit, excessive humility, self-depreciation, or lack of self-reliance. A man may habitually hate and despise himself,—a healthy attitude if he has been doing wrong, and is thereby led to a thorough moral regeneration, so that his sentiment justifiably changes from self-hatred to self-respect. Religious conversions of the type where the penitent undergoes a strong conviction of sin are of this type.[21] Since we know ourselves by knowing others, and know other persons by knowing ourselves, sentiments analogous to those built up about the self as object of the impulses of self-assertion and self-respect are developed toward other persons. *Respect* for other persons who deserve it is a virtuous sentiment, and there is an ethical sense in which the humanity in even the most contemptible of men deserves a certain measure of respect. Condescension, scorn, toadying, excessive admiration, and hero worship are examples of wrong sentiments toward other persons in which the positive and negative self impulses play prominent parts.

V. Complex Impulses and Emotions

Man has so many impulses and emotions that he seldom experiences any of them singly. When two or more impulses and their attendant emotions are simultaneously aroused, they are likely to blend into a more complex process. Some such complex impulses and emotions occur, according to Professor McDougall, without being connected with sentiments. "Admiration", he believes, is a combination of wonder and submission, as in the case of a child who exclaims "Oh, how wonderful"! or—"Oh, how clever"! or "How did you do it"? "Awe" is admiration tinged with a little fear, as in contemplation of physical nature in sublime action, like a magnificent thunderstorm or the Victoria Falls. On the other hand, "reproach" can only be experienced with reference to the object of a previously formed sentiment. It is a fusion of anger and tender emotion stimulated by the conduct of a person toward whom one has the sentiment of love. "Oh, how could you do it"! is the natural exclamation of reproach on the part of a mother whose little son has been cruel to an animal. If a person has become the enduring object of a sentiment of hatred, the impulse and emotion felt toward him may no longer be simple pugnacity and anger, but an ardent desire for "revenge" and a "vengeful emotion". The "bashfulness" of a little child too small to have developed very much of a self-regarding sentiment is a complex emotion due to a conflict between self-display and shyness. "Shame", however, is bashfulness felt by a person with a developed consciousness of himself, who has felt a severe blow to his sentiment of self-esteem because of some discreditable action on his own part. Professor McDougall gives other illustrations of complex emotions; while a wealth of them, many taken from literature, have been carefully described and analyzed by Mr. Alexander F. Shand.[22]

Regarding the analysis of human impulses and emotions, three observations are pertinent at this point. First, we should always be careful not to make too simple and crude an analysis of human conduct, whether of ourselves or others. Since we ordinarily experience several impulses and emotions at a time, the motives actuating our conduct are usually mixed. It is likely to be an over simplification to charge any action to a single primary impulse, even if it is the action of an individual. Biographers sometimes make this mistake. Still more is it erroneous to impute a single motive to any large group. A corporation, a labor union, a church, or a nation, is composed of many individuals with varied impulses and sentiments. The collective action of such a group is inspired by the wishes of many individuals with diverse motives. On the other hand, a few motives may be dominant in the majority, and determine the general course of action by the group. It would be fallacious to make motives more heterogeneous than they really are in such cases. Secondly, while some complex impulses and emotions appear in the absence of sentiments, none can be repeated very often with reference to the same object without the formation of at least a rudimentary sentiment toward it. Once a sentiment is formed, the complex impulse and emotion are modified. To admire a single action of a person is different from the impulse and emotion evoked after repeated experiences of admiration for the same person, who has come to be regarded as somewhat of a hero.

Thirdly, a complex impulse and emotion are more than the mere sum of their constituent processes. New qualities appear in the combination, and it has a certain uniqueness. The situation is not altogether unlike that in chemistry. In water qualities are observable that are not found in either hydrogen or oxygen taken separately: yet it is of value to know that water is the product of their combination in accordance with the formula H_2O. So it is illuminating to be able to analyze complex impulses and emotions into their constituents; it affords better understanding and control of them. On the one hand, we must avoid the fallacy of refusing to recognize the fact that a complex emotion despite its uniqueness is a composite, which can only appear and endure while all of its constituent processes are in operation. On the other hand, we must avoid the opposite fallacy of fancying that we have fully explained a complex emotion when we have analyzed it into its constituents. As a complex emotion it is unique, and its constituents themselves in some ways function differently because of their combination. It is an instance of an organic whole. Such a whole is more than the sum of its constituent parts; each part contributes to the whole and is modified by it.

VI. Sentiments Are Organic

A sentiment is another case of an organic whole. A sentiment is not a mere aggregate of simple and complex impulses and emotions directed toward a given object. To be sure, in its origin each sentiment is the effect of impulses repeatedly aroused in the same person by an object. But once a sentiment has become established it largely determines what future impulses shall be evoked by the object.

As an illustration, let us suppose that Mr. A, who is a very rich eastern banker, gives an immense sum toward some secular charity. Mr. B, who has a deep sentiment of friendship for Mr. A, in which respect, admiration, affection, gratitude, and confidence are combined, has profound admiration for Mr. A's generosity, and sincerely praises his act to every one whom he meets. His previous sentiment for Mr. A has become intensified. Mr. C is an old enemy and business rival of Mr. A, and hates him heartily. The gift of Mr. A consequently arouses his anger and checks his own self-assertion. He feels that Mr. A is going to get a lot of applause that he does not deserve. Mr. C's emotions are combined anger, jealousy, and perhaps reluctant admiration at what he believes to be a clever piece of advertising. Mr. D does not know Mr. A personally, but he is greatly interested in the particular benevolence to which Mr. A has contributed. In him are therefore aroused favorable impulses and emotions toward Mr. A, and he acquires a sentiment of respect and affection for him. Mr. E is an ardent young radical who hates eastern capitalists, the class of which Mr. A is a member, although he knows nothing of Mr. A individually. To Mr. E, the action of Mr. A shows him to be a dangerous corrupter of the people by insidious gifts calculated to blind them to the harm that "the interests" are doing to the country. So in Mr. E are aroused emotions of fear, anger, and moral indignation toward Mr. A, now become for him the object of a new sentiment of hatred directed toward him personally, in addition to the general sentiment of hatred that he feels toward his class. The fact that Mr. E is not acquainted with Mr. A personally, and knows of him only in connection with certain activities to which he is opposed on what he believes to be moral grounds, makes his sentiment toward Mr. A more unqualifiedly hostile than even that of Mr. C, who knows him very well and cannot help respecting him in many ways although he is a business rival. We might go on to imagine the various impulses and emotions inspired in others by Mr. A's act,—his admiring and devoted wife and daughter; his extravagant and impecunious son-in-law, who fears that Mr. A is beginning to give away the bulk of his fortune; his pastor, who approves of philanthropy, but prefers charities in the control of his own church; etc.

As Mr. Alexander F. Shand has said, "every sentiment tends to include in its own system all the thoughts, volitional processes and qualities of character that are of advantage to it for the attainment of its ends, and to reject all such constituents as are either superfluous or antagonistic". [23] Selfish men grow hardhearted because the sentiment of self-love gives little place for tender emotion; if a selfish man is a pleasure lover, he tends to lose pride because this is an obstacle to sociable entertainment; while a selfish man who is ambitious has to maintain his power and superiority in the face of opposition and becomes proud. The sentiment of love develops sincerity, gentleness, kindliness, loyalty, courage, and forgiveness toward the object of this sentiment. So a dominant sentiment organizes extensively the various impulses and emotions into harmony with itself. At first this organization goes on with the person himself hardly aware of it. Later on, he becomes conscious of the impulses and actions characteristic of his sentiment, reflects upon them, and tries to cultivate them. For instance, the lover forms ideals of how he should feel and act toward his beloved, and so his tenderness and loyalty toward her increase. His ideals inspire a feeling of obligation and duty to realize them. His conscience reproaches him if his conduct falls short of these ideals. So each sentiment tends to develop a "relative ethics" of its own.[24]

The sentiments must not be exclusively considered as mere aggregates of impulses, and the self must not be supposed to be simply a combination of sentiments. It, too, is an organic whole, greater than the sum of its parts. The sentiments constitute the self, so far as it is an organized moral whole; on the other hand, the self directs the sentiments. I am my arms and legs and other bodily organs, my memories and thoughts and impulses and sentiments,—there is nothing else that I could be. And yet I can and do move my arms and legs as I please. I recall this memory, and I determine to act on that impulse rather than on a conflicting one. I criticize my sentiments. I decide that I should no longer hate that man, for after all he has many excellent qualities and the injury that he did me long ago may now well be forgotten. I determine to pay more attention to music and art, in which I have been little interested in the past; and if I am young enough and determined enough, perhaps I shall succeed in developing a sentiment for things artistic that will at least be sufficiently intense, refined, and discriminating to make me fairly respectable, so long as I do not visit Boston.

This brief account of sentiments in their relation to impulses, emotions, habits, reflexes, and the self, though quite superficial, may suffice to introduce us to the psychology of the virtues,— the distinctively moral sentiments. The chief caution, again to be repeated, is to remember that human nature is far more complex than psychological analysis can reveal. Some essential traits of human character may be indicated, but all the finer shades and nuances in human character could only be appreciated by the study of individual persons. Every human being is a unique personality; no general rubrics can do him entire justice. He has thousands of sentiments toward objects of all conceivable kinds, and no two of his sentiments are alike. No sentiments of two individuals are identical; it is an exaggeration when two persons say that they have the same sentiment toward some subject. Every sentiment of every individual both helps to determine, and also is determined by, his character as a whole. The psychology of ethics, therefore, is no exact science. However, it can suggest ways of approach that will give us a better understanding of ourselves and of others.

REFERENCES

* William McDougall, *Outline of Psychology*, chaps. V, XVII. *Introduction to Social Psychology*, esp. chaps. II, III, VI. *Psychology* (Home University Series).

* William James, *Psychology*, Briefer Course, chaps. X, XXV. *Principles of Psychology*, II, IV, XXIV, XXV.

  G. F. Stout, *Manual of Psychology*. *Analytic Psychology*.

* J. R. Angell, *Introduction to Modern Psychology*.

* W. S. Hunter, *General Psychology*, Part I, chap. IV; Part II, chap. III.

  A. G. Tansley, *The New Psychology*.

* John Dewey, *Human Nature and Conduct*, Part II.

* T. De Laguna, *Introduction to the Science of Ethics*, chap. XV.

  A. F. Shand, *Foundations of Character*.

  Adam Smith, *Theory of the Moral Sentiments*.

* C. L. Sherman, *The Moral Self*, chaps. II, III.

Additional references are given in the Notes to this chapter.

CHAPTER IX

VIRTUES

I. VIRTUES AND VICES IN GENERAL

A person has as many sentiments as there are objects about which any of his impulses have become habitually organized. Whenever primitive men first came to recognize that some sentiment was a particularly good and praiseworthy trait of character to possess, the evolution of virtues began. The recognition of a virtue implies the beginning of self-consciousness and introspection, and the capacity to pass moral judgments on personal characteristics. Multitudinous as are the sentiments of different individuals, most of them fall into general types which can be recognized and classified as morally good, bad, or indifferent. The types which the moral consciousness of a society considers good are called virtues, and individuals feel under moral obligation to acquire them. Sentiments that are strongly disapproved are known as vices.[1]

All virtues are sentiments, and imply an habitual organization of impulses toward some object. Being sentiments, all virtues are acquired, and none are innate. Virtues are never attained without effort. While the more primitive virtues originated under kinship organization and group morality, no virtues are wholly unreflective. They all imply thoughtful recognition and appraisal of personal traits. However, with the advent of reflective morality and increased powers of criticism, it became possible to study the various types of character more thoroughly, so that virtues increased in number and became richer in content. As Aristotle observed, many virtues imply a nice discrimination, called the "golden mean", between two opposite tendencies, one excessive and the other defective,

221

virtues are all acquired. Nat. man has no good.

known as vices. Cowardice and foolhardiness are vices, between which lies the virtue of courage. Self-reliance is a virtue midway between boastfulness and excessive self-depreciation. The mean does not lie at the same point for every one, and cannot be calculated mathematically. Circumstances, responsibilities, talents, and opportunities differ.

A *virtue* may be defined as *a sentiment that effects the rational control of one or more primary impulses in response to the demands of the whole self*. Since the self is social, this means that a virtuous sentiment is consciously cultivated in response to the demands of the groups with which its possessor is identified, so that it brings him into *harmonious and coöperative relationship with society*. (*If moral of group is good.*)

Virtues, as has been said, are deliberately and reflectively cultivated. Through them a person realizes most fully his highest interests and capacities as an individual and as a member of society. On the contrary, no one ever deliberately cultivated what he at the time considered to be a vice, or sought to overcome what he believed to be a virtue. Vices are often habits into which impulses develop inadvertently, with such driving power that the individual finds it almost impossible to control them by the time that he realizes their true nature. An evil sentiment that has great driving power, because it consists of extremely powerful impulses, may come to dominate the character of the person. In such cases he is liable to be impervious to social criticism, and to deceive himself into believing that his ruling vice is a virtue. Thus the miser regards himself as a worthy man who is making prudent provision for his old age. A gossip imagines that she is performing a social service in spreading news that all ought to know. An obstinate man thinks that he is firmly standing by his principles, in fidelity to the dictates of his conscience. Others may condemn the selfish lust that prompts a man to invade the sanctity of another man's home, but the adulterer himself probably believes that he is manfully affirming the sublime rights of love in the face of artificial and unjust conventions. Men readily believe what they wish; so pseudo-rationalizations easily convince the wrong doer of his own integrity, and make his vices appear to him in the semblance of virtues. When vices are deliberately cultivated, it is in ignorance of their true nature. For instance, if a young man with great difficulty persists in acquiring the ability, and later the habit of drinking liquor to excess, in order to win the approval of a social set to which he aspires, he supposes that he is aiming at a praiseworthy accomplishment,—in other words a virtue. He thinks that it is only old-fashioned elderly people who fancy that drunkenness is a vice. No one is more foolish, unsophisticated, and addicted to pseudo-rationalizations than the gilded youth who is sowing his wild oats.

As an individual cannot make an entire moral consciousness for himself, he accepts as virtues the sentiments approved by his contemporaries, and seeks to acquire them. It is almost impossible to find a good man in a thoroughly evil environment. The story of the righteous Lot in Sodom only becomes plausible because we are told that he was not a native of that city, but entered it with sentiments already acquired elsewhere. People in every age need to be morally reflective, at once appreciative and critical of the sentiments which they approve as virtues and condemn as vices. The individual should be reasonably sensitive to the moral evaluations of his character by those who know him best and are themselves men of integrity. Social groups should be responsive to the judgments passed on them by other groups. This applies to families, cities, clubs, colleges, churches, nations. Broadway and Main Street should mutually profit by each other's appraisal; endowed colleges and state universities have different virtues and vices; Catholicism, Judaism, and Protestantism each has its own peculiar merits and limitations; the United States of America can learn much from European and Asiatic commendations and criticisms. A generation or a century may well inquire how other ages, past and future, would evaluate its character. Have we really advanced in our moral sentiments beyond the Victorians, at whom it has become more or less the fashion to smile or to *put Him by Himself*

sneer? And what would Pericles or Socrates think of us? How would Confucius, Buddha, (Jesus,) and Mohammed evaluate us? Would Washington, Madison, Hamilton, Marshall, and Lincoln be pleased with what we have made of the federal republic inherited from them? And what will the closing decades of the twentieth century think of us?

II. Objectivity of the Virtues

Are the virtues subjective and transitory, or are they objective and permanent? It is evident that the moral judgments of no individual nor group of individuals, nor even the prevailing opinions of any generation of mankind are infallible. How then can we determine what really are virtues? Or must we simply say that virtues are what the individual, or his group, or his epoch, believes them to be, and that no further objectivity can be sought? Well, none of us possesses divine omniscience, and can define and delimit the virtues for all time and eternity. However, it does not follow that the virtues, as the moral philosopher describes them, are entirely subjective and transient. In Part I, the course of social and moral evolution was indicated in a very general way. We have now reached the relation of Citizenship and reflective morality. In the preceding chapter were listed the principal primary impulses that have thus far played the chief rôle in human conduct. If these primary impulses are indeed instincts, they cannot greatly change unless man were to evolve into a new species. Even if they are habits, they will not change rapidly. Some of these impulses, like pugnacity, fear, sex, and self-assertion, in many circumstances prove too vehement and unruly for the conditions of life under Citizenship. They must be governed by sentiments so that their driving force can be kept within individually and socially useful channels. Others, like the social, constructive, and acquisitive impulses, in the majority of persons need stimulation and incitement through sentiments that will urge them into greater activity. Some impulses are ordinarily neither too intense nor too weak, but need training, to keep them from developing into improper sentiments. Left to itself, curiosity may develop into vicious sentiments of prying meddlesomeness and gossip, instead of virtuous habits of thoughtfulness and observation, and the pursuit of theoretical knowledge and practical wisdom.

So long as associated life shall retain any form analogous to Citizenship, and so long as the principal primary impulses remain as they practically have been since the beginnings of recorded history, the virtues which men ought to acquire cannot become greatly different from those outlined by the moral philosophers of our own and preceding ages. To be sure, experience will reveal new modifications in details, as conditions change; but the Cardinal Virtues in most of their prominent features will persist. In this sense it can be said that the Cardinal Virtues are *permanent* and *objective*.[2]

III. CARDINAL VIRTUES

Lists of the cardinal, or more important virtues, vary somewhat. Most moral philosophers, though, have agreed upon what are the desirable forms of conduct, and the chief difference has merely been under how many heads they have thought it convenient to enumerate them. The virtues overlap, and no rigorously logical classification seems possible. However, additional light is thrown upon their number and character, when they are interpreted as rational and socially approved sentiments that regulate the expression of the principal primary impulses. Here we shall notice some of the more important and more generally recognized virtues, and their constituent impulses. Each virtue is theoretically consistent with the others. Perfect possession of any virtue would mean inclusion of all, in a completely unified and coherent personality. That is, however, only a theoretical ideal. As a matter of fact, no individual manifests complete integration of all the virtues and entire freedom from any vice.

Those men whom the world has most esteemed for goodness have possessed all the virtues, though each has been noteworthy for superiority in one or more specific virtues. Socrates, Plato, and Aristotle, each in a somewhat different sense, was wise. Amos and Isaiah I. possessed high moral courage. Ezekiel was reverent. Ezra understood justice, and set forth the Law. Jesus and Paul loved all mankind. Marcus Aurelius was conscientious. Yet all of these men possessed all the virtues in an eminent degree. On the other hand, many great men have been esteemed for their excellence in certain virtues, although they were conspicuously lacking in others. Francis Bacon, Voltaire, Napoleon, Goethe, and Bismarck would serve as examples of very great men to whom the world owes much, but whom few would be disposed to call good men. Even certain great and thoroughly righteous men, like Gladstone and Woodrow Wilson, seem in some way lacking; few would be disposed to place them on a moral plane with, say, Abraham Lincoln.[3]

1. *Courage*

Perhaps the first virtue that primitive man learned to recognize was Courage. This seems to have been the original significance of the Greek and Latin words for virtue (*areté, virtus*). In battle and on the hunt a man must be daring, venturesome, and persistent. He must subdue his fears. The man who habitually excelled in these respects became a leader and a hero. Others emulated him. As men became introspective, these qualities of the leader who was foremost in danger were carefully discriminated, and known as "virtue". Later, when other mental traits also were commended, this first of the virtues received the specific designation of "courage". In its simplest psychological form, courage is the habit or sentiment in which the pugnacious impulse overcomes that of flight or fear. A man sticks and fights even if he would fain run away and hide.

In its later developments this virtue has become more complex. *Physical* courage—the daring of the soldier, the athlete. the explorer, and the aviator—continues to be commended. *Moral* courage is the pugnacious attitude of the man who stands

for what he believes to be right in the face, not so much of
physical danger as of moral opposition,—abuse, ridicule, slander,
and social persecution of all kinds. The psychology in both
types of courage is the same up to a certain point; in each,
pugnacity overcomes impulses to retreat. But the objects of
opposition and the modes of defense in the one type are directly
and overtly physical and muscular, and in the other more reflectively moral and social. As a rule, the boy who acquires
physical courage in his plays and games will not be found wanting in moral courage, while the boy who is afraid to fight a
bully on the playground will be morally a coward in later life.
However, there are exceptions. Billy Brown, let us suppose, is
a universal favorite at school because of his daring successes on
the ski jump. Timothy Smith is generally regarded with indifference, because he is physically weak and unprepossessing, and
at the slightest provocation his knees shake and his teeth
chatter. Which of the two would be the more likely to prove a
moral hero, should he ever be called upon to stand by what he
believed to be right, at the cost of general ridicule and possible
ostracism? We should on first thought guess in favor of Billy,
but he has been the best liked boy in his group, and has never
known what it is to endure unpopularity. He might lose his
nerve at the prospect. Poor Timothy, who has never known
what it is to be liked, might prove the braver in a moral crisis.
Fear is usually most intense in facing dangers unencountered
in the past and so never withstood; hardships greater only in
degree to those we have endured before are less formidable.

The two vices, between which the virtue of courage is the
rational mean, are foolhardiness and cowardice. It is fool-
hardy and vicious to take unnecessary risks for causes that are
of little consequence. Nor is it courageous to be fearless because ignorant of the existence and nature of danger, or because angry and provoked enough to be reckless. On the contrary, courage implies full knowledge and fear of dangers, and
prudent provision to avert them. "Thus he who faces and
fears the right things for the right motive and in the right way

and at the right time, and whose confidence is similarly right, is courageous; for the courageous man in his emotions and actions has a sense of fitness and obeys the law of reason". [4] The virtue of Courage in all cases is a rational balancing or coördination between the conflicting impulses of pugnacity and fear, neither of which should be allowed wholly to dominate. It is enlisted in behalf of some cause in which a person is and ought to be interested and ready to contend. Such a cause obviously appeals to other impulses,—social, sex, parental, self, acquisitive, constructive, or what not—else a person would not be interested in it. So the exercise of this virtue implies a coördination of other impulses in union with the central two.

If courage is really good and a virtue, it is employed in *loyalty* to, and with *respect* for, causes and persons that are *just* and *benevolent;* the means employed are *wise, temperate*, and *economically* practical; and no other persons, causes, ends, values, or interests that ought to be taken into account have been overlooked. The courageous action, in other words, is an expression of all the virtues, in the interests of the whole self of the individual and the common good of society. Or, if this is not literally true, the action is at least the closest approximation to this ideal that is humanly possible in the given circumstances.

2. *Honor*

In its earliest form, Honor was probably simply the virtue of Courage with the added impulse of self-assertion. The warrior felt it a duty to be courageous on all occasions; to fail to be so would have contradicted his ideal of himself as he wished to be, and wished others to regard him. He must ever maintain manfully his rights, and resent any personal affront; by combat when necessary. With further rationalization and socialization, this type of honor includes due regard for the rights and dignities of others,—a qualification that implies negative self-feeling or deference to superiors, mutual respect for equals, and sympathy for all, including consideration for inferiors who ought not to be humiliated.

Honor early came to be a virtue also expected of woman. In her case it was preceded by the virtue of chastity,—a control of sex impulses in accordance with the mores. The unchaste woman lacked the virtue expected of her, and therefore lost her honor. The conduct of an unfaithful wife was a stigma upon her husband's honor; it seemed to imply that he lacked courage in maintaining his conjugal rights. He could only remove the stain by inflicting vengeance upon her seducer. This explains the psychology of the duel in such cases; it was a rationalized means of vindicating a man's honor by the demonstration of his courage. Even if the mores of the times had given a wife the moral right to expect her husband to be faithful, which was not the case in Europe in this stage of moral development, his infidelity would not have been regarded as a stain upon her honor, as a woman could not be expected to fight.

The virtue of honor, in those in whom it has become well established, probably exerts the strongest impulsive strength of all the cardinal virtues. To appeal to the honor of an individual, a family, a labor union, or a nation is to evoke powerful emotional responses in the self impulses and the self-regarding sentiment. Everybody wishes to be able to respect himself, and to be respected by others. Workingmen and their unions take pride in keeping their agreements, and conducting their work as craftmen in a business like manner. If employers can learn how to give their various kinds of workers just and proportionate recognition for their different services, and a reasonable voice in the conduct of their work, the men will gain increased self-respect and a higher sense of honor.[5]

College students have been known to respond marvelously to responsibility intrusted to them and appeals made to their honor. Student self-governing councils often prove efficacious in removing abuses with which faculty committees have been unable to cope. The whole moral tone of the students of a college is heightened as they acquire the virtue of honor in their collective capacity. In no way can colleges more surely develop the characters of their students than through successful "honor systems" applied to the various details of student conduct. A faculty cannot, however, impose an honor system on a student body that does not wish it. A common college consciousness and collective self-respect must develop to lead students to desire an honor system, or become capable of using it. However, it would seem that whenever students have a strong enough collective consciousness to desire athletic victories ardently, and to feel deep chagrin at athletic defeats, they ought to be capable of developing a collective moral consciousness and a sense of honor.

Marvelous progress has been achieved in the reformation of hardened criminals through honor systems. A criminal is an offender who has proved lacking in his sense of social responsibility. If, during a period of imprisonment, it proves possible to awaken in him an appreciation of his social responsibilities, self-respect, and a sense of honor, his character will largely be reformed, and he will leave prison with the steadfast determination of becoming a good citizen. Thomas Mott Osborne and others have shown that to a large extent it is practicable to put the inmates of a prison on their honor in their collective capacity, so that the lack of good faith on the part of any individual (e.g., in the abuse of privileges given to the body as a whole), will be generally felt to reflect on the honor of the whole group. Under such circumstances a high degree of moral responsibility and trustworthiness often develops in a class of human beings among whom such a development would seem least possible.[6]

The virtue of honor to-day no longer demands that an individual man involve himself in physical combats to show that he is courageous in maintaining his rights. Personal fights are honorable only in frontier communities, and the latter no longer exist in the United States. Dueling has long since become extinct in Anglo-Saxon countries, and is on the wane everywhere. As courts of law have developed, men have learned that it is no reflection on their honor to bring their disputes before them, and have them adjudicated in accordance with the principles of justice and equity. To refuse to do so rather arouses the suspicion that a man has not acted honorably, and is unwilling to have his conduct subjected to an impartial investigation. However, a man who does not, in matters of consequence, defend his good name, property, and other just rights, in courts of law and by other socially approved measures, is still regarded as lacking both in courage and in honor. He fails in his duty to himself and to society.

3. *Temperance*

Temperance, as conceived by moral philosophers, in accordance with its Greek and Latin equivalents (*sophrosyne, temperantia*) might more properly be denominated "self-control". It means *the rational control of all impulses*, especially of the more vehement and unruly ones, *in the interests of the whole self and the social good*. Certain instinctive impulses with a massive bodily basis, known as appetites, like hunger and sex, were probably the first to be controlled. Among savages, the consumption of food takes place at regular times, usually at a social meal, in accordance with a rude etiquette; and often, as among the early Semites, it has been regarded as a sacred act. The custom of saying grace at meals is a survival of this view. Greedy manners at table have always been regarded with disgust, and moderation thought merely decent. Gratification of sex impulses has never been left wholly to the caprice of individuals, but has always been subjected to strict regulation in order to promote what was believed to be the ultimate good of individuals and of the group. Other vehement impulses have often been subjected to conventions. In all ages, every one has been expected to keep his temper and to restrain his self-assertiveness within the limits of good manners. Etiquette sometimes seems to us artificial; however, its underlying aim is social; due respect for others as well as for oneself. Such respect requires self-control, the suppression of all contrary and inappropriate impulses.

The more vehement impulses are, and the more dangerous if unregulated, the more important become the conventions, customs, and laws by which society attempts to induce individuals to cultivate the virtue of temperance.

In our own time rude and vulgar displays of the impulses of food, temper, and self-assertiveness are well controlled by public opinion. Our chief problems to-day are connected with sex and alcohol. Sex can be more conveniently referred to Chapter XVIII, with the simple observation here that conventions in this connection should not be despised. While they have naturally varied somewhat from one generation to another, as social conditions change, conventions of some kind have always proved necessary. The young and inexperienced, at the age when passions are violent, need to be protected from irreparable harm to themselves. Those who refuse to respect such conventions must in extreme cases find themselves punished by social disapproval and even ostracism.

The use of alcohol in early times performed a social service in promoting good will on festal occasions, and it furthered group loyalty. This remained the situation among primitive peoples down to our own times, so long as they were confined to beverages of their own manufacture, usually not very powerful, and scanty in amount. The complete demoralization of native races resulting from the plentiful supply of spirits by white men has been swift and terrible. Among civilized races, the moderate consumption of alcoholic drinks has been of service in affording relaxation, in promoting sociability and good will, and in brightening life under conditions otherwise dull and drab. It is significant that the use of wine has been sacramental in various religions,—the heightened consciousness and conviviality induced by the common cup being thought promotive of a higher life. However, even under the most favorable conditions, alcoholic indulgence often led to deplorable consequences.

In our own time the majority of the thoughtful are everywhere coming to the conclusion that the practice should be abandoned. Safer modes of relaxation and conviviality are now available. In the strain of modern life every one needs to be at his best. Even extremely moderate drinking,—a liter of beer or a few glasses of wine in a day—has been shown experimentally to reduce mental accuracy and other forms of efficiency, and to be liable to produce bad physiological effects, including diminished resistance to disease. And in modern conditions, at least in America, moderate drinking has become increasingly rare. Our unusually stimulating climate, subject to greater extremes of heat and cold and more sudden shifts from day to day in all seasons than most of Europe, is probably less conducive to the moderate consumption of alcoholic drinks. Our liquor traffic, highly commercialized in the days of the bootlegger even more than in those of the saloon, has done its best to increase profits by tempting patrons to excessive drinking. It has also been prone to alliances with those gainfully interested in the exploitation of other vices like prostitution and gambling. The fact that alcoholic indulgence removes normal inhibitions, stimulates sexual appetite, and makes men reckless, has rendered this kind of alliance natural enough. The liquor traffic, too, in our country has for generations been allied with corruption in politics,—both as regards officeholders and voters—and with the promotion and protection of criminal activities of every kind.

The chief danger of alcohol lies in the fact that it is a habit producing drug that rapidly and insidiously creates in many of its consumers an inveterate craving of which they are ordinarily unaware until it has become virtually uncontrollable by themselves and often incurable by the best medical treatment. The news of college alumni is confined to the activities of the virtuous and successful, so that nobody knows how many of them ultimately go to physical and moral ruin as the result of habits of drinking and "going down the line" acquired while undergraduates—vices that grow on them in after years and make them objects of worry and often shame and sorrow to their relatives and friends. The habitual and even the periodical drunkard often becomes a victim of general mental and moral degeneration, and his early death is a profound relief to all interested in him.   Young men go to college under the supposition that an education will increase their chances for success in after life.   Why do a few of them while in college run the risk of acquiring vices liable to render them many times more harm than a college education could possibly benefit them!

It needs to be pointed out that temperance, like all other virtues, is a sentiment that can only be acquired by individuals of their own free will and intelligent choice.   Conventions and laws can force no one to be virtuous.   What public opinion and legislation can do is, first, to arrange social conditions so that virtues will appear attractive, and vices as little tempting as possible; and, secondly, by education to make clear to all that the cultivation of virtues and avoidance of vices lead to the largest satisfactions to individuals, and promote the general good.   None cultivate vices knowing them to be such, and few will be misled if commercialized agencies for the exploitation of vices are not permitted to trap the unwary.   The substitution of attractive and morally wholesome means of recreation accessible to all classes in the community greatly avails to prevent dives, dance halls, gambling dens, and other haunts of vice from alluring those who have not already become vicious. The activities of social settlements, institutional churches, municipal playgrounds, community centers, and like agencies, do valuable constructive work along these lines.   The details of such work belong rather within the domain of the sociologist than of the moral philosopher.   The latter, however, insists that while legal and social agencies are bound to fail so far as they attempt to compel people to be temperate as regards sex, alcohol, or gambling, they are right in attempting to educate people to judge rightly what is virtuous and what is not, to prevent the commercialization of every vice, and to provide means of amusement that will be favorable to the acquisition of virtues and avoidance of vices.[7]

4. *Justice*

Plato and many others have regarded Justice as the one all inclusive virtue both for the individual and for the social order. Understood in this broad sense, this entire chapter is an exposition of justice for the individual, while Part IV treats of justice for the social order. In the narrower and more specific sense, *Justice*, for the individual, connotes *fairness and equity in all of a person's dealings with others, in accordance with the principles established by law and custom.*

Justice is rendering to every one his due. It implies impartiality in the treatment of others,—both conscientious fulfilment of obligations, and appreciation of services rendered to oneself. The just man always carries out his legal obligations, as well as the moral obligations that custom, good faith, and fairness lead others to expect of him. His word is always as good as his bond. He is ever reliable. He never fails to keep his promises, which he does not make lightly. His statement of facts is always accurate. He imputes motives to people carefully and correctly, never giving undue praise or blame; and he considers all aspects of a situation before he renders his opinion. He is equally candid and impartial in his evaluation of his own conduct, claiming credit for his own deserts in a modest way, and avoiding exaggeration. He is the foursquare man whom all know how to appraise. If he possesses wisdom commensurate with his justice, he is a man in whom all place implicit confidence, and to whom they come to seek advice, and to arbitrate their disputes.

The impulsive basis of Justice is complex. It may have originated with the need of effecting a proper balance between resentment and the social impulse in the attitude to be taken toward those who had offended tribal custom. A has wronged B, and B is angry and seeks vengeance. The other members of the group sympathize with B, and are angry at A and desire his punishment. At the same time, A is a fellow tribesman with whom they feel social ties, and they do not want A punished out of proportion to his deserts. Such a balancing between the two impulses is *moral indignation*, and is the root of punitive justice.[8] To feel moral indignation and not unrestrained rage when a wrong has been done to a person became a virtue which it was the duty of all to cultivate in the interest of general good will. Another way in which the sentiment of justice early took root was the problem of effecting such a distribution of goods captured in the chase or in war, that each would receive his fair proportion. Here the impulses to be coördinated were the acquisitive and social impulses. Or the problem may have been to give each individual hunter or warrior due praise and blame for his conduct; if so, the impulses of self-assertion, self-abasement, and the social impulse were chiefly involved. It will be observed that the problems mentioned all have to do with the rudiments of social or political justice, rather than with the conduct of the individual. Probably the conception of the individually just man is a later derivation from earlier established customs defining social relationships. The latter originated first. When increased individualization ensued, and persons became more self-conscious, it became every person's duty to acquire sentiments in harmony with the spirit underlying the customs of the group.

Justice arose in larger social groups than the family and the circles of close friendship. It is the basis of the more impersonal relations that we have with all who are not more closely bound to us in ties of affection. To be sure, even among friends and relatives this virtue has its place. The parent must be just and impartial in his treatment of his children. But it is with those with whom we have more impersonal relationships that justice is the virtue of chief importance. Laboring men, for instance, who are working for a large corporation wish to be treated justly by it; they neither love the stockholders nor expect to be loved by them. Any self-respecting man, as a matter of justice, wishes his deserts to be recognized; it is only in cases of dire misfortune that he seeks for charity or benevolence.

Since justice is the virtue that connotes what our sentiments should be to most of mankind in most of our relationships, it is in many respects the most important of all the virtues. In their moral aspects it is the basis of law and government, and of the economic order. In a just social order all men will prosper in accordance with their talents and efforts; in an unjust social order few will prosper materially, and none can gain well balanced characters so as to enjoy true happiness or attain the highest virtues. A just social order is possible only if individual citizens are just, and *vice versa.*[9]

5. *Love*

An individual has as many sentiments of love as there are objects toward which he has habitually become attracted through impulses of tenderness, sociability, or sex. *Sexual love* in its highest form of *romantic love* includes tender emotion, subjection, self-assertion, sex, pugnacity, acquisition, and other impulses all sublimated and united in complex emotions and sentiments of admiration for the beloved,—pride at having won her favor, humility at one's own unworthiness, loyalty to her, courage in her service, and the like. Only the poets and writers of romances can adequately portray the beauty and comprehensiveness of this sentiment, one of the chief influences that has led men and women to their finest achievements and afforded them the greatest happiness in life.

Hardly less intense in most fathers and more intense in most mothers is love for their own children. To whatever extent maternal tenderness originates as an instinct, under ordinary conditions it soon becomes and remains the ruling passion in the life of a mother while her children are small and dependent upon her, and it normally receives little abatement throughout life. A man ordinarily loses the best friend of his life at the death bed of his mother. Second only to the mother's love of her children, and to the father's love of her, is his love of their children. The impulsive basis of a father's love for his children is likely to be his original love for their mother, which leads him to love the children whom she has borne him.

The love of children for their parents combines impulsive tenderness with feelings of dependence and gratitude, sociability, and comradeship. It might well contain more of the impulse of submission and the complex emotions and sentiments of awe, respect, and obedience than it commonly does in twentieth century America, although no one desires that our children should literally carry out all of the precepts of Confucius and Mencius. The generation responsible for the Great War can make no large pretense of wisdom, and perhaps deservedly finds its children lacking in filial awe and veneration. It can only hope that the generation of the present "youth movement" will prove wiser when it reaches maturity, and be more able in its turn to maintain parental authority and prestige.

Within home and family the finest sentiments of love ordinarily develop. Next in importance are the friendships formed with other individuals. To the profound commentary of Aristotle on Friendship it is possible to add little of consequence.[10] The social impulse is the original one, and is combined in different proportions in different cases with the self impulses and various of the others, and with the sentiments, ideals, and aspirations that friends share in common. Friendships are virtuous when friends are coöperating for purposes that are good, and each is unselfishly finding joy in common undertakings. A friendship in which each friend finds delight in the other's companionship, and help from sharing his deepest confidences, is morally better than one in which each is in a more self-conscious manner attempting to "do good" to the other. People ordinarily do not wish others to come to see them with the purpose of "doing good" to them, and friendships of the highest order do not ordinarily come about in that way.

One of the chief contributions of Christianity to our modern moral development was in the widening and deepening of the virtue of Love in its application to mankind in general, as charity, love of neighbor, benevolence, and altruism. (See Chapter VI, above.) We ought to feel toward all mankind somewhat of the sentiment that we feel to the members of our family and to our close personal friends. We ought to be ready and willing to render services within our power to any one in need of them. Envy, jealousy, and ill will leading to strife, fights, strikes, lockouts, and wars between individuals, groups, and nations would cease, if we could learn to love our neighbors as ourselves, and to consider all mankind our neighbors. But it would not be ethical for a person to feel and act from a sentiment of love to all mankind in the same ways that he does toward his own wife and children. It would hardly be right, in order to contribute money to save Asiatic children from dying of starvation for him to deny his own children the chance of a high school education. Excess of altruism toward strangers at the cost of service to those bound to us by immediate ties of love is too rare a vice, however, to require much comment. We more often fail in not loving sufficiently those with whom we have no personal contact. Excessive affection toward children, and near friends, spoiling them by unappreciated sacrifices that they take for granted and do not need, is a more common vice than is usually realized. To make children inconsiderate, selfish, and lacking in initiative and self-reliance is not virtuous love for them. The negative rule here holds, that it is never virtuous to render services to others that it is not virtuous for the others to receive. A similar remark applies to charity. To pauperize the poor through humiliating forms of patronage that deprive them of self-respect and initiative is not the virtue of charity.[11]

The relationship between the virtues of Justice and Love might be expressed in this way. Justice, a pagan virtue recognized by Plato and Aristotle and their contemporaries, consists in rendering to others in fairness and equity what society has found in its experience to make for the general good in the long run, and so has embodied in law and custom. Love of neighbor, charity, benevolence, altruism, or whatever it may best be called, is an added Jewish and Christian virtue that urges us to feel tenderness and comradeship to all mankind, and to render to them more than justice demands. Just how much more cannot easily be defined, so love of neighbor has been called a virtue of "indeterminate obligation", as opposed to justice, which is of "determinate obligation". It is clear that there is a margin beyond the limits of definable justice over which altruism should extend, and that both within the range of justice and within the margin a feeling of tenderness ought to be applied toward all mankind. It is never right, however, to be benevolent to some at the cost of being unjust to others. Robin Hood and St. Crispin were not virtuous in stealing from the rich in order to benefit the poor;[12] nor are modern radicals right in advocating dishonest expropriation of the wealthy in order to ameliorate the condition of the masses. In an ideal social order justice and benevolence would become identical. And in progress toward such an order, requests that previously in a vague way might be advanced in the name of benevolence or charity are becoming more precisely defined and assuming the form of justice. Public provision for the deserving poor has already passed within the domain of justice and taken the place of indiscriminate almsgiving in the name of charity. Pensions for the old and helpless, and the widowed mother, and insurance for workers against sickness, serious accidents, and involuntary unemployment are rapidly passing within the domain of determinate justice.[13]

6. *Loyalty*

On the whole it is convenient to distinguish between love and loyalty, and make of them separate virtues, although in ordinary language they rather overlap. When distinguished, Love is said to be felt toward individuals, and Loyalty toward groups. A man *loves* each separate member of his family as an individual; he is *loyal* to his family as a social unit, and to each member of it because of his membership in it. Powerful certainly are the sentiments that bind a man to the social groups with which he identifies himself—his immediate family, totem, and clan in the case of the primitive man; his family, church,

city, college, fraternities, profession, and nation in the case of
the civilized man.   The basic impulses in his sentiment for
his family include tender emotion and sex.   The self impulses,
too, are here strongly operative; his self-assertion is strengthened
by emotions of pride, and his self-abasement by humiliation at
the behavior of his family as a whole.   Other groups evoke
analogous sentiments; the social impulse, however, taking the
place of the parental and sex impulses.   Each group to some
extent has its own mores; each makes its own demands; and
a man joyfully serves each of his groups and feels pride if commended, and shame and sorrow if condemned, by any of them.

The virtue of *Loyalty* is *the rational control and organization
of the sentiments felt toward the different groups with which a person is identified.*   Theoretically, the sentiments felt toward each
of these groups should complement those felt toward the others,
and in no way conflict with them.   A man's loyalty to home and
family should lead him to be loyal to the city, "state", and nation which sustain and protect his family life; as he serves each
larger group he should be serving and doing honor to the smaller
ones.   The same is true of other groups of a different character,
—like his profession and his religion.   Obviously in our imperfect society, loyalties often seem to conflict.   Can a man best
serve his family by laying down his life for his country?   Can
he best serve his college by vigorously denouncing and expos-
ing to the world its faults?   Ought he to defend his profession
unqualifiedly, because he believes it mainly right, even though
on a particular issue he knows it to be wrong?

However, it has probably become the fashion to exaggerate
the frequency of such instances.   In many cases, the best heritage a patriot could leave his sons would be the memory of his
supreme sacrifice in the cause of their country,—to make it a
better place for them to live in.   The best service to a college in
the long run may well be a frank exposure of its faults to the
public.   The members of no profession can realize their own best
good so long as they remain blind to their faults.   Service of no
group is likely to conflict with service of other groups in ways in

which they have rightful claims upon one. Love of one's beloved can never conflict with love of truth and honor; love of God and country imply love of humanity; loyalty to any cause is moral provided only it is in harmony with loyalty to larger and more inclusive causes. So, if we define Loyalty as a virtue, this virtue tends to embrace in a common and coherent whole all the sentiments by which an individual is attached to different groups. So far as these sentiments seriously conflict with one another, they are not virtuous, and are not Loyalty.[14]

7. *Economy*

The sentiment which prompts to the acquisition of private property is old in the human race. It is not wholly lacking even in the primitive horde, although it does not gain full force until private ownership of large property—cattle or land—first becomes established. Besides acquisitiveness the sentiment includes the following impulses:—constructiveness; fear of future need and consequent desire for security; self-assertion (because of the expression of personality that property makes possible, coupled with the satisfaction at the respect which its acquisition and successful management give the possessor); the family impulses (leading one to desire to provide for wife and children); and pugnacity (because of the competition and rivalry of economic activities).

No sentiment needs more careful criticism in order to assure its becoming a virtue. Those successful in the accumulation of wealth are liable to be addicted to greed, avarice, dishonesty, cruelty, selfishness, arrogance, and lack of refined appreciation for culture of no obvious economic worth. The poor are in danger of becoming victims of the vices of jealousy, lack of self-reliance and self-respect, discontent, toadying to the rich, and failure to appreciate the simpler joys that are available to every one.

Economy as an individual virtue implies *rational control of the sentiment prompting to the acquisition and care of property, and the expenditure of income. The individual should so use his property that it will enrich his own life in all the best ways, and at the same time be of service to the social order.* The economical person is a benefactor to society. His capital makes possible the employment of others who would be less profitably occupied if it were not available. It facilitates the production of goods that enrich the lives of consumers. The total amount of the national income,—even in the richest countries of the world, no matter how equitably it were divided, would not at present be sufficient to enable all to enjoy the comforts that modern civilization ought to make available to every one. The more the total capital in existence can be increased, other things equal, the larger will be the opportunities afforded to every one. Whoever at the present time saves part of his income and invests it in ways that are socially productive is therefore rendering a public service.

More persons in America are now able to save than ever before. Whoever does so is developing in himself thrift, self-control, and foresight; he is gaining firmness and consistency in his character, and becoming a man of strength and integrity. There was a certain truth (although of course exaggerated) in the identification of "the rich, the wise and the good" by the Federalists in the earlier decades of our republic, in a period of large and undeveloped resources when the accumulation of property was possible to all who were industrious and provident. To-day such opportunities in a different way have again become accessible to large numbers of our people in consequence of unprecedented high wages, and the availability of good securities to all savers who seek the advice of reliable investment bankers. The time is not far distant when it will be a mark of moral weakness for any American in good health, with fair natural abilities, and free from unusual misfortunes, not to be an accumulator of at least a modest amount of capital.

Economy as a virtue refers not only to the accumulation and care of capital, but to the wise expenditure of income. The economical man knows how to spend money so that it will afford to him and others the largest satisfactions. He provides for the necessities of life before the luxuries, and shows good taste in clothes, books, furniture, amusements, works of art, and all his expenditures. He inspires emulation in others to select what is both useful and beautiful. He divides his time rationally into hours of work, rest, and refined leisure—a feat possible on different scales for those with modest as well as large incomes. He is generous, too, in his benevolences. Economy in benevolences does not mean small gifts, but it does mean that the giver sees that his benefactions become of the greatest possible service to worthy causes and to the type of persons for whom they are intended.

The importance of the virtue of Economy in our modern capitalistic and largely industrial society can scarcely be overstated. Unless wealth exists in large quantities and is wisely employed, the comforts of life cannot be enjoyed by the many, much less secondary and higher education and the larger and richer cultural life that they afford. Aristotle was wrong in fancying that the poor man of his own time could not be virtuous. But even to-day the full development of life in all its possibilities is hardly open to those who are not able to enjoy moderate incomes. The opportunity for every one to make the most of his life is increased to the extent that all persevere in the accumulation of incomes and in the expenditure of them in ways that increase general appreciation of useful and well made commodities, genuine art and music, good literature, beautiful architecture, and all expressions of clear thinking and high living.[15]

8. *Wisdom*

The *conscientious* man *carefully weighs ends and means, compares values, and ever seeks to do that which will promote the most good.* The *wise* man *habitually does all this successfully.* Conscientiousness is wisdom in the making; wisdom is conscientiousness achieved. Every one can rightfully be expected to be conscientious; only experience, talent, and long perseverance render anyone wise. However, every one can learn to be docile, to realize his own limitations, and to seek the counsel of the wise. And most people are intelligent enough to learn who are wise and competent. Plato realized that only a few are wise; he thought that if these could rule and all obey their behests, all would act wisely. In a modern democracy, there is faith that the voters, most of whom are not very wise, will be guided by the judgment of those whom they know to be wise, and accordingly vote for the best men and the best solutions of issues. How far this faith is justified, the reader may well consider.

Conscientiousness implies intellectual integrity. No one can progress on the path to wisdom who does not look facts squarely in the face and recognize them for what they are, declining to confuse them with his own wishes or ideals. Men should have aspirations and ideals of course; and they should learn how to realize them. But it is sheer intellectual dishonesty to assume that anything is practicable just because its attainment would be a desirable ideal. Religion especially in our time is suffering from obscurantism in the confusion between ideals and realities. To observe frankly and to think consistently are essential. So far as a college really teaches its students to do so, it can truthfully claim to be successful in the upbuilding of character. For most wrongdoing implies self-deception. The man who lies or cheats or is slothful or self-indulgent is dishonest with himself, and does not frankly call his acts by their right names, even to himself. To spend a short time every day in meditation, honestly taking account of one's own moral attainments and deficiencies is highly to be recommended. To know oneself is to make solid progress on the road to wisdom.

The impulsive basis of wisdom and conscientiousness is curiosity or wonder. This impulse prompts to observation and reflection in order to satisfy the desire to know and to understand. Other impulses prompt to the pursuit of various ends not always in harmony with one another, and to the employment of means not always likely to prove successful. The sentiment that leads one to evaluate means and ends with careful accuracy is conscientiousness or wisdom. So important is it that the ancient Hebrew writers of the "Wisdom" books as well as the Stoics and Epicureans thought wisdom the supreme virtue. If a man could attain this virtue he would be certain to gain the rest.

Wisdom in modern conditions must not be confounded with erudition and technical skill. Men who possess these are not always wise. On the other hand, the wise executive is often simply the man who knows how to pick out experts, and to make practical use of their advice. Nor is conscientiousness the virtue *par excellence* of the fanatic, the bigot, or the "conscientious objector". If the first two were really conscientious, they would not be so lacking in wisdom. The last is sometimes a stubbornly conceited individual who fancies himself to be a heroic martyr for the sake of his principles, when he refuses or neglects to seek and be guided by the judgments of the wise and competent.

9. *Respect*

As a social being, a growing boy is extremely sensitive to the behavior of his fellows. When their conduct is superior to his own in any way, his impulses of negative self-feeling and wonder are aroused in the complex emotion of admiration; or to this reaction may be added a dash of fear, and so constitute the emotion of awe. If a boy habitually feels admiration or awe toward another person he acquires the sentiment of respect for him. If the boy, in his own turn, manifests excellence in any way, he finds himself an object of respect to those younger than himself. Thus his own positive self-feeling is stimulated and gratified. Thus made overconfident, perhaps he seeks to display his own strong points rather ostentatiously, and presently his hasty pride undergoes a fall. His performances do not equal his expectations; or some boy of his own age proves more proficient than he. So experience teaches him caution, and his growing sentiment for himself presently acquires a healthy mixture of pride and humility. As boys grow into manhood, especially with the increased self-consciousness that comes in adolescence, they become discriminatingly critical, both of other persons and of themselves.

The *virtue* of *respect* is *a rational sentiment in which regard for personality is wise, just, benevolent, and honorable.* It is a duty to respect others and to respect oneself, to give praise and blame to others and to oneself in accordance with real worth and character. A large part of ethics could be included within this virtue.[16] As compared with the virtue of love or friendship, respect is more dispassionate and equitable in its judgments. It involves a certain amount of sympathy in the technical sense,—ability to feel, understand, and evaluate the emotions and sentiments of others, and to put a correct appraisal on the worth of one's own as well. Implying, as it does, evaluation of other virtues, respect emerges after other virtues have already appeared, and it continues to develop with them.[17]

10. *Reverence*

Respect and Reverence are sometimes regarded as synonymous. Here, however, it will be convenient to distinguish between them, and to define *Reverence* as *the extension of the virtue of respect to a Being superior to man, who arouses in him complex emotions of admiration, awe, love, and gratitude, and also, probably, of mystic rapture and devoted loyalty.* In the old pagan religions such emotions, or some of them, were aroused by a great variety of supernatural beings. In *Christianity and Judaism, there is but one supreme object of religious reverence, namely, God.*

Some highly moral persons are not at all reverent in the religious sense. They have true respect for other human beings and social groups as well as for themselves, but they are neither religious by sentiment nor conviction. On the other hand, most people have more or less well developed religious sentiments. In profoundly devout persons the religious sentiment is the ruling passion in their lives, and all other sentiments and virtues are included within it. However, the religious sentiment is not necessarily a virtue. The bigot and the fanatic have strong religious sentiments, but these are not virtues. A virtue, we must remember, is rational, social, and moral, and a mean between two extremes. Whether a person's religious sentiment is virtuous, depends in part on his conception of God. For the religious person tends to become like his notion of the God whom he worships and seeks to follow. If he conceives of God as angry and jealous, a vindictive hater of heretics, and intolerant to all who do not literally accept the creed of a certain sect to which the person adheres, his religious sentiment will lead him to imitate in his own life and character what he believes his God to be, and to require of him.

For this reason, among others, even religion must be subjected to reflective moral criticism. Religion must itself be moral, and the God of religion must Himself be the supreme exemplar of all the virtues which man has thus far learned to respect. The lasting superiority of Christianity and Judaism lies largely in the fact that in the history of these religions the conception of God has constantly become enlarged and enriched. In contrast to the old Greek and Roman religions especially, the time has never come when Christians and Jews in their own lives have aspired to higher reaches of morality than they have been able to attribute to God. There is no reason to fear that Christian or Jewish ideals of God will ever become hardened and crystallized into doctrinal statements incapable of further interpretation in the light of advancing experience. Were this to occur, these religions would become morally doomed. Man would outgrow them.

With the understanding that God is conceived as the supreme Person who possesses all the moral virtues in superhuman excellence, and that He expects man to imitate Him, and with His help to cultivate all the virtues, Reverence may be rightly regarded by the religious man to be the highest of all the virtues, because it includes them all and gives them additional sanction. The truly religious man who has acquired the virtue of Reverence will then excel in courage, temperance, honor, justice, love, loyalty, economy, wisdom, and respect. For him, religion is the highest morality, and comprehends within itself all that is valuable in life.[18]

REFERENCES

Aristotle, *Nichomachean Ethics. Eudæmean Ethics.*

* F. Paulsen, *System of Ethics*, Book III.

* S. E. Mezes, *Ethics, Descriptive and Explanatory*, chaps. IX–XIV.

* J. Dewey and J. H. Tufts, *Ethics*, chap. XIX.

* M. W. Calkins, *The Good Man and the Good*, chaps. VI–X.

* Durant Drake, *Problems of Conduct*, chaps. XVI, XVII.

* H. W. Dresser, *Ethics*, chaps. XX–XXIII.

* Theodore De Laguna, *Introduction to the Science of Ethics*, pp. 80–98, 296–323.

H. W. Wright, *Self-Realization*, Part Four.

C. L. Sherman, *The Moral Self*, chaps. IV, V.

CHAPTER X

THE SELF

I. Unity and Diversity of the Self

In philosophy and psychology, the term "self" is used in many different senses.[1] First, there is *the unity of self-consciousness,* which Kant († 1804) and those who have come under his influence have emphasized.[2] All the experiences that we undergo form a unity. You could not recognize an object that you had perceived before, nor could you awaken in the morning out of sound sleep and know yourself to be the same person that you were yesterday, unless present and past experiences formed a unity, and were known by a common mind. This unity of self-consciousness in the adult is only rendered possible by the continuous existence and integral unity of the brain and nervous system. When this latter is broken down interruptions in memory are liable to occur, objects not to be recognized, illusions, and delusions to be accepted as known facts; in aggravated cases, insanity ensues. However, to escape the fallacies of materialism, it is necessary to remember that consciousness cannot be *identified* with the brain and nervous system. Whatever consciousness may be, and closely related as it undoubtedly is to material processes, it is nevertheless unique and *sui generis.*

Secondly, there is *the transcendental or pure Ego,*—a silent spectator of all a person's sensations, memories, emotions, and judgments. The existence of this "I" as Descartes († 1650) showed, cannot be doubted, because in the very process of doubting it there must be an "I" that doubts. Yet a person is not usually aware of the "I", and it is often only on reflection that its presence is found to be implied. The "I" cannot be identified with any particular sensation or image or

other content of consciousness; as Hume († 1776) pointed out,
the latter continually come and go in an ever shifting stream;
yet the "I" persists. This "I", always present, and always a
subjective observer and never experienced object, has been
compared by Shakespeare to the eye of vision, which perceives
external objects constantly, but cannot directly look at itself.[3]
The Platonic doctrine that this pure Ego is the manifestation
of some simple, underlying, and indestructible soul substance,
though held as recently as the eighteenth century by Berkeley
and others, is generally thought to have been refuted by the
attacks of Hume and Kant. [4]

Thirdly, there is the more concrete conception of the self, *form*
often called *"the empirical me"*. This, especially in its moral
aspects, is far more important for ethics than the unity of self-
consciousness or the pure Ego. It is with this conception that
we shall be chiefly concerned. Subsequent references in this
volume to *"the self"*, *"selfhood"*, *"personality"* or *"character"*,
*without further specification, will be understood to have reference
to this third conception of the self, the empirical me.*

The empirical me is harder to define than to describe, although it is much like the common sense view of what is meant
when one says "I", or "myself", "you", "he", "she", "persons", or "people". There is really nothing very involved or
technical about it. The expression "empirical me" simply
means that it is the plain "me" of ordinary experience, as distinguished from more abstruse and elusive conceptions of the
self. When we first try to describe what we mean by our
own selves or those of other people, we are likely to mention
physical characteristics. "He is tall and strong." "He is fat
and homely." "She is a pure blonde." But we soon find
that *mental and moral characteristics* are more important aspects
of the self. "He is kindly and good natured, and very sympathetic; you need not hesitate to ask his assistance." "He
is boorish and sarcastic; don't approach him in the matter."
"She is a very domestic woman, wrapped up in her family;
she wouldn't be interested in a book on feminism."

*Empirical = experimental ; Empirical me = the part that
can be reached by experiment.*

Body & Mind problem by James in "Psychology"

A living man's self or personality—his empirical me—certainly includes his body, which is the bearer and sustainer of his spiritual life. The body must be properly fed, clothed, and cared for if the self is to be normal. A person's moods and temperament, his whole emotional life, and to some extent his moral character, are dependent on the functioning of various glands, as recent research has established.[5] But *sentiments* are what we chiefly have in mind when we think of the self from a social or moral standpoint. All that a man values and about which his sentiments accordingly develop, profoundly affect his self. His vocation and his avocations, the wife whom he cherishes and the children whom he has begotten, the church, school, hospital, and other philanthropic institutions to which he has devoted time and money, the book he has written, the business he has built up, the enemies with whom he has contended, the political party which he has supported and the one which he has opposed, the principles which he respects and those which he abhors,—every thing, person, institution, and abstract conception or ideal with reference to which his primary impulses have become organized in sentiments:—all these make a man what he is, and determine the nature of his self.[6] So we may say that *a man's sentiments chiefly make him what he is, or in other words constitute his empirical self.*

As the objects to which a man devotes himself prosper, his self or personality expands and becomes assertive; as they decline his personality becomes contracted and abased. He is angry at an attack on any of them, and springs to their defense. He feels curiosity regarding all matters that affect these objects in any way, he is acquisitive and constructive in their behalf, his social impulse is satisfied in the companionship of those who are also interested in these objects. A man's ruling sentiments, when any decisive test comes, reveal themselves in his conduct. A man's behavior is a surer expression of his self than his introspections or professions; in crises his sentiments and self reveal themselves in action. "If you love me, love my dog": this is as much as to say that the love of my dog is one of my ruling sentiments, and no one can love me who does not love the object of this sentiment. If you are aware of my sentiment, and do not love my dog, it is manifest that you cannot love my self.

If a man's sentiments, as disclosed by what he does, are mainly virtuous, he is a good man; if they are mainly vicious, he is a bad man; if they are partly one and partly the other—which is really the case with most persons—he is in some ways good and in other ways bad. When we appraise a man's *character*, we are evaluating *the moral worth of his sentiments*. It is important to remember that not only do a man's sentiments constitute his character, but a man's character determines his sentiments. A wise man who loves his country has unfavorable sentiments toward the principles and expedients that traitors and ill-advised patriots advocate.

The unity of the empirical me, no less than the unity of self-consciousness, depends upon the integral action of the brain and nervous system. Lesions of any kind are liable to impair it. Functional disturbances may cause breaks in memory, and give rise to alternating or multiple personalities,—strange pathological cases in which consciousness and memory are divided between two or more selves that in turn control the body, but have largely different memories, interests, and sentiments.[7] The *moral* integrity of the self depends, of course, on the coherence of its sentiments; when sentiments are virtues they promote the complete good of their possessor and the common good of humanity.

II. RÔLES OF THE SELF

The self, as empirical me, plays various *rôles*. The same man may act in the different rôles of a devoted husband and father, an honest and successful business man, an earnest church worker, an active promoter of various movements of municipal interest, a loyal adherent of his political party, and a patriotic supporter of his country. Such a man may have a fairly consistent character. His sentiments may all be virtues that do not often conflict with one another. Yet even such a man would show different sides of his personality to the different groups with which he is related. After his death, his widow and children will be comforted as well as surprised at heartfelt tributes of appreciation from persons whom they do not know and groups with which they have slight acquaintance. And they would have been even more surprised if while he were living they had witnessed his speech and behavior in each of these relationships, in ways that might have aroused their approval and admiration, but certainly were vastly different from the rôle which fell naturally to him in the home. The virtuous man may not fear to let all of his friends witness all of his activities; but no acquaintance who knows him in only one of his rôles could in advance predict just how he would appear in any other.

Many men would be reluctant for all of their friends in one of their rôles to know them in certain of their other rôles. In such a case, the man in some of his rôles may be playing parts that he is aware are morally unworthy of the self he manifests in more favorable rôles. Illustrations would be that of a kind father and husband who is a brutal employer, or a delightfully good fellow at the club who reserves his spells of bad temper for the privacy of his home. Or a man may be playing rôles which he does not believe to be morally blameworthy, but which some of his more narrow-minded associates in other rôles might condemn. A clergyman in a narrow sect may find it necessary to smoke surreptitiously in the attic, or visit the plays of Shakespeare or Ibsen in cities where he is not known. Many politicians, capitalists, and labor leaders are forced in public to oppose unqualifiedly persons and principles that in private, to those whom they can trust, they concede to have considerable merit. Such men are usually not hypocrites. Most of them are conscientiously rendering to society the services needed of them; which they could not do if they did not play these rôles in the manner expected of them. The real hypocrite is the man who plays inconsistent rôles in order to further his selfish interests at the expense of the groups whom

he professes to serve. The line between adaptability and hypocrisy is not always easy to draw, and many deceive themselves
by pseudo-rationalizations into thinking that contemptible
deceit is kindly tact and wise diplomacy.

Does a man's self as a whole select the rôles which he plays,
or do the rôles make the man's self what it is? Partly one and
partly the other. A young man, governed by his sentiments
at the time, chooses his profession, his wife, and the various
groups and principles with which he identifies himself. But
the governing sentiments that constitute his personality when
he makes these choices are the outgrowth of his previous associations, in many of which he was born and bred without conscious
choice. And in after life each of his rôles puts its stamp upon
him, not only upon his body in physical appearance and facial
expression, but upon his character in habits, convictions, tastes,
and sentiments. If he plays his rôles successfully, he will live
himself into them, and ultimately become what they determine
him to be.

III. Social Nature of the Self

Selfhood or personality is not innate; it is acquired in a
social environment. A little baby has no self; he is merely a
"candidate for personality". The infant of two or three years
is already, however, in the process of its acquisition. He
imitates older children as well as adults in his little plays, and
so learns his mother tongue, and also his first moral—or quasi-
moral—judgments which consist of emotions of approval and
disapproval of various actions which he sees approved or
disapproved by his elders. He engages in activities that bring
him applause, and desists from those likely to bring a frown or
a spank. As he grows a little older, he continues through imitation, sympathy, and suggestion to adopt the likes, dislikes,
and general behavior of his elders. He practices on those still
younger than he, playing that they are his children or pupils,
domineering over them, and often exploiting them. With his
peers—other children of like age and attainments—he asso-

ciates on equal terms, now taking the lead, and now following, now fighting with them, and now coöperating for common purposes. His earlier sentiments are thus formed. They may be virtuous within his capacities:—courage in defense of his little sister and his dog, obedience and docility to teachers and fair play to his comrades,—rudimentary forms of justice and conscientiousness; temperance, in refusing to eat sweetmeats to an extent that parents and experience have taught him are liable to lead to indigestion. Although the vices of infancy and childhood—unbridled temper, greed, cowardice, lying, bullying, jealousy, and spite—do not begin so early as St. Augustine supposed, they emerge soon.

All the sentiments, good and bad, are acquired in a social environment. The child is no wax tablet, to be sure, passively molded by parents, teachers, and associates as they will. The primary impulses, if not innate instincts, at any rate are stubborn and vigorous, and they delimit the possibilities of moral training. One child has a powerful pugnacious impulse; it is impossible to train him to be a gentle soul; yet he can be prevented from developing into a bully. Instead he may be taught to become a heroic champion of fair play and a fighter of iniquity,—first in the nursery, later in the schoolroom and on the playground, and, when he becomes an adult, in public life. Another child, who manifests constitutional timidity, will never have it in him to be a hard fighter for any cause, good or bad, but he need not become a sneak or a coward. As a boy, he may learn to be a prudent counselor who influences his playmates against hasty and ill-considered projects; as a man, he may prove to be one of those wise conservatives who keep well meaning but hot-headed radicals from plunging society into downfall and ruin. The primary impulses of no two children are equal in relative strength; the virtues and vices into which their sentiments are likely to develop are diverse. Yet the social environment, if wisely controlled and directed, will facilitate the growth of children into useful men and women,— even in cases in which physical heredity is unfavorable.

Since anyone's personality is the outgrowth of interaction between his primary instincts (or impulses) and his social environment, it is not surprising that his own consciousness is a quasi-social affair. A man's thoughts are a perpetual conversation. If the reader will watch his own mental processes for a day, he will be surprised to see how true this is. He will find that he is constantly praising, condemning, and reasoning with himself,—just as if within him were an ego and an alter, two different personalities. He will find that his ego or "I" will say to his alter or "myself",—"You had better study tomorrow's logic lesson, and not go to the movies this evening". Possibly "myself" humbly replies, "Yes, perhaps you are right", or more spiritedly rejoins, "No, you have studied enough for to-day, and you need the recreation". "Myself" says to my "I",—"I made a great hit with Miss Smith at the dance last night", while "I" retorts, "No, you didn't; she thought you a great clown, and you stepped all over her toes!" "Myself" crestfallenly admits that such is likely true. "Myself" fortunately has some sense of humor, and can laugh at his own shortcomings; moreover he is sure that "I" is not infallible, and sometimes too severe in judging "myself". That is rather a pity, for "I" is probably the most indulgent critic that "myself" possesses.[8]

Sometimes the individual who watches such conversations going on within his own mind will identify himself with one, and sometimes with the other of the speakers. In moral struggles he may bewail with Ovid, St. Paul, and Faust that two souls dwell within his breast, and that while he sees and approves the better course he follows the worse.[9] In former times, a man might have identified himself with the better of the two contestants in an internal moral struggle, and think of the other as a devil who was tempting him; or he might think of himself as the baser of the two, and believe the other to be an angel, or even God Himself. Both ego and alter, from a modern psychological standpoint, must be considered quasi-persons into which the whole self is temporarily divided, each representative of sentiments for the time in conflict. A man is responsible for all that goes on within his mind, both good and bad. Between two conflicting selves, it is within his power to identify himself with, and permanently become, whichever he really chooses. If a moral decision is virtuously made, it is a reconciliation of opposing impulses in the interests of the whole self, with proper recognition of the claims of society upon him. His self advances to a higher plane. If the decision is wrongly made, the self is further disorganized, or becomes coördinated on a lower moral plane, so that the man emerges from the crisis a person of lower character than he might have become.

IV. Sympathy

Sympathy, as we have seen in Chapter IX, is the experience of the emotions of others. Since man is an animal with powerful social instincts or impulses, he readily experiences the emotions of his fellows, especially of the social groups with which he identifies himself. Even in a crowd, impulses and emotions of fear, anger, laughter, and curiosity are extremely contagious, and become intensified as they spread. A crowd may degenerate into a mob, carried away by such emotions, and perform acts of brutality, and more rarely of generosity, of which its members would have been incapable as individuals. Lynchings culminating in burning victims at the stake, enlistments in a volunteer army, and religious pseudo-conversions are instances. Such sympathetic emotions induced in crowds are likely to prove transient, and to have no permanent hold upon individuals, once the crowd has been dissolved. The individual on reflection regrets the brutal lynching into which crowd excitement drew him. He may have to stay in the army, but he regrets that he was carried away by the music and the speeches, and he feels that he would have been a better soldier if his patriotism had been appealed to more rationally. The victim of the religious revival on deliberation is likely to laugh at his pseudo-conversion, and to regard revivalists as clever impostors or strangely deluded fanatics. It is worth debating to what extent organized cheering and singing at athletic contests develop enduring sentiments of loyalty and affection for the college or university, notwithstanding the violent emotions which they evoke at the time.

In groups more coherently and permanently organized than crowds and mobs, the emotions sympathetically experienced by the different members become knit together into sentiments. The members are thus effectively united, with common traditions, ideals, hopes, and aspirations. A liturgy, as in a church or lodge, may be employed to arouse such emotions and permanently attach them to common objects of loyalty. Patriotic exercises may strengthen national sentiment.[10]

Sympathy plays an important part in the moral life. Every one, to some extent, craves the sympathy of those to whom he is attached. Some persons become selfish in the assertion of what Professor McDougall calls "active sympathy",[11] and insist on recounting their worries and joys to others whom they expect to be responsive, and to participate in their emotions. Such a man may prove a positive bore to his friends, and he may bring his wife to nervous prostration. Within moderate limits, however, every person needs to share his emotions with his friends. He thus gains relief from anxieties which become lighter when shared, increased joy from pleasures which are renewed and enhanced when recounted, and greater devotion to ideals which are clarified and strengthened as they are dis-cussed.

The development of character and the acquisition of virtues are furthered through motives induced by sympathy. A person desires to share the sentiments of his groups; and as he does so, he acquires their likes and dislikes, their moral judgments, and, in time, their virtues. Without sympathy, moral conduct and social life would be impossible. Unless members of groups mutually shared each other's emotions and acquired common sentiments, there could be no common values which they could seek, and no traits of character that they would generally approve and cultivate as virtues. Sympathetically experiencing the suffering of another person prompts to tender emotion and pity for him, and so to the virtue of charity or benevolence. Knowledge of the wrongs of another through sympathy arouses anger at those who have injured him; and this, coupled with social feeling for the offender himself, tempers anger into moral indignation and so leads to the virtue of justice.

Desire for sympathy is the principal motive impelling most persons toward righteous conduct, though probably it is not the exclusive motive in any human action. The child understands his mother's emotions more than she realizes. He fears her anger or disgust not merely nor chiefly because of possible punishment, but because he wishes her love and confidence. As he grows up, he wishes the good will of his groups, avoids the vices that would make him an object of their dislike, and cultivates the virtues that win their approval. As he becomes more reflective, the sympathy sought may not be so much that of the persons immediately in his vicinity as of the more competent ones of his profession or religion or other specialized group. Or he may become religious enough to be satisfied with believing that he has the sympathy of God; or like Adam Smith, philosophical enough to be content to believe that a purely ideal spectator who thoroughly understood the situation and was completely competent to judge, would sympathetically share his sentiments and approve his conduct.

The cases supposed in the last paragraph increasingly imply an advance beyond a moral outlook based exclusively upon sympathy, if by the latter is meant the mere participation in common emotions. Discrimination is made in those whose sympathy is sought. This implies reflective criticism. A person may ask himself on this level: "Do I *deserve* sympathy?" This means that he wishes his emotions and sentiments to merit endorsement on moral grounds. His emotions must become rationalized, socialized, and individualized, in order to warrant sympathy on the part of competent judges.[12]

What psychological principles will effect this rationalization? It has sometimes been affirmed that it can be effected through an appeal to pleasure. It will therefore be necessary to consider the psychological interpretation of pleasure.

V. PLEASURE AND UNPLEASANTNESS

We have seen that the basic springs of moral conduct are the principal primary impulses and the sentiments in which these impulses are organized. When an impulse is in the process of satisfaction pleasure is experienced; when it is in the process of being thwarted or obstructed, unpleasantness is felt. While a person is succeeding in activities concerned with the object he loves, hates, or respects, his feeling is pleasurable; when the reverse is true, his feeling is unpleasant. If a person could be conceived as absolutely devoid of impulses, he would be totally apathetic, incapable of feeling either pleasure or unpleasantness. Most of the time people do not directly desire the feeling of pleasure itself or directly avoid the feeling of unpleasantness. What is ordinarily desired is some object to which an impulse or sentiment impels; and because the person already desires the object, he is capable of experiencing pleasure or unpleasantness with reference to it.

To make this clearer, we must first eliminate *pain* from consideration, and get some idea of the psychological functions of pleasantness and unpleasantness. *Pain* is a specific organic sensation comparable to the various sensations of sight, hearing, taste, smell, temperature, and pressure. It has definite nerve fibers and end organs scattered throughout the body. Its function is to evoke movements of withdrawal, both reflexes and conscious acts, when bodily tissues are being injured or seriously disturbed. Pain, thus understood as an organic sensation, is not much discussed in ethics. When the word occurs in ethical treatises it usually refers to what recent and more careful usage no longer calls pain, but unpleasantness or disagreeableness.

Pleasure or *pleasantness* and *unpleasantness* or *disagreeableness* (not "displeasure") on the other hand, are not specific organic sensations at all. They are technically known as *Affection* or

Feeling. The neural basis of affection may be the general character of nervous reaction as a whole, or it may be undifferentiated nerve cells; the authorities differ on this question. At any rate, affection is the general tone or quality of the whole condition of consciousness at a given time, and not, like pain and other sensations, a constituent element or process within consciousness. When a child tastes candy, he has a sensation of sweetness and a feeling tone of pleasure; when he tastes quinine, he has a sensation of bitterness and a feeling of unpleasantness. All persons experience the same sensations when they taste mustard, but some persons find these sensations agreeable and others find them disagreeable.

Sensuous pleasure attends the satisfaction of organic impulses or appetites, such as the eating of well prepared food when one is hungry, warming oneself before the fire when chilly, and the like. *Sensuous unpleasantness attends the thwarting or obstruction of organic impulses or appetites,* such as the taste of poorly cooked food when hungry, the oppression of foul air which one is forced to breathe in a subway, etc. There is some experimental evidence in favor of the theory that sensuous pleasure is attended by expansive movements in the muscles, the flow of blood to the surface of the body, and increased respiration, while unpleasantness is attended by the opposite phenomena. It seems to be agreed that sensuous pleasure is likely to be attended by bodily movements of expansion and approach, and that it is an index of normal and efficient neural action; while sensuous unpleasantness is likely to attend movements of bodily contraction and withdrawal, and that it marks excessive or defective nervous reaction.

In general, sensuous pleasure attends processes that are immediately favorable to the welfare of the organism, and sensuous unpleasantness those that are not so. The exceptions to this rule are mostly instances of the general principle that "the senses are not prophets"; affection, like a thermometer, registers present and not future conditions. The immediate organic reactions from eating lobster salad and drinking intoxicants freely are favorable and so pleasurable; if poisoning effects develop later they will be registered in disagreeable affection, as well as in sensations of pain, when and not until they occur. The function of sensuous pleasure is therefore to reinforce the impulses that are being gratified and to encourage their continuance. The function of unpleasant sensuous feeling is to retard impulses that are being hampered, or to cause the efforts to satisfy them to take some other form.

Ideational pleasantness and unpleasantness are the concomitants of mental activity that is either successfully or unsuccessfully carried on. If mental activity is at once being stimulated to greatest intensity while obstacles are being consistently overcome, the feeling tone is pleasurable. Æsthetic pleasures are afforded by works of art that produce the greatest unity in the greatest variety. A strikingly short, direct, and simple solution of a mathematical problem affords æsthetic pleasure, as does a scientific experiment that solves a perplexing problem by a simple and effective device. Any theory is beautiful and pleasant that brings under one point of view a multitude of seemingly disconnected facts, and so gives coherence to our understanding. A literary style has a pleasant charm if it is clear and compact. Pleasant is the concurrence in rhythm between two distinct processes, like the correspondence between sound and sense in poetry, or dancing to music. A lecture is pleasant when the listener's thoughts move concurrently with the speaker's; the latter does not bore him by dwelling too long on any single point, nor does exposition proceed so rapidly that it is difficult to follow. A well constructed drama or novel holds the attention pleasurably; the action is stimulating because complex and rapid, while at the same time the plot is solved clearly and convincingly, without irrelevant digressions. A game or contest is pleasurable, no matter who wins, provided it calls forth the skill of well matched opponents, and enables each to do his best. A humorous story evokes pleasure by arousing the close attention of listeners, and suddenly satisfying it in a manner that is both apt and unexpected.

On the other hand, when mental activity is not sufficiently stimulated, the resultant feeling tone is unpleasant. Unceasing monotony for this reason is always disagreeable,—whether in a landscape, a building, a novel, or a poem. If mental activity is stimulated only to be thwarted or baffled, the feeling tone is even more unpleasant. Simple illustrations would be arrangement of things of any sort in a disorderly manner, say heaps of stone and rubbish, books and clothes scattered about chaotically in a room, a neglected garden overgrown with weeds and underbrush, or a book consisting of miscellaneous anecdotes and comments of no great intrinsic interest and bearing no common significance. Material of any kind that is so intricately put together that a person cannot grasp its meaning will be disagreeable to him; although it may afford high intellectual pleasure to a better informed person who can understand and appreciate it. Mystical poems and dramas and difficult classical music will serve as illustrations. A lecturer is disagreeable if he bores his audience by frequent digressions, unnecessary pedantry, and elaborations of the obvious, or if he makes himself incomprehensible by too rapid exposition of difficult points. Badly constructed plots are unpleasant to follow, because they arouse interest only to tantalize it by long digressions. A one-sided game is unpleasant; the skill of the superior contestant is not evoked, while the inferior is hopelessly baffled. A humorous story is a failure if its point is either obscure, too obvious, or too long delayed; such a story is decidedly unpleasant, and the attempt to laugh at it out of courtesy is disagreeable.

The acute suffering caused by a recent bereavement is due to the fact that thoughts of the deceased are constantly called forth by everything that occurs, as a result of past associations, and such thoughts are only brought to mind to be crushed. In the process of time, thoughts of the deceased are no longer connected with present plans and purposes, and everyday living, and they become mere memories. As such, they are less hard to bear; gradually the feeling aroused is connected with emotions of tender sadness. Finally, memories of the dead, now simply precious and comforting, become pleasurable, and stimulate instead of repress mental activity. Sorrows of bereavement again suddenly become acute when there is some vivid reminder of the one who has been lost, so that for the moment he almost seems to be present, only to be followed by the bitter realization of the actual facts. Unexpectedly coming across personal letters written by the deceased, or sudden waking from a dream in which his companionship has been enjoyed, may have this consequence.[13]

VI. HEDONISM

Psychological Hedonism maintains that all that men ever desire are pleasant feelings, and all that they ever seek to avoid are unpleasant feelings. In the light of the preceding section, the reader will perceive on a little reflection that this doctrine cannot be true. It is because impulses prompt men to desire objects that it is possible for them to feel pleasure if they are successful in their efforts to obtain them, and to feel unpleasantness if their efforts are thwarted. Yet it would be going too far to contend that people *never* seek to repeat pleasant feelings simply for the sake of their pleasantness. Pleasant dishes are eaten again when opportunity offers. A man may repeatedly engage in athletic sports for the pleasurable excitement that they afford him. Indulgence in sensuous pleasures for their own sake, if done in moderation, is not necessarily wrong. Only ascetics have fancied this to be true. But the improper cultivation of sensuous pleasures for their own sake leads to the vices of *sensuality*, like gluttony, drunkenness, and sexual debauchery, or the milder vice of the man who becomes absorbed in athletics to the neglect of any serious interest in life. Under this head perhaps should be classified the vices of gambling and excessive love of excitement, such as that of the woman who spends all her mornings reading fiction, and all her afternoons and evenings playing bridge; although the pleasure in such cases is to some extent intellectual.

Ideational pleasures are sometimes cultivated for their own

sake. A poem is reread, a melody played or listened to once
more, a foreign city is visited again and again,—all purely to
revive agreeable feelings of an intellectual character. In moderation, this, too, is defensible. Carried to excess it is the vice of
æstheticism, or that of *love of mental excitement*. In the course of
time sensuous and æsthetic pleasures sought for themselves alone
cease to satisfy. The jaded sensualist and the blasé æsthete are
defeated in their pursuit of pleasure and become pessimists.

Attention should be called in passing to what has come to
be known as the "paradox of hedonism". Pleasure is most
keenly felt when attention is not directed upon a person's
feelings, but upon something more objective. To feel pleasure,
don't think about it. Who, for instance, would keenly enjoy
witnessing a lively athletic contest if he kept thinking constantly
of his feelings, kept hugging himself and inwardly ejaculating
"What a wonderful time I am having!" Only as a person for-
gets himself in the excitement, and is absorbed in intense desire
for the victory of his team, can he get much of an inward thrill
from watching a game. The same remark applies to all pleasures, sensuous almost as much as intellectual. A man must
discriminatingly observe the excellent qualities of food, wine,
and cigars if they are to afford him much pleasure. The novel
reader and the bridge player forget themselves and their inward feelings of pleasure, and become lost in exciting events.
The lover of the arts must be intent upon the harmonious
composition of the musical tones, the rhythm of the poem, the
symmetry and proportion of the cathedral, if he is to feel keen
æsthetic pleasure from them.

Ethical Hedonism defines good and evil in terms of pleasantness and unpleasantness; men ought to seek what will most
promote pleasure and diminish unpleasantness. The critical
discussion of ethical hedonism will be reserved for Chapter
XIII. In the present connection, however, three observations
may properly be made. First, since psychological hedonism is
largely false, a case for ethical hedonism cannot be deduced
from it. Secondly, the fact that constant and deliberate culti-

vation of agreeable feelings for their own sake is liable to lead
to the vices of sensuality and æstheticism, makes it doubtful
whether an entirely satisfactory standard for moral judgments
can be found in the injunction that the object of every action
should be the promotion of pleasant feelings. Thirdly, since
sensuous pleasure is in the majority of instances the concomitant
of processes that really promote bodily welfare, and since ideational pleasures attend activities that are successful in achieving the purposes to which impulses and sentiments prompt,
ethical hedonism cannot be wholly off the track. Any action
that would have as its ultimate effect the increase of the pleasure of mankind would be very likely to be morally desirable;
any action that would have the opposite result would in all
probability be morally undesirable.

VII. Duty and Conscience

To achieve the satisfaction of any of his impulses, a man is
dependent on his physical and social environment. So even
primitive men and small children feel external restraints or
sanctions to act in certain ways rather than in others. *Physical
sanctions* force men to protect themselves against cold, storm,
and drought, to work harder than they would otherwise do, and
to deny themselves indulgences. The physiological requirements of his organism enjoin upon a man both indulgence and
restraint in food, drink, sex, rest, exertion, and sleep. *Political
sanctions* include the restraints of the government on the
individual; he must obey the laws on penalty of punishment.
Social sanctions (the adjective is not very apt) are the coercions
of public opinion; man is ever anxious to have the good will and
moral approval of his fellows, and to escape their censure and
dislike. *Religious sanctions* influencing conduct are the result
of man's concern to be in harmony with the spiritual forces in
the universe external to him, *e.g.*, the result of his fear and love
of ancestral ghosts, nature spirits, and gods in many primitive
religions, and of the one God in the case of Christianity and
Judaism.[14]

What has been true of the race continues to be true of the modern individual child. He is led to act in certain ways and to refrain from acting in others, because of his desire to please his elders and playmates. "Good" and "bad" for the little child are respectively the actions that arouse favorable and unfavorable responses from those who control his environment. Fear, filial affection, desire for comradeship, self-assertion and submission make him seek the "good" and avoid the "bad" as he conceives them.

Conscience, in the light of what has just been said, *in its more rudimentary forms*, includes the intellectual recognition of what the sanctions just mentioned require of the individual. It also includes a complex emotion, in which fear, love, the social emotion, and submission are contained. *Duty* is felt when there is a conflict of impulses and emotions within the self, between the demands of conscience and contrary desires. The feeling urges the self to the performance of the obligations recognized by conscience. Thus conscience and duty emerge in their rudimentary forms, in the evolution of the race and in the development of the modern individual child.

As the race became reflective, and as the modern individual child grows older, duty and conscience come to mean something more than impulses to conform to the physical, political, social, and religious environments. It comes to be consciously perceived that certain things *ought* to be done, and certain virtues *ought* to be acquired, and that certain other things *ought not* to be done, and certain vices *ought* to be avoided, simply and for no other reason than that one form of conduct is good and right, and the other is bad and wrong. "Good", "bad", "right", and "wrong" are unanalyzable intuitions that animals do not have, that savages and infants very slowly acquire, but that the moral consciousness of the reflective man frankly recognizes. Just as colors as we sense them are not the light waves that stimulate the retinæ of our eyes, and sounds as we hear them are not the air waves that beat upon the drums of our ears, so these intuitions are something different from the sanctions that evoke them within us. And when reflective man recognizes these intuitions he feels it is his *duty* to conform to them, and his emotional state is unsatisfactory until he does so. His conscience "troubles" him.

What particular moral judgments a man makes, except so far as physical sanctions tend everywhere to be similar, depends on the *moral tradition* with which he has come into contact. No man, as Thomas Hill Green remarked, can make a conscience for himself. He acquires the moral tradition of his group, and makes moral judgments and feels moral obligations accordingly, in much the same way that he learns to speak the language of his group. Yet the modern man's conscience is not absolutely determined for him by the moral traditions of a single group. We inherit many moral traditions—Hebrew, Greek, Roman, Medieval, Protestant, and others. The Enlightenment has taught us to think, and the industrial revolution has rapidly changed social life and customs. Consequently many diverse moral judgments are in the air, and every one is prompted to reflective choice among them. Perhaps the inhabitants of the United States differ almost as much in their consciences and their moral judgments as they do in their physical features. The outcome is, that each of us has a conscience which more or less critically and intelligently passes moral judgments that he feels it his duty to obey.

Awareness of duty is most acute when there is a conflict within a man's self between the impulse to act in accordance with his conscience, and impulses that prompt him to act in some other way. Many writers confine the feeling of duty and obligation to such situations. Such conflicts become rarer as a man grows older. His character develops, his habits become fixed, and his self more unitary. To some extent this means that he has become a better man. Men who have reached middle life ought to be, and usually are, better men than they were as youths. They have had the opportunity through years of experience to become so. On the other hand, as men grow older and more addicted to routine, they become less sensitive to moral problems. Lofty ideals and heroic sacrifices are likely to appear visionary and impractical, and their consciences not to trouble them if they act in ways that have become habitual with them, and are generally regarded as respectable. Perhaps this is not true of the saint, or other person of unusually fine moral sensitiveness. As such a person grows older, and has clearer moral perceptions with added experience, he realizes more painfully the deficiencies in his character that are not yet overcome, and to the end of life he grows steadily in all the virtues, remaining humble because he sees the path of duty extending infinitely beyond the point he has been able to reach.[15]

VIII. REASON AND VOLITION

The whole of this volume is intended to be a discussion of reason in ethics. In this particular section, however, certain aspects of reasoning in connection with volition and the self need to be indicated briefly.

Reasoning in moral decisions includes the employment of the ordinary logical processes of deduction and induction. Established moral principles need to be applied to particular problems, consequences of possible courses of action need to be thought out carefully. Means and ends both require evaluation.

A rational decision in a moral situation implies a coördination of all the instincts and emotions involved. A stranger makes a very insulting remark in your presence. Your first impulse—resentment—is to knock the impertinent fellow down. If you remember the injunction to count ten when angry, and so give an opportunity for other ideas and impulses to come to consciousness, you probably will not do so. This is a public place, and you have no desire for a lot of notoriety, explanations to the police, and loss of time from your engagements. You have never seen the man before. He has either mistaken you for some other person or he is drunk or crazy. So you decide to leave him alone. Your other impulses and sentiments thus overcome the immediate impulse and save the situation for you. You act rationally, and avoid making a fool of yourself.

Reason in morality is closely related to volition. Each implies the coördination of impulses and sentiments in response to the whole self. Spinoza thought of will and reason as identical; while for Kant the will is the practical reason, *i.e.*, reason in conduct.

When a person has to make a moral decision between the call of duty and conflicting impulses, if his choice is right he seems, as William James observed, "to act along the line of greatest resistance". The still voice of duty sounds weak and repellent, while the voice of contrary inclination is strong and seductive. It would certainly seem as if he, by sheer force of will power, does what his strongest impulses oppose.

The fact of the matter is, of course, that any decision, good or bad, if freely made by a sane mind, is the person's own act, and he is responsible for it. A hasty action prompted by a single impetuous impulse like pugnacity or self-assertion, is usually wrong. A carefully deliberated action is much more likely to be right. If deliberation occurs, there is time for all the impulses and sentiments to assert themselves. The seductive temptation, though gratifying to certain impulses and sentiments, conflicts with the virtues that the person possesses, and especially it may be, with his respect for himself and for others. When he carefully considers all the consequences that would follow from the contemplated act, the possible or even inevitable injury to others or to himself, it is not the sort of thing that he can do in consistency with his ideal of himself,— with the kind of man that he hopes that he is. So, in the end, he simply cannot do the act which he clearly perceives to be wrong. Or, in case he is contemplating a good, perhaps generous or heroic act that calls for sacrifice, he finds that he simply must do this thing; he is the kind of man that "can do no other". In either case the man acts in accordance with the demands of his whole self, so far as they can be given expression under the circumstances. His action, after all, is in the line of least resistance.[16]

IX. Self-Realization and Self-Sacrifice

In this connection can be briefly indicated the respective places of Self-Realization and Self-Sacrifice. Some ethical writers have said that the moral good can best be considered in terms of *Self-Realization:* each individual, remembering, of course, that he is a social being, should seek the fullest expression of his whole self, of his entire personality. He should, for instance, select the vocation in which he can bring his talents to fullest expression. He should choose as his wife the woman to whose personality his own most fully responds. Since he is a social being, the man who thus seeks self-realization will find that he must be of service to others. For instance, the successful physician must conserve the health of his patients; the successful merchant must offer his customers the goods they desire, in good variety, with honest representation of their character, and at the lowest prices. The successful husband must be a faithful, loving, and considerate helpmate. And no man's life can normally be wholly restricted to the demands of his vocation and of his wife. He can realize himself in work and play only by performing numerous services to many persons and groups in many ways. To the extent that a man realizes the best that is within him, he renders greatest service to others and leads the good life in accordance with the demands of duty and conscience.

The advocates of *Self-Sacrifice* state a contrary view. They quote Scripture to the effect that he who would save his life must lose it. Ascetics have made a virtue of self-denial for the mere sake of enduring privations. The truth between the two positions is clear. It is impossible to realize all of a person's interests in any situation. One must always choose. For instance, in selecting any vocation and making a success of it, a man must concentrate his time and attention upon it, often to the sacrifice of much that he values. Darwin, for instance, largely lost his enjoyment for music as a result of the concentration of his attention upon biology. Yet he realized himself more fully by so doing, and he rendered a far greater service to humanity than he could have done if he had retained his musical gifts at the cost of dilettantism in biology. A man who marries sacrifices his bachelor independence and has to adapt himself to domestic life, while a woman leaves behind her the joyous and care free years of girlhood. Both assume increased responsibilities. In a happy marriage both find that they have gained many times what they have lost. Self-sacrifice is justifiable only when it promotes some greater good. Self-realization and self-sacrifice should not be conflicting principles. Each implies the other. However, self-realization is the positive good, and self-sacrifice a necessary evil,—the cost that we have to pay for the good.

In choosing a vocation, no one should ordinarily select a career for which he has no liking, simply because he sees that there is need for the services of men along that line. No one, for instance, should become a minister or a foreign missionary just because the world needs such men, and the life is accompanied by many hardships and privations. He should only enter such a calling because the opportunities for service that it affords seem so attractive to him that the hardships and privations appear negligible in comparison; and after having chosen such a calling, he should be careful to select a wife whose evaluation of his profession, including its opportunities and sacrifices, agrees entirely with his own. Only a person who can realize himself in a calling is likely to be of much service to others in it. This is true most of all in professions like the ministry, in which the services required include frequent demands for the full and free expression of sympathy,—entering into and understanding the emotional needs and sentiments of all sorts and conditions of men. The man who does not have unusual capacity for sympathy, and love of the other services that the vocation calls for, and merely enters the ministry from a sense of duty and self-sacrifice will later be judged by his suffering parishioners to have missed his real vocation.

Men who have talents for leadership, and can best express their personalities in directing other men, should qualify themselves for executive positions. Men with more drab and impersonal natures, who like best to work by themselves, and neither disturb others nor be disturbed by them, if not brilliant may find themselves happy and useful in work of a routine character; while brilliant men of this type who engage in scientific or other important research sometimes prove to be the greatest men of their generation.

There are, of course, cases in which it becomes the duty of a person to make a sacrifice for the sake of others, without any apparent chance for proportionate self-realization. For instance, two brothers have dependent upon them a widowed mother in poor health. Each boy is quite capable of working his way through college; but one of them will have to stay at home and engage in manual labor in order to support the mother. Which shall it be? The more generous one, who feels more attached to his mother, and to whom it will seem less of a sacrifice? To say this seems to put a premium on selfishness. Yet it is clear that the more affectionate son is the one who would prove of greater comfort to the mother. And, perhaps after all, he will be the one to realize the finer and nobler self. Fame, riches, and power are not the highest values for which to strive. More numerous, however, are the cases in which a selfish person demands disproportionate sacrifices from others. A selfish mother who imagines herself an invalid, and prevents her children from marrying or going into professions because she "needs them at home" might be stronger physically, mentally, and morally if she would sacrifice her caprices for the good of herself as well as of her children. Again, the over-sacrificing mother who spoils her children is mistaken in thinking that she is enabling them to realize their selves to the best advantage.

While, therefore, there are exceptions, the principle usually holds that if each person conscientiously seeks to realize his more important capacities to the full, sacrificing other capacities only when necessary for that purpose, he will thereby best fulfill his duty to others as well as to himself. As Professor A. K. Rogers wisely says, "A man who actually does something worth while for the world is in almost every case the man who works primarily because he likes it, and not he who flatters himself that he is 'doing the world good'".[17]

X. FREEDOM AND RESPONSIBILITY

The student of ethics makes it one of his fundamental assumptions that men are morally responsible for what they do. If this were not true, moral judgments would have no justification. We do not think of the motions of plants and inanimate objects and the behavior of animals as moral or immoral. If everything that a man does were *mechanically* determined, like the rolling of a stone down hill, logically we could neither praise nor blame him for anything that he did, nor pass a moral judgment of any kind on him. If he did something annoying, society might imprison him or execute him, in order to get him out of the way, just as one would pull up a weed by the roots, and either confine or kill a dangerous dog, without implying any moral censure of the weed or dog. But it would obviously be absurd to treat a rational human being in such a manner.

Our general practice is, to hold adult human beings morally responsible for their actions, provided that they are sane, and under no unusual or abnormal coercion. This practice assumes *Psychological Freedom*, *i.e.*, a person's actions are the outcome of his own mental processes, so that it is his own self that has decided them. So *Psychological Freedom* and *Moral Responsibility* can be regarded as synonymous: each implies the other, and the absence of either implies the absence of the other.

The technical criteria for determining whether an adult is sane and morally responsible for his acts, lie within the fields of law and medicine, and cannot be outlined here. In law, some allowance is made for those who do wrongful acts under extreme provocation, under circumstances in which a normal person might be expected to be unduly excited, and complete self-control to have been impossible. Such considerations mitigate the severity of penalties, since the crime was not willful, malicious, or premeditated. Children are held morally responsible for what they do in proportion to their age and experience. A common sense criterion is whether the child realizes clearly the rightfulness or wrongfulness of a given action. This should as a rule decide whether he deserves moral praise or blame with reference to it.

Freedom of the will, when defined as psychological freedom and moral responsibility, has been affirmed by the moral judgments of human society in all ages, and has the authority of all responsible writers on Ethics. This is the prior fact, to be recognized. The only question in which dispute is possible is the *nature* of human freedom.[18]

In ethical theory, there have been two different schools on the question of the nature of human freedom, the *determinists* and the *indeterminists*. The position of the former is, whenever a person is free, his actions are *determined by his own mental processes exclusively*, *i.e.*, his own impulses, instincts, habits, sentiments, and self, in such a way that he, being the type of person he is, could not have acted otherwise than as he did. He might have acted otherwise so far as external conditions dictated. If he were an honest man he could not steal the purse, let us say, because of his character; while if he were a weak and self-indulgent man now hard up, it would be impossible for him to resist the temptation to appropriate it, given the opportunity. This doctrine is not *mechanical* determinism, which no serious writer in ethics can maintain: a man is not a weed or a dog, much less a stone or a clod: his actions are not determined as theirs are. On the contrary, this view is *self-determinism*, or *teleological determinism:* a person's actions are determined by his self and his purposes,—by the kind of character he has, and the plans and ideals that actuate his life. It is just because he is a person, and his actions are determined by his personality, that they are praiseworthy or blameworthy. The reader will note that the advocates of self-determinism fully recognize psychological freedom and moral responsibility, and endeavor to account for it.

Indeterminists advance a different explanation of psychological freedom and moral responsibility. Each time a person makes a choice, his decision is not entirely determined by his heredity, environment, and previously acquired habits. On the contrary, there is a locus of free choice before him, affording alternatives between which he can make a selection independent of his heredity, environment, and habits. To be sure, this locus is restricted. A person will ultimately decide upon that course of action to which he gives most attention; but he can to some extent choose to what he will give attention. On a certain day, two boys have before them options, to go to school or to idle in the streets. Each boy is free to select,—neither heredity, environment, nor past choices absolutely determine his decision, although of course they influence it. John chooses to go to school, Thomas to be idle. Next day, the same two options face the two boys. John and Thomas repeat their choices of the previous day. In time, it becomes habitual for John to go to school and for Thomas to play truant. Some years afterward, John has before him two options, to go to college or to enter business. Thomas also has two options, to take a job at unskilled labor or to become a pickpocket. The two boys no longer have the same options; each has by his past decisions determined the general course of his development and the locus of possible future choices open to him. Yet, throughout every man's life, situations occur which are not wholly determined by the past, and which afford him a locus of possible choices. The way in which he makes these choices largely decides his future character and prospects. We make the habits which in later life bind us for good and for evil. We are the architects of our own fortunes.

Neither determinism nor indeterminism is an entirely satisfactory explanation of the psychological freedom and moral responsibility which both affirm. The determinist finds it difficult to show that the "self-determination" of which he speaks affords the individual any real choice after all. Is he not the slave of his own self? Could he possibly have done otherwise than he did; and if not, is he really free? On the other hand, the indeterminist finds some difficulty in meeting the charge of believing in chance. If a person's decisions are not determined by his character, what does govern his choice? Himself? If so, indeterminism becomes determinism. If not, then the decisions are effected by some alien and contingent force which is not the person's own impulses, sentiments, and character, and over which it is hard to see that the man has any real control. The author does not profess to know how to solve such difficulties as these. Determinists solve them to their own satisfaction in one way, and indeterminists in another. The literature on the subject is voluminous, and much of it is very interesting. The reader will find himself convinced by either position if he takes care not to read much on the other side.[19]

The author is disposed to what he believes to be an healthy agnosticism on the issue between determinism and indeterminism. Our wills certainly are free in the sense that we are morally responsible. Our whole social life takes this for granted, and human society could not remain on the basis it now is and always has been if it were not true. Otherwise we could not praise or condemn ourselves or anyone else for anything anyone ever did, and it would be impossible to make moral judgments at all. There could be no such study as ethics. The very fact that society has proceeded successfully on the hypothesis that men are morally responsible when their actions are determined by their own mental processes is a practical proof that the hypothesis must be true. And if ethical theory has thus far failed to explain how it is true, ethics is in no worse case than the more developed special sciences. No mathematician knows what space and time are, yet there is a science of mathematics. No physicist knows what matter and energy are; no biologist knows what life is. Psychologists are undecided whether theirs is a science of behavior or of consciousness; and no psychologist knows what either of these are. Economists cannot define value satisfactorily; political scientists cannot answer many questions as to the ultimate nature of the state; sociologists do not know what society is. Yet each of these sciences has been highly successful; and no reasonable person doubts that there are such things as space, time, matter, energy, behavior, consciousness, value, society, and the state. So we may not feel unduly disturbed at the fact that ethics cannot explain, and yet has to assume, the fact of moral obligation and freedom.

Ethical Freedom must be carefully distinguished from the psychological freedom already discussed. We are only free ethically when we decide to do what is right,—in other words, to do what is *the expression of our entire selves*. And since we are social beings, this means that an *ethically* free act is *in accordance with the common good, with social welfare*. Hasty acts prompted by isolated but violent impulses are neither ethically free nor rational, although we are psychologically free when we perform them, and it is right that we are held morally responsible for them. Ethical freedom is an ideal, which each of us realizes more or less imperfectly. If a man in his every act expressed a complete coördination of all of his impulses, under the guidance of the virtues, and if he lived in a society where every one else did likewise, he would be ethically free in a complete sense. To this ideal goal individuals and society are slowly and painfully advancing. The progress will be more rapid if each of us exercises his psychological freedom, in the choices he makes, in the direction of the highest self-realization and ethical freedom for himself and the common good of humanity. It will also be more rapid if progress is made in social amelioration, so that each individual will be afforded educational, industrial, and economic opportunity to develop his talents fully. Even in our present imperfect social order, the great economic progress since the industrial revolution has made available to the masses more material comforts and more educational and cultural opportunities than were ever accessible to the entire population of any nation in previous history. So the vast majority of mankind, at least in America, are to-day enjoying more *real free-dom*—in the sense of opportunity for self-realization—than was ever the case in the past. We should not congratulate our-selves over much, however. There is still a great deal of room for improvement. Our country as well as the rest of the world is full of social injustices, and denial of freedom and opportunity commensurate with the resources of modern civilization.

REFERENCES

* J. Dewey and J. H. Tufts, *Ethics*, chap. XVIII.
* M. W. Calkins, *The Good Man and the Good*, chap. II.
* Warner Fite, *An Introductory Theory of Ethics*, chap. XI.
* H. W. Wright, *Self-Realization*, Part III.
* William James, *Principles of Psychology*, chap. X. *Briefer Course*, chap. XXVI.
* C. L. Sherman, *The Moral Self*, chaps. VI, VII.
* Hastings Rashdall, *Theory of Good and Evil*, Book II, chaps. II, III.
  J. A. Leighton, *Man and the Cosmos*, Book IV.
  T. H. Green, *Prolegomena to Ethics*.
  F. H. Bradley, *Ethical Studies*.
  W. E. Hocking, *Human Nature and its Remaking*.
  Warner Fite, *Moral Philosophy*.
  J. E. Turner, *The Philosophic Basis of Moral Obligation*, chap. IX–XII.
  Paul Fauconnet, *La Responsabilité*.

Numerous other references, popular and technical, will be found in the Notes to this chapter at the end of the volume.

PART III
SYSTEMATIC ETHICS

CHAPTER XI

INTUITIONISM

I. Classification of Ethical Systems

Each of the great classical systems of ethics has been an attempted philosophical explanation of the nature and significance of moral judgments. Each system has in its own way offered solutions of problems that can be brought under four general heads: (1) the explanation of the objective character of moral judgments in view of their *source* in the mind, and the process by which they are discerned; (2) the *criterion* by which the moral is distinguished from the unmoral and the immoral; (3) the relationship between the *individual* and *society*, and upon which of the latter two emphasis should be placed; and (4) the *psychology* of moral conduct.

The last of these four heads has been discussed in the preceding Part, and will only be noticed here as consideration of other problems necessarily involves it. Regarding the first of the heads, all moral philosophers have in some way recognized the objective character of moral judgments, and have insisted that moral obligation is not a matter of subjective caprice, but that ethical principles hold alike for all. The systems have differed greatly, however, as to the *source* in the mind through which moral principles are known. *Intuitionism* has maintained that the basis of moral judgments is to be found in a kind of mental perception; the mind directly cognizes the distinction between good and evil, much as it perceives the difference between blue and yellow, or between identity and difference. While the source of moral judgments is attributed to a native capacity of the mind, intuitionists have differed among themselves as to how much of the content of morality is im-

283

Emerson was the strongest intuitionist U.S. produced. books in lib G.E., Transcendentalism.

mediately perceived,—whether a considerable portion, or little more than the abstract distinction between "good" and "bad", "right" and "wrong", "ought" and "ought not". For the intuitionist, moral distinctions when rightly apprehended are objective. Although they are recognized by a capacity of the mind, their validity does not depend on the accuracy with which particular individuals apprehend them. $7 \times 9 = 63$; if some school boys calculate the product to be 62 or 64, this does not alter the truth in the case. In a similar way, moral principles hold absolutely; once an individual has correctly perceived the elements of right and wrong by intuition, and has made the proper application to his own problems, he should go ahead and do his duty, without much regard for consequences to himself or to others.[1]

Opposed to Intuitionism are the diverse systems that do not put their reliance on any innate capacity of the mind for moral intuition or perception; but instead insist on the necessity of *calculating the probable consequences that would follow from the performance of this or that action*. General rules, of course, are permissible; and since exceptions, if too frequent, would lead to more harm than good, they should be rare. But the general rules themselves hold because they lead to the best results in the long run. In systems of this type, therefore, the proper *end* of all human action is first defined; the morality of general rules and specific actions is then determined with reference to whether they will promote this end. Such systems are therefore called *teleological* (from *telos*, end or purpose). *Ethical Hedonism* (from *hedone*, pleasure) is the kind of teleological ethics that finds the supreme end of all moral conduct in *the maximum of pleasure and minimum of unpleasantness*. Acts are accordingly judged right or wrong in the light of their probable consequences with reference to this end; sentiments and habits are virtuous provided they favor it, and vicious if they do not. *Egoistic Hedonism* maintains that the sole concern of any individual should be to gain most pleasure and least unpleasantness for himself. The ancient Cyrenaics affirmed this doctrine with little thought of social consequences. Thomas Hobbes († 1679) and others who have maintained a similar view in modern times have believed that each individual is impelled to seek exclusively his own pleasure (psychological hedonism), and that if everybody would only calculate intelligently how he can best obtain it, and would act consistently with this end in view, the general condition of mankind would be greatly improved. *Universalistic Hedonism*, more commonly known as *Utilitarianism* on the other hand, teaches that the criterion of human morality, by which every individual should be guided in his personal conduct, is that which will bring most pleasure and least unpleasantness to humanity in general.

The teleological systems that do not accept the hedonistic criterion have received various designations, common among which are *Eudæmonism, Perfectionism, Energism,* and *Self-realizationism.* Eudæmonism will be the term adopted in this volume to designate them. (The word comes from the *eudaimonia* of Aristotle, see page 117 above.) Pleasure and the absence of unpleasantness is conceived by writers of this type to be either an inadequate or a false designation of the supreme end of human conduct, which latter had better be called *welfare, perfection, self-realization,* (or possibly happiness, provided the meaning of this word is not that given to it by hedonists who confuse it with pleasure). A man should seek the symmetrical development of all of his capacities; the virtues should be cultivated and coördinated in a coherent self; such an end is good in itself, and not merely because its attainment is likely to be attended by a pleasant life. Pleasure is not the most important aspect of welfare; the realization of all one's capacities is more essential. It might be possible for eudæmonism to assume an *egoistic* form, *viz.:*—each individual should concern himself exclusively with his own highest development or welfare. But as a matter of history, nearly all eudæmonists have been *universalistic,* teaching that in order to judge what is good and bad the individual must act in accordance with the general rules that have been found by experience most likely to further the welfare of mankind universally. So in this volume, "eudæ-monism" and "eudæmonia" will be understood to refer to the universalistic form of the doctrine.

It is therefore possible to give a rough classification of most ethical systems in a comparatively simple table. Taking as the first principle of division, the *source* of moral judgments, *Intuitionism* may be distinguished from *Teleological* Systems. The latter can be subdivided according to the *moral criterion* recognized, into *Hedonism* and *Eudæmonism*, each of which, in accordance with the relative emphasis on the *individual* or on *society*, falls into *Egoistic* and *Universalistic* varieties.

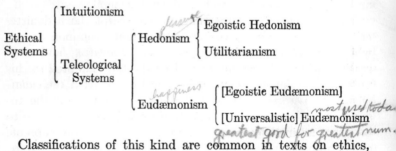

Ethical Systems
- Intuitionism
- Teleological Systems
  - Hedonism *(pleasure)*
    - Egoistic Hedonism
    - Utilitarianism
  - Eudæmonism *(happiness)*
    - [Egoistic Eudæmonism]
    - [Universalistic] Eudæmonism *(most used today)* *(greatest good for greatest num.)*

Classifications of this kind are common in texts on ethics, and they are convenient. Without some sort of classification the great variety of standpoints held by moral philosophers would be hopelessly bewildering, and it would be impossible to compare them. The classification just given calls attention to some of the most important issues in the history of ethics as well as at the present time, and it discloses the more important standpoints taken on these issues. But any classification has its limitations. Some of the greatest moral philosophers have been more concerned with other problems than the ones on which this classification is based. Furthermore, no tabulation can give any idea of the inspiring personalities of many great philosophers, the beauty of their literary style, and their penetrating insight into the problems of life. The following account of some of the principal problems in systematic ethics cannot serve as a substitute for an acquaintance with the writings of the great masters themselves. It is hoped that it may prove an incitement to their study.

II. Intuitionism and Common Sense

A simple form of Intuitionism bases its argument upon plain common sense. Most moral judgments, so it is urged, are obvious to any one with reasonable intelligence. They do not need to be demonstrated, because they are self-evident. Everybody with the slightest powers of moral perception knows that it is wrong to lie and to steal, to commit murder and adultery, to be envious, covetous, and malicious. On the contrary, it is equally certain that it is good and right to be brave, truthful, chaste, generous, loyal, wise, and just. Every man has a natural right to what is his own,—including his life, his liberty, his family, his property, and his reputation. It is clear that every one should claim these rights for himself, and respect them in others. Such moral judgments are included within the Golden Rule, that a person should treat others as he wishes them to treat him. Moreover, if a man knows that it is his duty to do this thing or that, he should go ahead and do it regardless of consequences to himself or to others. And he should do it from good motives,—because he knows that it is the right thing to do, not because he can profit by it in some way. Most moral judgments are self-evident, and are perceived by any honest and unprejudiced person as clearly as the differences between black and white, sweet and sour, that a whole is greater than a part, and that it is impossible for something to be both A and not to be A in the same sense and at the same time and place. This is because man has a moral sense or faculty, or conscience, by which he perceives the difference between right and wrong and feels the force of moral obligation.

Such common sense Intuitionism as has been sketched in the preceding paragraph may be criticized in various ways. If correct moral judgments are axiomatic, why is it that they have not been universally recognized? Some savages think that stealing and killing are meritorious. There is, or used to be, a religious order in India devoted to such activities, known as the Thugs. Cannibalism is common in the savage world. In Borneo there are tribes of head-hunters who regard as a hero a man who has intrepidly slipped into the territory of hostile neighboring tribes and returned with an armful of bleeding heads of women and little children. Perhaps all races have always regarded chastity as a virtue; but the kinds of conduct which it implies have certainly been extremely diverse, when we take into account group marriage, polygamy, concubinage, and temple prostitution.

To a large extent conflicting moral judgments are to be found among ourselves. Conscientious people disagree on whether it is right to play golf and go motoring on Sunday afternoons, to eat meat on Fridays, or pork at any time. A few thoughtful people believe that defensive warfare and the execution of murderers are wrong. Patriotism is denounced by some reformers as "vicious nationalism". There are people who think that the ceremony of marriage is an evil custom, and who defend the righteousness of free love. Perhaps it is axiomatic that "every one has a right to his own"; but if one were to cite this maxim to prove that wholesale confiscation or expropriation of private property would be wrong, there are radicals who would reply that all wealth belongs to the people collectively, that all private ownership of property is theft, and that all exactions of rent, interest, and profit are forms of robbery. Even the Golden Rule can be construed (mistakenly, of course) to teach that a man has a right to engage in what other people call sins and vices because he is willing and desirous that others should participate in them along with him.

In cases like these, where conflicting moral judgments are asserted with sincerity, it would appear impossible to claim that the correct moral judgments are as obvious as plain common sense, and are intuitively known by all persons of moderate intelligence through a native capacity of the mind. The Intuitionist might reply that those who make erroneous moral judgments reason incorrectly. The simple principles of morality are clear, but it is possible, especially when blinded by passion or prejudice, to misapply them in false deductions. To affirm this, however, is to concede that the fundamental principles known intuitively do not cover all cases in an obvious manner, and that it often takes mature experience and trained reasoning powers to apply them correctly. There are accordingly limits to the scope of Intuitionism in its rôle of axiomatic common sense.

III. Intuitionism and Conscience

Intuitionists sometimes urge that a man's conscience is an authoritative guide to right conduct. The ordinary precepts of morality, such as the Ten Commandments and the Golden Rule, are quite clear and intelligible, in their applications to the affairs of everyday life. Our consciences, guided by these precepts, tell us clearly enough what we ought to do in most of our daily activities. It is only when some unusual problem arises that we are in doubt, and in such instances we should seek the counsel of those who have had more experience than ourselves. The plain man, for instance, knows that he ought to pay for goods that he and his family have purchased at a retail store. That is obvious. But just what are a man's rights and his obligations in a complicated contract, when new conditions have arisen that were not foreseen when the contract was drawn up, and about which nothing was stipulated? He can perhaps find out his legal rights and obligations by consulting attorneys. If he is conscientious, however, this will not suffice. He will not only wish to know the law in the matter, but what in the general practice of the trade has been regarded as equitable under the circumstances. He will ask the opinions of others in whose judgment he has confidence, in order to decide what he ought to do. He does not wish to take advantage of legal technicalities, but to act fairly and honorably.

Intuitionists are largely right here. Most of us know well enough what we ought to do in most of our daily activities. True, it is only when some unusual problem arises that we are in doubt, and in such instances we can and should always ask the advice of those who have had more experience. However, Intuitionism overlooks the real reason why many moral judgments appear self-evident and obligatory, and why we spontaneously pronounce them. Comparative ethics shows that such judgments are part of the moral tradition that is handed down, with comparatively slight modifications, from one generation to another. Intuitionism has sometimes given the impression that there is something almost infallible about the deliverances of our consciences. On the contrary, our consciences are simply the products of our social environments and our past experiences. To be sure, they are usually right and ought to be followed, especially if the only reason for not doing so is some personal impulse or passion which probably could not be rationally justified. For when the dictates of conscience are in opposition to strong inclinations, it is tempting to try to refute them by means of pseudo-rationalizations.

Intuitionism is warranted in insisting that the dictates of conscience ought not to be disregarded unless there are sound logical grounds for suspecting them. And the individual cannot easily discover these grounds alone. He should seek the counsel of other persons who are wiser and better informed, and ascertain whether his reasons for challenging the moral tradition, as voiced by his own conscience, are convincing to them. He may find that there are better grounds for the moral tradition than he had suspected. The presumption should always be in favor of conscience and tradition; in this intuitionism is right. Yet conscience and tradition are sometimes wrong. When this is the case, reflective criticism will discover it. But reflective criticism will always, if it is sound, convince other persons who are competent to judge. And it must be remembered that an unreliable conscience is a serious moral liability; its deliverances are not to be trusted, however intuitive and axiomatic they may appear to be to its possessor. Every one's conscience is at times fallible. Whenever a person has occasion to suspect that his conscience may be at fault, his remedy is to appeal to the reflective criticism of others. Thus he will grow in moral discernment and his conscience will become trained.

IV. ETHICAL AXIOMS

Henry Sidgwick, († 1900) though in the main a Utilitarian, conceded to Intuitionism that there are three ethical axioms known by intuition to have real clearness and certainty. The axiom of Justice he stated thus: "whatever action any of us judges to be right for himself, he implicitly judges to be right for all similar persons in similar circumstances", or more briefly, "similar cases should be treated similarly". His second axiom, that of Prudence, is "I ought not to prefer a present lesser good to a future greater good", but show "impartial concern for all parts of [my] conscious life". The third axiom, that of Benevolence, is "I ought not to prefer my own lesser good to the greater good of another" since "each one is morally bound to regard the good of any other individual as much as his own, except in so far as he judges it to be less, when impartially viewed, or less certainly knowable and attainable by him". These three axioms Sidgwick believed to be as intuitive and self-evident as the mathematical axiom that "if equals be added to equals the wholes are equal".[2]

The truth and fundamental importance of these three axioms or principles in our modern moral life (organized as it is in terms of Citizenship) is indisputable. However, the principle of Benevolence could hardly have been accepted (unless understood in a quite different way) in a highly aristocratic civilization; while it seems doubtful whether any of the three would have seemed very clear, let alone self-evident, in times of primitive turbulence and confusion. We might imagine the writers of the biblical book of Proverbs gravely assenting to these three axioms, but could the people who lived in the times of the Judges even have understood them?

Sidgwick probably would not have been disturbed by such an objection. He discovered these three axioms himself only as the result of a profound and extended investigation into the methods of ethics. He might have been willing to agree that, like the fundamental principles of mathematics, ethical axioms are first discovered by the scholar, and only afterwards apprehended by persons of some intelligence. But he might have added that when they are once brought to the attention of the trained mind, their axiomatic and logically irrefutable character becomes manifest.

It may further be observed that these axioms are highly abstract, and treat chiefly of the quantitative side of ethics. They do not state what is good in specific instances. They merely teach that a greater amount of good, whenever, or wherever, or to whomever it is available, is always morally preferable to a lesser amount; persons, places, and times are to be viewed impartially. It seems to us to-day that the highest form of social organization is that of Citizenship, and that it will never be succeeded by a form that would be indifferent to moral axioms like these. We may therefore accept Sidgwick's three axioms as certainly true to-day, and probably true for all future human ethics.

V. ABSTRACT ETHICS

Various writers (some of whom would not on other points be classified as Intuitionists) affirm that the ultimate basis of moral judgments rests on certain simple intuitions that are axiomatic and not further analyzable. "Good", "right", "better", "ought", and their opposites are instances. They cannot be reduced to anything else, such as "pleasure", "unpleasantness", "ultimate interest", and the like. In this they are comparable to simple sensations, and to the axioms of mathematics.

Such intuitions are occasionally reported even among the lowest savages. For instance, Howitt reports that he once discussed with a young Australian savage whether it would not be right for him, if he were hungry, to eat prohibited food during an initiation ceremony provided that no one knew about it. He replied, "I could not do that; it would not be right." He insisted that it would not be right, although he could give no other reason except that it would be wrong to disregard the customs of his people.[3] Probably all human beings but no lower animals have intuitions like this.

On the basis of a few intuitions—axioms and postulates—mathematicians are able to deduce elaborate systems. Authorities are not agreed in all respects with just which axioms and postulates they shall begin; but other principles can be deduced in any event from those assumed to be rudimentary, and each of the various systems derived can successfully explain our spatial and temporal experiences. Would it be possible, in a similar way to start from axiomatic moral principles and derive a comprehensive system of ethics? The advocates of what it will be convenient to denominate Abstract Ethics have believed that this question should be answered affirmatively. The procedure of Spinoza († 1677) is the most famous modern classical instance. Starting with highly abstract axioms, postulates, and definitions he proceeded in the course of five books of theorems to outline a system of ethics, employing a method imitative of geometry. However, as critics point out, before the end of the fifth book Spinoza had unconsciously modified many of the conceptions with which he began. Besides, in the course of the argument he was obliged to inject many new principles. What he really did was to supplement a few intuitions with a wide range of added information. The latter he in no way mathematically deduced from these intuitions, but drew from his empirically obtained knowledge of science and of life.

Contemporary representatives of abstract ethics are more cautious than Spinoza. They admit that after the ultimate ethical principles have been carefully discriminated, only a portion of ethics can be logically derived from them, and that chiefly on the purely logical and quantitative sides. It is necessary to look to experience—away from abstract to concrete ethics—to determine the actual content of the good, and how it can be obtained.

It is not yet certain what, or how many ultimate intuitive

principles should be recognized, nor what are the types of good to be brought under them. Does the good, for instance, include the virtues, or are virtues merely instruments for obtaining it? Is character an intrinsic and ultimate good? Is this true of love, æsthetic experience, or social justice? If very much content is brought within the intuitive good, it will be hard to derive it logically and mathematically from elementary principles. If virtues, duties, and character are excluded from the intuitively known good, and classified as merely means for gaining it, the content of abstract ethics becomes rather slight, obvious, and unimportant, and almost the whole subject matter of the ordinary book on ethics proves to be concrete ethics. Concrete ethics, it is agreed, must derive its observations from a study of the actual problems and conditions of life and conduct, aided by the empirical sciences, such as psychology, sociology, and economics. Since concrete ethics cannot be derived from abstract ethics it becomes clear that the value of the latter is considerably restricted.

We concede to the advocates of abstract ethics that the ultimate principles of ethics, which all moral judgments imply, are intuitions that cannot be further analyzed, but are self-evident and must be accepted. "Good", "right", and "ought" are examples. However, we do know something about the processes of evolution that brought these moral intuitions into existence. What particular acts will be attached to these moral intuitions in the case of any individual? This depends chiefly on the moral tradition by which he had been surrounded. We know to some extent how that moral tradition has arisen and grown in Europe and in countries settled by Europeans during the past three thousand years under Hebrew, Greek, Roman, Christian, and modern secular influences. We can form some idea of the service which that moral tradition has rendered in the past, what have been some of its limitations, and how it can further be criticized and perhaps improved. We know to some extent how the child of to-day in a civilized society acquires a moral consciousness or conscience, and how it grows.

We know that an individual is aware of a moral struggle when there is a conflict between his impulses. We know how his impulses become organized into sentiments, some of which are virtues and others of which are vices. We know that the sense of duty and the voice of conscience are experienced on the side of the virtues that most adequately express the whole self or character of the individual as he would have it be. We therefore are beginning to understand under what circumstances the moral consciousness is handed down from one generation to another, how it takes root and develops for good and for bad in the minds of individuals, how it should be trained, and made better. Successful moral and social education in our age will hasten moral progress.[4]

Here Tuesday

VI. MOTIVES

Intuitionism places emphasis on the *motives* that prompt men to act. For Kant an act can have moral value only if it is done from the motive of doing what is right. Actions from other motives are either unmoral or immoral. Other Intuitionists have usually been less rigorous, and have attributed moral worth to several motives. James Martineau († 1900) made a famous classification of motives in the order of their comparative ethical merit, which (condensed) is:

Lowest
1. Censoriousness, Vindictiveness, Suspiciousness
2. Love of Ease and Sensual Pleasure
3. Appetites
4. Spontaneous Activity
5. Love of Gain
6. Sentimental indulgence of sympathetic feelings
7. Antipathy, Fear, Resentment
8. Love of Power or Ambition; Love of Liberty
9. Love of Culture
10. Wonder and Admiration
11. Parental and Social Affections; Generosity; Gratitude
12. Compassion
13. Reverence
Highest

Diff. people would define these diff.

In accordance with this table, Martineau believed that he could formulate an exact definition of Right and Wrong: *"Every action is* RIGHT, *which, in presence of a lower principle, follows a higher; every action is* WRONG, *which, in presence of a higher principle, follows a lower."*[5]   He gives various illustrations. Regulus was right in returning to death at Carthage, because the Reverence for veracity which prompted him to do so was a higher motive than Fear or personal Affection, which might have prompted him to do otherwise. Peter was wrong in denying Christ because the Fear to which he yielded was lower than the motives of personal Affection and Reverence for Truth which he disregarded. The act of missionaries of mercy, like Florence Nightingale and Livingstone, is right because impelled by Compassion, a higher motive than Love of Ease or of self Culture. The manufacturer of adulterated or falsely labeled goods acts wrongly, because he is moved by Love of Gain, an inferior incentive to good faith and Reverence for Truth. Only the lowest motives in the table are invariably wrong and only the highest invariably right; in the case of the others it is a matter of comparison. It is well to choose a vocation in life in which choices will usually be between motives high rather than low in the scale.

A little reflection will convince us that the morality of actions cannot always be decided by reference to this table. For one thing, motives are often mixed, and a person might feel impelled to one action by motives both very high and very low in the scale, and to a contrary action by motives lying in between. (*E.g.*, combined resentment and reverence for justice might prompt one to prosecute a wrong doer, while compassion might influence one in his favor.) Moreover, as recent psychology has taught us, it is hard for a person to know his real motives, especially when he is under the sway of strong emotions, and it is easy for him through pseudo-rationalizations to deceive himself as to their true character. Again, there are times when it is right to act in accordance with a motive lower rather than one higher in the scale. A person must at times satisfy his appetites for food and rest and his love of gain if at other times he is to be in a physical and economic condition to indulge in love of culture and generosity.

However, Martineau's table, while by no means infallible, is often useful. It gives recognition to the importance of motives and of character. In planning our lives and in considering social problems, it is of some service to have such a test before us. Other considerations that would have to supplement this test and would sometimes overrule it, would be the effects upon one's life as a whole, and upon other persons, that a contemplated action might produce.

VII. CONCLUSION

Intuitionism can be credited with many merits. It rightly calls attention to the fact that in the ordinary affairs of life a man can trust his conscience and his common sense to tell him what it is right for him to do. These are often likely to guide him better than an ethical formula, which he might not rightly apply. Intuitionism has always put great emphasis upon purity of motives and integrity of character. A man is not likely to go far wrong if he acts with a clear conscience from motives that he knows to be good, and if he seeks the counsel of others whom he deems competent in regard to matters with which he is inexperienced.

It must be conceded, too, that there are intuitive principles underlying all ethical theory. "Good" and "bad" cannot be defined in terms of anything else. The sense of duty, too, is unique and unanalyzable. The intrinsic worth of the virtues is known intuitively. There are certain moral axioms that can be apprehended intuitively.

On the other hand, Intuitionism is in some ways superficial. It cannot afford a complete point of view for ethics. The conscience of the plain man is not infallible. The student of ethics needs to understand the origin of the deliverances of conscience and how to criticize them reflectively. While perceptions of goodness and duty are unique and unanalyzable experiences, it is illuminating to know the conditions under which these experiences emerge in the evolution of the race and the development of individual life. Intuitions cannot serve as a substitute for the study of comparative and psychological ethics. Moreover, moral axioms, like those of Sidgwick, are of limited practical application, and at best cover only the quantitative side of ethics, the side on which there usually is least difficulty. Attempts to deduce a system of ethics from intuitive principles like those underlying mathematics and formal logic have thus far proved limited in their usefulness.

In this chapter little attention has been given to the more formal type of Intuitionism, that seeks to discover intuitively some one principle that can be applied to all moral problems universally. The most famous attempt to do this will be discussed in the following chapter.

REFERENCES

* F. Thilly, *Introduction to Ethics*, chaps. II–IV.

* W. Fite, *An Introductory Study of Ethics*, chap. IX.

* M. W. Calkins, *The Good Man and the Good*, chap. I.

* H. Rashdall, *Theory of Good and Evil*, Book I, chap. IV.

* Durant Drake, *Problems of Conduct*, chap. VI.

A. K. Rogers, *Morals in Review*, chap. XII.

James Martineau, *Types of Ethical Theory*, Part II, Book I.

Henry Sidgwick, *Methods of Ethics*, Book III.

G. E. Moore, *Principia Ethica. Ethics.*

[handwritten: less Friday]

CHAPTER XII

FORMAL ETHICS: KANT

I. Intuitionism and Formalism

Formal Ethics, or Formalism, is usually classified as a species of Intuitionism. A formula in mathematics or logic is literally formal; it has no specific content of its own, but will hold true *[handwritten: only form]* of any content to which it may be applied. "If equals be added to equals, the result will be equal." This formula will apply to all finite quantities, no matter what their contents: that is, whether the "equals" referred to are gold coins, diamonds, brickbats, or ballots. The law of Contradiction in formal logic affirms that two judgments which are logically opposed to each other (such as "A is B", and "A is not B") cannot both be true. There is no need for inquiring to what kinds of objects A and B refer; in any case whatsoever, no object or class of objects can both be and not be some other object or class of objects. John Smith cannot both be and not be a native American; that planet cannot both be and not be Mars; that poem cannot both be and not be a sonnet; and so on.

Suppose the proposition "All S is P" to be true. It follows from this, as a matter of purely logical consistency that at least some P is S, and that there are no cases of S that are not P. It makes no difference in the least to what classes of objects the symbols S and P refer. No matter what these may be, provided "All S is P", the other two propositions inevitably follow. Suppose now, some one informs us that "All the Baganda are natives of Uganda". We may never have heard of the Baganda before, and we may only have the vaguest notion that such a country as Uganda exists somewhere, perhaps in Africa. Nevertheless we are assured, without knowing anything in detail about either the Baganda or the country of Uganda, that if the

[handwritten: Don't read own reactions into Kant.]

proposition be true, "All the Baganda are natives of Uganda", it necessarily follows, as a matter of logical implication and consistency, that at least some of the natives of Uganda are Baganda, and that there are no Baganda who are not natives of Uganda. The implications of the logical formula "All S is P" apply to "Baganda", "natives of Uganda" and any other content that could possibly be given to S and P.

Is it possible to find similar formulæ in Ethics,—principles that must apply to all possible cases that might ever arise, so that it would not be necessary to consider details or consequences or anything else besides the bare form of the action so as to bring it under the formal principle? Ethical Formalism answers this question affirmatively. It is a kind of Intuitionism, because the formal principles adopted are believed to be self-evident intuitively, in the same way that the axiomatic principles of mathematics and logic are self-evident; not that every child and savage knows them, but that every one with sufficient intelligence to understand them will be infallibly convinced of their truth, once his attention has been called to them.

The most successful as well as the most famous attempt to construct a system of Formal Ethics was made by Immanuel Kant. It will be impossible to consider all aspects of his system of moral philosophy, and attention will be centered on those connected in a general way with its formalism. In exposition the author will freely advance his own interpretations and illustrations of what he believes to be Kant's meaning on doubtful points. He will offer criticisms of Kant as he proceeds, in the endeavor to extract what he believes to be the points of truth in Kantian ethics. The reader is advised to be critical of the author's evaluations at every point, but to make sure that he understands what the author means before he decides whether or not to agree with him.

II. The Categorical Imperative:—First Formulation

"No thing," says Kant, "can possibly be conceived in the world, or even out of it, which can be called good without quali-

To fit mould of transcendentalism, he had to make his ethics one of duty.

fication, except a Good Will" (or, as we should say, a good character).[1] Intelligence and perseverance are often good, but not necessarily so; they may be employed in some villainous undertaking. Gifts of fortune, like power, riches, honor, and even health and happiness, may inspire pride and presumption, and therefore not be good. Only a good will can be absolutely good, without qualification. Even if through misfortune and unfavorable circumstances, this will should be wholly unable to accomplish its purposes, although it summoned all the means in its power, still like a jewel, it would shine by its own light as a thing which has its whole value in itself. (We commend the goodness of a man who does his best, with all the means in his power, to accomplish a worthy end. Even if he completely fails, we say that he is a good man and has done his duty. And we respect his character and pronounce it of intrinsic value.)

The good will can be known to be good by the principle on which it acts. This principle, the "*moral law*", is self-evident when it is understood. It is *Categorical*, since it holds absolutely and without qualification. It is an *Imperative*, since it is a command that ought to be obeyed. The Categorical Imperative is *rational*, since it is apprehended intuitively by the reason and is logically consistent. It is *a priori*, since it can be known in advance to apply to every possible problem that may arise in experience. $7+5=12$; this formula is known *a priori*; it is universal and necessary; whenever seven objects are added to five objects the sum will always be twelve. The moral law is similarly *a priori;* it indicates what *ought* to be done under all circumstances. Other imperatives are *hypothetical, empirical*, and *a posteriori*, since they apply only conditionally and are known only posterior to similar experiences that have taken place in the past. To do one's duty is a categorical imperative that is rational and *a priori;* one ought to do one's duty under all circumstances whatsoever; this is intuitively evident to the reason; it is known to be true in advance of any specific situation that may ever come up. On the contrary, what particular kinds of food ought to be eaten, because they taste good and afford pleasure, are instances of imperatives that can only be known as an outcome of previous experience and so are empirical and *a posteriori*. Such imperatives are hypothetical because there is no need of eating them unless one desires the pleasure that they afford; there is no moral obligation of any kind in the matter.

Kant states the Categorical Imperative in three different ways that need to be distinguished here. The first is this: "*Act only on that maxim whereby thou canst at the same time will that it should become a Universal Law of Nature.*" (In other words, you should always act on principles that you would be willing should govern the principles of every one else in all places and on all occasions.) Kant gives four illustrations of violations of this principle. (1) A man driven to despair by successive misfortunes is tempted to commit suicide. The Categorical Imperative makes it clear that it will be wrong for him to take his own life, because he cannot consistently will it to be a universal law of nature that everybody should commit suicide; if that were the case there would soon be no person left to commit suicide. That would be bad; and a man cannot, in the light of this Imperative do himself what he sees that it would be wrong for every one else to do. (2) A man in desperate financial circumstances is tempted to borrow money, which he knows he can only do by promising to repay it in a definite time that will be impossible. However, it could not become a universal law of nature for everybody to attempt to borrow money with false promises; because nobody would ever lend money under such conditions. Such a law would be self-contradictory and could not become universal. A few people can borrow money fraudulently only because most people are honest and act in good faith.

His other two illustrations of wrongdoing Kant himself concedes are not wholly self-contradictory. (3) A man has great natural talents which, if cultivated, would render him a useful man in many ways. He is tempted not to cultivate them, however, because he is lazy. Kant concedes that a society could indeed exist (like that of the natives of the South Sea Islands) where everybody lived in idleness. But as a rational being, Kant says, a man could not will that everybody should live in that way. It is wrong for a man to choose for himself a manner of living that he would condemn in others, and could not desire to become a universal practice. (4) A man in prosperity sees others about him in wretchedness whom he could easily assist, but he declines to do so. Kant says that his action is wrong; for while the human race could continue if nobody ever helped anybody else, Kant thinks that no rational man would wish to live in such a society, because he knows that he may some time in his own turn need the help of others.

In criticism of Kant, it is obvious that the latter two illustrations are not perfect examples of purely formal logical consistency. The forbidden acts could theoretically become universal laws of nature. We would not wish them to become such, however, because they conflict with the kind of society that we really want. While not formally inconsistent, these acts are inconsistent with our moral tradition and ideals, with the sort of persons that we wish others to be, and that therefore we ought to strive to be ourselves.

The first two illustrations might possibly come under the test of formal logical consistency. It is obvious that if every person committed suicide, presently there would be no persons left to do so, and that if everybody attempted to borrow money under false representations no one would ever lend money to another person. Still, we may well ask Kant whether this is really the reason why suicide and fraudulent borrowing are wrong. Suppose a man were a thorough pessimist, and believed that it would be much better that all human beings should perish. Would it not be right for him to take his own life after he had persuaded as many other persons as he could to do likewise? Such a man could wish suicide to become a universal practice. And if a person were to become thoroughly convinced that all private property is the result of fraud and injustice, and that the world would be better off without it, ought he not to borrow money fraudulently, and do everything else in his power to overthrow the financial system? Such a person would be acting on a principle that, if it were to become a universal practice, would render loans impossible. The truth of the matter seems to be, that those who commit either of these sins do not really desire that life or credit should become extinct. That is why their actions are wrong; they are inconsistent with the continuance of a social order which they know to be good. They wish to indulge themselves in ways from which they wish other persons to refrain. The cheat wants other men to be honest in order that he can exploit them without being taken advantage of in his own turn. The suicide wishes other people to live and to work for the further advancement of humanity while he shirks his own part of the common task. Fraud and suicide, in other words, are wrong, but not because they are inconsistent with a formal ethical principle like the laws of logic and mathematics. They are wrong because they are inconsistent with our ideals of life.

To generalize. Kant in this first formulation of the Categorical Imperative has not succeeded in discovering a purely formal law that will apply to all human conduct *a priori*, independent of all experience and consideration of consequences. What he has chiefly done is to establish two important principles. (1) We ought always to act in a manner harmonious with our ideal of what human society should become. (2) As social and rational beings we should judge ourselves and other persons impartially; it is wrong for us to do what it would not be right for other persons to do under similar circumstances. However, our ideals of human society are necessarily based on an intelligent criticism of the moral tradition, and so are the result of human experience, that of others and of ourselves. These two principles are neither formal nor *a priori*. In considering whether what we would like to do would be right for others to do also under the same circumstances, we must take all aspects of the situation into account, including possible consequences. To do this is not formalism.

III. Humanity as an End in Itself

Kant's second formulation of the Categorical Imperative is: *"So act as to treat humanity, whether in thine own person or in that of any other, in every case as an end and never as mere means."* (In other words, always respect yourself and other people.) The same four illustrations of forbidden acts are employed. To commit suicide would be inconsistent with the ideal of humanity as an end in itself. It would be treating one's own self, not as of intrinsic value, but as a thing, a mere means of selfish enjoyment. So, when one's life is likely to afford one more misery than pleasure, and to be negative from the standpoint of personal enjoyment, one is tempted to do away with it, and not to respect one's own moral personality. To make lying promises to a creditor is to use him as a mere means to one's own profit, and not to respect him as a person with moral rights equal to one's own. To refuse to develop oneself is to lack self-respect; it is to treat one's own person as a mere means to idle enjoyment; it is to ignore every man's vocation to realize the best that is within him. To refuse to assist others is to lack respect for them, and not do what one can to promote their welfare.

In the application of the second version of the Categorical Imperative to these illustrations, it is hard to see how Kant supposed that he had discovered a purely formal law of logical consistency, by which moral judgments can proceed like those of mathematics. $7 \times 9 = 63$ always; any attempt to make the product 62 or 64 is formally inconsistent with the numbers employed, and the rules of multiplication. It is unnecessary to inquire to what objects 7 and 9 refer; the answer in every case is *a priori*, universal, and necessary. There certainly is nothing analogous in Kant's illustrations. In the case of each of them the test is not logical consistency. On the contrary the criterion is consistency with the moral ideal as we have come to recognize it and act upon it,—an ideal that includes respect for humanity as an end in itself, and never subordinates one's own personality or that of any other human being to petty ends out of harmony with the highest good of self and society.

With the purely formal element eliminated, and respect for personality emphasized, it is possible to accept Kant's second formulation of the Categorical Imperative. In this modified form it is one of the most fruitful that has ever been advanced in ethics. It is capable of endless illustration. The college student, the business and professional man and woman, the husband, wife, parent,—each may properly ask himself or herself: "Am I respecting my own personality and making the most of it? Or am I allowing myself through idleness, selfish enjoyment, and irrelevant distractions to become less of a real person than I owe it to myself and those dearest to me to become? Am I respecting the personalities of those about me, contributing to their happiness when I can, and making it easier for them to make the best of their lives? Or am I selfishly exploiting those about me for my own advantage and at their real cost? Am I treating them as mere means, or as ends in themselves?"

The principle has been applied since Kant's time to many social problems. Slavery was wrong, because the slave was exploited for the profit of others, and he was not treated as an end in himself. Prostitution is wrong; because in it a woman is treated as a mere means to man's pleasure at the cost of the degradation of her own personality. The fact that she consents to her own degradation only signifies that she also violates the moral law, since she does not respect her own personality. Free love is wrong; because the man and woman in such a relation do not truly respect themselves, and they refuse to develop their own characters in a manner best in the long run for themselves and for society. Drinking and gambling are wrong for similar reasons. Mere idleness in college, or absorption in extra-curricular activities to the extent that the student cannot get a real liberal or professional education, are cases of lack of self-respect.

Employers who refuse to give workingmen fair wages, reasonable hours, protection so far as practicable from accidents while at work, and some voice in the direction of the industry at the point where it most affects them personally, are treating their men as means to their own profit, and not as ends in themselves. Workingmen who idle when the foreman is not looking, waste materials, break their contracts, and in other ways obstruct rather than coöperate in making production efficient, are regarding their employers as mere means to their own profit, and do not accord the respect and thoughtful consideration morally due them.

In political relationships, a corrupt or time serving politician fails to respect himself and the community. In the government of colonies, and the guardianship of backward races, the moral issue always is: Are the subject peoples respected, treated as ends in themselves, given favorable opportunities to develop their own capacities? Or are they being treated as mere means, mere sources of revenue to outside investors?

Two corollaries of the principle we have been considering may be mentioned in this connection. First, as Kant pointed out, it is our duty to promote the happiness of others, not to try directly to improve their characters. Character must be a development from within, sought by the person himself, and not something imposed upon him from without. Ignoring character and motives, legislation must be confined to encouraging actions that are desirable, and to discouraging actions that are undesirable, in their externally observable effects. Laws can forbid murder and theft for instance, and they can require children to be sent to school. But laws cannot make people benevolent and honest in their motives and inward characters; laws cannot make people virtuous. It is not the business of a college faculty to try to make the students good, nor of an employer to make his workmen good, nor of a mother country to make its colonists good. Nor is it the business of an individual to go about trying to make other people good. Did you ever enjoy having some one come to you and say that he is "going to do good to you"? Do you enjoy having people, for that matter, try to be very tactful with you?   On the other hand, we can endeavor to make external conditions surrounding other persons favorable to moral welfare.   College trustees and faculties should do what they can to make the campus and its surroundings morally wholesome and intellectually stimulating.   Employers should be concerned about the living and working conditions of their men.   Imperial governments should prevent traffic in spirits and opium in backward countries subject to them; they should promote sanitation, and afford educational facilities.   In our own country, there is much difference of opinion as to where the line of legitimate governmental activity should stop, how far it is possible to try to regulate external conditions so as to make them favorable for the good life without actually attempting to "make people good by law".[2]

The other corollary is, that while a person should never treat other persons *merely* as means, it is morally right and proper that he should profit in his relations with them, provided it is not at their expense.   Two friends ought to benefit by their mutual relationship.   A husband and wife should both gain by their marriage, and become better persons in consequence of it.   A fair commercial transaction is an economic benefit to both buyer and seller.   If employers pay just wages and otherwise respect the personalities of their men, it is right for them to make profits in their business.   If merchants and investors in a mother country are making fortunes and laboring men are getting employment as a result of colonial undertakings, while the people in the colony are also benefiting by the development of their own country, there is no violation of this principle. Profiting is not necessarily profiteering; only the latter is a violation of the categorical imperative.

IV. Autonomy and the Kingdom of Ends

A sublime conception in Kant's ethics that follows as a corollary from his conception of humanity as an end in itself is his doctrine of *Autonomy*.   A person who acts in conformity with the Categorical Imperative is ethically free, since the law that he obeys is a law of his own highest nature as a rational being. *He gives himself the law that he obeys.* This is stated by Kant in a formalistic manner, connected with his system as a whole, into which it will be impossible to enter here. Divorced from the formalism, however, it can readily be seen that since the moral law implies self-respect and respect for others, and since man is a being who can only realize himself in a social life in coöperation with his fellows, this law is really of his own making. No one who actually knows what he wants desires to commit suicide or fraud or be idle or ungenerous, or in other ways to refuse to realize himself and to lead a socially useful life. Ethical freedom can be found, and only found, in a good life.

Connected with this is Kant's third formulation of the Categorical Imperative: *"Act according to the maxims of a merely possible kingdom of ends"*. A "kingdom of ends" would be a society in which every one were at the same time both sovereign and subject. If we could conceive of a society in which every one always acted in a rational way, in accordance with the Categorical Imperative, every one would act in harmony with every one else. The law would be both willed and obeyed by each and all. Kant thought of this in terms of formal logical consistency; if everybody reasoned logically all would come to the same conclusions. (Just as in a schoolroom where every pupil did his sums correctly all would get the same answers, so in a society where all thought rationally, all would pronounce the same moral judgments.) As we have seen, the moral law cannot be regarded in this way, as a formal logical principle from which conclusions can be abstractly deduced to cover every possible situation. On the contrary, we have seen that Kant's categorical imperative must be revised to mean, that every action should be done in accordance with our conception of the highest good of individuals, and the common good of society. And this conception becomes modified in the course of moral evolution. However, with this revision, the third formulation of the Categorical Imperative can also be accepted. The personal and social ideal implies that all of any person's actions will be in harmony and coöperation with those of all other persons for the common good. Since this common good is the good of all, both as individuals and collectively, every one in so acting would in an ideal society be both sovereign and subject.

We have no such ideal society to-day, but to approximate it is the effort of Citizenship. Kant conceived what he called a "republican" form of government to be the best. Its laws are theoretically, at least, supposed to be for the common good. No individual and no class of individuals should seek or be permitted to benefit at the expense of any other group; all should be treated as ends in themselves. Such ideals are not likely to be realized in a pure democracy, which latter would be subject to gusts of popular passion. Conditions would be more favorable in a "republican" form of government, by which Kant meant a representative system. In such a representative system citizens would not legislate for themselves, but they would elect representatives at times and under conditions that favored deliberation. Executive, legislative, and judicial functions would be carefully separated and yet coordinated; through them the deliberate and hence rational will of the people would be expressed.

Kant hoped that ultimately—although he realized that this could only come to pass in the distant future—all the nations of the world will be brought into agreement, and settle their disputes peacefully and lawfully, in accordance with reason and justice; thus wars will cease and an era of permanent peace will at last arrive. In this way a "kingdom of ends" will no longer be a mere ideal, but actual reality; and when it comes, every man will be citizen and sovereign in the free commonwealth of mankind. In the meantime, in all our personal and social relationships, we should remember that respect for self and for others implies a spirit of reason, mutual understanding and good will, and that to the extent that we realize these, our personal freedom and sovereignty—our autonomy—will be

attained.[3] (In this and the preceding paragraph the thought
of Kant has been stated in more modern language, but the
author does not believe that he has read into it more than
Kant really intended. Kant's conceptions seem greatly in
harmony with our American constitution and ideals—themselves products of the liberal political thought of the time in
which Kant was writing,—the latter portion of the eighteenth
century.)

V. THE COMPLETE GOOD

The *supreme* good, according to Kant, is doing one's duty,
fulfillment of the Categorical Imperative, a life of virtue. The
complete good, in addition to virtue, includes *happiness*, conceived by him in hedonistic terms. The only acts that have
moral worth are those done in accordance with the moral law—
i.e., the Categorical Imperative—and done from a sense of
duty—*i.e.*, done because they are in accordance with the moral
law and not from other motives. Kant's implication seems to
be, although he never definitely seems to say so, that where no
moral situation is involved, it would not be wrong to act from
other motives, such as desire for pleasure. But such actions
would have no "moral worth"; that is, they would not be moral
in the narrower sense, they would be unmoral. Yet those who
are virtuous and carry out the moral law *ought* to be happy,—
a consideration from which Kant drew theological arguments for
belief in God and immortality. With theological considerations we are not concerned at this point; but it is worthy of
note that for Kant virtue is not the whole good of man, though
it is the most important part of it; the complete good includes
happiness also.

Kant makes the complete good too narrow, in restricting it
to virtue and happiness. The complete good of man includes
intellectual, æsthetic, and religious values that do not in all
respects readily come under these heads. If we call these values
unmoral, we confine the scope of ethics too closely. Ethics
ought to take account of all the values that constitute portions of

the well rounded life that every one should seek to realize. To give each value its due attention in a well ordered life is certainly a task that all ought to attempt; it would seem that this is a moral obligation. Nevertheless it is true that in attacking many moral problems it is sufficient to take into account the probable effects of acts on human character and human happiness. In Part IV we shall frequently find this to be true, in dealing with current domestic, political, and economic problems.

VI. FURTHER CRITICISMS

Kant confines virtue to obedience to the moral law from a sense of duty. As we saw in Chapter IX, a virtue is a sentiment that makes for individual and social good and is coördinated with other sentiments in a harmonious character. It follows that any act prompted by one of the virtues is a moral act, whether done from a sense of duty or not. Consciousness of duty only arises in the presence of conflicting impulses,—desires in antagonism to virtuous action as well as in its favor. One in such circumstances feels it his duty to do what is right, and his self-regarding sentiment—his self-respect—is on the side of virtue. As character becomes established, it is easier to act in accordance with the virtues, and moral conflicts involving the sense of duty become rarer. Kant fails to realize this because of his imperfect psychology. He supposes that all human inclinations, with the single exception of respect for the moral law, are desires for pleasure. Consequently he seems unable to conceive of a human being performing an action in accordance with the moral law without feeling contrary inclinations in the direction of personal pleasure. To be sure, he mentions the notion of a *holy* will, that would always act in accordance with the moral law, with no opposing inclinations to overcome; but only God has such a will apparently. That men sometimes act rightly because their virtues so impel them, and that they feel pleasure in so doing, he does not seem to recognize. Acts of courage, generosity, loyalty, love, and justice done joyfully and with no thought of duty would at best on Kantian principles have to be called actions without moral worth (*i.e.*, unmoral), since they are not done from regard for duty.

In this connection we can give Kant credit for emphasizing one important truth. Acts performed from selfish motives certainly do not have equal moral worth with acts done simply because they are right. Kant is justified in making virtue the supreme good, and in not attributing the highest moral worth to actions prompted by other than virtuous motives, although to the external observer—as in the case of the merchant who gives honest measure merely as a matter of good policy—the action appears the same as if it had been done from motives of integrity as a good in itself. But Kant is wrong in attaching to such actions no moral worth whatever.

This brings us to another criticism of Kant's ethics. His extreme formalism leads him to affirm, even more emphatically than most other Intuitionists, that in making moral decisions consequences need not and should not be taken into account. All that is necessary is to ask whether an action could become a universal law of nature; if so, it should be done, and not otherwise. Perhaps it has become sufficiently clear that this test of formal consistency is not sufficient. Kant himself does not adhere to it completely in some of his own illustrations, as we have seen. He could not have defended his own bachelor life on this principle; for if all mankind, like himself, were celibates, there would soon be no one left to practice celibacy. It is hard to see how he could have defended the economic division of labor.

He was occasionally driven into rather tight corners in his defense of his formalism. For instance, a critic urged that if a would be murderer came to a man's house and asked if the man whom he was pursuing had entered the house, it would be a duty to lie to him in the endeavor to save a human life. Kant had to reply that veracity is a universal law to which there can be no exceptions whatever, since if telling lies whenever convenient became a universal practice, no one could ever tell them successfully.[4] Again, Kant's doctrine of formal consistency forced him to adopt without qualification the vindictive theory of the punishment of criminals, and to reject the reformatory and deterrent theories. A criminal should be punished in retaliation for his wrongful act; it is a universal law of nature that the evil deed ought to be made to rebound upon the doer. So if a people dwelling on an island should resolve to disperse and scatter to all parts of the world, it would be their duty first to execute any murderer among them that had received the death sentence.[5]

But perhaps enough has been said to make it clear that the rightfulness and wrongfulness of actions cannot be decided purely from a formal principle like the categorical imperative, without regard for consequences. On the contrary, possible consequences need to be considered,—how the act will affect the character, happiness, and other values of all concerned, whether the effects of it will further or hamper the advance of the good life in individuals and in humanity. Consequences can be calculated only in the light of past experience. And if consequences are taken into account, no rule can be formulated— other than abstract rules like the three axioms of Sidgwick— that does not have at least a few exceptions. If we say that murder is always wrong, this is only because we have already defined murder so as to leave out the cases in which it is deemed right to take life (in self-defense, warfare, execution of murderers, etc.). Unless we were to define lying so as to exclude justifiable cases of making false statements with intention to deceive (among which most of us would include the case denied by Kant) we could not say that lying is always wrong.[6]

VII. Conclusions

Formalism, as found in Kantian ethics, is an impossible position. No moral principle can be devised that will apply formally and universally to all situations that may ever arise, without regard to attending circumstances and consequences. No such principle can be discovered intuitively, or in any other way, that will carry us much further than Sidgwick's axioms, and these apply chiefly to the purely mathematical or quantitative side of ethics. What is true of Kantian ethics would be found to hold of other formalistic systems, none of which is so meritorious on the whole as Kant's. [7]

On the other hand, the Kantian ethical system is fruitful in moral insights, once formalism has been removed from it. The three versions of the Categorical Imperative should be revised to mean consistency with, and respect for, a high ideal of personal and social life. They then become richly suggestive, and capable of application in almost an infinite number of ways. We should do only what we can see would be right for others to do in similar situations. We must be impartial in judging ourselves and others. We must respect humanity as an end in itself, wherever we find it, in our own selves and in the humblest as well as the most exalted of our fellow human beings. We should think of morality as a law of our own making, the expression of our own wills when rational and intelligent.

We should think of an ideal society as a commonwealth of wills all working for a common good, so that every one would become both sovereign and subject. This ideal of society we should try to realize in our families and local groups, and the nation as a whole. We should look forward to the time when it can receive international application, and we should now take what steps we can in that direction.

We should endeavor to promote the happiness of others, and to surround them with favorable environments in which they will of their own free choice seek the good life. The complete good includes as its chief constituents character and happiness, as Kant saw. It also includes other elements not easily reducible in all respects to these two,—among which are some aspects of intellectual, æsthetic, and religious values. This complete good we should seek in our own lives. We should work for an improved social order, in which the complete good will be available to all who are willing to make earnest effort to attain it for themselves.

REFERENCES

I. Kant, *Fundamental Principles of the Metaphysics of Morals*, and *Critical Examination of Practical Reason*. (Both translated by T. K. Abbott in *Kant's Theory of Ethics*.)

H. Rashdall, *Theory of Good and Evil*, Book I, chap. V.

* W. Fite, *An Introductory Study of Ethics*, chap. X.

* J. Dewey and J. H. Tufts, *Ethics*, pp. 241–246; 309–317.

* W. G. Everett, *Moral Values*, chap. II.

* F. Paulsen, *System of Ethics* (trans. by Thilly), pp. 194–203; 350–363.

* Durant Drake, *Problems of Conduct*, chap. IX.

E. Caird, *Critical Philosophy of Kant*, Book II, especially chaps. II, VI, VII.

F. H. Bradley, *Ethical Studies*, Essay IV.

J. Seth, *A Study of Ethical Principles*, pp. 163–180.

A. K. Rogers, *Theory of Ethics*, pp. 60–68. *Morals in Review*, pp. 342–357.

F. Paulsen, *Immanuel Kant* (trans.), pp. 296–342.

W. K. Wright, *Ethical Significance of Feeling, Pleasure and Happiness in Modern Non-Hedonistic Systems*, pp. 57–71.

CHAPTER XIII

UTILITARIANISM

I. ETHICAL HEDONISM

If it were possible to find some universal quantitative standard, with which all moral actions could be compared, moral
judgments could be rendered with accuracy and precision.
Ethics could become a special science, as reliable on its theoretical side as mathematics and in its applications as engineering. Ethical hedonists believe that they have discovered
such a standard. "Good" is pleasure, "bad" is unpleasantness.
Whenever it is possible to make a choice between different
courses of action, the one should be chosen which will produce
most pleasure and least unpleasantness. (Writers on this
subject generally speak of "pain" instead of unpleasantness
because of their ignorance of psychology; unpleasantness is
really what they mean. See page 261 above.) A life in which
nothing but pleasure were experienced, and unpleasantness and
pain entirely absent, would be one of perfect "happiness"; for
hedonists differ from other schools in using pleasure and happiness as synonymous terms. (Since, as the author believes,
the words "happiness" and "pleasure" are *not* synonymous
terms, he has in this chapter written "happiness" in quotation
marks wherever it is employed in accordance with hedonistic
usage, as synonymous with pleasure.)

Ethical hedonists during the last hundred years have ordinarily been Utilitarians. The good to be promoted is the
universal pleasure (or "happiness") of mankind. The "happiness" of each individual should count equally with that of
every other one. Any moral problem thus becomes quite simple,
theoretically. The action that will add most to the aggregate
of "happiness" experienced by mankind, or will most diminish

317

the total "unhappiness" and misery in the world is right; the contrary action is wrong. Therefore, what we need to do is to consider the consequences of possible actions, and to determine how far they will be pleasant or unpleasant.

Bentham believed that all pleasures differ only *quantitatively;* between two pleasures or "pains" (states of unpleasantness) we need only to compare their intensity and duration.[1] Suppose, of two possible courses of action, each could have several pleasant and unpleasant effects, and we could represent the pleasant effects by positive numbers and the unpleasant ones by negative numbers, and compare the algebraic sums. We should then know which to prefer. For instance, studying to-morrow's ethics lesson might be calculated to have the pleasant effects of a good recitation, of a slight step in the attainment of a liberal education, and of following the wishes of one's parents, to which we might assign, say, the positive hedonic values of 2, 5, and 4. It would have the unpleasant consequences of a dry and stupid evening, and annoyance at a pleasure missed; these might be evaluated at -5 and -3. The total hedonic value would therefore be 3. Compared with this, the total hedonic value of going to the movies, instead of studying, might be found to be -2, since in such calculations future as well as present pleasures and pains (unpleasantnesses) are to be counted as of equal value.[2] Bentham's famous lines give the principle:

> *Intense, long, certain, speedy, fruitful, pure,*
> Such marks in *pleasures* and in *pains* endure.
> Such pleasures seek, if *private* be thy end;
> If it be *public*, wide let them extend.
> Such *pains* avoid, whichever be thy view;
> If pains *must* come, let them *extend* to few.

The question arises whether it is possible to measure all pleasures quantitatively. Is the pleasure of reading a good book or of performing a generous action simply more or less of the same kind of experience as that of eating a well cooked and juicy beefsteak when one is hungry? Or do such experiences differ in *quality?* John Stuart Mill, in opposition to Bentham, believed that pleasures differ *qualitatively*. We infinitely prefer some pleasures to others, because there is no basis of comparison between them. Only a fool or a pig could think otherwise. We all prefer the intellectual discontent of a Socrates to the satisfactions of the fool and the pig. And if the latter do otherwise, it is only because they know no better. The wise man knows his own pleasures as well as those of the ignorant and the vulgar; the latter know only their own side of the case.[3]

In criticism of Mill, it may be asked, if pleasures can be measured quantitatively, just what is the basis of measurement? It hardly seems possible to take seriously attempts to represent by algebraic sums different amounts of pleasure and unpleasantness. If there really were any accurate scientific method of measurement, by which different amounts of pleasure could be calculated and compared with one another, ethical hedonism would receive more serious consideration than it now does, although there would remain other difficulties to be removed before ethics could become an exact science like engineering. If pleasures cannot be measured quantitatively, because they differ in quality, how then, are they to be compared? Moreover, would it not be quite impossible both for want of time and knowledge, to calculate all the pleasant and unpleasant consequences of every possible course of action that might be pursued?

In reply to such objections, the Utilitarian is obliged to confess that he cannot make ethics so accurate a science as mathematics or engineering. He has to be guided on ordinary occasions by the general rules formulated out of his own experience and that of others through past ages. The ordinary judgments of the moral tradition have been tested many times, and in general they are reliable. Where certainty cannot be known, one can decide according to probabilities. We should on every occasion select the act whose presumption of "happiness" is a maximum; just as we should, if we were seeking the maximum amount of money or soap or other commodities in a commercial transaction. The code of the banker is "to make all the money possible"; likewise the Utilitarian is guided by the principle, "make all the happiness possible". It might be hard to calculate the exact amount of unpleasantness involved in cutting off one's leg; but it would be easy to decide that there would be less unpleasantness if an anæsthetic were used. It would promote more "happiness" in the end to instruct school children in the rules of health, and to imbue them with healthful habits than not to do so.[4]

It thus becomes evident that, once Formalism is rejected,—as it must be—there is no possibility in our present state of knowledge of making ethics an exact science. All teleologists, both Utilitarians and Eudæmonists, are obliged to trust to observation and experience in judging of the possible consequences of actions, as well as deciding what course is the more likely to promote the end desired. The issue between Utilitarian and Eudæmonist therefore becomes this:—can all actions be judged better by the amount of pleasure that attends them than in any other way? The answer obviously will be in favor of the Utilitarian, if he can prove either that all values are different amounts of pleasure and nothing else, or that the amount of pleasure is the best available gauge of the amount of value in any course of action.

II. Egoistic Hedonism

Utilitarians have often attempted to prove their own position by a preliminary evaluation of Egoistic Hedonism. The latter doctrine is now rarely if ever held by moral philosophers, but Utilitarians think that its refutation logically leads to their own position.

Egoistic Hedonism is the ethical doctrine that everybody should seek the greatest amount of pleasure for himself, regardless of other persons. The argument for this position would presumably be *psychological hedonism*. The latter doctrine asserts it to be a fact that every one (at least when cool and reasonable and not carried away by some passion) does desire his own pleasure, and judges and acts solely with reference to it. This fact, that every reasonable person desires his own pleasure, is proof enough that it is desirable. The older Utilitarians conceded the truth of psychological hedonism. But they did not think that the egoistic form of ethical hedonism is a necessary consequence of psychological hedonism. If it could be shown—and they thought it could—that in order to gain his own pleasure or "happiness" a man must seek the greatest "happiness" of the greatest number, then egoism and altruism would coincide. Egoistic Hedonism would be merged in Utilitarianism.

But, as we saw in Chapter X, psychological hedonism is not true. Pleasure and freedom from unpleasantness are not the ends to which we are usually prompted by our desires and impulses. On the contrary, pleasure is the affective tone that accompanies successful effort, and unpleasantness is the affective tone of thwarted or obstructed effort. If we did not already desire objects and so strive to attain them, we should make no efforts at all, and could not experience the pleasures and unpleasantnesses that constitute good and evil according to ethical hedonism. Therefore all the attempts of the older Utilitarians to prove that good and pleasant are identical because men always desire pleasure are fallacious. Pleasure is neither the only, nor is it the chief, object of desire. However, opponents of Utilitarianism have been mistaken in supposing that they can completely dispose of Utilitarianism by refuting psychological hedonism. Although pleasure is not the sole object of desire, it might still be true that pleasure and the absence of unpleasantness affords the most satisfactory standard or criterion of goodness and obligation.[5] It might be true that the goodness and hence moral desirability of objects could be calculated by the amount of pleasure that their attainment brings.

The older Utilitarians were right in believing that a truly enlightened egoism leads to recognition of the common good. It was difficult for them to show this convincingly, however, starting as they did with psychological hedonism as the first step in the argument. Bentham enumerated four *sanctions* that impel men, desirous of pleasure, to act morally. The *physical* sanction makes it to men's personal interest to keep themselves in bodily health and intellectual vigor; most pleasure and least unpleasantness come from obeying this sanction, and cultivating the virtue of temperance. The *political* sanction makes men obey the laws, and the *moral* (or, as we might say to-day, the *social*) sanction leads people to seek the good side of public opinion. To conform to these sanctions leads to pleasant consequences, and to disregard them leads to unpleasant ones. The *religious* sanction impels men, in view of prospective divine rewards and punishments, to adopt courses of action that will earn for them divine favor. Spencer, in the light of evolutionary considerations, was able to present a stronger though more involved argument for the reconciliation of egoism and altruism.[6]

The resolution of an enlightened egoism in the social good becomes clearer in view of the social nature of man, which requires the good will of his fellows for the realization of his own capacities. The really successful man in any vocation or avocation is the one who is of most service. And such a man, other circumstances equal, will be the one who gains most pleasure and leads the happiest life. This is not a Utilitarian way of putting the argument, but it seems to the writer at least, that if psychological hedonism be rejected, and if the end of man be viewed as self-realization, it can be shown that since self-realization implies social service, the successfully realized life will be likely to be the happiest one. Seek first the virtues and happiness will be added unto you.

III. Other Utilitarian Arguments

The remaining Utilitarian arguments are for the most part intuitive or pragmatic. It is self-evident that the pleasant is the good and the unpleasant is the bad; this is intuitive. It is a pragmatic argument to urge that some actions are called good because they afford men pleasure, and others are called bad, because they render men miserable. This is the reason why honesty and truth telling are right, for they cause pleasure in the long run. If people received pleasure by being told lies and having their purses stolen from them, such conduct would be right; it is because the contrary is true that it is wrong. Pragmatic reasoning of this type confirms the intuition that the pleasant is the good and the unpleasant is the bad. If other moral philosophers say that the various virtues are good, the Utilitarian heartily agrees, and he thinks that he can explain pragmatically why they are good. Courage, temperance, and the other virtues, he claims, are habits that usually increase "happiness" and diminish misery. That is precisely why they are virtues. Nobody would call them virtues otherwise. In most cases the actions to which these virtues prompt are good from a Utilitarian standpoint. Therefore people have very properly been taught to cultivate these virtues. In the course of time, however, these virtues have become mistaken for ends in themselves instead of the means for the promotion of "happiness" that they really are; just as the miser comes to love gold for its own sake in place of the uses to which it can be put.

The reply usually given to the Utilitarian's explanation of the virtues is intuitional. Courage, temperance, wisdom, justice, and self-respect are intuitions perceived to be intrinsically good. We esteem them on their own account, and not merely because they produce happiness. If the Utilitarian rejoins that his critic is naïve, since he does not see that they are mere habits like the miser's, with only instrumental value, the critic can only respond that it is the seeming sophistication of the Utilitarian that really is naïve. With psychological hedonism excluded, the Utilitarian can only reiterate that to him it seems axiomatic that pleasure is good and good is pleasure, and that both are identical with "happiness". All other values, he feels confident, he can reduce to this equation. But this identification of good and pleasure, the critic urges, does not seem axiomatic to mankind generally.

Most philosophers, like most people who are not philosophers, have failed to become converts to Utilitarianism. Goodness and pleasure are not synonymous terms, so most people think. And happiness is not identical with pleasure. A happy life would not necessarily be the life of most intense and long continued pleasures, and fewest unpleasantnesses. A life of much struggle, anxiety, and many disappointments, in which great force of character is manifested, would be judged by many to be happier, and by most to be better, than a life of unending pleasures. For instance, the lives of Abraham Lincoln and Robert E. Lee would be agreed by all to have been good lives. Most would not, however, consider them happy lives. Yet all, probably, would pronounce such lives morally preferable to a life of as nearly unalloyed pleasures as an individual could experience. In reply, the Utilitarian might possibly urge that the life of Lincoln was good, not for its own sake since it was not "happy", but because it rendered great services to mankind; he freed the slaves and saved the Union. The life of such a man is morally preferable to a life of unalloyed pleasure because it does more to increase the total bulk of "happiness" in the world and to diminish the total bulk of unpleasantness.

But what of Lee? Lee was on the wrong side; he failed; and it is good that he did fail. Yet we praise Lee for his sincerity, his courage, his gallantry, his lovableness, and his loyalty to duty and right as he saw them. So we say that Lee was one of the finest exemplars of manhood America has ever produced. Is the Utilitarian's explanation convincing, if he says that we praise the virtues of Lee because such virtues usually bring with them happiness to self and others, although they did not do so in this exceptional instance, in which devotion was directed to a mistaken cause? Can the Utilitarian persuade us that our error in this case is like the miser's, who comes to think of gold as valuable in itself, and not merely for the pleasures that can be gained with it? Is this the reason why we have come to think virtues valuable intrinsically, and not simply for the pleasures that their general practice affords? Can we believe it to be only a matter of expediency and good policy to praise virtues like those of Lee because they usually increase the bulk of human "happiness"? Or could it be said that the æsthetic value of Lee's career affords so much pleasure that the misery that it brought to himself and countless others is less in comparison, and for this reason it should be pronounced good?

In discussing the lives of such men we have to fall back upon introspection, and we shall not be unanimous in our answers. But most of us, it is probably safe to say, will be of the opinion that there was something about the characters of both Lincoln and Lee that we deem intrinsically good, and that we cannot logically reduce to the pleasures that those men personally felt or communicated to other people. Their lives were of instrumental as well as of intrinsic value; and the instrumental value in each case in considerable part has been the moral inspiration that they have afforded others, and by this we mean something different from the total bulk of positive pleasure in the world.

It might be noted in passing, that while Utilitarian writers insist that "happiness" and pleasure are identical terms, or different only in the sense that "happiness" connotes more explicitly the more permanent and extensive pleasures, they often drop "pleasure" from their pages and speak only of "happiness". Now all of us would agree that the promotion of human happiness is a more convincing moral end than the promotion of human pleasure. But is not this just because the word happiness is often used to designate aspects of life other than pleasurable feeling? Does not the word happiness imply the ideal of Eudæmonism—perfected mental and physical well being? Suppose one were to read any Utilitarian classic, like Mill's famous essay on *Utilitarianism*, or a contemporary exposition like Mr. James MacKaye's lucid and closely reasoned *Logic of Conduct*, and to substitute "pleasure" wherever the word "happiness" appears. Would not much of the plausibility and attractiveness of such arguments disappear? [7]

There are other pragmatic arguments in favor of Utilitarian-

ism. The slogans of "the greatest happiness for the greatest
number" and "each to count for one and none for more than
one" have a convincing ring. Bentham and his followers in
using them helped to effect great reforms in the interest of social justice. Such principles were easily understood. Old and
unjust laws favoring privileged classes, with no better argument in their favor than mere use and wont, had to give way
before such a movement. It could clearly be seen in England
that to allow free importation of food, to afford workingmen
living wages and reasonable hours of labor, to abolish slums,
to afford opportunities of education to all, to permit unions to
have the right to organize and carry on peaceful strikes, and
to extend the suffrage, would promote the greatest happiness
of the greatest number of people. Eudæmonistic arguments
would have been more subtle and less convincing to the general
public.

It must be conceded, the author believes, that there is much
force to these pragmatic arguments. The advantage of Utilitarianism, however, on these lines, he thinks is chiefly with
reference to social movements. It seems doubtful whether the
individual will in his own life be so likely to seek high ideals
if he applies Utilitarian standards in the choice of a vocation,
and in other important decisions.[8] He will be liable to think too
highly of immediate and tangible pleasures, and less of the finer
satisfactions that a respect for virtues and for the intellectual,
æsthetic, and religious values as ends in themselves might
afford him. The Utilitarian may reply that this is not the real
meaning of his doctrine, that he is quite willing to concede the
superiority of these higher values, and that they afford the
greatest pleasures in life, once the material necessities have
been provided for. However, we are here considering Utilitarianism practically; it can hardly be gainsaid that the actual
tendency of Utilitarianism has been to fall short of a full appreciation of these higher values.

It would probably be possible to contend that the influence
of Utilitarianism has been in the direction of identifying prog-

ress too much with material and bodily comforts, and to lose sight of the higher life. So long as the masses of the people were without adequate food, clothing, and shelter, and obliged to live and to work in conditions unfavorable to bodily health, "the greatest happiness of the greatest number" was a proper moral maxim. Until these conditions had been remedied, it was not possible to expect the masses to be interested in the higher aspects of the good life. But, at least in America, such unfavorable conditions for the most part no longer exist. On the other hand, we are charged with neglecting the higher cultural interests. Economic activities occupy too much of our thought and attention. Utilitarianism, therefore, does not seem to be pragmatically the best moral philosophy for Americans in the twentieth century.

IV. CONCLUSIONS

Utilitarianism, in making the universal diffusion of pleasure the moral ideal, affords a roughly accurate moral standard, useful for some purposes and on some occasions, but too inaccurate to be universally trustworthy. The reason for this is, that pleasure is not generally the direct aim and object of impulses and desires; in other words it is not itself the good. On the other hand, pleasure is the concomitant of healthy bodily activity and the successful attainment of ends, and unpleasantness of the opposite conditions. So pleasure is an indication of the presence of the good, *i.e.*, of bodily health, and successful attainment of ends, *i.e.*, welfare. This is especially true in the case of bodily and economic activities. The pleasures connected with these are intense and to a considerable extent sensuous. It requires no very nice discrimination to distinguish them and to contrast them with the opposite states of unpleasantness that attend ill health and economic deprivations.

The ordinary follower of Utilitarianism is liable to think of the good chiefly in such terms. To possess in abundance food, clothing, amusements, stocks, bonds, real estate, farms, factories, retail stores, banks, automobiles, yachts, and private railway cars, and to have good health to enjoy them, is to lead a happy and successful life as an individual. To promote the production and consumption of such utilities widely throughout the country, and to make their distribution as general and democratic as possible, is likely to seem to the Utilitarian layman the most commendable social ideal. The classical exponents of Utilitarianism,—Bentham, the Mills, Sidgwick, Spencer, Stephen, and the others—were by no means so narrow in their conception of moral values. But the influence of Utilitarianism has been to put insufficient emphasis on the intellectual, æsthetic and religious values, the intrinsic worth of character, love, friendship, and like goods which are attended by pleasures less tangible and less easily discriminated and evaluated by introspection.

Since, for the Utilitarian, virtues are only good because they are instrumental in the increase of pleasures and diminution of unpleasantnesses, the influence of Utilitarianism is toward more laxity in moral issues than would meet the approval of other schools. Lying is wrong, willful divorce and remarriage is wrong: on such assertions Utilitarians and Eudæmonists are agreed. That there are exceptions to such principles they are also in accord; only the most rigid formalists contend that moral principles can be laid down so as to admit of no exceptions whatever. But Utilitarians seem to other moral philosophers to find exceptions too readily. Since for Utilitarianism lying, marital inconstancy, and killing are only wrong because they tend to diminish "happiness", exceptions ought to be admitted whenever more pleasure will thereby be afforded.

To be sure, in such cases the Utilitarian would not confine himself to a consideration of the persons immediately concerned. He would observe that it is necessary to make general rules, and that law and custom have deterrent effects that promote the general "happiness" in the long run. If exceptions to the duty of veracity became too common, there could be little faith in another person's word. If everybody thought it right to lie whenever in his private opinion it would increase the total bulk of pleasure in the world for him to do so, lies would be extremely common. Nobody would have much confidence in what anybody said. The loss on the whole would exceed occasional benefits in particular instances. Similar considerations would influence the Utilitarian in the other two illustrations. He is fully aware that hard cases make bad law. Nevertheless, he would admit exceptions to such virtues and duties as veracity, the indissolubility of marriage, and the preservation of life, whenever the exceptions, if they became generally recognized, would in his opinion tend to increase rather than diminish the general "happiness". Weakening of respect for virtues would not seem to him an evil, unless it had the effect of diminishing the total amount of pleasure and increasing the total amount of unpleasantness in the world.

The Eudæmonist would be more conservative. Since he admits that no virtue is absolute, he is willing to concede that there are a few rare cases in which a lie is necessary to prevent harm to the virtuous lives of other persons. Similarly, there are cases where prohibition of divorce would lead persons to bitterness of heart and baseness of conduct, and where permission of divorce and remarriage would further the cause of virtue. He would want the laws and customs carefully defined in these instances, however. The Eudæmonist would probably agree with the Utilitarian that there are exceptional cases where it is right to take life. A newborn infant, misshapen and bound to grow up a helpless idiot, who can only be kept alive by the constant care of two attendants, had better be permitted to die. A physician would perhaps be justified in not prolonging with all the means at his command the life of a hopelessly incurable invalid who is in constant and intense suffering. The test that the Eudæmonist would apply in cases like these would be the effects upon the characters of all persons concerned. No less than the Utilitarian, he would insist on the necessity of general rules, and would consider the influence of these rules upon the common good. Both Utilitarian and Eudæmonist would insist that a man cannot be judge in his own case, and that individuals must submit to hardships when making exceptions in their cases would tend to break down morality in general. There would be this difference. The Eudæmonist would think principally of the effect upon the characters of people in general, and only incidentally upon their pleasures, while the Utilitarian would consider pleasures alone.

It is true that in most cases that might arise the moral judgments of Utilitarian and Eudæmonist would agree. The point is, that the Eudæmonist is the more careful of the two to maintain high moral ideals; since he takes character into account, as well as the intellectual, æsthetic, and religious values where they apply, and makes pleasure a subordinate consideration.

All this is another way of saying that the Utilitarian pays scant attention to the motives that prompt men to act. He makes a sharp distinction between the *intention*,—that which a man wills to do, and the *motive*, the desires that impel him to perform the action. A man *intends*, for instance, to represent truthfully the nature of the goods he offers for sale; that is all the Utilitarian asks, in order to determine whether the act is right or wrong. That he intends to be honest merely because honesty is the best policy, and not because of his respect for honesty as a virtue, according to the Utilitarian, has nothing to do with determining the morality of his action, although it has much to do with judgment of his personal character. The Eudæmonist would not be willing to distinguish so sharply as this between agent and action. Motives impel to acts; hence it is of the greatest importance that people act from the right motives. It should be the great concern of moral education to inspire in children love of the right motives. Can this be done if they are left out of account in the formation of moral judgments upon conduct?

Nevertheless a concession should be made to Utilitarianism at this point. We should judge not that we be not judged. We cannot discern the thoughts of men's hearts. In many cases we cannot penetrate with certainty beneath overt acts and the obvious intentions with which they are performed. In law, motives as distinguished from intentions do not ordinarily enter into account, although they do in serious crimes. But in the moral judgments we pass upon ourselves, and in exercising influence upon those with whom we have close personal friendship, we ought to set high value upon such motives as love of the virtues, and of æsthetic, intellectual, and religious values. We cannot praise these too highly.

It is necessary to commend the praiseworthy insistence upon the part of the Utilitarian school that animals should be treated with kindness. The highest good is often defined by this school as the general "happiness" of all sentient beings. This is because animals as well as men experience pleasure, unpleasantness, and pain. Since animals do not have virtues and character, other schools have not called attention so often to their welfare. The Utilitarian, of course, recognizes the justification of vivisection when performed as humanely as possible by experts in scientific research; the consequences are liable to increase general "happiness". And he is not a vegetarian; for the lives of domestic animals used for food are on the whole pleasurable, while their deaths come quickly and are not anticipated. The lives of these animals, apart from their utility to human beings, add to the total amount of pleasure in the world. If they were not eaten for food many of them would not exist at all. The Eudæmonist can fully recognize that the Utilitarian is right in urging humane treatment of animals. He can add another reason for this to those given by Utilitarians: kindness to animals is itself an aspect of the general virtue of benevolence, and cruelty to animals reveals a real defect in the character of the person guilty of it.[9]

Utilitarianism has, as a matter of history, rendered a great service in moral advancement. In order to increase general "happiness" its adherents have helped to remove great injustices. It is impossible reasonably to oppose any reform that will clearly afford greatest "happiness" to the greatest number of people, in order to preserve privileges to a few. And it is difficult to think of clear cases where a public measure whose effect would be to diminish the amount of happiness in the world ought to win support on the ground that it would promote the common good in some other way.[10] While pleasure is a normal concomitant of good living, it is not the sole nor chief constituent of the complete good of mankind. Since it is a constituent, however, and has the advantage of being comparatively simple and recognizable, pleasure can often be used as a rough standard for the measurement of good. In most instances moral judgments rendered in the light of Utilitarian tests will be right. However, the Utilitarian standard is only an approximate and not a perfect test. At times it is likely to prove misleading. It is not a good standard to preach in periods in which bodily and economic necessities are generally accessible, and emphasis should be upon the cultivation of higher moral, æsthetic, intellectual, and religious values. The thoughtful student of ethics will recognize that a more accurate definition of good will have to enumerate other and more important values than pleasure, values whose successful attainment is indeed attended by pleasure, but whose relative worth pleasures do not always accurately gauge.

REFERENCES

* Jeremy Bentham, *Principles of Morals and Legislation.*
* John Stuart Mill, *Utilitarianism.*
* F. Paulsen, *System of Ethics* (tran .), Book II, chap. II.
* J. Dewey and J. H. Tufts, *Ethics,* chaps. XIV, XV.
* F. Thilly, *Introduction to Ethics,* chaps. VI, VIII.
* W. G. Everett, *Moral Values,* chap. V.
* J. S. Mackenzie, *Manual of Ethics,* Book II, chap. IV.
* Warner Fite, *Introductory Study of Ethics,* Part I.
* James MacKaye, *Logic of Conduct. Economy of Happiness.*
* James Seth, *Study of Ethical Principles.*
* Durant Drake, *Problems of Conduct,* chaps. VII, XII.
* G. S. Fullerton, *Handbook of Ethical Theory,* chap. XXV.
  Henry Sidgwick, *Methods of Ethics.*
  Herbert Spencer, *Data of Ethics.*

Leslie Stephen, *Science of Ethics. The Utilitarians.*

Hastings Rashdall, *Theory of Good and Evil,* Book I, chaps. II, III; Book II, chaps. I, II.

F. H. Bradley, *Ethical Studies,* chap. III.

E. A. Albee, *History of English Utilitarianism.*

G. E. Moore, *Principia Ethica,* chaps. II, III.

F. C. Sharp, *Ethics,* chaps. XIX, XX.

A. K. Rogers, *Morals in Review,* chaps. XIII–XV.

CHAPTER XIV

EUDÆMONISM

I. Introductory

Eudæmonism has already been referred to frequently in this book, and some of its principal points have been mentioned in the five preceding chapters. The accounts of the virtues and of the self were eudæmonistic in tone, as were most of the criticisms directed against Intuitionism, Formalism, and Utilitarianism. The present chapter, therefore, will to some extent be a review of ground already traversed. In addition, the author will endeavor to state his own version of Eudæmonism in a connected way, and to make clearer some of its implications.

Eudæmonism, as the author subscribes to it, identifies the good with *welfare, the full and free development of all capacities, and the attainment of all values.* Values are *intuitively* recognized by men when they emerge upon a sufficiently high level of development; but the means by which these values can be successfully attained can only be learned through observation and experience, and the calculation of consequences. Eudæmonism is therefore intuitional in its recognition of values, and teleological and empirical in its formulation of moral judgments. Virtues are those sentiments, or habitual traits of human character, which make men capable of attaining values for themselves and for others. In this sense virtues are *instrumental;* they are also *intrinsically* valuable. Virtues and other values can be attained by individuals only as they coöperate with other individuals in a *just social order.* Eudæmonism, therefore, seeks that social order which will be most favorable to the general attainment of individual welfare. A life of welfare is an *active* life; man finds his good in advancing with struggle and effort from lower to ever higher levels of attainment. It is also a

334

happy life, since it is accompanied by the satisfaction that attends full and free expression of one's personality in harmony with others. Happiness according to Eudæmonism and in opposition to strict hedonism, cannot be reduced to a quantitative aggregate of pleasures.[1] Happiness accompanies the harmonious synthesis of all impulses and sentiments in a unity. It is highly desirable. It would be more accurate to say that happiness is the *highest* pleasure, rather than the greatest bulk of pleasures measured by intensity and duration.

Eudæmonism conceives of the good as an ever growing ideal, that gains fuller content as man advances in moral insight. This ideal, consequently, has never been attained completely in any human life. Every individual and every group of individuals is imperfect; no one's impulses and sentiments are entirely coördinated; no group of persons are in complete harmony with one another and with other groups. But as mankind has advanced in past moral history, there has been better understanding of values and virtues, and more success in their attainment. We estimate moral growth by the twentieth century standards at which our own reflective morality has arrived. We do not possess eternal and absolute standards by which to measure it. No doubt there will be better standards in future centuries, which will have grown out of our standards, enlarged and corrected by further experience.

II. EVOLUTION

If there were no minds and wills with impulses and desires, there could be no values. In an absolutely dead universe it would not matter what happened; nothing could be desirable or undesirable in any way. In a world in which there were only plants and animals, there would be struggle for survival, and conditions might be favorable or unfavorable to the life of this or that species; still, in such a world there would not be the conscious and critical comparison of objects and actions with which ethics is concerned; there would not be values in the human sense. The history of values on the Earth only begins with the emergence of man, whose impulses can be guided by his reflective consciousness and moral judgments.[2]

The values of the lowest representatives of the human race are largely those connected with survival: food, sex, victory in war, safety from storms, earthquakes, pestilences, wild beasts, and hostile men. It is with bodily and economic values that primitive religions are mostly concerned. Yet, as we saw in Chapters II and III, even the least developed men recognize moral values. For in the primitive horde, the lowest kind of social organization, consisting merely of a few families living in huts or caves in the same vicinity and subsisting on what plant and animal food they can gather together with their hands, we found the moral consciousness. Such virtues as courage, veracity, chastity, respect for property rights, hospitality, generosity, and kindness are appreciated and practiced.

We must conclude that at some prehistoric date, after man had advanced beyond the plane of intelligence of his anthropoid relatives but before he reached the level of the lowest savages now in existence, there dawned in his mind a moral consciousness. He knew intuitively the distinction between good and evil, experienced the feeling of moral obligation, and made his first moral judgments. This is the truth in Intuitionism. Why is it better to survive than to perish; to have food than to go hungry; to have a mate, children, and fellow clansmen than to live in solitude; to be courageous, honest, chaste, hospitable, generous, and kind? To say that the preferable alternatives are likely to afford more pleasure and less unpleasantness and pain is only part of the correct answer. It does not explain why one morally *ought* to seek pleasure for oneself and others, and to avoid unpleasantness and pain. The complete answer to the question is, that there are values that man has intuitively perceived ever since he has been human—goodness, oughtness, pleasure, and their opposites. The principal primary impulses, —such as fear, anger, sex, tenderness, sociability, self-assertion, submission, curiosity, acquisitiveness, and constructiveness— lead men to desire certain objects or ends. With the dawn of moral consciousness, man intuitively perceives that these ends or values are good; they ought to be sought and conserved. As man becomes sufficiently discriminating, he learns that it is good that impulses be rationally coördinated and harmonized in sentiments, and so become virtues.

The recognition of virtues has been a gradual process of moral evolution, not yet complete, and that perhaps never shall be complete. Courage and honor were probably the first sentiments to become rationalized, individualized, and socialized as virtues. The rest in due course followed. All the virtues have become enriched in content, and this process continues throughout human moral development. Recall how each form of social organization has appeared and in its turn given way to a higher one. The earliest form, based on Kinship, passed through the successive stages of primitive horde, mother right, and father right. In the course of the second form, resting on Authority, men were disciplined into obedience to a common despot, under whose rule precedents presently gave way to law, and reflective morality emerged from the level of custom and group morality. During the present form of social organization, that of Citizenship, men are gradually learning to govern themselves, to preserve individual rights and a common good. Each form has marked an advance in recognition of the values that man ought to obtain in order to secure full expression of his capacities, and of the virtues that he ought to cultivate in this effort. The Hebrew, Greek, Roman, Germanic, and Christian roots of modern western civilization have contributed values and virtues which the Renaissance, the Enlightenment, and the subsequent period have enriched, both in their ideal significance and in practical means for their attainment.

So the whole history with which comparative ethics is concerned has been a process in which welfare has been advanced, in which there has been a development of human capacities and the attainment of values. The same is true of the psychology of individual moral development. In the years of infancy the primary impulses make their appearance; in later years these become organized in sentiments which become moralized as virtues, and in their organic unity constitute the self, character, or personality of the adult.

III. A CLASSIFICATION OF VALUES

It is impossible to arrange human values in a hierarchy of increasing dignity and importance. However, Professor W. G. Everett has furnished a serviceable classification of the goods of human life.[3] He places at the bottom the *economic* values, because all others depend upon them. Life itself is impossible without means of subsistence. Character does not reach its best development in dire want, with little opportunity for recreation and the enjoyment of friendships; nor can education, art, and religion thrive without economic support. Next come the *bodily* values, since physical health and vigor are needed if the other values are to be cultivated under favorable circumstances. Then the values of *recreation, association,* and *character* come in order, and are followed by *æsthetic, intellectual,* and *religious* values.

An *intrinsic* value is of worth *on its own account,* an *instrumental* value *because of its consequences.* That *economic* values are *instrumental* is obvious; all other values are rendered attainable by means of them. Are economic values also *intrinsic?* Professor Everett thinks not; wealth should never be regarded as an end in itself, but merely as a means to the attainment of other goods. In one sense this is true. But in another sense it seems to the author that economic values are intrinsic. Is there not an intrinsic good in successful and productive economic activity? The artisan who has done a skillful job at small expense of time and materials has proved himself something of an artist; his achievement is an expression of character, it is an intrinsic good. The farmer, the small merchant, the great captain of industry, whoever handles his affairs successfully from an economic standpoint—other things equal—deserves commendation for successful creative effort. Such men find their vocations of intrinsic interest and value. And surely it is not a mere New England prejudice to affirm that nothing should be wasted, even when there is abundance! Prodigality and wanton destructiveness spontaneously evoke moral condemnation. People who cannot keep a proper balance between their incomes and their expenditures seem somehow lacking in moral fiber. Persistent and productive activity combined with self-denial in expenditures and foresight in investments is the virtue of economy. The unproductive hoarding of the miser is neither instrumentally nor intrinsically virtuous. It seems to the author impossible to think of a case where economy would be of instrumental value where it would not also be of intrinsic value.

The *bodily* values, most modern men would agree, are intrinsically good. Health and vigor afford delight to their possessors and all who know them. To have a symmetrical body and to keep it in good condition is worth while for its own sake. And yet not for its own sake alone; since the chief reason for having a good body is its instrumental value,—it enables a person to use it in pursuit of the other values of the good life. The calling of the physician is one of the noblest. Those of the athletic coach and the professional athlete deserve commendation; since they to some extent are serving others in ways that promote the general welfare. But the man who devotes his whole life to amateur athletics and has no serious interest except to keep his body fit, deserves even less approval than the man who thinks and cares about nothing but money getting. The latter, if he is engaged in economically productive processes, is increasing the total amount of wealth in existence, which is a service to the community; the former is a mere waster.

Next in order come the values of *recreation* and *association*. Play for the mere joy of playing is intrinsically worth while, within proper limits. And sport engaged in because a person loves it has high instrumental value also. The man who plays for the sheer love of the game will benefit more instrumentally in improved health and efficiency, than one who dutifully devotes time to recreation because his physician prescribes it. Association with others, including the values of comradeship, friendship, and love, affords experience of the values that in this world are both instrumentally and intrinsically of most worth. He who neglects this side of his nature misses the well rounded life that is the complete good of Eudæmonism.

The values of *character* are the virtues, and the self in which they are organically united. These are of both intrinsic and instrumental value. Courage, wisdom, love, justice, and the other virtues we admire and revere as good in themselves as well as for the other goods that accompany them. The virtues were discussed at length in a previous chapter.

Æsthetic values are of intrinsic worth. They are often said to be wholly disinterested, and their value to be entirely in themselves. While enjoying a landscape or a painting, a person does not ask who possesses it, nor does he wish to own it himself; at least, not so far as his appreciation is purely æsthetic. Æsthetic interest is free from economic and selfish considerations. Yet æsthetic values are also instrumental. Nothing is beautiful that is constructed merely to be beautiful, and that has no further purpose. A façade added to a building for pure ornament, pillars that hold nothing up, but are inserted with the idea that they will look well, anything in architecture that has no purpose except to be beautiful,—these are not beautiful. If an architect were asked to design a merely beautiful building,—one to serve no specific end but just to be beautiful—he would reply that it would be impossible. The same principle holds in all the fine arts—belles lettres, music, sculpture, painting, what you will—in every case the artist in some way endeavors to accomplish something more than the production of æsthetic pleasure. He interprets life or nature in some way, leads us to a better understanding of ourselves and of others, or indicates what is really most significant. His art serves humanity in some instrumental way. And it would not really be art if it did not do so. Art for art's sake exclusively is not good art.

John Ruskin, and more recently, Professor Dewey, have

lamented that in our specialized industrial society economic and æsthetic activities have become divorced, to the detriment of each.[4] Toil in factories and mines has little that is beautiful about it; sculpture and painting are of slight utility. The industrial worker can only enjoy beauty in hours of recreation, and the æsthete, in order to remain a real man, must in some extraneous way make himself economically useful. It would be better if manufactured articles could be made more beautiful, and if works of art might serve more utility in our modern life. Every artisan should to some extent be an artist, and every artist an artisan. Hideous articles are ugly because they are clumsily made, and ill-suited to the purposes for which they are designed: they are not beautiful because they are not useful. We should have both more beauty and more utility in human personalities and in human commodities if the activities of art and life were more organically related.

Intellectual values are obviously instrumental. Knowledge is power. Human life and health have been lengthened and improved, material comforts have been multiplied, human culture has been enriched, education has become more accessible, and welfare in every way has been advanced with the progress of knowledge. All learning is of intrinsic value, interesting for its own sake. Research in any subject becomes fascinating to those who have any aptitude for it, and are willing to persevere through the initial drudgery until they arrive at the point of insight. From an hedonistic point of view, the delight that comes to the investigator when he is making a new discovery is among the keenest pleasures that man can know. Any philosopher can understand why Aristotle thought intellectual pursuits constitute the supreme happiness of the gods.

However, there is useless knowledge. Some research would be unfruitful, and ought not to be undertaken, not withstanding the pleasure it might afford the individual investigator. The pursuit of knowledge ought to be carried on in directions that promise most for human welfare in its entirety. This is not to say that all scholarship should be concentrated into fields whose utility is most obvious to the layman. But it would be well to discontinue any investigation that serves no purpose except to complete the requirements for a doctoral dissertation, or to satisfy the curiosity of specialists in some sterile field of inquiry. The way to decide whether a man is a scholar or a pedant is to ask whether his learning contributes to a well rounded life in which all values find place; or whether he is accumulating erudition without any definite purpose in view except the satisfaction that may come from its mere possession. Scholarship promotes the general welfare, while pedantry serves no human good.

The *religious* values are of preëminent importance in a good life. "Thou hast made us for Thyself, and our souls are restless until they find their rest in Thee" is a profoundly true saying of St. Augustine. The intrinsic value of religion is not always appreciated. Prayer and praise are good for their own sakes, and divine communion is the highest form of love and blessedness. In our own time we overlook this, and over emphasize the instrumental side of religion. We are disposed to seek through ecclesiastical means to reform politics and industry, at times when secular agencies would be wiser and more efficient. Some of our preachers discourse so much on economics, war, and international relations (regarding which they are often incompetent), that they neglect to cultivate in their listeners appreciation of the love of God and the spiritual life.

Other ages have occasionally made the opposite mistake. Religion was divorced from the problems of life. Suppression of all other interests—asceticism—became a common practice. Even in recent times cultivation of the religious life upon Sundays often seemed to have no bearing upon a man's conduct in business. The same principle holds in religion as elsewhere. Religion should be of both intrinsic and instrumental value; it cannot be one without also being the other. In consequence of his communion with God, the religious man should be an abler and better man in every task that he undertakes. The influence of church and synagogue should point men to higher spiritual values and inspire them to make this a better earth for humanity to live upon. Love of God and service of humanity are indispensable aspects of the religious life; neither can be neglected without impairment of the other. In saying this, allowance must be made for differences in duties and capacities. Mary and Martha put different emphases on values; but each was of both intrinsic and instrumental value. St. Francis of Assisi and St. Dominic each in his own way served both God and man, as did also Brother Thomas à Kempis and St. Thomas Aquinas.

IV. VALUES AND VIRTUES

The virtues bear a certain relationship to the values. However, lists of virtues and values are constructed on different principles. In cataloguing virtues, it is necessary to keep before the mind what traits of human character are good, and to trace their growth from impulses and sentiments. In classifying values, the problem is more comprehensive. Man lives in an environment. What objects, in this environment, as he comes into interaction with it, does he find good? What traits of his own personality does he find good in this connection? All values therefore imply interaction between men and nature, in which each is modified by the other.[5]

All virtues are values, both intrinsic and instrumental. Men intuitively approve of courage, honor, wisdom, and love; like jewels they shine in their own light. All virtues are instrumental also; they promote the welfare of individuals and of society.

To every value there is a corresponding virtue. For the continued pursuit of any value implies a habit or sentiment, and if the value is rationally pursued, the sentiment is a virtue. Thus the proper pursuit of economic goods is the virtue of economy. The cultivation of friends, devotion to wife, and tender care for children are manifestations of the general virtue of love or benevolence. Corresponding to the intellectual and religious values are the virtues of wisdom and reverence. Cultivation of the bodily values comes under the head of the virtue of temperance; with attention upon this fact temperance is seen to be a positive virtue, and not exclusively negative and inhibitory in character.

It is more difficult—though possible—to indicate virtues parallel to æsthetic values. Artistic creation is constructive; the artist interprets some aspect of experience that is in a way complete and harmonious in itself. Æsthetic appreciation is passive; the spectator or auditor who contemplates beautiful objects is taken out of himself and his ordinary range of desires and activities, and for the time he is absorbed in a larger experience valuable for its own sake. So far as such æsthetic activities and experiences disclose knowledge, they appeal to the impulse of curiosity or the will to understand, and their virtue is wisdom. For beauty is sometimes truth. As we have seen, there is a sense in which æsthetic values are instrumental. An æsthetic experience is the completion and fulfillment of some interest. Any primary impulse may be evoked, and the appropriate virtue come into play.

Not all æsthetic value is moral. Works of art that are of exquisite beauty may be unmoral or even immoral. So far as works of art are really immoral, they should be excluded from life, regardless of their beauty. However, it must be remembered that occasionally books and plays that have deep moral significance, when rightly understood, are unjustly denounced by the prudish and superficial. We should take the trouble to understand a work of art before we proceed to pass moral judgment upon it. At the same time censors and courts have to decide whether the general public will appreciate moral facts expressed with unconventional frankness, or whether they will interpret the work of art in a morally unwholesome way. It is not so much a question of the artist's intention, as the significance which his work will assume in the minds of those to whose attention it will come.

Art that is unmoral is often of greatest value. In fact, most would agree that art that does not preach is of more intrinsic value than art that loses its attractiveness because it is heavily loaded with moral instruction. Moreover, the instrumental value of didactic art is often not of a high order. There are exceptions, of course, notably among the great poets. But the reader is advised, as a rule, to study ethics and other philosophy in technical treatises, and for leisure hours to seek the values of æsthetics in works that do not propose to solve the problems of the social sciences and moral philosophy.

How much of a person's time should be devoted to æsthetic concerns depends on his tastes and interests, and his responsibilities. In a well proportioned life, some leisure time is devoted to the disinterested enjoyment of nature and of art. It may be conceded that some people err in trying to cultivate æsthetic tastes of which they are naturally incapable. William James remarked that some people in Boston would be much happier if they would only honestly and shamelessly confess that to them a symphony is an unmitigated nuisance.[6] But most of us make the opposite mistake. We fritter away many a leisure hour in recreation devoid of æsthetic value that we would really more enjoy if it were occupied with the appreciation of natural scenery, belles lettres, music, or the fine arts.

V. Values as Intrinsic, Absolute, and Eternal

Are any moral values wholly intrinsic, absolute, and eternal? Values that are *wholly intrinsic* would be of worth entirely for their own sake, and would in no way be instrumental to the advancement of other goods. *Absolute* values would be of ultimate and unconditional worth; such values could never be regarded as relative, subordinate in some cases to other values. *Eternal* values could never change or evolve into different values than they now are.

In a sense, it seems to the author that all of the virtues are *intrinsic:* courage, honor, temperance, wisdom, justice, economy, loyalty, love, respect, and reverence: they are all good for their own sakes. But no virtue is exclusively intrinsic. Every virtue is also instrumental,—it serves the good life. Character or personality—the self as a whole—is a synthesis of the virtues. Courage is a virtue because it is exercised in good causes, and in a wise manner, so as to serve the good of the individual self and of society. Resolute daring, if for a bad purpose, or if exercised unwisely, is not virtuous and is not of value, intrinsic or otherwise. Courage is not of intrinsic value unless it is also of instrumental value. Love is of intrinsic value, for he who truly loves is not seeking ulterior advantages; yet he would not truly love who was willing to do nothing for his beloved except love her. True love implies service in other ways; it is at once intrinsic and instrumental.

But is not personality, character, or selfhood an intrinsic good? Yes, if one's character is social, *i.e.*, if the good life of the individual self is also instrumental, in the sense that it is of service to the common good of humanity; but not otherwise. Must we not say, however, that the common good of humanity is an intrinsic good? Yes, for the common good of humanity includes and furthers the good life of each individual, and in that sense is instrumental to individual goods. Therefore, however considered, good is always both intrinsic and instrumental; it cannot be the one without to some extent being the other also.

Some values, in comparison with others, are relatively more intrinsic and less instrumental. Economic values are more instrumental, while the values of character, culture, and religion are more intrinsic. No life is well rounded in which any virtues or values are lacking. He who is unduly concerned with money getting should be led to appreciate the values of character, culture, and religion. On the other hand, there seems to be a tendency in some quarters to belittle the characters of those whose economic activities make possible our churches, art galleries, and colleges, and to overlook the intrinsic as well as instrumental value of their services. Most college students expect to go into business. They ought to respect themselves as future business men, and to realize that their future work will be of intrinsic value; they ought also to expect to appreciate and personally enjoy the "higher" spiritual activities that their economic contributions will make possible.

Are any values *absolute?* Any sentiment can be carried to the point where other and greater goods have to be sacrificed in its behalf, and it then evidently is not an absolute good. Most of us, for instance, would say that if the sentiment for veracity were carried to the point where a person refused to tell an untruth, when by doing so he might avert a shock to a sick person whom it might kill, the sentiment would not be an absolute good; indeed to act upon the sentiment for veracity in such a case would seem to make one morally responsible if the sick person were to die as a result of the shock. We can, therefore, think of cases where veracity would not be a moral value. In the field of business ethics, Professor James Melvin Lee, quoting with apparent approval the opinion of Professor Jenks that "the greatest business sin is a lie, and the greatest business virtue is truth," expresses his belief that the concensus of opinion among writers on ethics affirm that a bad promise is better broken than kept, and that the absolute duty of truth telling is limited to that field where men and women have a moral right to know the truth.[7] Modesty is ordinarily virtuous; but if two girls in a boat were to refuse to rescue a drowning man because they discovered that he was naked, their modesty, carried to this extreme, would not be of moral worth.

We have defined a virtue as a sentiment that is moralized by being rational, individual, and social. If a virtue is completely moral, this means that it is entirely harmonized with other sentiments so that it will invariably promote the good life. Thus defined theoretically, a virtue is conceived to make provision for emergencies and exceptional cases; only as it promotes welfare is it a virtue at all. In this sense veracity and modesty carried to immoral extremes are not virtues. Thus theoretically defined, virtues may be said to be absolute. Any rule that provides for all exceptions to the general principle that it lays down may in a sense be regarded as an absolute rule. But such a conception of absoluteness is rather paradoxical; it savors of rather fine hair splitting, not to say sophistry.

It must be added that no virtues have as yet become entirely harmonized and coördinated with one another, even in theory. For instance, we do not yet wholly know how to reconcile national patriotism and international good will (two aspects of the virtue of loyalty) either theoretically or in practice. What we designate as virtues to-day are the closest approximations to such complete coördination that we have thus far been able to achieve. These approximations are of course sufficient for most of the ordinary problems of individual conduct, and they are constantly being improved with experience and reflection.

What has been said of virtues applies to all values. No value can be said to be absolute, unless it is understood in all cases to harmonize with all other values in the complete good, comprising the common welfare of humanity and the individual welfare of every one. And such an ideal reconciliation of all values is a goal toward which humanity should ever aspire, but which has as a matter of fact not yet been wholly reached, either in theory or in practice, although constant progress is being made in that direction.

Are any values *eternal?* If so, which ones? Love? Beauty? Personality? Democracy? Reverence? These are the instances perhaps most often cited by those who believe that some values are eternal. When we review the course of moral evolution, we at once see that these values have been variously conceived in past ages, and even to-day there is no complete unanimity among moral philosophers regarding their definition.

There are and have been many different kinds of Love—toward parents, children, wives, mistresses, war, peace, science, art, humanity, and God. He would indeed be an hardy moral philosopher who would venture to set forth a definition of Love that he could claim to be a perfect ideal of eternal validity. What Beauty is, the writers on Æsthetics have by no means made clear. The objects to which æsthetic value has been attached have varied greatly from one age to another, and there is much diversity of opinion among artists and critics to-day. While it is not true that there is no disputing about tastes— there is plenty of such dispute, and some of it is well reasoned— still, no standards of æsthetic judgment have yet been formulated that can be confidently claimed to be eternal. As to Personality. What is it to be a person? And how define what aspects of a person are of eternal value? Decidedly heterogeneous traits of personality have been esteemed in the civilizations that the earth has thus far known. What is the eternally valid norm of personality? Who knows? Or is there any? As humanity continues its moral evolution, may not different types of persons be required at different stages of future development, so long as man continues to inhabit the earth?

Democracy in our American history has been an ideal championed by every one, and preëminently by certain of our great national heroes—Jefferson, Jackson, Lincoln, Roosevelt, Wilson, and others. It has been responsible for some blunders and for much lasting good. Sometimes the word is understood to connote political rights, and sometimes to signify greater opportunity (if not entire equality) in social and economic relationships. Some profound thinkers still regard Democracy in both of these senses as a doubtful experiment. What rational thinker—even one who thoroughly believes in Democracy and is ready, if need be, to die in its cause—will avow that any definition of Democracy that has yet been reached ought to endure eternally!

To the deeply religious man, God may seem to be the Eternal Value, embracing all other values, and Reverence toward Him (understood to mean complete organization of all the virtues in a harmonious whole in devotion to God) may be the supremely eternal virtue of humanity. But consider past, including very recent, evolution of the idea of God, and of the virtues that He has been believed to require of men, and to afford them grace to obtain! We see that both the conception of God and the corresponding virtue of Reverence have been and still are undergoing great and rapid alterations in their significance.

Who can as yet define either God, or Reverence for Him, in any eternal sense, valid for all time?

We must conclude that moral philosophy is at present incapable of defining any eternal values. To be sure, human knowledge of values has been evolving, and our corresponding advance in the attainment of virtues has been following this progress slowly and painfully but with some success. Whether there are Eternal Values subsisting independent of change and evolution in some abstract realm of being, like the Platonic ideas, or more concretely, in the mind of God, is a question for theologians and metaphysicians. But so far as human ethics is concerned, moral philosophers confess that they do not as yet know how to define any value in a sense that they can claim to be eternal. Nor can the Eudæmonist except welfare as he has been able to conceive it, from the limitations of human knowledge. It, too, is only an approximation, although he believes it to be the most adequate conception of the good available for present human ethical theory.[8]

VI. Conclusions

Eudæmonism is perhaps most often attacked on account of its indefiniteness. Formalism sets forth exact imperatives that are to be carried out under all circumstances. Utilitarianism has one common standard of all good,—pleasure. But the Eudæmonist speaks very vaguely of "welfare"—of attaining all values and realizing all capacities. He does not advance a comprehensive and all embracing definition of welfare.

The Eudæmonist would reply, that his standard is as definite as known facts permit. Other schools sometimes have gained more apparent precision, but it has been at the cost of being too narrow, and leaving out considerations that cannot be ignored if moral judgments are to be correct. It is impossible in all cases to decide what is right by mere intuition, or by a barely formal rule in which consequences are ignored. We saw that defenders of Intuitionism, including Formalism, really introduce teleological considerations in their interpretation of the good. We also saw that Utilitarians are unable to make pleasure a perfect criterion; it is only a rough gauge of right and wrong. So the Eudæmonist believes that no standard can be correct that is less comprehensive than his; to attempt to reduce goodness to some simple principle like formal duty or pleasure is to lose out of vision much that is good. It is better to include all good within one's standard at the expense of some vagueness, than to be more definite at the cost of leaving out much that is relevant.

Moreover the Eudæmonistic ideal is not vaguer than human experience itself. We have learned to distinguish a variety of virtues and to note some of the contents of each. We have observed that the desirable proportion of values is not the same for all. Some individuals should devote more attention to some values than should other persons. Which virtue should be the more emphasized depends on the individual. In part this is a matter of native instincts or early acquired impulses, and in part of the conditions that surround him. So one man should be chiefly concerned with religion, another with art, another with science, and most with economic production. One man ought to be notable for his daring, another for his prudence, a third for his justice, and a fourth for his loyalty. Such specialization is proper if not carried too far. The test is, whether the individual's own life is symmetrical, and whether he does his part in society in promoting the common good. This test can be applied to any given case in the light of experience and common sense, and the answer is usually clear, once all the relevant facts and considerations are carefully taken into account.

The Eudæmonistic ideal cannot be stated in a formula because human knowledge of values is constantly increasing. Corresponding to this increase in understanding of values there must be modifications in the virtues desirable in human character, so that the right values may be sought in due proportion. Human social conditions have been altering with very great rapidity, especially since the industrial revolution, and the consequences of an act have constantly increased in complexity. An ethic that does not take consequences into account is bound to be inadequate. Eudæmonism, which keeps modifying its conception of the good in order to keep pace with moral evolution, is therefore to be preferred. As values, virtues, and social conditions change for man, the moral standard must change with them.

While Eudæmonism is therefore claimed to furnish the moral standard, other schools are conceded to have their merits, and to have brought forth aspects of morality that might otherwise have been overlooked, although when once recognized these merits and aspects can properly be included within Eudæmonism. Intuitionism is right in affirming that "good", "right", "ought", "better", and their opposites are self-evident principles known intuitively, and irreducible to anything else. To this Eudæmonism can assent, adding, however, that what particular acts are good, right, and what ought to be done, can only be known through considering the consequences of the actions, *i.e.*, whether and to what extent they further welfare. It must also be conceded to Intuitionism that the knowledge that virtues and values have intrinsic worth rests finally on intuitions. This concession includes the intrinsic worth of welfare itself. But how virtues and values can be pursued, and how they can be coördinated in a self can only be ascertained by a consideration of consequences.

The ethics of Kant, too, has been seen to have great merit. It calls attention clearly and emphatically to the principle that what is right or wrong for one is equally right and wrong for all, circumstances remaining the same. The impartiality of moral judgments is thus emphasized. The various Kantian formulations of the categorical imperative were found, however, really to owe their chief merit to the implied values of Eudæmonism, which are disclosed when the formalism has been eliminated from Kantian ethics.

The values that most often need to be considered in moral problems are character and the virtues, and pleasure and happiness. Since welfare is a pleasurable condition of existence, it is conceded to Utilitarianism that pleasure furnishes a rough measurement of right and wrong that is sufficiently accurate for many purposes, and at times therefore pragmatically preferable to the less simple standard of Eudæmonism. What can be seen to promote universal pleasure in the long run is very likely what ought to be done. However, this test may at times prove misleading when it is a question of intellectual, æsthetic, and religious values, and the virtues. So the final criterion of moral judgments should be that of Eudæmonism.

There are circumstances and occasions when the criteria of other schools may well be employed, in order to test the conclusions to which Eudæmonism seems to point. If the other criteria confirm the conclusions of Eudæmonism, we can feel more certain of their correctness. If they contradict them, it becomes apparent that the problem is complex, and needs to be reconsidered. It is *prima facie* doubtful whether anything is right that contradicts the precepts and customs of the moral tradition which seem self-evident to the simpler types of Intuitionism, or wrong that agrees with them. This sometimes occurs, especially in our rapidly changing social conditions; but well established moral judgments should not lightly be set aside before all available evidence has been taken into account. It is also doubtful whether moral judgments should be adopted that would not be willed to be universal laws of nature, that do not respect humanity as an end in itself, or that are incompatible with a kingdom of ends; such can never be the case when the Kantian tests are employed with the formalism eliminated and the eudæmonistic conception of values and welfare substituted. It is probably never true that a moral judgment would be valid that would be opposed to the promotion of the happiness of humanity as a whole; but as we have seen, a quantitative estimate of comparative pleasures will not always indicate whether this is the case. The eudæmonistic criterion is the final one—at least at present—and other tests must in the last analysis yield to it.

The author has not meant to be dogmatic in his advocacy of Eudæmonism. He has admitted its principal weakness—the vagueness of its criterion, which it is impossible to express in a formula. He has found real merits in the simpler and more definite criteria of other schools, and he has admitted that it is always best to test moral judgments by these criteria as well as by those of Eudæmonism.

In Part IV, in considering the moral problems of the family, the state, international relations, and the economic order, the criteria of Intuitionism, Kantianism, and Utilitarianism, as well as of Eudæmonism will be implied, though it will not ordinarily be necessary to refer to them explicitly. Fortunately, in this field, conclusions rendered in the light of these different criteria usually agree. Unfortunately, advocates of both sides of unsettled issues are often able to quote and apply these criteria with more or less plausibility. This is not, however, so much the fault of the criteria themselves, as a result of the lack of sufficient knowledge of facts and consequences. It is impossible to be sure that the result of a simple sum in addition is the true answer if it is uncertain whether the numbers added correspond to the facts. The conclusion of a logically valid syllogism may not be a statement or fact, if one of the premises is not certainly known to be true. In unsettled questions, the facts themselves are usually in dispute, and until these can be fairly accurately established, the standards and formulæ of no school of ethics can be applied with certainty. Let us therefore approach the problems of Part IV with reasonable confidence in the criteria of the great ethical systems. Provided facts are reasonably certain we can depend on the conclusions to which ethical theory leads us. Those forms of family life, of political organization, of international relationships, and of economic activity that conform to our intuitive moral judgments, that agree with the Kantian imperatives (the formalism eliminated), and that promote universal happiness will ordinarily be those that will advance universal welfare conceived in the spirit of Eudæmonism.

REFERENCES

* F. Paulsen, *System of Ethics*, Book II, chap. I, II, VII.
* F. Thilly, *Introduction to Ethics*, chap. V, VII, IX.
* W. G. Everett, *Moral Values*, chap. VII.
* Warner Fite, *Introduction to Ethics*, chap. XI.
* J. S. Mackenzie, *Manual of Ethics*, Book II, chap. V.
* H. Muirhead, *Elements of Ethics*, Book IV.
* James Seth, *A Study of Ethical Principles*, Part I, chap. III.
* J. Dewey, and J. H. Tufts, *Ethics*, chaps. XII, XVIII.
* H. W. Wright, *Self Realization*.
* J. A. Leighton, *The Individual and the Social Order*, chaps. XXVII–XXXI.
* C. L. Sherman, *The Moral Self*, chaps. VIII–X.
  Hastings Rashdall, *Theory of Good and Evil*, Book I, chap. VII.
  T. H. Green, *Prolegomena to Ethics*.
  G. E. Moore, *Principia Ethica*, chap. VI.
  F. H. Bradley, *Ethical Studies*.
  Warner Fite, *Moral Philosophy*.
  R. B. Perry, *General Theory of Value*, chap. XXII.

PART IV

POLITICAL AND SOCIAL ETHICS

CHAPTER XV

THE STATE

I. Citizenship

In this Part, we shall consider the problems of political and social ethics, chiefly as they confront us in our own country at the present time. We are living in the relation of Citizenship,—in which government, wholly in theory and largely in practice, carries out the will expressed by the people, and in which the ethical ideal of the state is the protection and furtherance of the rights of individuals and the promotion of the common good.

Citizenship, as we have seen, is a late type of social evolution, which in the form of national states (as distinct from city-states) is limited to modern times, for the most part to the last two centuries. For the sake of brevity, a state in the relation of Citizenship will be referred to as a "free" state,—in contrast with the Authoritarian and Kinship types of social organization. The term state, as employed in this chapter, will be understood to refer to the whole political structure of a people,—both local and national; unless reference is made to the "states" of the United States of America, in which case "state" will appear in quotation marks.

For a people to carry on successfully a state organized on the principle of Citizenship, those who are citizens must exercise political intelligence and discrimination in voting for candidates, political parties, and issues. They must have moral discipline, and with general unanimity abide by the decision of the majority. They must always seek changes in the personnel of the government by constitutional means, and never by civil wars, revolutions, or any methods of violence, terrorism, or intimidation. Citizenship as a fact cannot exist among illiterate populations, nor where the outcome of elections is dictated by physical force. Wherever national Citizenship really exists in the world to-day, a people before entering it had passed through a preliminary preparation centuries long under Authority, during which they had developed a comprehensive body of written law, that they knew how to respect and obey. Popular education in political matters had become extensive. People settled their disputes in the courts, respected one another's rights, and coöperated for public purposes. This prior evolution under Authority made it possible for them to take the reins of government into their own hands, and to assume the responsibilities of a free state. In order that a state may be free, most—though not all—of the following conditions must be present: the sense of a common nationality based on a common language, history, culture, and traditions; similar mores; economic interests that can be harmonized; similar racial characteristics; religious confessions that are mutually tolerant, and do not clash in their fundamental moral teachings.

The sentiment that citizens feel toward a national state may be called *nationalism*. When this sentiment is a *virtue*, it is *patriotism*. (Nationalism as a vice is chauvinism or jingoism, and will be discussed later.) When citizens lack patriotism, and so are indifferent to the welfare and security of a national state, refuse to obey its laws and support its authority, the state cannot long remain both united and free. Under such conditions, internal dissensions may either result in a disruption into two or more separate though possibly free states, or in reversion to authoritarianism under the rule of a dictator, or in conquest by a foreign power.

Patriotism in its simpler forms, to be sure, antedates the appearance of Citizenship. It may emerge in any type of social organization in which individuals are conscious of their membership in a group, and feel devotion to it. The sentiment develops from the gregarious instinct or impulse, through which members of a group feel a common "consciousness of kind."[1] With gregariousness as its nucleus, other impulses later become included within the sentiment,—self-assertion or pride because of the excellent characteristics that its members believe their group possesses, pugnacity in defending the group against its enemies within and without, fear of disasters that might bring it ruin, curiosity to know more about the land and history of the group in matters of geography, literature, customs, industries, and other characteristics and activities of every kind. Patriotism as thus far analyzed would prove a sufficient psychological support for a national state in the relation of Authority. But for a free state, a further development of the virtue is necessary. In addition to being patriotic in the ways already mentioned, citizens of a free state must be respectful toward the law, intelligent in discussion of political problems, willing to take time and thought to vote wisely, and ready to engage in political activities. All must regard office as a public trust. Majorities must be just and generous; minorities must cheerfully submit to majority rule and support the state loyally.

So complex a sentiment as the patriotism requisite for a free state does not develop rapidly. Each of our original thirteen colonies had a long history of exploration, settlement, struggles with the hardships of nature, the menace of savages, and a political and legal tradition extending a thousand years back to the Anglo-Saxons. A patriotic sentiment toward the local "state" developed prior to the Revolution in each colony, which already enjoyed most of the features of Citizenship. It took the Revolutionary War itself and the difficulties that followed it, to make possible the extention of "state" into national patriotism. Through the efforts of Washington, Hamilton, Madison, Marshall, Webster, and others, a federal government finally emerged, supported by a national virtue of patriotism sufficiently strong to induce the citizens in a majority of the "states" to support the Union when its integrity was threatened in the time of Lincoln. Among the citizens of the "states" which then attempted to secede, the nation was still invested with a weaker sentiment of patriotism than the "state". From what has been said, it is evident that a very large portion of the earth is inhabited by populations that are incapable of Citizenship now, and that probably cannot be rendered capable of it for generations to come, if indeed ever at all. At present, the only possible rule for such peoples is authoritarian. The only debatable question is, whether the great mass of such people in any region will be happier, develop more rapidly, and suffer less injustice under the benevolent imperialistic rule of one of the free national states, than under the rule of an aristocratic and intelligent minority who are natives of the country. If this native minority is of the same race and religion, speaks the same language as the majority of the people, and shows itself humane in its attitude toward them, something can be said in favor of intrusting the government to it. Lack of political experience, capital, and economic efficiency may possibly be offset by their patriotism.

In our times we hear much denunciation of imperialism, especially when it is combined with economic advantage to a ruling country. An imperial system in which natives were put to the lash, forced into slavery, and otherwise cruelly exploited in order to raise tribute for their foreign rulers would be outrageous. But it is hoped that such conditions do not exist today in the possessions and protectorates of any free state. There is no injustice in the mere fact that civil servants, capitalists, and industrial workers of a ruling country gain their livelihood directly or indirectly through the government and economic development of a colony. If the subject people themselves share equitably in the labor and profits of the development, if they are better off economically and culturally than they would be if the ruling nation were to withdraw and leave them to their own resources, and if they are acquiring the capacity for self-government as rapidly as their native intelligence allows, imperialism may be of inestimable benefit to them.[2]

II. SOVEREIGNTY

In recent years, there has been much discussion among political philosophers whether the modern free national state possesses the absolute powers of the despot of authoritarian times, or whether its sovereignty is limited. Advocates of the doctrine of absolute sovereignty claim that there must be one supreme authority to adjudicate all disputes and preserve order. The state is an involuntary association, into which one is born, and which one is forced to obey so long as one remains within its boundaries. Advocates of the doctrine of limited sovereignty point out the fact that the government of no free state has ever dared to interfere with all of the activities of its citizens. The conduct of family life, churches, labor organizations, and business firms has actually been regulated by the state only to a limited extent. The people prefer to express themselves in many activities through other forms of association than the political state, and they confine the interference of the latter to the minimum necessary for the maintenance of order, and the rendering of such services as can best be performed by it.

Space does not permit an adequate discussion of this controversy. The writer, however, will make a few observations. In the first place, the types and subtypes of social organization that preceded Citizenship are so different from it, and from one another, that it is almost impossible to advance any blanket definition of sovereignty that will cover them all. The ancient city-states, though a form of Citizenship, were too unlike our modern national states for any definition of sovereignty to be equally applicable to both. It is even doubtful whether any single theory of sovereignty could be devised that would be applicable to all modern national free states,—so widely do the latter vary in their legal and constitutional traditions, customs, and modes of political thought and action.

If we confine ourselves to the situation in the United States of America, the facts seem clearer. The people in their federal and "state" constitutions have carefully defined the powers intrusted to the executive, legislative, and judicial branches of government. In disputed cases, the courts determine the limits of the powers. The exercise of official powers, already strictly limited by the constitutions, is still further restrained by public opinion. No official under ordinary conditions dares to exercise his full prerogatives. No official, or all of them put together, is an absolute sovereign. It has been pointed out that the people can, in the manner prescribed in the various constitutions themselves, through amendments or through the adoption of new constitutions, increase the scope of governmental authority indefinitely. In this sense therefore can it be said that the people are themselves ultimately an absolute sovereign? As a matter of fact, the American people thus far in their history only in extreme cases have either through their officers of government or by constitutional amendment interfered with what minorities believed to be their personal and property rights.[3] The American people seemingly do not think that in their collective capacity as a national state, nor as local "states" they either are in fact, or in ethical theory ought to be, an absolute sovereign.[4]

III. Natural Rights, Political Rights

There are certain natural rights which a free state is morally obligated to assure to its citizens. The doctrine of natural rights has had a long and interesting history. This begins with Stoic conceptions of the Logos and with the notions of natural right and natural law developed by the jurists of the Roman empire. It continues in the discussions of medieval philosophers. The doctrine was revived in a modified form by Grotius and the other founders of modern international law. In the course of the seventeenth and eighteenth centuries it was further developed by Hobbes, Locke, Rousseau, and others. It was asserted by representatives of peoples in the American Declaration of Independence, and in the French Declaration of the Rights of Man. To-day the related doctrine of a *social contract* (into which men in early times were supposed to have voluntarily entered in order to form a government for the maintenance of their natural rights) can no longer be regarded as an historical fact. The evolution of Citizenship, as we saw in Chapters II and III, was a gradual and largely an unconscious growth. Nevertheless, considered as a *fiction*, the conception of a social contract is valuable. Each individual citizen, in return for protection of his indispensable rights, morally obligates himself to obey the laws and in other respects fulfill the duties required of him. He is a party to an implicit moral contract with his fellow citizens and with the state,—a contract which is for their mutual benefit. On this ground, he must pay taxes and fulfill his other civic obligations; and he has no reason for complaint if the state, after due legal trial, finds him guilty of infractions of laws and punishes him accordingly.

Natural rights may, for our purposes, be defined as *those claims which a free state is morally bound to assure to its citizens, as indispensable conditions for satisfactory living.* "Satisfactory living" may be understood in the Utilitarian manner as the enjoyment of happiness, or Eudæmonistically as the realization of the essential virtues and other values of the good life. Perhaps all natural rights can be brought under the three heads enumerated by Locke,—"life, liberty, and property"; or by Jefferson as "life, liberty, and the pursuit of happiness".

Under the right to life and limb, the state must make every endeavor to protect citizens against assault, murder, and needless danger on streets and highways and in public conveyances. It should also enforce regulations to assure the sale of pure food, and the labeling of poisons. It should take sanitary measures to safeguard the public health. Physicians, nurses, and pharmacists should be legally certified. Other applications of this right will occur to the reader.

The state under the right of liberty assures its citizens freedom of locomotion—to travel as they please; freedom of contract—to make agreements regarding the purchase and sale of commodities, terms of employment and other personal and business relations; and freedom to marry whom they will and to conduct their family affairs unmolested. This is in contrast to slavery, to serfdom, to the condition of "status" under which such rights were curtailed by the feudal system, and to the special privileges and monopolies which the Stuarts, Bourbons, and other royal houses used to give to their favorites. Under this general head, too, come the rights to mental activity—freedom in the exercise of religion, speech, publication, and association.

The rights of property include protection against theft, enforcement of contracts, and the rights of inheritance and bequest. A person has a property right in the products of his own mind, which is protected by patents and copyrights.

If an enumeration of such natural rights as these seems trite, it is only necessary to turn to the pages of history in order to realize how recently they have been won anywhere; while treatises on comparative law and politics reveal how imperfectly they are protected, even on paper, in any except the most advanced states.

Corresponding to every right there are *duties* that a citizen owes to the state and to his fellow citizens. These duties are of a twofold character. First, a citizen must exercise his rights in such a manner that he does not trespass upon or endanger the equal rights of his fellow citizens. His right to life implies that he will do nothing to imperil the lives of his fellow citizens,—such as careless use of firearms, disregard of traffic regulations, etc. His rights of liberty do not give him immunity if he attempts to incite workingmen to riot during a strike, or soldiers to desert in wartime. The right to property does not give him a valid claim to possession of goods obtained in a fraudulent manner.

Secondly, a citizen may be called upon by the state to assist in the defense of the rights of all. Since the state endeavors to protect his own life while in danger, he may be called upon to assist in the protection of others, and be drafted into service as a deputy sheriff or a soldier. Since the state assures his property rights, he must pay taxes and fulfill other obligations as occasion arises.

No individual has a right *against* society. He cannot expect to be protected in a privilege which is detrimental to the public good. He cannot maintain his property in a manner that creates a public nuisance. The state may take possession of his land by its right of eminent domain, affording him compensation, if it is needed for a railway, a highway, a public park or building, or similar purposes. His property may be heavily taxed for schools, hospitals, libraries, and other undertakings deemed of great public good, regardless of whether he may personally care for them or make use of them. As a matter of ethical theory, socialists would be right in proposing that the rights of inheritance and bequest be abolished altogether, and all property revert to the state on the decease of its present owners, provided only that they could really prove that such a course would be for the public good.[5]

Political rights—to vote and hold office—historically have not been regarded as the natural rights of all citizens in a free state. It is for the government to decide in the public interest on which of its citizens such privileges and responsibilities should be conferred. In the course of the last century, they were gradually extended to workingmen, while women have come into general possession of them during the present century. The general principles of Citizenship logically lead to the conclusion that political rights ought to be conferred upon every citizen capable of using them for the common good. The state will be more secure and of greater service if this is the case. A citizen needs these rights so that he can more confidently rely upon the government to protect his interests. A disfranchised class is liable to be neglected in a democratic government. Minors, felons, idiots, unnaturalized inhabitants, and persons who have lived too short a time in a place to be likely to know its problems, are not capable of exercising political rights intelligently, and so should not possess them. However, all such persons have natural rights.

Political rights imply political duties. Even at the cost of considerable sacrifice, every citizen is under a moral obligation to take the time and trouble to inform himself on candidates and issues and go to the polls and vote.[6] This remark applies to women. The ballot is not a mere privilege; morally it is as much a duty as it is a right, although few states have yet found it practicable to impose a legal penalty for failure to perform this obligation. The common good which it is the purpose of the free state to assure its citizens cannot be achieved unless the more intelligent citizens vote and take a reasonable amount of interest in politics.

The right to hold office implies a certain duty also. Citizens who are qualified often owe it to society to enter politics and to seek office. If all the best men refuse to do this, society must suffer misgovernment at the hands of the less conscientious and competent. A citizen who neglects his political duties is deficient in the virtue of patriotism. The least that a conscientious citizen can do is to express appreciation and to give moral and political support to those who consent to accept office and who perform its duties faithfully.

Whether an educated citizen should identify himself with a political party, or be an "independent" voter, must be decided according to his convictions, talents, and opportunities. It is usually difficult to gain much political influence or leadership without working with a political party. Primary elections are often of great importance, in some "states" more important than the regular elections. Most men and women should be sufficiently associated with parties to vote at primaries, but independent enough to "scratch" their party tickets when decidedly better candidates are available.[7]

IV. FORMAL FREEDOM AND REAL FREEDOM

The rights enumerated in the preceding section are in general all those which the older individualistic writers like John Stuart Mill and Herbert Spencer thought it the duty of the state to maintain. These rights are said by Professors Dewey and Tufts[8] to constitute *formal freedom*. The older individualistic view was, that if a state assures these rights to its citizens, they will by their own efforts be able to succeed in life in proportion to their merits; or, at any rate, that they will be more likely to do so than they would under the paternalism of a feudal system, an absolute monarchy, or any form of collectivism,—all of which interfere with the freedom of individual initiative.

In contrast with formal freedom, thus conceived as consisting of natural and political rights, Professors Dewey and Tufts advance their conception of *real*, or *effective, freedom*. A man does not have real freedom unless he is actually able to share in the benefits and privileges of modern civilization. The mere possession of formal freedom, the fact that a man has the legal right to buy and sell as he chooses in competition with others, to travel wherever he pleases, to seek employment wherever and at whatever occupation he prefers, will not afford him real freedom if he has no money with which to buy, nothing to sell, and in a period of economic depression no one is able and willing to employ him. In our modern society persons are born and educated under unequal conditions. They do not start in the competition of life under equal terms. Many have little real freedom in the selection of what they shall do in life, either in their vocations or avocations.

What else ought a free state to undertake in order to afford real freedom to every one? Such states very generally endeavor through provision of free schools and compulsory attendance laws to assure a good elementary education to every child. Free public high schools and junior colleges and practically free state and municipal universities and colleges provide secondary and higher education to a larger proportion of youth in this country than has ever been done elsewhere. Schools in the trades and professions also have become more widely accessible than ever before. Libraries and museums of art are maintained at public expense and are open to all. Public parks, playgrounds, and places of recreation are provided in our cities. National and state departments of agriculture distribute literature and selected seeds to the farmers, while many state agricultural colleges furnish them with free analyses of soil, and give personal advice regarding their problems. The national government has brought into existence a system of banks that make them loans at reasonable rates of interest. Legislation has been passed to protect workers against dangerous machinery and unsanitary conditions. Women and children in some "states" are to some extent protected against excessive hours of labor and working conditions dangerous to health and morals; although much more needs to be accomplished in many places. Consuls in foreign lands supply information regarding favorable openings for commerce. These are a few of the many ways in which the state is endeavoring to go beyond the traditional limits of formal freedom in order to afford more real freedom.

What additional steps the state should take to open wider the doors of opportunity is a matter of controversy. Should workingmen be insured, through the efforts of the state, against accident, sickness, unemployment, old age, and death? These are misfortunes against which it is hard for them to provide with their own resources. Medical attendance and hospitals are now free to the very poor; should such facilities be extended to include all whose limited means make their cost a heavy burden? Should our cities, like many in Europe, subsidize theaters and operas?

Meritorious as such projects seem to be, it has to be remembered that they would be expensive, and that the money for their maintenance would have to be raised by public taxation, and that the state is seldom economically efficient in any of its undertakings. If those whose industry, thrift, and ability have won them a place among the tax paying class were extremely heavily taxed for the benefit of the less industrious, less thrifty, and less able, would that be just? Or would it put a premium on idleness and extravagance, and discourage personal initiative? If intelligent and ambitious people with moderate incomes who wish to give better opportunities to their children are heavily taxed, they will postpone marriage and have even smaller families than at present. College graduates do not now reproduce themselves. Shall subsequent generations be bred from those who at present are less intelligent and successful, from those who are contented with lower standards of living and education for themselves and their children?

It will be widely conceded that in a prosperous country like ours more than has yet been done can be properly undertaken by the state in order to afford real freedom to all. The general principle is clear. The more the national wealth increases the more the state should attempt along the lines mentioned. That there must also be a limit at any given time to the extent of such state activities will also be conceded by most persons. Only by experience can the proper limit be discovered. It is some comfort to remember that through scientific farming, high wages, and the general standards of living and of saving which they make possible, the American farmer and laborer enjoy more real freedom than men in their occupations have known elsewhere. Further reference to the problem of real freedom will be made, from another angle, in the following chapter.

V. Law and Justice

The evolution of justice from the primitive horde, in which each individual had to enforce his own rights, through the later forms of kinship in which the group came to his aid, and the relation of Authority, in which courts arose and gradually extended their jurisdiction, is long and interesting, but too lengthy to be outlined here.[9] We have learned to distinguish in law between *crimes* (like murder, rape, arson), which are injuries of such consequence that the state prosecutes the accused, *torts* (like libel and trespass), lesser wrongs in which the injured individual of his own initiative seeks redress, and *contracts*, whose interpretation in doubtful cases may be brought before the courts for determination. The court is an impartial tribunal, before which legal talent representing opposing sides presents evidence and arguments. The judge decides in accordance with law and precedent, regardless of his own feelings and intuitions. In some instances, the decision regarding matters of fact is referred to a jury, consisting of twelve representative citizens, who listen to the evidence which is presented to them in accordance with the rules of procedure which long experience has shown most trustworthy. After hearing this evidence they retire from the court room, and, removed from popular disturbance, deliberate on the evidence; if one side has clearly established its case, they are able to arrive at a unanimous verdict.

Popular legislation is occasionally declared unconstitutional by the courts, although this does not occur so often as is frequently supposed. In most such instances in the past, historians find that the legislation was hasty and ill-advised, and that we owe much to the courts for having annulled it. To satisfy popular clamor, politicians sometimes pass bills that they know to be unconstitutional as well as undesirable. They thus escape the wrath of their constituents and force the bench to bear the odium of popular indignation.

Twenty years ago there were numerous complaints against the courts on the ground that judges usually came to the bench after legal practice in defense of large business corporations, and so were unduly prejudiced in their favor. Courts pronounced unconstitutional measures that required shorter hours and more sanitary working conditions, or protected women and children, on the ground that such laws interfered with the right of freedom of contract for those who were willing to accept employment without such safeguards. We hear of fewer such decisions to-day, and more legislation along such lines has been sustained by the courts in recent years. Labor leaders complain that unduly sweeping injunctions are sometimes issued during strikes; but in such instances there are usually two sides to the question. We now realize that strikes, especially those carried on by unions not affiliated with the American Federation of Labor or the Railway Brotherhoods, are often under the influence of agitators who urge destruction of property and violent assaults upon strike breakers, and who are more concerned to hasten the "social revolution" and the advent of communism than to promote the interests of the particular men on strike. Under such circumstances we appreciate that injunctions sometimes may be necessary.

The impartial American can hardly believe that peaceful

picketing should ever be forbidden by courts; but he realizes that the line between this and intimidation is not always easy to draw. Courts may sometimes decide against workingmen because the latter have less able counsel and fail to get their side adequately presented; here there may be real ground for complaint. But few, except the radicals, believe that the courts are now willfully prejudiced against labor. At present public opinion seems decidedly opposed to drastic changes in our judicial system, such as the recall of judges, the recall of judicial decisions, and the election of all judges by popular vote for short terms. On the contrary, it is felt to be important that judges perform their work free from popular excitement and clamor, guided solely by the law in rendering their decisions.

There is more justification for criticism of the jury system as it now exists. Juries are often carelessly chosen. In many "states" they are still expected to pass upon technical matters beyond the comprehension of laymen, such as pleas of insanity in criminal trials. Lawyers are permitted to make emotional appeals to juries. Historically and theoretically, juries should be a protection against the prejudices of judges, and they should be representative of general public sentiment. Practically the present tendency seems to be to make less use of them, until reforms can be effected.[10]

It is frequently claimed that our court procedure affords too many advantages to those on trial for crimes, making conviction of the guilty very difficult; and that, to offset this, the police frequently revive medieval methods of torture in the endeavor to extort confessions from those under arrest. Perhaps every one as soon as arrested ought to be examined in open court, and required to testify regardless of whether his evidence may be unfavorable to himself. It seems questionable whether under any circumstances a witness ought to be permitted to refuse to answer questions on the ground that his replies might tend to incriminate himself. No honest man would seem to need such immunity, and no others should be allowed it.

The most serious criticism of our judicial system, of which

the author knows, is the expensiveness of litigation and the long delays which often make it difficult if not practically impossible for a poor man to obtain justice in the courts. In a civil suit the poor cannot afford the best trained lawyers, so that their causes are not adequately set forth; the wealthy, on the other hand, through appeals and continuances, can keep a case in the courts for years, until a poor man's resources are exhausted. In criminal cases the poor man is unable to secure in his defense a lawyer who is at all a match for the district attorney;[11] a wealthy defendant can engage the best legal talent in the country, with whom the district attorney probably cannot compete in skill. A little has been done in our large cities to alleviate some features of this situation, by providing informal courts in which small debts can be collected quickly and inexpensively; while legal aid societies afford assistance to the poor. But changes of a very sweeping character seem inevitable before it will be true that all classes of people will be on a level of equality when they appear before the courts. Until this is done, the power of the purse will continue at times to tip the scales of justice.[12]

The moral philosopher must regard the law with high respect. So long as laws exist they should be obeyed. The security of society and the general welfare depend upon them. It is very rare in a free state that a conscientious objector is justified in disobeying them. He should, instead, argue for their revision or repeal. Where freedom of speech and publication are assured, it ought not to be difficult to arouse public opinion regarding real wrongs.

Moreover, no one can study statute law, still less the common law, without being impressed by their fundamental wisdom in most respects. The ethics of the common law is objective, based on experience in judgment of actual cases by countless courts for generations and centuries. It is the expression of more extensive reflection in contact with actual life, than any system of ethics deduced in his study by a moral philosopher can possibly be. One American teacher, at least, has believed that the study of court decisions furnishes the best introduction to ethics.[13] The chief limitations of the law as a source for ethical study are, that it is inevitably conservative, revealing only those thoroughly crystallized moral judgments that have had time to be embodied in statutes and judicial decisions, that it deals chiefly with prohibitions of overt offenses that can be proved in courts and punished by the means available to them (chiefly imprisonment and fines), and that it can only to a limited extent take account of motives, or reckon with the higher values. Law, therefore, is by no means the whole of ethics, but it contains a basic portion of it.

VI. CRIME AND PUNISHMENT

When animals or men are thwarted by others in the expression of any deep-seated impulse, they feel the emotion of anger, and an impulse to fight. The pugnacious impulse has a biological basis, and is of value in the protection of species. But fighting for the sake of fighting is neither instinctive in animals nor men; it occurs only in the defense of values threatened or in retaliation for injuries already received.[14] The pugnacious impulse is capable of education in modes of its expression and in the organization of sentiments. This is why there has been an evolution in the human attitude toward punishment, so that the resentment of a social group has come to supersede individual resentment in the punishment of crimes, and fighting has become confined to the expression of national resentment in wars.

When a member of the primitive horde is injured, as we have seen, he unaided fights his enemy and tries to revenge the wrong. Under mother right and father right his kin through sympathy share his anger and assist him to revenge himself. If, however, the offender is also a member of their group, the gregarious impulse tempers anger. Then punishment must be measured, so that vengeance will not be out of proportion to anger felt. To imitate the offense in the punishment often seems satisfactory. Perhaps this is the origin of the *lex talionis*—an eye for an eye, a tooth for a tooth, a life for a life. The authoritarian court was more reflective, probably, than the kinship chiefs whom it succeeded. Gradually customs were reduced to written laws and were codified. The Laws of Hammurabi and the Mosaic codes reveal the justice of early civilizations. The psychology underlying them is for the most part simple and logical; punishments are proportioned to public indignation at wrongs committed.[15]

As morality reached higher stages of reflection, it no longer seemed right to punish offenders simply as an expression of public anger. Some more adequate ethical basis for punishment had to be found. Many theories on the subject have been advanced by moral philosophers. Most of the truth in them can, the author believes, be brought under four heads, to which he will give arbitrary names as a matter of convenience.

First, and most important, is the idea of *moral education and social condemnation*. The simplest illustrations of this principle can be found in the nursery and schoolroom. If one child bloodies the nose of another he needs to be punished in order that both he and the other children will be morally educated to know that the act is wrong and to condemn it. Otherwise the children would not realize that the act was wrong; some of them would probably approve of it; and a bad precedent would be set for the future. A wise parent or teacher, who is a good disciplinarian, leads children to share his own indignation at misdeeds as well as his willingness to forgive those who are penitent and have made reparations.

The same principle holds on a larger scale for adult society. Punishments educate people to view crimes with moral indignation. An offense that is never punished ceases to receive serious moral condemnation; many people fail to realize that it is wrong. Most persons want to do what is right, and voluntarily refrain from what they realize to be social wrongs. If they are taught to discriminate correctly, they can be depended upon to act accordingly. Furthermore, if an offender can also be led to see the wrongfulness of his act—and he often can, especially if he is young—he will repent and may reform. On the other hand, if he were not punished for his crimes, he would hardly realize that he had been guilty of serious misconduct.

Punishments on this or any other theory must not be harsher than public opinion will support. A teacher whose pupils think that he punishes with too great severity will be regarded as a tyrant, and his victims will be deemed heroes and martyrs. Such punishments are futile and even harmful from the stand-point of moral education. If the state enacts penalties severer than public indignation warrants, police will be slow to arrest, grand juries will not indict, petit juries will not convict, and governors will pardon. On the other hand, if public indignation is great, and crimes are frequent, while arrests and convictions are few and uncertain, and punishments are mild, the public will become impatient. Those suspected of crime will be lynched. Ku Klux Klans and like organizations will run out of town those whom they fancy to be undesirable citizens. Vigilance committees will seize authority and mete out rough handed justice. The trouble with such extra-legal forms of justice is that the accused are not given fair trials, the innocent are often punished, and the guilty escape. Worst of all, the community loses its respect for law. The aims of moral education are defeated.

Second in importance is the principle of *deterrence*. While most persons will do what is right, if they know it,—otherwise courts and police officers would be insufficient—a minority exists who are grievously tempted to commit what they know to be crimes. For this minority, the risk of apprehension and punishment is necessary for deterrence. In cities and countries in which the prospect of swift convictions is high, crimes are few; while in localities in which convictions are rare, crimes are frequent. Although minor causes enter, this seems to be the chief reason why homicides and robberies are many times more common in the United States than in Great Britain and most other free countries. In order to secure moral condemnation by the general public, a fairly severe penalty is impressive and has high value, provided the measure of severity does not exceed public approval. On the other hand, strong probability of arrest and conviction, even with a mild penalty, is a stronger deterrent to would-be offenders than a severe penalty rarely enforced. It is said that in the days when a pickpocket was occasionally given a public hanging, but when pickpockets usually were not caught, the pockets of the spectators at such an execution were often picked.

The two principles thus far discussed are based primarily upon the public interest. This is ethically defensible on the ground that no one has rights against society, least of all those who have transgressed its laws. First consideration must be given to the common good. The two remaining principles, of subordinate but real importance, call attention more directly to the offender himself.

The third principle is that of *prevention* of further crimes by the convict. Obviously the only absolutely sure means is execution. Imprisonment is efficacious during the term of sentence, as long as the convict does not escape or secure a pardon. A milder penalty is a fine; it is even fondly believed that this punishment is efficacious in causing persons guilty of speeding to be more careful about endangering human lives. An offender may simply be censured, with the hope that fear of punishment for his next offense will restrain him. Or he may be placed under surveillance, *e.g.*, put under bonds to keep the peace, or required to report to judge or police station at stated intervals, with the hope that the knowledge that he is under observation may prevent him from engaging in further crime.

Fourthly, punishment may have as its motive the *reformation* of the moral character of the criminal. If during his imprisonment he is taught an honest means of livelihood, and inspired with higher ideals, he may be reclaimed for society. Dr. William R. George[16] through his conduct of the George Junior Republic has had remarkable success with adolescents guilty of minor misdemeanors. In this institution boys and girls, while engaged in economic production, largely govern

themselves and acquire a fine sense of honor and social responsibility. Thomas Mott Osborne [17] had remarkable success in
carrying out similar ideas with adult offenders in the state
penitentiaries of New York. Hardened offenders placed on
their honor and made collectively responsible for good behavior
while enjoying special privileges proved trustworthy to a remarkable degree. Many of them afterwards became useful
citizens. A criminal is such because he has failed to acquire the
moral judgments and virtues of society; if he can be placed in
a society in which he will acquire appreciation of good faith
and of the moral approval of others, he can be redeemed. If
reformation can be effected, the purpose sought in the prevention theory is also accomplished.

It is possible to educate the general public to feel greater
indignation at some offenses than is now customary, and less
resentment at others. For instance, the public is capable of
learning to become more angry at political corruption, manipu-
lation of the markets, exploitation of child labor, bootlegging,
and other serious evils. On the other hand, public opinion is
learning to be more tolerant of Sunday amusements, and of
women who disregard minor conventions.

While mankind in the reflective stage of morality realizes
that anger is not itself a sufficient justification for punishment,
it insists on satisfying its resentment when such a course may
be justified on principles like moral education, deterrence, prevention, and reformation. But society will consent to no application of these principles that proceeds further than is necessary to justify its resentment. For example, it might seem to
be a logical application of the idea of reformation to confine
vagrants and drunkards for long periods; for otherwise they
are not likely to be cured. Again, it might logically be argued
that deterrence would be more effective if the families of
criminals were executed or imprisoned together with them.
Society would never sanction such measures as these, which
carry the idea of deterrence to extremes that exceed social resentment. Many murderers take life under peculiar circum-

stances, and if they were free, they would never commit another crime; logically the theories of prevention and reformation might seem to imply that they ought not to be punished at all; but society would never allow its resentment to be denied satisfaction because of such considerations. Some criminologists think that their diagnoses show that certain first offenders guilty of trifling crimes are irreformable, and ought to be confined for life; it hardly seems likely that the general public can ever be led to approve of such drastic treatment. Public indignation is the mainspring of all prosecution of criminals. Society will not sanction punishments either milder or more severe than those for which its resentment calls.

There will always be cases in which public indignation cannot be restrained. For instance, if a President of the United States is assassinated, or a white woman is raped by a negro, or a country banker embezzles the savings of his community, the guilty person if caught is sure of punishment, regardless of whether he is entirely sane, or whether there are extenuating circumstances. Perhaps this is not altogether to be regretted. A psychiatrist has informed the author that mentally deranged people are morally responsible to a certain limited extent, and that deterrence is operative among them to the same extent. The mental and moral condition of such persons is benefited if they are held morally responsible so far as practicable. It is disastrous for them to come to think that their mental condition affords them complete moral immunity. If deterrence is operative to some extent even among the partially insane, they as well as other persons tempted to do wrong under extenuating circumstances can often be deterred, if they know in advance that the crimes to which they are tempted would not be forgiven. If the half crazy fanatics in the country generally knew that if one of them were to kill the President, he could escape with a plea of insanity, would the life of any President be safe for a week?

As a general principle, with a very few possible exceptions such as the preceding paragraph suggests, only persons who are undoubtedly sane and morally responsible should be punished by the state. Other persons, who have committed what would have been crimes if they were morally responsible, may need to be confined for the safety of society and for their own good. They should be placed in sanitariums and hospitals, given medical treatment, and released only when, if ever, it is safe to do so. Some psychiatrists in recent years have claimed that the number of mentally unbalanced offenders is greater than is usually supposed, and that the ordinary legal tests for sanity and moral responsibility are inadequate. Psychiatry is as yet by no means an exact science; but there seems to be ground for the belief that many unfortunates who were not morally responsible have been unjustly punished in the past, and for hope that in the future many similar persons can be cured and made useful members of society.

Society is partly responsible for the fact that some boys and girls go wrong. Born and bred in slums, with no playgrounds but city streets during childhood, with only vicious places of amusement accessible when older, with scant opportunities for a useful education, and with few resources for making an honest livelihood, they drift into crime. On the contrary, it should be pointed out that many persons who have grown up in such unfavorable circumstances, notwithstanding have led useful lives, while a few, despite their handicaps, have risen to posts of eminence.[18] No one is wholly the victim of his environment. No person should be encouraged to pity and excuse himself, and to believe that he is a victim of circumstances.

Without for a moment denying the moral responsibility of sane persons for their own acts, or condoning their crimes, it should be recognized that society ought to do all it can to assure every child and young person a favorable moral environment. The abolition of the saloon has been a step in the right direction. Improved housing conditions, more schools, and better homes, more active churches, are needed. A new municipal recreation center or social settlement will often make an enlarged jail unnecessary.

In concluding this section a few words may be added on the problem of capital punishment. It is generally agreed that this penalty should only be imposed in cases of willful and premeditated murder, treason, and similar extreme offenses. Those who believe that capital punishment should not be imposed even in these cases urge that it is brutal, shocks the sensibilities of the public, creates maudlin sympathy for those sentenced, has a bad influence on the moral education of the public, and makes juries reluctant to convict when they think it likely that judges will impose death sentences. Those who argue on the other side say that only the most depraved type of offender receives capital punishment in our time. If given life imprisonment such a man is often ready to kill his guards in the attempt to escape. If he has wealth or influence he is likely to employ questionable methods to secure a pardon. It is urged that to keep a person in prison for life is really more cruel than to execute him. Modern methods of execution are the most painless science can devise, far more so than most natural deaths. It is expensive to the public to keep an offender in confinement for years; the same amount of money diverted to schools and recreation centers might save several boys and girls from ever going to prison. It is further argued that if capital punishment were not imposed in the most aggravated cases, the public would not realize how wrong they are; execution of the worst offenders is sanctioned by public opinion and has a salutary influence on moral education. In some aggravated cases, if capital punishment could not be imposed, an enraged public would lynch the offenders. While the author is personally inclined to favor capital punishment in extreme cases, he admits that the question is debatable, and one difficult to consider dispassionately.

VII. War

War has played important functions in moral and social evolution as a socializing, an individualizing, and a rationalizing agency.[19] When the call comes, men lay aside their ordinary individualistic pursuits, forget their jealousies, and sacrifice all, if need be, to work and perhaps to die for the common cause. It has been chiefly through wars that larger social groups have been brought together under a common rule and nations have been formed. This has made possible greater facilities for trade, specialization of industries, the rise of the relation of Authority, and the appearance of civilization. The two ancient and modern peoples who were blended from the most warlike stocks, the Romans and the English, have contributed most to the development of law and government, just because they were the most pugnacious peoples with the greatest number of quarrels to be settled. Folk by disposition more peaceable, like those of India and China, have been less successful in political development.[20]

War has been an individualizing agency of great importance in history. It evokes the exertion of one's powers of initiative and endurance to the utmost, whether he be officer, common soldier, ambulance driver, executive, surgeon, manufacturer of munitions, or producer of supplies that directly or indirectly are of aid in the common effort. The same is true of women, whether they serve as nurses, do useful work of various kinds at home to help the men at the front, or engage in the necessary economic tasks that men would do at ordinary times. Men insignificant in peace suddenly become aroused, and accomplish achievements of which no one had deemed them capable. Cromwell and Grant are notable instances. Every one can recall men of his own acquaintance of whom this has been true in less degree.

War has also been a rationalizing agency. Most inventions during the classical period of Greece and Rome, and much of the progress in the arts and crafts in all ages has been induced by the necessities of war. Military art and science call for the highest powers of reflection and ingenuity. Much that is great in literature, music, architecture, painting, and sculpture has been produced because of war.

And yet the great costs in human suffering, in economic exhaustion, in the breeding of hatred and ill will, have long led war to be regarded as the most terrific scourge which has afflicted the human race. The ancient Greeks recognized these evils, and their public conscience began to disapprove of wholesale massacres and enslavements, at least when fellow Greeks were concerned. In consequence they made the first attempts in Europe to establish leagues, arbitration courts, and international law. As the Romans became more cultured, their consciences, too, revolted at the needless cruelties which their generals and armies had perpetrated. They manifested a high sense of honor in obtaining treaty relations with other peoples. During the Roman empire the areas which it included enjoyed peace for longer periods than ever before, or than they have experienced since its fall.

Many of the early Christians seem to have been pacifists, and to have disapproved of war altogether, and some of them preferred martyrdom to service in the Roman army. After Christianity became the ruling religion of the empire, its attitude of necessity had to change. St. Augustine and other Fathers of the Church approved of war in defense of the empire against the inroads of the barbarians, and for such other reasons as seemed to them morally justifiable. With the coming of the middle ages, the Church was forced to make still further concessions. It was impossible to convert the barbarians to pacifism or even to exclusively defensive warfare. So the Church did what she could. She exalted the peaceful life of the monk as a counsel of perfection, while she gave to the layman the ideals of chivalry. The investiture of the knight was a religious ceremony, in which he vowed to fight only for worthy causes, and covenanted "to defend the church, to attack the wicked, to respect the priesthood, to protect women and the poor, to preserve the country in tranquility and to shed his blood in behalf of his brethren." The Church had more or less success in instituting the "Truce of God" in some parts of Europe, according to which peace was to be observed during Lent and Advent and for portions of every week throughout the year. Popes endeavored to mediate between warring princes, and sometimes succeeded in effecting peace. The Church, however, did not disapprove of wars against infidels and heretics.

With the coming of the Renaissance the evils of warfare were seen to be an impediment to the progress of commerce and the arts, as well as the higher and more cultured standards of life. As early as 1461, Poebrad, king of Bohemia, proposed a federal state, to consist of all existing Christian states, with a permanent congress at Basle. Similar proposals were subsequently made from time to time, but nothing came of them. With the Reformation, religious wars of unparalleled ferocity and destructiveness ensued, of which the worst was the Thirty Years' War.

During the course of this war Grotius published his *De jure belli et pacis*, the foundation of modern international law. In the cause of peace he appealed to a law of nature more fundamental than the laws of any earthly state, which God Himself must obey, and which alone makes society possible. He also tried to formulate rules limiting the justifiable causes for war, and prescribing greater humanity in the conduct of warfare. Grotius had marked influence. States thereafter tried to follow his principles, or at least made a pretense of doing so. Instructions were issued by most states to their military officers modeled along the lines of his work.

By the time of the Great War of 1914, the following seemed to have become established moral judgments in the conscience of Europe: (1) Treaties should be faithfully kept; otherwise, there could be no international good faith whatsoever. (2) Warfare should be resorted to only after all other recourses have failed, and then only for morally justifiable reasons, such as national defense, national independence, and the protection of citizens; but not for conquest, glory, or economic expansion. Public opinion was undecided to what extent it was right to engage in war to liberate another nation, or to protect the property of a nation's citizens in other lands. It was the duty of a state to come to the support of another state that had already been attacked, to which it was bound by treaties of alliance for mutual defense. Once a state had entered war, the rights of neutrals were to be respected. Warfare should be conceived to be between governments and not individuals, from which it followed:—that women, children, and other non-combatants must not be molested, provided that they should faithfully obey the regulations announced by the invaders; that no private property might be destroyed except for military necessity; that pillaging and booty should be forbidden; that no unfortified places might be bombarded; that quarter must be given if asked in good faith; that prisoners must be treated humanely; that no one should be compelled to serve in military operations against his own country.

Probably the people of no country believed that they entered the Great War of 1914 in violation of these principles. Whether and to what extent rulers knew differently is a matter of controversy, and it is not the author's purpose here to express his opinion regarding the amount of "war guilt" that should be charged against any European government then in existence. That is a problem for the historian rather than the moral philosopher. He will, however, dogmatically state that he believes that it was the duty of the United States of America to enter the War, in the manner that they did, in 1917.

The rules for the conduct of war were probably observed most of the time during the course of the War of 1914. They were frequently violated, however, because each side believed that the other had already broken them and that reprisals had become necessary; and because "military necessity" proved too elastic an excuse. Since all the largest states were drawn into the War, neither side felt compelled to keep within bounds in order to retain the good will of great and powerful neutral nations. The few smaller nations, like Holland, Switzerland, and the Scandinavian countries, that remained neutral, were able to exercise comparatively little moral influence.

New moral problems arose because the methods of warfare had changed since previous wars, and some conventions formerly agreed upon were no longer clearly applicable. The invention of new poisonous gases, and the development of submarines and aëroplanes are illustrations. Then, too, all the resources of every nation were called forth to an unparalleled extent in the conflict, and questions arose whether the inhabitants of occupied territory could be called upon for activities, not of a definitely military character, yet which would indirectly assist an invading enemy in the conduct of the war.

Certain moral benefits have come from the Great War,—for instance, more peoples enjoy Citizenship in free states; treaties will henceforth be more faithfully kept; there will be less secret diplomacy and intrigue. But if there had been no conflict, these benefits would have come in time, and at less terrific cost in human life and welfare. Social and moral evolution will go on more swiftly in the future if perpetual peace can be maintained. Moral equivalents for the high idealism, self-sacrifice, and courage that war involves will, it is true, need to be found. William James was right in pointing out these benefits of wars in past history, and in raising the problem of "a moral equivalent for war", even if he did not succeed very well in proposing a solution.[21] This, we hope, will be a problem that our descendants shall, as a result of enduring peace, have occasion to solve.

What practical steps should be taken now and in the immediate future to avert war belong rather in the provinces of students of diplomacy, international law, political science, economics, and modern history than in that of the moral philosopher. However, the latter may make a few observations. He may, for instance, plead for more mutual tolerance between the advocates of different remedies. Nothing is more unfair than for the partisans of certain policies to accuse their opponents of the lack of moral principles and ethical insight. Those in our own country who plead for moderate military preparedness, including compulsory military training in some of our schools, are no more and no less moral than those who advocate pacifism. Both desire universal peace; they differ only in their practical judgment how to bring it about. Both those who affirm that the United States should enter the League of Nations and the World Court and those who believe that America should remain officially independent, but should unofficially coöperate with Europe, are sincere. Both are actuated by the moral conviction that our government should at once protect the freedom and security of our people and also coöperate with other nations for the welfare of our common humanity.

Most to be censured from the moral point of view, is the unconscious national egotism of those who assume that the people of the United States are superior in moral wisdom and integrity to the citizens of other free states,—whether from this they draw the inference that we should therefore keep aloof from Europe, and not allow ourselves to be contaminated; or whether they draw the opposite conclusion and say that we ought to send representatives to Europe to tell the people there how to manage their own affairs. In view of the fact that we insist upon a great navy, although oceans separate us from any power of comparable strength, we are hardly in a moral position to reprove the British for naval preparedness, or the French for their standing army. More humility would become us as a nation.

VIII. INTERNATIONALISM

Patriotism, as we have seen, is the virtuous form of the sentiment of nationalism. The patriot loves his country, so he is faithful to his civil and political duties. He votes conscientiously and intelligently. He pays his taxes and other financial obligations. He obeys the laws and does what he can to promote the welfare and increase the happiness of fellow citizens in his immediate locality and in the nation. He is willing to enter politics, if he is competent and his services are needed. He is ready to serve his country in war time, laying down his life in its behalf if necessary. The true patriot is proud of his country. For this reason, he is jealous of its honor and insistent that his national government should be scrupulously just and generous in its dealings with other nations, both small and great. It would be intolerable for his government to slink among other nations as a coward, or to play the part of a braggart or a bully. Just because he is a patriot, he respects other free nations. He is sympathetic but not condescending in his attitude toward nations that have not yet attained the plane of Citizenship. He realizes that other nations often lead in culture, science, and art, in which he desires his fellow citizens to emulate them. He is also aware that his own nation may be superior in other ways, for instance in initiative and invention, in maintenance of high standards of living made possible by economic efficiency, and in wide diffusion of education and other forms of opportunity,—in short, in those features of democracy which are most important. He is never ashamed of his country, and never boastful of it.

Just because a man has the virtue of patriotism, it is possible for him to extend this virtue and to become an internationalist. The same psychological principle applies to patriotism that we have observed with reference to other virtues. Parents through love of their own children—a sentiment with tender emotion as its nucleus—learn to love children in general, and to be supporters of measures for the promotion of child welfare. People who are thrifty in management of their own affairs acquire the virtue of economy, and appreciate sound financial management in governmental undertakings. In like manner, the gregarious impulse in the development of the individual and the race acts as a nucleus for a sentiment of loyalty to clan or village or city; it later becomes extended to the nation as patriotism; it is capable of further extension to include the whole of humanity. He who does not love his own country is hardly capable of appreciating the sentiment that other men have for their countries, or the common devotion that all men may sometime have for a commonwealth of nations.

Opposed to virtuous nationalism or patriotism, on the one hand, is vicious nationalism or chauvinism, and on the other, cosmopolitanism. Chauvinism or jingoism is the vice that prompts a man to glorify his nation by running down other nations. It is the vice of the man who goes about Europe telling everybody how much better everything is done in America, and who can himself learn nothing from a tour of older and in many ways more cultured nations. The American jingoist looks down upon foreigners in his own country as "micks", "dagoes", "wops", and "hunkies"; he can see no good in them, and feels no humanity toward them. He wishes history taught to show that all the heroes of his nation have always been right and that its opponents have always been wrong. He thinks his government should grab all the territory that it can, and that the inhabitants of exploited countries have no rights that his needs respect. His alone is "God's country", and he is a "hundred percenter".

Cosmopolitanism is the contrary vice. The cosmopolite looks upon national patriotism as an outworn and provincial superstition. The American cosmopolite is seldom home to vote. He often prefers to live in Europe, but keeps his citizenship in the United States, to escape taxation in the country where he prefers to spend his time. He is ashamed of his fellow Americans, and imitates European manners. He believes that if nobody cared for any country any more than he does for his, there could be no wars for nobody would be willing to fight. His remedy for national rivalries and jealousies is national apathy. He believes himself to be unusually broad-minded and tolerant. To the people of the country in which he stays he is naturally a foreigner; when after long years abroad he returns to his own country conditions have so greatly changed in certain directions and his own point of view in others that he finds himself unable to understand his boyhood friends or they him. He has expatriated himself. He has become the most pathetic of all persons, a man without a country.

The patriot who becomes an internationalist is the person whose sympathy and vision are broad enough to enable him to appreciate that the people of other nations love their countries and have equal rights with him and his country. He seeks to understand other nations and to help them to understand his own. He believes that national rivalries, ill will, and wars are in large measure due to lack of understanding and not to malice. He believes that if all men were intelligent patriots, all would see that the ultimate interests of their own nations can only be realized in a world of international security, justice, and good will.[22]

Internationalism is being promoted in the world in many ways at the present time. There is more interchange of ideas through increased study by each free nation of the languages, literatures, and scientific contributions of the others. There is more foreign travel by the citizens of each nation, this being particularly true of students, teachers, and merchants. International athletic contests promote good will. International aërial flights have attracted wide attention everywhere, and have helped to bring the world together in sympathy. Christianity has always professedly been an international religion; world conferences representative of the religious denominations of different countries are bringing Protestants everywhere into better mutual understanding. The Roman Catholics have always maintained allegiance to an international church. There are a multitude of international conferences every year, representing all kinds of human interests and activities.

As the inhabitants of the earth become more internationally minded, it will be easier to remove causes of friction between states. Each nation groaning under heavy burdens of armament deemed indispensable for safety will realize that neighboring peoples are only enduring military burdens because of reciprocal fear, are equally deploring the cost of military preparedness, and would be glad to unite with them in steps toward mutual disarmament. Nations that need markets in order that their working people may find employment in industries are capable of appreciating similar needs in other nations; they ought therefore to be able to arrive at a mutually satisfactory understanding regarding the exploitation of undeveloped countries. People in the latter need capital, and as they become more politically experienced and self-controlled, they will gladly offer terms favorable to foreign investors, and will keep faith with them. Most conflicts between nations as well as between individuals are due to lack of thought and understanding, failure to appreciate the interests and point of view of others. Once people in different nations really understand one another, they will soon become able to adjust their relations amicably.[23]

International sentiment, the author believes, can be promoted in many other ways. Just as now there are national patriotic songs expressing love for country, there might be international songs expressing love for humanity. There ought to be an international flag, symbolic of our common human brotherhood. Auguste Comte devised a calendar, in which every day of the year was commemorative of some one who had served mankind notably. Some such calendar should be drawn up by international agreement. Newspapers each day all over the world could then call to the attention of their readers the name of the great man to be remembered on that day; school children could learn what he did for the world. Statues of Humanity might stand in public parks everywhere, side by side with statues of the particular country—America, Britannia, la France, Deutschland, Italia, etc., as the case might be.

The ultimate step in social evolution—it may be many centuries before it arrives—would be the federation of all nations into a world state. Just as clans and village communities became consolidated into little authoritarian kingdoms, and these into national states, so the logical inference is that the latter will sometime become united into a world federation. The majority of consolidations in the past were the result of conquest; but there have been exceptions. The United States of America and Switzerland originated as voluntary federations of free "states" and cantons, and the larger patriotism has strengthened and not annihilated attachment to the lesser unit. So the international loyalty, whenever it shall come, will not appear in the guise of cosmopolitanism, but of an internationalism that will satisfy national patriotisms, because the desire of every patriot is for the ultimate security and full development of his own nation. New York, Texas, and California are all greater "states" because of the Union; Geneva, Luzern, and Lugano are stronger, safer, and more prosperous because of their membership in the Swiss Confederation. Every nation will not only be more secure, but also will have a fuller opportunity for the expression of its own genius, when, at last, all national states shall have advanced far enough in the spirit of internationalism to be ready for a federal union.[24]

REFERENCES

* J. Dewey and J. H. Tufts, *Ethics*, chaps. XX, XXI.

* J. A. Leighton, *The Individual and the Social Order*, chaps. XXXIV–XXXVI.

* T. V. Smith, *The Democratic Way of Life*.

* J. H. Tufts, *Our Democracy. The Real Business of Living*.

* S. E. Mezes, *Ethics, Descriptive and Explanatory*, chapter on Justice.

* L. T. Hobhouse, *Morals in Evolution*.

* J. S. Mill, *Liberty. Representative Government*.

* J. H. Wigmore, editor, *Rational Basis of Legal Institutions*, Parts I, V.

* Marcus Kavanagh, *The Criminal and His Allies*.

* H. Baker-Crothers and Ruth Hudnut, *Problems of Citizenship*, chaps. XXIV–XXXI.

W. E. H. Lecky, *Democracy and Liberty*.

T. H. Green, *Principles of Political Obligation*.

Herbert Spencer, *Justice*.

Henry Sidgwick, *Elements of Politics*.

W. W. Willoughby, *Nature of the State*.

W. A. Dunning, *History of Political Theories*.

References to special topics are given in the Notes to this chapter.

CHAPTER XVI

DISTRIBUTIVE JUSTICE

I. The Relation of Ethics to Economics

Distributive Justice demands that every one obtain the share in the values of life that he individually deserves, and that it will promote the common good for him to receive. It matters little, whether with the Utilitarians, it is asserted that all values can be comprehended within happiness; or whether, with the Eudæmonists, a diversity of values is thought essential to complete welfare. In either case it is impossible to think of happiness, character, and culture as if they were commodities that could be distributed among people; the problem of distributive justice is not this, but how to assure to every one a real opportunity to acquire these values by his own efforts. Since it is with reference to economic conditions that the social order is both most subject to criticism and also most capable of improvement, the discussion of distributive justice centers chiefly, though not wholly, about the ethical side of economic processes. In criticism of the economic system, it is not the province of modern ethics to propose idealistic social arrangements that are impracticable because they are in violation of economic laws.[1] But within the range of economically practicable possibilities, it is the duty of ethics to consider what is morally preferable.[2]

Let us try to illustrate very simply how the range of ethical inquiry is limited by economic conditions. It would be morally desirable, if it were economically possible, that every man, woman, and child should have just as large a share in all the goods of modern civilization as would most further his welfare and happiness. This would probably imply that every one receive the equivalent of at least five thousand dollars a year, at the present level of prices. The present *per capita* national

income in the richest country of the earth is, of course, not
nearly so much.[3] So the problem of distributive justice, confronted by economic realities, becomes something like this:—by
what arrangements can the present national income be distributed in order to accomplish two purposes: first, to afford
most opportunity to each individual now living, and secondly, to
stimulate production so that there will be a larger and more
adequate national income in the future? Neither of these two
ends must be overlooked in consideration of the problem as a
whole.

II. PROPERTY RIGHTS

The oldest theories of the rights of property were intuitional
and authoritarian. That "every man has a right to his own"
is self-evident; the word property means "one's own" (*proprius*).
"Thou shalt not steal" is a Hebrew commandment. "Render
to each his due" is an old precept in Greek thought, which
Roman law came to recognize as one of the three essential
principles which comprise all justice.[4] That theft and embezzle-
ment are morally wrong is obvious to almost every one. While
all radicals condemn our present system of property rights,
very few of them would defend an individual who appropriates
the property of another. All must play the game according to
present rules until it has been agreed to change them. The
reason is evident. There could be no social or personal security
at all, if every individual were thought justified in laying his
hands on anything that he chose.[5]

The question may be raised whether the rules of the game
are fair, or whether they might be improved. What is the
ethical justification for the system of private property as we
know it to-day?

The first famous attempt to answer this question in modern
times was made by John Locke († 1704).[6] He succeeded in
showing that, under primitive conditions, a man can acquire a
property right by appropriating goods, of which no one has
possession, and mixing them with his own labor. Thus a savage

could collect some apples or acorns in a wood, heap them in a pile, and they would rightfully be his property. Locke added the stipulation that the savage would not be right if he appropriated more than he could use, and that there must be abundant goods left, which others could appropriate if they made the necessary exertion. Locke's principle works out satisfactorily under simple pioneer conditions. In it we can see the justification for the national homestead laws, which provided that a settler could enter a claim for a quarter section of public land, and after putting a certain amount of labor in clearing, cultivating, and otherwise improving it, gain a title. But it was harder for Locke to apply the principle to the conditions of his own time, and it would be still more difficult to do so to-day.

Every one will admit that a man is morally entitled to the whole product of his own labor. It is also his right, and it may be his duty, to preserve part of this, and so to acquire capital. If he lends his capital to others, it is right that they should pay him for the use of it. And it is his right to bequeath his capital to his heirs, and their right to inherit it from him.[7] But what is the product of one's labor? The older individualists took it largely for granted that the property that a man holds, can be presumed, in the lack of evidence to the contrary, to be the product of his own labor, thrift, and self-denial, or that of those from whom he inherited it. But if land values increase, through no effort on the part of the holders, but by the growth of the community, is not the increased increment unearned by its holders?[8] And how far ought the rights of inheritance to extend? Have the descendants of a man who has amassed a fortune the right to hold it forever, and live in economic idleness upon its income, provided that they keep it productively invested?

Consider the price paid for a commodity. Suppose a man buys a suit of clothes at an agreed price. How much of this cost to the consumer represents the labor respectively of the man who raised the sheep, of those who scoured the wool, of those who made it into cloth, of the tailors who cut and sewed the garments, of those engaged in the transportation and sale of the materials as they passed from one stage to another in the industrial process? How much should be reckoned as the proper earnings of land and capital? There are few articles of consumption to-day which do not pass through many hands between the producers of the original raw material and the seller of the finished product. How much has each producer contributed, and how much of the final selling price ought he therefore to receive? It seems impossible to determine. Perhaps you say, as the classical economists did, that with free competition between those engaged in each step of the process, each will receive approximately his proper share. However, who knows this? The farmer may have had to sell his wool at an excessively low price, because of temporarily unfavorable market conditions. Workingmen cannot readily move from one place to another to seek work where wages are highest; and if they have specialized trades there may be only one possible employer for them, some powerful corporation. And what ground is there, anyway, for claiming that the law of supply and demand under free competition measures the value of services?

From what has been said it will be seen that it is impossible in our complicated social and economic order to determine on intuitional grounds "what is one's own", or what is "the whole produce of labor" to which one has a natural right. Consequently no decision upon the justice of our present system of property rights, whether favorable or unfavorable, can be reached by way of Intuitionism.

So we must consider the justice of the economic order, including property rights, from the teleological standpoints, Utilitarian and Eudæmonistic, and ask, "Is human happiness increased and is human welfare furthered by the present system more than it would be by any practicable alternative?"

An economic system that is efficient in producing the goods that society wants can claim to be effective in increasing human happiness. Every one has been greatly benefited by the industrial revolution and the development of machinery. We are better fed, clothed, and housed; books and newspapers are cheaper and more plentiful; a multitude of recreations are possible for leisure hours; efficient production is constantly shortening the necessary hours of labor. Man no longer works from sun to sun; while a woman whose home is supplied with modern electrical apparatus finds her work quickly done. Better living conditions and the development of medicine and surgery have greatly lengthened the average duration of human life.

The effects of the economic process on character are important for the Eudæmonist. On the side of production, the virtue of economy is encouraged. Families are knit together in love and loyalty, as the father provides and the mother expends the family income for the good of all its members. On the side of consumption, the possession of property gives freer scope to the development of personality; a man and his family are not completely at the mercy of changing circumstances; temporary unemployment does not mean destitution. Life can be planned with forethought; children can be educated and given a start in life; means for the expression of tastes and talents are available. A business that a man has built up, and a home that a woman has made beautiful and helpful to its members, are both expressions of human personality, forms of self-realization; each generally implies the possession of property. A permanent position and a calculable salary in some ways are a substitute for capital, since security is afforded, and life can be planned intelligently. But there is a certain development of character acquired by the self-denial, foresight, and business judgment implied in the accumulation and investment of even small amounts of capital, that can be gained in no other way.

On the other side of the account, it may be replied that only a minority of the population is able to accumulate property, and to obtain the benefits that come from its possession. Moreover the wealth in existence is most unevenly distributed.[3] A few persons are spoiled by riches, and would be better and happier if they had to work for a living. A large proportion are forced to toil for mere pittances, and cannot count on regular employment. Under our present capitalistic system men are incited to economic effort by the desire for profit for the benefit of their families and themselves, and not by the disinterested wish to serve the common good.

As a rejoinder it may be urged that it is better that some rather than none should possess property. The existence of capital makes large scale production possible. Every producer is in some measure better off than any person doing the same work was in the era before the industrial revolution and the consequent creation of capital on a large scale. The wholesale destruction of capital would be a calamity to every one. A better life is opened to all by the presence in the community of some persons with wealth, and the culture that it can afford to its possessors and those whom they employ. A poor farmer who cannot afford to send his own children to the state university is better off because of its existence, and the presence of liberally and technically educated persons in the community.

It may be asked, however, whether communism, socialism, or some other form of collectivism might not assure a more just social order than we now have. Before facing this question, it will be necessary to find some canon of distributive justice in the light of which we can consider the respective merits of capitalism and collectivism. First of all, we must formulate the underlying principle on which such a canon can be based. This principle is equality of consideration.[9]

III. Equality of Consideration

In our time and country, it is unnecessary to refute the type of aristocratic philosophy which affirmed that the perfection of a few is of greater good than the well being of mankind in general.[10] Nobody believes this to-day, at least in America. So we can safely assume that all readers will agree that *equality in economic and all other activities and rewards is morally desirable*, and that privileges should be afforded to a few only on condition that the happiness and welfare of all will thereby in the long run be promoted more than by absolute equality.

The primary good is the happiness and welfare of all; equality is to be preferred to inequality, *except when the latter will be the more conducive to this primary good.* The burden of proof must rest upon the advocate of preference or privilege in any form.

First, absolute equality cannot be afforded every one if the monogamous family is allowed to remain in its present form, and parents are permitted to bring up their own children. Some fathers and mothers are far more competent than others, so that their children have an enormous advantage. But if all children were taken away from their parents at an early age and brought up in institutions where impartial nurses and governesses would give absolutely equal opportunity, it is safe to say that the great majority would grow up under far more unfavorable conditions than now. There are indeed a few vicious or totally incompetent parents whose children ought to be taken from them and put into institutions; or, still better, adopted into homes where they will receive love and care.[11] Fortunately such cases are rare; for most children their own parents and homes, however humble, are better than any substitute.

Secondly, absolute equality would imply that all persons receive exactly the same education. This is obviously absurd. But it may be asked,—"Ought not all to receive as much education as they wish, and are mentally able to acquire"? The reply would be, that no nation is wealthy enough to provide this as yet. Perhaps we should regard it as an ultimate goal. We are certainly moving in this direction, in comparison with previous generations, although we still have a long way to go. In the meantime, it is better that a few of those who are competent to become physicians, lawyers, engineers, architects, poets, painters, university professors, and clergymen should receive the best training which human knowledge and economic resources make possible, rather than that no one should be permitted to specialize. Everybody in the nation is benefited in this case by the privileges of the few.

Thirdly, it is better for society in general that men who have the ability to carry on farming, manufacturing, commerce, and other forms of production under just conditions should be allowed the use of capital and the employment of workers. Such captains of industry increase the total amount of useful goods in existence, and so advance general happiness and welfare.

Fourthly, it is of benefit to all that there should exist classes who as a result of inheritance possess "leisure" in the economic sense, *i.e.*, who have independent incomes and do not have to be economically productive. A society would be unendurable in which all wealthy men had started with nothing and built up their own fortunes entirely. Many self-made men, indeed, perform great services and we are proud of them and grateful for their achievements. But most self-made business men are somewhat limited in their outlook; rarely are they good judges on questions of science, religion, politics, architecture, painting, drama, literature, music, education, and other fields unrelated to the business activities in which their experience makes them high authorities. Men of inherited wealth and economic leisure more often are intelligent on these subjects. Much æsthetic achievement in the past has been possible only because such men appreciated good work and gave it their patronage. Will the great masses of a democracy ever be good judges in matters of culture? Is not the support and prestige of the leisure class the main hope that the arts will not all become hopelessly mediocre? The possession of independent means has enabled men to lead careers of social usefulness to an extent that otherwise would not have been possible. Charles Darwin, Theodore Roosevelt, Andrew D. White, and William James will serve as illustrations.[12]

Fifthly, a large amount of liberty of initiative is incompatible with equality. If society were to attempt to give every child an equal start, no persons of lower than average intelligence could be permitted to marry and have children; since their children would not be equally bright with the rest. The size of families would have to be regulated by the authorities. In a state where absolute equality of economic goods were assured to all, everybody would have to be compelled to work; vagrants and tramps would receive condign punishment. Where liberty exists, it is bound to be abused by many. Under the present system those who abuse it are allowed to suffer the consequences. But under a system of perfect equality where all received equal rewards, every one would be compelled to work under supervision. There are ardent collectivists who profess to be willing to give up their personal liberty entirely, and to have all their activities determined by officials, in order that absolute equality of reward could thereby be assured. Most of us, however, believe that we would be both better and happier with more independence. We are not willing to sacrifice liberty for equality in cases where the two are incompatible.

In the preceding chapter we saw that every right implies a duty. This applies emphatically to every possessor of any special privilege. Any person fortunate enough to be born of wise and gifted parents in an exceptionally good home is one of the most highly privileged persons in the world. More than all others, he should lead a life of service. Every person with a good secondary or higher education has received benefits that cannot be provided to the majority; society has a right to expect much of such persons. Every individual who has been able to amass a large fortune for himself or to inherit one from his ancestors is also privileged. The least that he can do in return is to keep his capital invested productively. He ought not to spend the whole of a large income in self indulgence. He either should reinvest most of it, or else contribute freely to the promotion of the arts or to philanthropy. If the inheritors of great wealth do not show that they are willing to use it in ways that benefit society, they must not complain if presently they find that most of it has been taken away from them through income and inheritance taxes. A leisure class of as little social worth as the French aristocracy before the Revolution will not be tolerated in the free states of the twentieth century.

There are privileged nations. Such morally owe a debt to humanity in return for their privileges. Here in the United States of America, a little more than one hundred million people are occupying a vast area with great natural resources, on which no doubt, at least four times as many people could live with standards of comfort and culture far superior to those now possible for the coolies of China and India. Yet we exclude these latter from immigration into our country. Why, on the grounds of equality, is this just? The welfare and happiness of three hundred million people would be advanced at a sacrifice on the part of only one hundred million people. The only moral justification for our policy of exclusion can be, that we believe that we are effecting on this continent, in a free state, advances in science, culture, political institutions, and social welfare. By these the world as a whole in future generations and centuries will be benefited more than it would by the immediate relief of three hundred million Asiatics, at the cost of the submergence of the present American nation with its traditions and ideals. Our special privileges as a nation can be justified only on the presumption that through them we are rendering a compensatory service to humanity.

The implications of the principle of equality of consideration have now been indicated. It has been seen that mankind ought to be on an equal basis, except when for some reason the general happiness and common welfare will be further advanced by giving preference in some way to certain individuals. Such exceptions are justified on condition that the privileged persons render important services to society that could not so readily be obtained in any other way. Those favored should be chosen on some ground other than arbitrary partiality. The first and best reason for preference is the possession of unusual talents and the will to use them. Secondly, considerations of social expediency enter, such as the integrity of the family, and the encouragement of parents to endeavor to provide liberally for their children; and, thirdly, the unwisdom of too much public interference with individual liberty. In a society in which no one possessed special privileges except for such reasons as these, there would not be absolute equality by any means, but the social order would be just.

IV. A Canon of Distributive Justice

We have seen that it is impossible, in our complex economic system, to calculate the value of the services which each individual renders to society. We have also seen that equality of opportunity in cultivation of the values of life should be maintained, except when all, including future generations, will benefit by the bestowal of special privileges upon a chosen few. Our canon therefore follows: *A just distribution of economic and other goods will render to the members of each class of society the facilities and rewards requisite to enable and to induce them to render the services which society has a right to expect of them.* Men as a rule are virtuous and happy when they are successfully performing the services for which they are competent; so it can be assumed that *compliance with this canon will best assure the happiness and welfare of the individuals in each class of society.*

The significance of this canon can best be brought out by showing its application to different classes. Members of the professions should, if they are moderately successful, receive incomes sufficient to enable them to maintain the standard of living that will make them most efficient. This implies suitable facilities for work and for study, books, scientific apparatus, freedom from distracting monetary anxieties, and opportunity to travel in order to keep in touch with progress elsewhere in their professions. Brain workers are under severer mental and physical strain than manual workers; to keep fit, they need more opportunity for recreation, more varied and appetizing food, and homes or offices in which they can study in quiet. It may be an unnecessary convention that they need better clothes and household appointments than workingmen; but it is for the good of society that they have means for æsthetic gratification, since their class can and should do much to uphold standards of taste in the community.

If the professional classes are to be socially efficient, and the values of their homes are to be conserved, their families must share their standards of living. A successful man should be in a position to give an education equal to his own to such of his children as are desirous and capable of it. This does not entirely hold of course for the unsuccessful and inefficient, nor for those who have excessively large families.

It is not necessary that professional men become possessors of large amounts of capital in order to be able to serve society, nor is possible wealth the inducement that will make them most efficient. In the army and navy, government civil service, teaching, and the religious ministry permanent tenure under good behavior with pensions on retirement is perhaps a sufficient financial arrangement; although society may be benefited if these classes are enabled and induced to accumulate and to invest small amounts of capital. To do this last develops a certain integrity of character, practicality of judgment, and appreciation of economy in public affairs not otherwise obtainable. Those whose incomes consist of fees, as is the case with most physicians and lawyers, need to accumulate property to provide for emergencies and old age. It must be kept in mind that the rewards which incite to professional success are not chiefly financial; interest in the work, consciousness of service faithfully rendered, and appreciation by colleagues and the general public count for more with the best professional men.

How far do our present social arrangements comply with the canon, in case of the professional classes? The author supposes that physicians, lawyers, teachers in higher positions, and engineers in general have little ground for complaint. The salaries of government employees have not in most cases sufficiently advanced since the war; the same is true of some teachers, especially in elementary schools. The position of the average successful clergyman is most pitiful of all; his is the worst sweated industry in society to-day, measured by the canon. It is quite impossible for him and his family to maintain the standard of living necessary for him to render to society the services that might be expected of him were he adequately paid.

The function of the business man, whether merchant, manufacturer, or banker, is directly or indirectly to supply the public
with material commodities of good quality at reasonable prices,
and to afford to those who work for him just wages and working conditions. Wages are just, if they provide a standard of
living sufficient to enable workers to render to society the services expected of them in accordance with the canon. Just
working conditions include physically sanitary and morally
wholesome surroundings, and such a voice in management
and details of work that will give them self-respect and a sentiment of loyalty to the business. To do all this, the business
man requires capital and credit. He should therefore receive
profits commensurate with the service he is actually rendering
to society. The captain of industry who is a manager rather
than owner should be able to pay customary rates of interest
to bondholders, and dividends to stockholders commensurate
with the service the business is actually rendering to society.
A business man's motives are, and should be, more frankly
economic than those of a professional man; under normal
conditions his financial success is likely to be a correct
measure of his services. The state should protect him from
unfair competition, including local price cutting, fraudulent
advertising, sweated industries, and like immoral and socially
pernicious practices. Business men's associations should, so
far as they can, formulate and promote codes of high moral
standards in matters that have to be left to public opinion rather
than to law enforcement.

The highly successful business man under a capitalistic system should be able to make substantial profits and become a
large property holder. His business success, under normal conditions, demonstrates his ability to handle large amounts of
capital wisely. He can be relied upon to invest his capital
productively; which will be of benefit to the public. Since such
a man's interests are largely material, the possibility of a somewhat lavish scale of living is often needed to incite him to his
best efforts. Usually a man with less education than the pro-

fessional man, and less capable of æsthetic forms of recreation at small cost, he needs more luxuries. Still, there are limits to the expenditures which he ought to allow to himself and his family. He should add considerable portions of his income to his productive investments, or expend them in benevolences. The general principle that should guide him is the canon of distributive justice; he and his family should only spend in their mode of living such sums as will render them most useful.

Does our present economic order comply with the canon of distributive justice with reference to the business classes? Most readers will probably agree that it does, in a rough way. Although small business men are sometimes worsted in competition with large corporations, the general public is less disposed to complain at this to-day than a generation ago.[13] There still are many openings left for small enterprises. Moreover, many a small business man finds himself more successful as an employe of a large concern. Take the case of a small merchant who has a staff of four or five sales people and a deliveryman. Such a merchant has to be a successful buyer, advertiser, floorwalker, salesman, personnel man and window dresser. If he does not sell exclusively for cash, he must be a credit expert. Since few small merchants combine all these qualifications, most of them in every generation have ultimately failed. Such men often have one or more of these qualifications, however, and are capable of rising to high positions in the employment of a corporation. The same principle applies to many small manufacturers and bankers. "Big business" has furnished opportunities to many who could not succeed in a small business. The whole question between big and small business is which is the more successful in serving consumers, giving better rewards to employes, and earning larger profits to investors. Whichever succeeds best in all these respects is ethically best. A moral philosopher hardly feels competent to judge; but the author supposes that the proportion of each now in existence approximates what it ought to be.

The workers deserve a standard of living that will enable

them to do best the work in which they are engaged. This means as high wages, short hours, and regular employment as industry in its present stage of development can afford. It also means decent homes and sanitary places of work with wholesome moral conditions, and access to suitable forms of recreation. Workers should be insured against accident and death; and, if it can be made practicable, against sickness and unemployment. It is undoubtedly a social injustice that the people most helpless to avert industrial depression suffer most in consequence of it. Child labor should be made impossible. Machinery should not be sped beyond normal powers of human endurance. All employed in any industry deserve respect. Wages paid for piece work should be justly proportionate to the actual skill and labor involved. There should be redress against arbitrary foremen. All this implies that workers should in some way be given a voice in the conduct of those details of industrial processes that directly affect them and about which they have some knowledge. Workingmen are often impulsive and idealistic. If they are made to feel that they are real participants in their industrial processes and not mere cogwheels in a machine, they become loyally coöperative, and take personal pride in the achievements of the firms which employ them.[14]

The condition of labor in most industries in the United States is highly favorable. The standard of living is the highest that the world has ever known. That there is much room for improvement, is implied in what has been said in the preceding paragraph. If such improvement is to take place, the canon of distributive justice implies that workers must do their part. They should not slack on the job; they must prevent waste; they must take pride in their work and be loyal to their firms; they must do their best in every way to make their industries successful. Unless a business is economically efficient, it cannot raise wages and reduce hours. Labor unions are coming increasingly to recognize that workers have duties corresponding to their rights; and that it is economically impossible for them to secure better terms unless they help to make business profitable.[15] It is conceded that unions are needed to protect workers in their rights, and to win for them a just share in the prosperity of their industries.

Much complaint is made, though more by theorists than by labor leaders or workers, that under large scale production labor is too monotonous. Instead of making a whole article—a watch, a pair of shoes, or what not, which in former times required high personal skill and craftsmanship, the worker constantly has to repeat the same stupid, monotonous task, perhaps every minute or once every ten seconds! This undoubtedly is a drawback in modern industry. However, the worker is compensated by shorter hours and higher wages. As a consumer he can buy articles at lower prices. From the old days of hand workmanship has come down to us the proverb that the cobbler's wife has no shoes. It is probable that the cobbler in those times was too poor to make them for her; it took costly leather and many hours of labor; while food and fuel were more pressing necessities that were very dear in terms of his real wages. A hundred years ago, a newspaper, or the postage on a letter, were luxuries that working people could hardly afford. Moreover, there must have been many workers in those times, just as there are to-day, who were incapable of good craftsmanship. The finest and not the average specimens of their work have been preserved for us to admire in museums. The ordinary laborer often has a mediocre mind, for which monotonous tasks are best suited. Intelligence tests show that the bulk of the population is not brilliant, and presumably would do nothing remarkable if engaged in craftsmanship. It is not true, as is sometimes alleged, that workers to-day can find nothing interesting in their work. If the humblest toiler can learn something of the complete operation of which his own task forms a necessary part, he will become conscious of the joys of creative work.[16] The main thing most workers wish, is to receive the recognition and appreciation, by their employers and by their own associates, to which their success at their jobs entitles them.

The farmer deserves an adequate standard of living, and expert advice about the use of fertilizers, rotation of crops, means of fighting blights and pests, and methods of accounting costs. He should have access to capital on low terms of interest, and be encouraged to save and eventually to own his farm. He should be assisted in coöperative marketing of his products, and coöperative purchase of his supplies, so that there will be few intermediaries between him and consumers on the one hand, and manufacturers on the other. The whole economic structure rests ultimately upon him. He deserves more consideration and respect than he sometimes receives.

It should be pointed out that the rewards of the farmer are not to be reckoned wholly in financial terms. Under favorable conditions, he is the most independent of men. He leads a healthy outdoor life, is his own employer, and can plan his work as he pleases. He is likely to be better read and more intelligent than the industrial worker. The social life of a country community is ordinarily wholesome, kindly and sympathetic, with high standards of moral integrity. Unlike the city, men are appraised by what they produce rather than by their expenditures. As compared with the city man with the same income, the farmer's children grow up under more favorable conditions, morally and physically, and are more likely to become successful men and women. Many of the eminent in every generation are born on farms. On the other hand, city populations never reproduce themselves in the long run, either in numbers or in ability. With the telephone, the radio, good roads, and motor cars, the farmer's life is no longer isolated. He can go and enjoy the amusements of the town when he chooses, and return to the peace and quiet of his home. It is his duty to be just to his employes. While farm labor cannot be standardized in hours and wages, it should not be unjustly exploited.

We have seen that our present economic order in part, but by no means wholly, meets the requirements of the canon of distributive justice. We have still to consider whether the canon may be more fully met by improvements in our present system that will keep it within the bounds of the relation of Citizenship and the capitalistic system, or whether the substitution of some form of collectivism would be preferable.

V. Capitalism or Collectivism?

Our present social structure, regarded from the economic standpoint, has been denominated *Capitalism*. Capital, mostly the fruit of previous labor, thrift, and industry, and held by individuals as *private property*, is an essential factor in production, and *the holders of capital justly receive private incomes from it in the form of interest, profits, and rent*. In opposition to Capitalism, the advocates of *Collectivism* believe that *all, or most, capital employed in production should be owned and managed by the people collectively*, and not held as private property. The income now received by property holders as profit, interest, and rent should all go to the people collectively.

On ethical grounds collectivists are united in the opinion that the present capitalistic system is bad, since the primary motive for production is self-interest and gain,—profit for the individual and a living for his family. For this they would substitute the motive of public service; all should work, not for private profit but for the general good. The social system should be so arranged that each according to his ability would contribute to the general welfare, economically as well as otherwise, and each would receive in accordance with his needs. Another criticism of Capitalism is, that the propertyless worker is obliged to accept employment where he can find it, and to do his work under the conditions laid down by his employer. This is "wage slavery". No one should have economic power over another. All productive property should belong to the people collectively; the individual should work for the collective group, not for the holders of private property.

Collectivists criticize the wastes of competition and advertising that are inevitable under Capitalism. Some claim that capital is being concentrated in fewer and fewer hands, and that workers are growing poorer and poorer. Many no longer make such sweeping assertions, and content themselves with pointing out the fact that most capital is at present owned by a small percentage of the population. All argue that a more nearly equal division of income would further human happiness and welfare. Collectivists are chiefly concerned with the condition of industrial laborers, who under past conditions were seldom property holders. It is from their point of view that collectivist attacks on Capitalism are usually made. The advocates of Collectivism profess to believe that farmers would be benefited by the collective ownership of land; but farmers usually own or aspire to the private ownership of the land which they work, and are emphatically individualistic. Collectivistic propaganda makes little headway among them.

Many not otherwise in sympathy with collectivists concede that they perform a service in calling general attention to serious evils and injustices. On the constructive side, collectivists are by no means in agreement with one another, either regarding the details of the new economic order which they desire, or the means by which transition to it can be effected. They wage countless controversies with one another; new divisions keep appearing among them; they often attack one another's programs with almost as much bitterness as they do Capitalism itself. However, four general types of Collectivism may be distinguished, and the statements following are believed to be as accurate as any that could be made in a short account, allowing for the great diversity of opinion among the proponents of each type. These four types are (1) Communism, (2) State Socialism, (3) Guild Socialism, and (4) Consumer's Coöperative Democracy.

1. *Communism*

The word Communism suggests an order in which all goods would be held in common; the social tie that binds each member of the group to the rest would be so close that each would joyfully contribute all that he had to the common good of all. A normal family is such a commune. Monastic orders are communistic. Settlements like the Oneida Community originated on a communistic basis. Historically, Communism in this sense has proved successful only in groups in which a strong tie of personal affection has bound members so closely that the good of each was of vital concern to the others, as in the family; or in groups in which devotion to a common cause like religion, has been so zealous that men were willing to sacrifice their individual interests. Communistic organizations other than the family have usually been celibate, or have practiced free love, or in some other way have avoided family ties. Family loyalties would have been divisive, and would have broken down the complete identification of private interest with the common good that a commune must insist upon.

Communists to-day, however, are not thinking of establishing religious orders or small self-sufficing economic communities. They aspire to seize the governments of present free states, overthrow the capitalistic system, establish the dictatorship of the proletariat (the working classes) under the control of the Communist Party, confiscate all private property, and abolish all class distinctions by compelling every one to work for the newly organized state. Thus universal equality, they think, will be established.

Ultimately, perhaps, some Communists say, every one will receive the same compensation for an hour's labor as every one else, no matter what the work has consisted of, nor how well it has been done. Why should one man, because he has greater natural talents, or more education, or because he is naturally industrious and likes to work, receive more pay than another man who is not so bright, has less education, and has inherited or acquired a disposition toward idleness? The necessities of both men are probably equal; the man who has the greater natural handicaps should not be discriminated against. This, however, is a detail that can only be decided after the Communist Party has been in power for a long time, and the minds and mores of the people have become thoroughly indoctrinated with Communism.

Communists are likely to be skeptical of evolution. It would take too long a time to convert an actual majority of the population to Communism, under the handicaps of the present capitalistic régime. Revolution will prove a swifter and surer method of inaugurating Communism. The Communist Party in every country must be well organized and thoroughly disciplined. No one is admitted to membership in the party who will not consistently adhere to its principles and obey orders. The party must spread communistic propaganda as widely as possible, especially in labor unions and in the army and navy; it may prove expedient for Communists to become members of these organizations in order to be able to spread their agitation by "boring from within". With laborers discontented, and the army and navy disaffected and unwilling to obey orders to suppress the Communists, the leaders of the well organized and disciplined Communist Party will be able to seize the government and industries of the country. Once in control, as much private property as is feasable will be confiscated, and the "dictatorship of the proletariat" will be established. Social classes will be abolished, for everybody will be a worker. Ultimately all private property and economic enterprise will be taken over by the state, although for a while concessions may have to be made to skilled workers, small traders, and farmers.

With the communistic party in power, the free—or as the Communists call it, the "bourgeois"—state, with its so-called civil and political rights, will be at an end. Communists will control education, speech, publication, and all associations including the churches. The coming generation will be thoroughly indoctrinated with the principles of Communism, and their minds will not be permitted to be confused as they grow up, by being allowed to hear or read presentations of the erroneous points of view of the defenders of Capitalism. When, after several generations, every one shall have become a Communist, as a matter of conviction, discipline may become more relaxed, and government more democratic. That can be decided in the future. The Communist Party of Russia and the Third

International are the most famous proponents of Communism in the world to-day.

Communism appeals most strongly in countries where wages are low and sharp lines differentiate workers from the rest of the population, so that they become class conscious, and believe that they have no interests in common with their employers, and that by the overthrow of the present economic order they could "lose nothing but their chains", which bind them to "wage slavery". Communism is not likely to spread in a country where workingmen receive high wages and continuous employment, are able to save and to invest in stocks and bonds, and are given some voice in management. Under the conditions just mentioned workers realize that they have a stake to lose in the overthrow of the present system, and they are ready to defend it.[17]

2. *Socialism*

There are many different kinds of Socialists. Some look forward to the same ultimate goal as Communists, but are ready to work for more immediate objectives by constitutional means, through books, pamphlets, and speeches in attack upon Capitalism and in favor of Socialism; by securing legislation pointing in a socialistic direction; by agitation within the labor unions;[18] by organizing political parties and winning elections. Since in any free country the people have the power by legislation and constitutional amendment to inaugurate any kind of political, social, and economic order that they desire, Socialists hope to persuade them to take steps in the direction of a socialistic commonwealth. Socialists are likely to begin by agitating for immediate government ownership and operation of railways, mines, and large electric power plants,—measures which naturally may gain the support of persons who do not regard themselves as Socialists. Next in the socialistic program would come government control of large industries, especially of those that tend to become monopolistic. Instead of endeavoring, like individualists who believe in Capitalism, to break down monopolies and to restore competition, Socialists would have the state take them over and run them.

Socialists believe that municipalities should own and operate all their public utilities,—water, gas, electricity, street railways, and the like. When all this has been achieved, commerce and agriculture should pass into the hands of the government. Present private owners might be pensioned during their lifetime, and their widows and minor children provided for. Ultimately, however, all or most private property used in production would be confiscated. To this end, heavy income and inheritance taxes should be inaugurated immediately, so that the wealthy, forewarned, will cause their children to be educated to earn their own living by economic effort.

The character of the socialistic state would become utterly different from the political state as we now know it; the latter would "wither and pass away", and a social organization would take its place in which all men would love one another as brothers, and work no more for profits but for service in the common good. If this last sentence is rather vague, it is only because the author has been unable to make a more specific statement to which he supposes that most Socialists would assent.

Many Socialists would leave the present family and the marriage system undisturbed. Others would have all women work except during pregnancy and lactation, and have children brought up in institutions under the charge of trained nurses and educational experts. Some would permit families to live together; others would have all live in barracks and eat at common tables. Some would permit families to own their clothes, household furniture, books, and inexpensive works of art. The great works of art, of course, would be owned by the public, and their enjoyment made accessible to all.

Some Socialists would even allow individuals to accumulate and invest property in speculative undertakings and small business enterprises in which it would either not be safe or else not worth while for the state to enter; individual freedom of initiative to that extent might make for progress.

In some socialistic schemes incomes of workers would be graded according to the worth of their services, in order to stimulate them to their best efforts. However, there would be no opportunity for hoarding or lending at interest, or inheritances. Many Socialists, on the contrary, think prizes, medals, and similar tokens of honor would be sufficient incentives to develop executives and inventors, in a social order in which no other forms of distinction were allowed.

There are Socialists who, like most Communists, regard religion with disfavor; it is an opiate that makes people content with bad conditions, because they hope for compensation in another life. Other Socialists are friendly toward religion. There are even Christian Socialists who claim that Jesus was one of their number, and who think that the early church in Jerusalem was a commune, and that the socialistic order will be an earthly realization of the kingdom of heaven, in which the precepts of the Sermon on the Mount will be practiced.[19]

Two criticisms of the general types of Collectivism thus far described will occur to the reader. Both Communism and State Socialism seem to contemplate a very highly organized officialdom, which would control all, or most, economic activities. States now are notoriously inefficient in their economic undertakings. Governments are distinguished for love of red tape. Officials are advanced largely by reason of seniority. They feel little incentive to avoid waste and produce cheaply, in sharp contrast to officers of corporations who must keep down expenses and earn dividends. Men more frequently get into elective or appointive offices because they are good fellows whom everybody likes, than because they are economically efficient. There is much race and religious discrimination in politics. On the other hand, in business, men are more likely to advance because they are economically efficient; stockholders and directors of corporations are more interested in that qualification than in considerations of political popularity, race, and religion. The consumer has influence upon production in the capitalistic system; manufacturers and merchants compete in offering him articles that he will buy; his dollars are more effective in making capitalistic production efficient than is his ballot in making governmental undertakings economical. For such reasons as these, it may appear doubtful whether either Communism or State Socialism would be economically efficient. In view of the fact that at present there is not nearly enough wealth in existence, to enable every one to enjoy the full benefits that ought to be afforded to all for the self-realization of Eudæmonism or the attainment of happiness which Utilitarianism seeks, it would not seem desirable to try a different economic order in which even less wealth would be produced.

The second criticism is, that both the socialistic and communistic orders would be arbitrary and paternalistic. No one would be free to come and go as he pleased, or to order his life according to his own wishes. His work and his play would be largely prescribed. Some men like army life and its discipline. They do not mind living under orders. They welcome freedom from responsibility, and the assurance of at least a plain living. Most men, however, though willing to submit to army discipline in a war for the common defense, are very glad when peace comes, and they can throw off their uniforms and no longer have to salute their officers. They had rather shift and fend for themselves; they believe that their chances for success are greater than their risks. Socialism has sometimes been called a philosophy of failure; it has been said that principally the timid and incompetent, who fear that they cannot succeed by their own efforts, desire to be taken care of under the regimentation of a socialistic state.

The advocates of the two forms of Collectivism that remain to be considered attempt to meet the criticisms mentioned. They believe that their schemes would make for economic efficiency, and escape bureaucratic incompetence and regimentation.

3. *Guild Socialism*

Guild Socialists propose that the workers in each industry, organized as a guild, should manage their own affairs, choosing foremen, managers, and general superintendents, fixing hours and wages, and prices charged for products. The political state would have less rather than more functions than at present, and in part these would be different. The state would continue to maintain order, punish crime, and provide for the national defense. In addition, it would adjudicate disputes between the different guilds. All productive property of consequence would be managed collectively, by the guilds themselves, who would either own it, or would be intrusted with its direction by the political state, which would finance the undertakings of the guilds. Thus each industry would be immediately under the control of those who would work in it, understand its conditions best, and be concerned to make it economically effective, in order that their own incomes might be as high as possible. The dangers of bureaucratic red tape, wastefulness, and regimentation would be escaped. All workers would have a voice in the conduct of their own industries, would take pride in them, and be loyal to them. At first, higher pay might have to be accorded in each industry to skilled workers, but ultimately there would be complete equality in this respect. The golden age of medieval craftsmanship would be restored by the guilds.

Guild Socialists are peaceable folk, and anticipate the transition to their system by constitutional means, the state gradually expropriating the present owners, and turning the industries over to the guilds. *Syndicalists* have a somewhat similar social order in view as their goal, but they are in more of a hurry to bring it about. They favor violent measures, such as a general strike in all industries simultaneously, which would terrify present owners, and force them to surrender their property to the ownership and management of their employes.

In criticism of Guild Socialism, it might be feared that the workers would vote themselves excessively short hours and high wages, and elect officers who were popular fellows and good politicians rather than skillful managers. This fear seems to be confirmed by the results of an experiment in this direction that was made in England shortly after the war, when certain building trade unions were given large government contracts, in which they failed.[20] Guild Socialists think that this experiment is inconclusive, and that the idea ought to be given another trial. The Syndicalists brought about a general strike in certain cities in northern Italy shortly after the war, with the result that the workers actually gained possession of several industrial plants. They soon found themselves unable to operate them to their own advantage, and were glad to return them to their former employers and work again under the capitalistic system. A violent reaction from Syndicalism to Fascism took place in the minds of Italian workingmen shortly after, and under Capitalism Italy at the present time seems to be making faster strides toward the economic prosperity of the workers than ever before in modern times.[21]

4. *Consumer's Coöperative Democracy*

In Denmark, England, and many other European countries, and to a considerably less extent in the United States, Consumers' Coöperative Societies have been developing. Danish farmers combine in marketing their produce, purchasing their supplies, and making loans, thus saving the profits of middle men. English coöperative societies, which include in their membership one third of the families in the country, carry on an extraordinary business, primarily retailing merchandise to their members, but also to some extent manufacturing the goods which they sell, and even importing on their own steamships tea, grain, and other products raised on their own plantations overseas. Earnings beyond the expense of management, interest on the capital invested, and a sinking fund, are returned to consumers in proportion to their purchases. The cost of living for the members is thus substantially reduced. The whole enterprise is carried on for service and not for profits.

One enthusiastic leader of this movement in America [22] believes that coöperative societies will in time take over most of the productive processes of the country. The majority of people will obtain employment in these societies and purchase their goods from them. The outcome will be an organization in some respects like Guild Socialism, except for the important difference that the ultimate control will be in the hands of consumers instead of producers. The political state will be governed by representatives of consumers and producers. There will be more decentralization of government and a closer approximation to pure democracy than we have at present.

The plausibility of Coöperative Democracy lies in the fact that it is a further expansion of a principle that has actually proved to work economically,—something that can hardly be claimed for any of the other forms of Collectivism which we have considered. But while coöperative societies have been of real service, experience seems to indicate that there are limits to the possible expansion of the movement. It seems risky for them to extend credit to retail purchasers, or to carry other than very stable commodities. It is hard for them to secure executives with the necessary qualities for business success. A few individuals of high capacity will work at the head of coöperative societies at small salaries, out of devotion to the cause. But most men of outstanding ability prefer to work for profit for themselves and their families. Like other forms of Collectivism, Coöperation does not offer sufficient incentives to evoke the highest degree of economic efficiency. It seems improbable that the expansion of Coöperation will ever proceed so far that it will revolutionize the economic and political structure of any free state.

5. *Conclusion*

It has been seen that Capitalism in its present form meets the requirements of the canon of distributive justice partially but not perfectly. On the other hand, all the types of Collectivism appear visionary, and it seems improbable that in our time, at least, any of them will supplant Capitalism,—certainly not in America, where the advocates of Collectivism are few and diminishing in numbers.[23]

However, there is no reason why American municipalities and "state" and national governments should not attempt ownership and operation of public utilities whenever and whereever private enterprise breaks down in efficiency and it seems probable that the change would be an improvement. The chief obstacle in the way of such attempts to-day arises from the fact that most voters are not property holders, do not pay taxes, are not efficient in their personal finances, and do not appreciate economical public management. There is hope that conditions may change in these respects. Workingmen are beginning to save. Labor unions have gone successfully into the banking business, and are helping their depositors to invest their savings in stocks and bonds. In other words, workers are becoming capitalists on a small scale. A veritable economic revolution in the distribution of wealth seems to be going on in our country to-day.[24] If this continues, the time will come when the majority of voters will be property owners and taxpayers. Then citizens who themselves possess the virtue of economy will appreciate economy in public undertakings. Thus the time may come when more economic processes can be undertaken successfully by the state than is now the case. But this does not mean that complete Socialism will ever come. State ownership and operation of economic enterprises can only be successful provided the majority of citizens are themselves possessors of the virtue of economy; the latter cannot be true unless they are private possessors of income producing property.[25]

It may be observed that to-day many persons in our nation are really working and living under collectivistic conditions. Judges of the United States Supreme Court, officers in the army and navy, employes of the civil service on permanent appointment, teachers in public schools and state universities, and many other persons, now hold permanent positions during good behavior and receive pensions on retirement. Their incomes are not large enough to enable them to become considerable holders of capital. In general, their positions are really

Socialized (using "Socialized" in the sense of "Socialism", and not in the broader sense of the chapters in Part I).[26]

It may be a question whether other professions might not also become Socialized advantageously. A teacher does not receive fees from his pupils; ought a physician or a surgeon to receive fees from his patients? Ought not members of the medical profession to be entirely free from financial interest in their relations with their patients, and receive fixed annual salaries as public servants, or as members of the staffs of endowed organizations, like colleges, hospitals, and clinics? And how about lawyers? We saw in the previous chapter the great inequality between rich and poor in our courts. Might not legal as well as medical services be maintained at public expense for all who need them? Ought not both professions to be placed on the same status as higher judges and teachers? Those who favor the present arrangement point out that in professions not Socialized, patrons enter into close personal relations with their advisers, and argue that collectively appointed officials would not have the same personal interest, and so would not perform their services so faithfully. Moreover, it is said that competition in these professions is necessary in order to key up their members to their highest efficiency. The author has no decided opinion to offer. It is clear that professional services cannot satisfactorily be measured in terms of money. A judge, a teacher, or a physician is not deemed successful by the evidence he displays of business ability. This is one important reason why it is possible for professions to be Socialized.

The situation is different in the case of business men, farmers, and workingmen. Their productiveness is directly economic, and is more readily measurable in economic values. It seems just that they should remain within the capitalistic system, and that their incomes should be proportionate to the economic services that they render. And while, as has been seen, our economic structure is too complex to make it certain that the laws of demand and supply and free competition assure that each will always receive rewards in accordance with his services, it seems questionable whether any form of Collectivism would make a better apportionment. Our present economic order conforms to the canon of distributive justice at least in one respect. It gives business men, farmers, and workers strong incentives to be economically efficient, and in the main it provides them the opportunity to become so. It therefore seems probable that evils in our capitalistic system can better be corrected by legislation, supervision by government commissions, and by higher ethical standards within business itself, rather than by the adoption of any system of Collectivism. Our next topic is a consideration of the ethical standards of business and the professions.

REFERENCES

* J. Dewey and J. H. Tufts, *Ethics*, chaps. XXII–XXV.
* J. A. Leighton, *The Individual and the Social Order*, chaps. XXXVII–XLIV.
* J. H. Wigmore, editor, *Rational Basis of Legal Institutions*, chaps. I–XXXVIII.
* T. N. Carver, *Essays in Social Justice. The Present Economic Revolution in the United States.*
* H. Baker-Crothers and Ruth Hudnut, *Problems of Citizenship*, chaps. XVII–XXIII.
* J. H. Tufts, *The Ethics of Co-operation.*
* C. Gore, editor, *Property, its Rights and Duties.*
* J. A. Ryan, *Distributive Justice.*
* Herbert Spencer, *Justice.*
* A. J. Eddy, *Property.*
* Whiting Williams, *The Mainsprings of Men.*
* L. D. Edie, *The New Economics*, chaps. I–VII, XI–XIII.
* F. W. Taussig, *Principles of Economics.*
* H. R. Seager, *Principles of Economics*, chaps. XXIX–XXXIV.
  L. T. Hobhouse, *Social Justice.*
  Henry Sidgwick, *Elements of Politics.*
  T. V. Smith, *The American Philosophy of Equality.*

Other references, some of a more technical character, will be found in the Notes to this chapter.

CHAPTER XVII

THE PROFESSIONS AND BUSINESS

I. Vocational Ethics

Vocational Ethics treats of *the rights and duties of the members of a business or profession with reference to one another, their employes, and the general public.* In previous chapters we have been concerned with moral principles that apply impartially to every one, or at least to every citizen. Now we are interested in the added privileges and obligations that an individual assumes when he enters upon a particular occupation.

Some moral obligations bind members of certain vocations more strictly than they do people in general. Thus every citizen ought to vote and take an intelligent interest in the political issues of the times, but the lawyer is expected to be more active and better informed. Every citizen should be concerned about the general health of the community, insisting that streets be kept clean, water and milk pure, and hospitals efficient. But in these matters physicians are more competent and responsible. Every one ought to practice the virtue of economy, avoid needless waste, and do what he can to increase the total amount of wealth in existence. Upon business men, however, chiefly rests the duty to keep the processes of production as stable as possible, averting panics, business depressions, and hard times. Every person should help to render town and countryside comfortable and beautiful; so that wherever people live and children are born and bred, their surroundings may help them to be healthy, happy, and virtuous. But specialists in architecture, engineering, the fine arts, sociology, and kindred subjects should lead movements in city and country planning.

Every one should cultivate all the virtues. Only in a well rounded life, where each virtue has its full development, can

425

happiness and self-realization be achieved. But certain virtues are more indispensable in some vocations than in others. All men ought to have courage, but the aviator, soldier, policeman, and fireman must excel others in this virtue. Every person should be reverent and sympathetic, but the clergyman particularly so. All need to be conscientious, but specialists must be wise in matters in which they profess to be experts.

The ethics of the members of a vocational group supplement and in many ways are stricter than the mores of society in general. Professional men are jealous of the dignity of their professions. A physician or a lawyer may not publish advertisements in a newspaper, other than a brief professional card. To do more would be *unethical*, according to the standards of the profession; although it could hardly be thought to be *immoral*, measured by the moral judgments of people in general. (*Ethical* and *unethical* are the adjectives applied by professional and business men with reference to the *actions that do or do not conform to the ethics of their vocations; moral* and *immoral* being reserved for *actions judged by the ordinary moral consciousness.*[1] This usage is followed throughout this chapter, but not elsewhere in this volume.) A minister,[2] and in some localities a teacher,[3] must not deliberately seek a call elsewhere at a higher salary, if he has no real intention of leaving, but merely desires to force a raise in salary in his present position. A banker must be extremely careful in recommending investments; in some cases he should not advise customers to incur risks that he would not hesitate to take himself with his own private capital. Men in every occupation, including business, must be guarded in their criticisms of their colleagues, when conversing with persons outside of the vocation; although they must protect its good name by taking such action as is possible against real offenders. The opposite conduct in the illustrations mentioned would not in all instances be immoral, but would be considered unethical.

On the other hand, vocational ethics is liable to be more lax in some respects than ordinary morality, although this is less true to-day than it was even a few decades ago. Immoral habits in drink and sex, if not notorious, may not seriously affect a man's standing in business and in many professions. They might not prevent professional or business relations with one whom a decent citizen would not care to receive socially in his home. The moral laxness of vocational ethics, when it exists, is partly due to the almost inevitable slant which the character of the vocation gives to its participants. Civil lawyers are prone to have a magnified notion of the importance of property rights and to fail to appreciate other human rights. A criminal lawyer is liable to develop too much sympathy for his unfortunate clients, to condone the wrongs that they have done, and under estimate their menace to society; although legal ethics is becoming stricter in this respect, and now forbids a criminal lawyer to seek the acquittal of a client whom he positively knows to be guilty.[4] A college teacher is prone to over emphasize the importance of intellectual interests and to undervalue the other interests of his students; this he does perhaps in self defense because alumni and even parents frequently exert their influence unduly in the opposite direction. Civil servants are inclined to make a fetich of seniority and red tape. Soldiers tend to make morality mere *esprit de corps*. Business men in the past were often too lenient upon exaggerations in advertisements and salesmanship; of late years they have been making sweeping reforms. Ministers have been over lenient in condemnation of plagiarized sermons. They have been so ready to write recommendations for every one that such a letter from a minister often has less weight than it deserves.

Vocational ethics seems justified in refusing to pass judgments on offenses that have nothing to do with efficiency and reliability in the vocation itself; these are matters for the public moral consciousness to condemn, and not the members of the vocation as such. On the other hand, in all conduct that concerns the professional or business trustworthiness and efficiency of any of its members, the vocation should be uncompromisingly severe in its judgments. The public has the right to expect the bar, the medical profession, and the ministry to protect it from shysters, quacks, and Elmer Gantrys. The stock exchange must exclude dishonest brokers and the floaters of fraudulent securities. Business men need to raise the general tone of advertisements. Unless the members of a vocation protect the public from the black sheep in their ranks, the whole vocation becomes discredited in the public mind, and cannot with full effectiveness render the services which society has a right to expect from it. Society in such cases is led to attempt through legislative and administrative action to force higher standards of conduct in matters that could more wisely and effectively be regulated by the members of the vocation itself.

II. Professional Ethics

The general line of demarkation between professions and business is fairly clear, although there are vocations that overlap. Clergymen, teachers, army officers, and civil servants are undoubtedly members of professions. Bankers, manufacturers, and merchants are business men. The work of the lawyer is mainly professional, although he sometimes acts as a business agent. Engineers and architects should be classified among the professions; realtors are business men.

The features that distinguish a profession from a business are chiefly these. A lengthy and specialized education is a prerequisite for membership in a profession. The work itself calls for highly technical training and skill. Such a group is, therefore, comparatively restricted in numbers, marked off from the rest of society by their work, and often—truly though subtly—by their habits of life, tastes, and personal demeanor. It does not take a Sherlock Holmes to distinguish a professional man, as he passes by on the street, and to decide to what profession he belongs. The relation between a professional man and those whom he serves is likely to be more personal than that between a member of a business firm and its patrons. Physicians and lawyers, for example, practice as individuals or in small firms; a patient or client when he calls, asks to see a particular person who gives special attention to his case. Professional men feel a certain pride in their vocations, and are capable of much group loyalty. They can readily organize themselves into associations with strong solidarity. Success is measured by technical erudition, and skill in applying it to specific problems.

The rewards of professional success consist very largely in the interest of the work itself, in the opportunity to devote oneself to its study and practice. The members of any profession have a certain prestige,—they enjoy cultivated association with persons of like minds and interests. The service that a profession renders is not easily measured by money; its contribution to the common weal is genuine and important, but it is not economically productive in the narrowest sense. No intelligent person would think that the success of such a man could be estimated by the amount of property that he accumulates. In a rough way, it can be said that the motive of service is more marked than in a business, and that considerations of private profit are more incidental; although, of course, the professional man must make a living adequate to maintain himself and his family on a scale that will enable him to be proficient, as well as to lead the manner of life that custom expects of him.

Certain professions, as we saw in the preceding chapter, are now Socialized. The member of a vocation of this type receives a salary, and often on retirement a pension. He should be able to devote his entire attention to his work, free from financial worry. His relation with those whom he serves is financially disinterested. In professions where a fee is received from patrons, professional men practice separately or in small partnerships; patrons engage their services as individuals rather than as a firm. The professional man should not make the amount of his fee the primary consideration in determining the amount of attention that he shall give to the case of any particular patron. He ought to be willing to serve with equal fidelity those who can pay little, or nothing at all. A lawyer or a physician often takes special interest in a case that calls for high professional skill in the solution of new legal or medical points, with little regard to financial remuneration.

Most of the professions have lengthy codes, drawn up by their respective associations, to which the interested reader can be referred.[5] A code sets forth the principles to which the members of the profession are expected to adhere, and it enumerates specific forms of misconduct that are forbidden.   Offenses deemed most reprehensible, or those which the members of their own initiative cannot prevent, a professional association will seek to have prohibited by law, with penalties attached. Such an association is likely to feel that there is a wide domain in which it can best by its own efforts prevent misconduct, or at least keep it at a minimum.   In the professions, as elsewhere, the principle of moral education applies.   Most men will respect the ethical standards of their social groups, if these are formulated and made known to them.   They want to do what is ethical, as judged by their colleagues. Would be offenders are deterred by fear of certain condemnation and possible ostracism by their fellows. A professional association is a better judge of professional propriety than are legislatures and courts. All the latter can do is to prohibit and punish offenses immoral enough to be classified as crimes and misdemeanors.   The association can maintain higher standards of conduct among its members.

It will be impossible to outline the codes of all of the professions.   A brief summary of some points in two of them will perhaps give an idea of their general character.

A physician is a member of a profession that "has for its prime object the service it can render humanity; reward or financial gain is a subordinate consideration". He should never reveal the confidences of a patient, nor flaws of character observed in him except when imperatively required by the laws of the state, or to take definite action to prevent the infection of a healthy individual. A physician is free to choose whom he will serve; but he must always respond to requests for assistance in an emergency. Having once undertaken a case, he should not neglect a patient because incurable, nor withdraw from the case without giving timely notice. He must not solicit patients by circulars, advertisements, personal communications, or interviews. He must not sell surgical instruments or medicines to his patients, nor receive rebates from those who sell them. Physicians should treat members of the families of other physicians when requested. They should assist in consultations. A physician should ordinarily avoid making social calls on the patients of other physicians; he should never take charge of a patient under the care of another physician until the latter has relinquished the case or been dismissed. A physician succeeding another in a case should not make criticisms of his predecessor. Physicians should treat the poor gratuitously. They should not secretly divide fees. They should not dispose of their services under contract in a way that would prevent adequate service to patients. They should coöperate for the prevention of epidemics. In general, the physician should behave toward patients, the public, and his fellow practitioners as he desires them to deal with him. He should always uphold the honor of his profession, and endeavor to serve the public.[6]

The lawyer should maintain a respectful attitude toward the courts; he should endeavor to prevent political considerations from outweighing judicial fitness in the selection of judges. A lawyer should avoid marked attention and unusual hospitality toward a judge; he should not communicate or argue privately with a judge as to the merits of an impending cause. A lawyer should be willing to serve as counsel for indigent prisoners. "It is the right of the lawyer to undertake the defence of a person accused of crime, regardless of his personal opinion as to the guilt of the accused; otherwise innocent persons, victims only of suspicious circumstances, might be denied proper defence." "The primary duty of a lawyer engaged in public prosecution", on the other hand, "is not to convict, but to see that justice is done." A prosecuting lawyer should not suppress facts nor secrete witnesses. A lawyer must not represent conflicting interests, except by the express consent of all concerned; he must not subsequently accept retainers or employment from others in matters adversely affecting any interest of his client. A lawyer should give a client a candid opinion of the merits and probable result of pending or contemplated litigation. Whenever a controversy will admit of fair adjustment, the client should be advised to avoid or end litigation. A lawyer should not directly negotiate with the clients of a lawyer on the opposing side. Money or other trust property belonging to a client should not be used by the lawyer.

A lawyer should fix his fees in accordance with the time and labor involved, the probable loss of other practice through taking the case, customary charges for such services, the amount involved in the controversy and the benefit received by the client, the certainty of compensation, and whether the employment is casual or for an established and constant client. "A client's ability to pay cannot justify a charge in excess of the value of the service, though his poverty may require a less charge, or even none at all." "In fixing fees it should never be forgotten that the profession is a branch of the administration of justice, and not a mere money-getting trade."

In supporting a cause, the lawyer should defend his client's rights to the utmost of his learning and ability, regardless of how it will affect his own popularity; all this must be within the bounds of the law, and he must not assist a client to violate the law or engage in any manner of fraud. "He must obey his own conscience and not that of his client." He should do his best to restrain clients from improprieties, avoid personalities with opposing counsel, treat witnesses with fairness and consideration, be cautious about discussing his causes in the newspapers, be candid and fair in his quotation of documents and testimony. He should not try to curry favor with juries, nor privately communicate with them. He should avoid all kinds of direct and indirect advertising, except ordinary simple business cards. He should not stir up litigation. He should uphold the honor of the profession, aiding the Bar against the admission of incompetent or morally unfit candidates, and he should expose before the proper tribunals corrupt or dishonest conduct in the profession. He should decline unjustifiable litigation. "Above all a lawyer will find his highest honor in a deserved reputation for fidelity to private trust and to public duty as an honest man and as a patriotic and loyal citizen." [7]

The value of professional codes like those summarized is to make clear to all practitioners what they may and what they must not do. Codes should not abound in moral generalities like the Golden Rule; professional ethics must be more specific. The service of a code is to afford definite guidance in the detailed problems of the practice of the vocation. A code may properly urge the profession to respect and obey the law; it should not mention particular laws in such a manner that the inference might be drawn that others need not be regarded so scrupulously. No code can pretend to be exhaustive; like the two cited, every code should explicitly state that it does not include all the duties and obligations of the profession. Codes should be revised from time to time as conditions change.

III. Business Ethics

A business, as distinct from a profession, is economic in the narrower sense. It is engaged in the production or sale of commodities rather than of services. It involves to a greater extent the investment of capital. Its success is more adequately measured by its profits; the most successful business man is he who has accumulated the largest amount of property, with the stipulation that he has done so in ways that are both moral and ethical. The stipulation is becoming increasingly recognized, and business associations, Rotary Clubs, and similar organizations are formulating codes containing ethical standards for the conduct of business, and they are endeavoring to enforce them. To that extent business is becoming professionalized. But business remains distinct from the professions in that comparatively little technical education is ordinarily required, and the chief incentive to activity is the desire to earn profits. The moral and ethical stipulation signifies that to deserve profits some real economic service must be rendered to the community. The most serious violations of business morality can be prevented by legislation, and by the regulation of federal and "state" trade and public service commissions. Ethical violations that have not been brought within the scope of governmental activity are prevented by the influence of the public opinion of business men and the efforts of business men's associations.

A good simple code of business ethics has been formulated by Mr. Edward A. Filene: "1. A business, in order to succeed, must be of real service to the community. 2. Real service in business consists in making or selling merchandise of reliable quality for the lowest practically possible price, provided that merchandise is made and sold under just conditions."

"Real service to the community" means that goods must be made that are best adapted for the particular uses for which people want them, and sold at just prices. Total profits must increase by the reduction of costs to the lowest practicable figure, and by large and frequent sales at a small margin of profit on each individual transaction. The "lowest practicable price" will vary somewhat in different years and localities, and will become increasingly lower with the progress of methods of manufacture and distribution. Merchandise must be maintained at the level of "reliable quality"; the lowering of prices through the substitution of inferior goods would not be real progress. "Just conditions" for the manufacture and sale of commodities exclude merchandise made or sold under "sweat shop" conditions, or by underpaid or overworked people; to lower prices through such methods would merely be to rob some people in order to benefit others. Good relations should be maintained with employes for the purpose that all may coöperate in service to the community. The business man should take an interest in promoting the welfare of the community in which he lives. He should give his support to efforts at civic betterment. With the reduction of prices under the conditions named, the necessities of life will become available to all for fewer hours of work, and men will gain more real freedom. It is not impossible that in time a man will only need to work five hours a day in order to provide a living for his family; he will then perhaps choose to continue eight or ten hours at his vocation in order to put his children through college, or to satisfy other desires. The merchant or manufacturer who best succeeds in these efforts at lowering prices by conducting business on a large scale will properly earn the largest profits because he is rendering the largest service to the community.[8]

In the preceding paragraph Mr. Filene's statements have been paraphrased for purposes of condensation; but it is believed that the import of his code of business ethics has been faithfully summarized. This code embraces the essential principles of business ethics, and properly marks off the differences between the ethics of business and the professions.

The development of business men's associations is one of the most remarkable moral phenomena of the present generation. There have been various causes for this development. Among them the following may be enumerated. The numerous exposures of bad business practices in newspapers and popular magazines during the first decade of the present century aroused the conscience of the business world, as well as of the indignant public. The moral idealism and championship of reforms advanced by Theodore Roosevelt, Woodrow Wilson, Robert M. La Follette, and many others, made an impression. There was the fear of bureaucratic governmental interference to correct abuses if the business world did not set its own house in order. The experiences of the War, during which business men often entered into whole-hearted and disinterested coöperation with one another, gave men a better realization of the possibility of competitors working together for the common good. The attempts of the churches to bring more Christianity into business helped. A contributing cause may have been the coming of prohibition, which led business men to seek the society of one another in lunch clubs and other places where conversation moved on a higher moral plane than it had in bar rooms. It would be pleasant to believe that the attention given to problems of distributive justice in college courses in ethics and the social sciences may have made some lasting impression on the younger alumni after they had entered the business world.

The outcome of it all has been that in this country there are now something like a thousand national trade associations, besides multitudinous state and district associations covering almost every field of business activity imaginable. Membership is open to all in good standing who are engaged in the business. Each association endeavors to promote the common good of its members. Manufacturers give one another information regarding trade conditions, stocks of goods on hand, and prices of raw material. This enables each firm to plan its operations more intelligently, and avoid over stocking the market. Industries suffer less from extreme fluctuations. Improved methods of accounting are made known to all. Each association studies new uses for the industry's product, and carries on advertising campaigns. It provides expert advice for members in their business problems.

The chief interest to the moral philosopher about these associations is the fact that they formulate codes in which the practices that are unethical according to the judgment of the association are explicitly enumerated and forbidden, and desirable practices are commended. Some associations are powerful enough to enforce their codes, because deprivation of membership would be a serious disadvantage. In any case the opinion of the association has considerable moral influence upon the conduct of its members.[9]

One of the great problems in business ethics with which the various associations are concerned is the definition and observation of truthfulness in advertising. An advertisement should be accurate in its statements about the nature of the article, the materials of which it is composed, the place where it has been made, and the benefits to be obtained from its use. Misrepresentations of an absolutely fraudulent character, now punishable by federal and "state" laws, are becoming rare as compared with a generation ago, or with some European countries at the present time. Advertisements that are gross exaggerations, or in offensively bad taste, although not necessarily criminal or immoral, are at any rate unethical, according to the standards of business men's associations. The better newspapers and periodicals refuse to publish them, because they weaken public confidence in all advertising, and so work injury upon those who advertise in good faith. To be sure, there is more of the element of suggestion than of strict logic in advertising, as the psychologists have long taught us; but business experience shows that the truth pays best in the long run, not only to periodicals but to advertisers themselves. It is impossible to fool all the people all the time; on the contrary, purchasers who find articles satisfactory will buy them again, as well as recommend them to others. Advertising is necessary in a capitalistic system; it introduces the public to commodities offered for sale; it makes larger scale production possible, and with it, lower prices. Contrary to popular impression, the cost of advertising is not excessive. Of the prices paid by consumers even for most of the very widely advertised articles, not more than five per cent can properly be charged to advertising.[10]

In business ethics—contrary to professional usage to a certain extent—the same price should be charged to every customer. Fixed prices—almost unknown when A. T. Stewart introduced the practice in New York in 1825,[11] have become the rule nearly everywhere in American retail trade. In all reputable retail stores the most ignorant purchaser can rely upon being asked the same price as the most persistent bargainer. Prices are commonly marked in plain figures; this is a guaranty of good faith on the part of the merchant, and it expedites trade by enabling the customer to look over goods and often make his selection while he is waiting until a sales person will be free to give him attention. Sales people truthfully say whether goods are made of cotton, silk, wool, or linen. They can be relied upon to measure thirty-six inches to the yard, sixteen ounces to the pound, and twelve units to the dozen. The dissatisfied customer can return goods and receive his money back without an argument; unless he has taken an unreasonable time to return them, has damaged them in some way, or bought them at a sale in which it was advertised that purchased goods might not be returned. In all of these respects American retail business has made great strides in recent years, and is far in advance of the smaller shops in Europe. Some of this progress must be credited to the growth of "big business". In large establishments uniform prices and consistent treatment of customers is more necessary than in a small shop in which the merchant, with perhaps one or two helpers, makes all sales personally. The progress in the ethics of salesmanship, like that of advertising, has come about because it pays; in successful business undertakings the largest profits go to those who render most service.

Another field in which there has been marked improvement in business ethics, although much further progress is needed, is in the definition and enforcement of the rules of *fair competition*. Profits, as we have seen, ought to be the reward of service. Competition in rendering services is fair. Efforts to outdo a rival and gain larger profits than he by some other method than that of rendering greater services are unfair.[12] The forms which unfair competition may assume are legion. Among them are: false and misleading advertising; misbranding articles offered for sale; combinations in restraint of trade; malicious disparagement by salesmen of competitors and their goods; attempts to deprive a competitor of his source of supply or place of business; price fixing; cutting prices below costs in certain localities in order to drive out small competitors and build up a monopoly; forcing retailers into keeping all the articles made by one manufacturer and none of a similar character made by others; adulteration; bribery of a competitor's employes to reveal business secrets; inducement of employes of a competitor to come into one's own employ by underhanded methods, for the purpose of getting his secrets and capturing his customers; and sending spies into a competitor's place of business.

Certain of the practices of unfair competition are punishable by law, and some progress has been made in prosecution of them. Others are subject to the control of federal and "state" trade commissions. All are denounced by chambers of commerce, Rotary clubs, and trade associations. Persistence in them brings an offender the ill will of his business associates and loss of their coöperation. This at least is unpleasant; in the long run it may prove a more serious loss than can be compensated for by the immediate profits gained by unfair practices.

The relations between business men and their employes have been steadily improving in recent years. The consciences of most business men are now awake, and they desire to be on terms of good will and coöperation with their helpers so that greater gain may result for both, with lower prices to the public. Business men are greatly improving conditions in stores and factories from the standpoints of sanitation, comfort, and convenience. Welfare work is carried on. Personnel workers endeavor to find for each employe the task for which he is best suited. Employers are learning to recognize labor unions, meeting them half way, and seeking to negotiate fair terms with them. Many unions are losing their belligerent attitude, and learning to respond in a cordial way. Shop committees and arbitration boards are supplanting strikes as means of settling disputes. In various ways workers are given a voice in the details of management that directly affect them, and regarding which they have knowledge. Employes are becoming stockholders in the corporations for which they work. This broadens their moral outlook, as they come to regard the business from an investor's as well as an employe's standpoint.

To-day perhaps the most difficult problem is to find some means by which in all portions of the country restriction will be enforced upon excessively long hours and low pay, dangerous working conditions, child labor, and the labor of women in circumstances detrimental to their welfare. It is unjust that in portions of the country where conditions hitherto have been good, workers should be thrown out of employment or compelled to accept unfavorable terms in order to make it possible for their employers to compete with regions where labor is cruelly exploited.   Perhaps in time the whole country will become sufficiently morally enlightened for this situation to be remedied, as standards of working conditions are raised to a common level by "state" and local action.   At present progress in this direction appears painfully slow.   To bring this field within the control of the national government by an amendment to the federal constitution seems to many contrary to our tradition of "states' rights".   Yet it must be remembered that it was only through such a course that free labor was finally freed from unfair competition with slave labor.   "States' rights" are only morally defensible when their recognition furthers and does not obstruct the advance of human welfare.

A word remains to be said about the duties of consumers. In retail stores it has become a common practice to assume that "the customer is always right" in all disputes.   The generosity of merchants in this respect has often been imposed upon.   Goods not wanted are not returned promptly, or are brought back in a damaged condition.   Credit privileges are abused.   Customers are often rude and inconsiderate, not to say cruel, in their treatment of sales people.   Consumers should avoid shopping at crowded times when it is possible for them to make purchases at earlier hours and seasons.   They should refuse to buy goods manufactured or sold under unjust conditions.   In many ways they can help the better merchants and manufacturers to maintain higher ethical standards in the business world generally.   Women's clubs, churches, and other organizations are doing much to enlighten the public in these matters, and they can do more.

IV. The Choice of a Vocation

It was said in Chapter X, section IX, that apart from exceptional cases in which self-sacrifice is called for, a person should choose the vocation in which he can best realize his capacities. Naturally this implies that the chosen vocation not only appeals to his tastes, but that he actually has talent for it. To be sure, tastes and talents are likely to go together. People can usually do best that which they aspire to achieve. But this is not always true; nor does manifestation of a little talent necessarily imply great possibilities of development. Not every bright clerk in a village could become a great merchant or banker if he were to go to New York. Nor does every girl who sings well in the choir of a country church merely lack training in order to be a prima donna.

In these days, when vocational counselors give information and advice regarding the outlook in the different callings, and psychologists are equipped with intelligence tests that throw light upon natural mental ability and special aptitudes, students have expert assistance available. The psychologists can claim fairly high coefficients of correlation favoring the accuracy of their tests, and their predictions regarding a young person's capacities are probably at least as trustworthy as the forecasts of the weather bureau.[13] The opinions of psychologists and vocational counselors should be supplemented by the advice of teachers and other older friends who are well acquainted with a student personally, and can take into account aspects of his character which mental tests are not apt to disclose.

It is the duty of every one to make his life of service to humanity. It does not follow that all who feel this obligation strongly should choose those vocations that are reputedly altruistic in preference to those popularly deemed selfish. A few years ago, a famous scientist asserted that a young man with ability for research could probably accomplish more that would be of wide benefit to humanity during the next generation by devoting himself to pure and applied physics than to any of the so-called "social sciences". He would be more likely to make discoveries himself, or help to apply the discoveries of others, in ways that would cheapen production and hence raise the standard of living for every one. In short, that the physicists are likely to accomplish more for the prevention of poverty than the sociologists and social workers. Shortly after the War, when, as a result of increased wages many people were for the first time learning to save and to invest, and it was of importance that they receive trustworthy advice, a great economist expressed the opinion that a young man could hope to do most good in the world by entering the field of investment banking. A student came into the author's office recently, full of zeal to help his fellow men. He said that he was thinking of going into the ministry, although he felt more attracted, so far as personal inclination went, to the career of an industrial chemist. It turned out that he did not feel drawn toward pastoral work, nor toward trying to preach spiritual messages that would bring men closer to God. To him, being a minister chiefly meant an opportunity to preach sermons on the "social gospel", which, he thought, might help to bring employers and employes closer together. He was told that as an officer in a manufacturing corporation he probably could do more to bring workingmen and managers together than he could by preaching sermons in a church; and that in his case the first step might well be to study industrial chemistry. Society not only needs social scientists, social workers, and ministers, but also physicists, chemists, and business men. One can be of great service to humanity in any of these callings.

To succeed in any vocation a man must enter into social relationships and be of help to others. A physician can only succeed as he heals his patients, a lawyer as he handles the business of his clients to their advantage, a merchant as he fills the demands of his customers. So in the long run and as a rule, the man who in his vocation renders most service to others should and usually does receive the highest rewards, honorific and pecuniary, that the vocation has to offer. There are exceptions, and it is the great problem of social control to eliminate them; but the statement holds true as a broad generalization. The conclusion is, then, that it is usually good advice to urge a young person to choose the vocation he most desires to enter, and in which he believes that he would most fully realize himself and hence be happiest. This is subject to four reservations: (1) the vocation must be an honest one, that renders genuine service to the community; (2) the individual must show some talent for it; (3) the vocation must not be overcrowded, there must be real openings in it for men with his measure of ability; (4) he must not shirk responsibilities; *e.g.*, a man with a family and without independent means ought not under ordinary circumstances to begin preparation for a learned profession.

A final observation needs to be made. A person in choosing a vocation in which he can realize the best that is within him, should avoid a calling in which his own weaknesses will subject him to undue temptation, or in which his virtues will not have a chance for expression. A man who finds it hard to be honest should not seek positions of trust. A man with a weakness for drink should not enter a vocation in which temptations of that kind will frequently be thrust in his way. An unusually generous and sympathetic person should not seek employment in a collection agency nor upon a detective force. An unsociable person should not seek an occupation that requires a great deal of good fellowship. Every one excels in some virtues more than in others. There are plenty of callings suitable for the prudent and for the daring; for the generous and for the thrifty; for those who love quiet study and research, and for those who like executive work; for realists who see things as they are and are always prepared for the worst, and for idealists whose ardent "will to believe" helps them to turn visions into realities.

REFERENCES

* Edgar L. Heermance, *The Ethics of Business. Codes of Ethics.*

* Carl F. Taeusch, *Professional and Business Ethics.*

* Clyde L. King, editor, *The Ethics of the Professions and Business.*
(Annals of the American Academy of Political and Social Science, May, 1922.)

James Melvin Lee, *Business Ethics* (especially chaps. V–IX).

Everett W. Lord, *Fundamentals of Business Ethics* (especially chaps. V, VII–XI, XIV, XV).

Richard C. Cabot, *Adventures on the Borderlands of Ethics* (especially chaps. II, III).

R. M. Binder, *Business and the Professions.*

Frank Parsons, *Choosing a Vocation.*

E. L. Bernays, editor, *An Outline of Careers.*

J. McKinney and A. M. Simons, *Success Through Vocational Guidance.*

H. L. Hollingworth, *Vocational Psychology.*

C. H. Griffiths, *Fundamentals of Vocational Psychology.*

CHAPTER XVIII

THE FAMILY, AND THE POSITION OF WOMEN

I. INTRODUCTORY

The Family is the primary human social institution,—first in origin and first in importance. The earliest forms of group life are based upon the relation of kinship. Even the primitive horde, as we saw in Chapters II and III, has learned what we still consider the most important moral judgments, from experiencing the relations between husband, wife, and children. Among civilized nations to-day the family in the form of ethical monogamy is the securest of all institutions. In the confusion at the close of the Great War, when the three most powerful authoritarian empires in Europe fell, and in several countries the state, the church, private property, and other long respected institutions were jeopardized, and in one partly overthrown, the monogamous family remained unattacked. The Russian revolutionists were indignant at the charge that they were contemplating its abolition.

Monogamy as an ethical institution, we saw on page 58, permits only the union of single pairs, who publicly vow life long fidelity to each other in a manner prescribed by law and custom, usually including a religious ceremonial. All other forms of marriage are forbidden. The triumph of monogamy has been the outcome of a long social evolution, in which other forms of sexual relationship were tried and found wanting. It cannot be said that monogamy is instinctive in the human race; but history has proved that through it human instincts and impulses are most adequately satisfied, and men, women, and children approach nearest to complete happiness and self-realization.[1]

In the earlier stages of biological evolution, sexual reproduction supplanted reproduction from a single parent through

445

fission, budding, and parthogenesis chiefly because the participation of two parents effects more numerous variations in the offspring.   In consequence, favorable variations more often appear and survive.   Defects of one parent are escaped by many of the progeny, through the inheritance of normal traits from the other parent.   With the appearance of sexual reproduction, therefore, evolution became swifter and surer.   The offspring of the higher vertebrates, especially birds and mammals, receive maternal care from their inception until infancy is passed and they can shift for themselves.   The longer the period of infancy, the more complex can brains and nervous systems become, and the higher is the resulting intelligence.   Most birds and many higher mammals mate when in their natural wild state.   The father sometimes assists the mother in care for the young; in such cases infancy becomes further lengthened, and is attended by a corresponding increase in intelligence.[2]   This seems particularly true of our nearest animal relatives, the anthropoid apes.[3]

Of all possible forms of human sexual relationship, monogamy most effectively secures the care of children by both parents through the long years before they are educated, ready to support themselves, and to establish homes of their own.   The more thorough the nurture that children can receive from their parents, the more capable they can become of high attainments, measured by welfare and happiness.   In this sense it can be said that *human monogamous marriage is a reflective continuation of processes already initiated in biological evolution.*[1]

The logically possible forms of sexual relationship are complete promiscuity and no marriage system at all; group marriage, in which several men are married to several women; polyandry, in which several men are married to one woman; polygamy, in which several women are married to one man; pair marriage, in which marriages usually occur between two persons for practical reasons, but in which other forms of marriage are not forbidden; and monogamy.   So far as is known, promiscuity has never been a morally approved institution.[4]   Something approaching group marriage has been reported among certain native tribes in Australia and elsewhere; the practice is infrequent, and it is not likely that it was ever general among primitive men.[5] Polyandry is very rare; it is caused by a scarcity of women and extreme poverty. Polygamy often occurs among chiefs, royal houses, and the wealthy during father right and less developed authoritarian civilizations; but in such instances pair marriage is the practice of the bulk of the population. Gradually, as we ascend the scale of social evolution, the practice of polygamy declines in frequency, and at last is forbidden; monogamy triumphs in moral teaching and legislation. Polygamy seems to have disappeared among the ancient Hebrews before the book of Proverbs was written, as there is no reference to it there. It has longest survived among Chinese and Mohammedan peoples; in these the movement at present is emphatically toward monogamy.

II. Historical

Our present laws and customs regarding marriage and the position of women can hardly be understood without reference to their history. They have had three principal sources: ancient Roman law, early Teutonic custom, and the teachings of medieval and modern occidental Christianity.[6]

During the earlier centuries of the ancient Roman republic, the marriage laws were the development of the paternal family system carried to its extreme logical conclusions. A man was the absolute ruler and owner of his family,—that is, of his wife, minor sons, and unmarried daughters. He could command them to do as he pleased, and punish them for disobedience, even putting them to death after he had consulted with a council of relations. There were three different forms by which a man might become married: one (*confarreatio*), sacramental and religious, in which he and his bride ate together a sacred cake and were thought to be mystically united; another (*coemptio*), which was imitative of the forms of a legal sale or contract; and a third (*usus*) less formal, but which implied a marriage agreement. The legal effect of all three was the same, the bride passed out of the power (*potestas, tutela, manus*) of her father into that of her husband. Divorce was possible for the man, but rarely occurred. A woman had no property or other civil rights. While the laws were not less unfavorable to her, the actual position of woman was much higher than in Greece or the Orient. Roman women were respected and esteemed by their fathers, husbands, and sons; they were their social equals and confidants. Marriage was strictly monogamous.

In the course of the last two centuries of the republic a change was effected. A modification of marriage by *usus* was devised, so that a woman after marriage could remain within the *manus* of her father. This resulted in her virtual emancipation. Her husband had no legal authority over her; and as she lived in her husband's home her father could rarely exercise much control, and ordinarily did not care to do so. During the Roman empire, a Roman matron acquired full civil rights. She could carry on business and legal transactions, and had control of her own property. She had more rights than married women had ever known before,[7] or were again to possess until the middle of the nineteenth century. Divorce could be had at the desire of either spouse, and became common. The position of the unmarried woman remained unchanged; she continued to be subject to her father. Whether or not the emancipation of married women was responsible, there was greater sexual laxity under the empire than the early republic.[8] However, it is probable that the Roman matron in imperial times remained as a rule the loyal and devoted counselor and friend of her husband that she had been in the earlier republican times when she was under his dominion.[9]

The Teutonic tribes which overran and finally subdued the Roman empire in the West, retained the customs of father right in a manner similar to the early Roman republic. A man was the absolute ruler of his wife and children, exercising over them the right of life and death,—the latter subject to some extent to the council of relations. Without necessarily consulting his daughters, he chose husbands for them, often receiving compensations from their bridegrooms. Pair marriage was the ordinary practice of Teutonic peoples, but chiefs and wealthy men were often polygamous. The Teutonic wife was expected to be, and usually was chaste. No corresponding moral requirement was expected of her husband. It is chiefly from Teutonic sources that the "double standard", allowing greater freedom to the man, has come down to us. On the other hand, the Teutons were pure minded, and respected decent women. Their early literature, including myths, is decidedly superior in this respect to those of Greece and the Orient.

The medieval Latin church fostered the Teutonic respect for women. As a result of the interaction between Teutonic and Christian tendencies, there arose the institution of chivalry which afforded them special protection and consideration. From this developed the romantic literature of the middle ages, and our modern ideal of romantic love, which has done much to idealize the relations between the sexes, and put them on a higher ethical plane. In the adoration of the Blessed Virgin Mary, the church taught exalted conceptions both of celibacy and of motherhood. Laymen learned respect for both nun and married woman. Marriage was a sacrament, blessed by God and the church, and reverence for it was impressed on the medieval mind. Polygamy entirely disappeared. Divorce came to be forbidden absolutely; the doctrine was that those whom God had joined in holy matrimony, men might not part asunder. However, it was often easy for a man of influence to discover or to manufacture evidence that would persuade an ecclesiastical court to declare his marriage null and void. For a marriage was not valid unless both parties had originally given their voluntary consent, and unless they were not connected within remote lines of relationship traceable through either their own parents or their god parents. Moreover, a marriage could be annulled if a man could convince the court that he had already been secretly married; for clandestine marriages were considered valid, although they were not favored by the church. While, therefore, divorce was forbidden in theory, annulments were common in practice.

With the development of feudalism, the lord claimed the right to dispose of the daughters of his vassals in marriage as he chose, and to receive payment for them. This practice the church resolutely fought. By the close of the middle ages she had succeeded in establishing for all classes of society, including serfs, the principle that the voluntary consent of the woman as well as of the man was necessary for a legally valid marriage. Their mutual consent was also sufficient; parents and liege lords could lawfully neither command nor forbid them to marry.

As a result of the Reformation, marriage from the legal point of view in all Protestant and many Catholic countries has become a contract under the control of the state, and not a sacrament under the dominion of the church. Divorce is legally permitted on some grounds in nearly all free countries, although it continues to be sternly disapproved by the Roman Catholic church. Since the Council of Trent, this church has forbidden clandestine marriages, and has eliminated the other abuses that had previously made annulments easy. Annulments are now rarely granted by the Roman Catholic ecclesiastical courts, and only on conclusive evidence.

Neither Catholic nor Protestant churches opposed the continuation and further development in European law of the doctrine originating in Teutonic custom that a wife is under the supreme control of her husband.[10] Until about the middle of the nineteenth century, a married woman had few civil rights, either in Europe or the United States. She could not hold property in her own name. Whatever she inherited passed into the hands of her husband. She could carry on no business transactions except under his control. A wife could rarely testify in court against him. She was sometimes not held responsible for crimes committed by her in his presence, on the assumption that she did them under his coercion. Down to the middle of the seventeenth century a man still had the legal right to beat his wife for the sake of discipline, provided he did her no permanent bodily injury.[11]   There was no legal way, until well along in the nineteenth century, by which a woman with a drunken husband could prevent him from appropriating the money that she earned with her own labor.   The husband had complete authority over the children until they came of age.   Divorce, in the countries where it was permitted, was difficult and expensive, and granted on terms more favorable to the husband; children were more likely to be committed to him than to their mother.

In England, at least, the unmarried woman in early modern times gained full civil rights as soon as she became of age. There, at any rate, the tradition of father right only persisted for the married woman, who on marriage passed under the control of her husband.

To the Christian church can be credited the logical deduction from the principle of monogamy that strict continence outside of the married relation is as obligatory upon men as women. This "single standard" of sex morality, hardly known by ancient Jews, Greeks, or Romans, and certainly not by Teutons, has been consistently taught by the Christian church ever since New Testament times.   While it has never won an entire victory over the "double standard" of morality, it is recognized by all honest men as right in moral theory.   Most men observe it in practice most of the time, and many men, at least in Anglo-Saxon countries, throughout their lives.   In having taught the single standard, and made considerable progress in bringing it into observance, the Christian church has rendered a service of inestimable value to women.   For this contribution alone, the church may be forgiven her failure to do more than she did in other respects to assist married women to regain the rights which they lost at the fall of the Roman empire, with the result that Griselda became the model of womanly behavior for the middle ages, the Renaissance, and the Enlightenment.

The humanitarian movement of the early nineteenth century gradually directed part of its efforts toward the betterment of the position of women.   Other voices were added to those of Mary Wollstonecraft, Frances Wright, and John Stuart Mill.[12]   Dur-

ing the latter half of the last century most free states removed
the majority of the restrictions upon the freedom of women
which had come down in law and custom from the traditions of
Teutonic father right. They have gained most civil rights.
They can hold property, carry on business, sue and be sued, no
matter whether married or single. Legally woman now is in
nearly all respects upon a parity with her husband in the direction of the home, and in decisions that concern the welfare of
the family. There still remain various details in which women
have not gained full civil rights, chiefly in matters that affect
comparatively few women and have not come to general attention; but the battle for sex equality can be said to have been
won in principle.[13] As a matter of custom in America and among
the American born, the wife is the supreme authority in household matters; here the immigrant is likely to be more conservative, clinging to the tradition of father right and thinking of
himself as "lord in his own house".

Slowly women gained the right to higher education on equal
terms with men. By the middle of the nineteenth century many
European and American universities and colleges admitted
women; and in those parts of America and England in which
coeducation was distrusted, new higher educational institutions
were established exclusively for women. It is now generally conceded that women are equal to men in intellectual ability.[14] In
the United States to-day, more women than men complete cultural courses in secondary schools and in colleges and universities.

Political rights were gained by women in a few European
countries and American "states" during the closing years of the
nineteenth century. The services performed by women during
the Great War of 1914 won general sympathy with the suffrage
movement, and in most free states to-day women have the
right to vote and hold office on the same terms as men.

III. The Ideal in Marriage, and Some of its Implications

The modern ideal in marriage is an ethical sacrament.[15] The
relation does not rest upon a magical bond,—it is not sacramen-

tal in that sense in the minds of most of us. But it is something more sacred than an ordinary business contract. It is a tie in which a man and woman are united in lifelong fidelity. Its emotional basis is a virtuous sentiment of love, in which impulses of tenderness, self-assertion, respect, sympathy, prudence, acquisitiveness, and constructiveness are powerfully combined with sexual attraction, and all sublimated into a common interest and common will.

The ideal family is the most beautiful and most sacred human relationship. The words husband, wife, father, mother, and child are freighted with utmost meaning and value. In the ideal home, every member finds his highest joy in working with the others for the good of each individual. Whatever interests one is of intimate concern to the others. Each can confide his private hopes and aspirations and count on the understanding and support of all. Each is stimulated to his best efforts by this common love. The success of each individual is a common triumph; the weaknesses and failures of any member are matters for mutual sorrow, but not bitter invective. All are ready to make every effort to help him to victory over self and circumstances. Husband and wife are free personalities, with equal rights, each expert in his own sphere, and secure of the help and support of the other. Each child accepts parental counsel and guidance with loving docility, and is assisted in gaining free expression in the development of his personality. All members of the family work together to enable each to realize his ambitions; every one gladly makes sacrifices for the common good. The greatest affliction that can come to an ideal family is found in the death of one of its members; immediate solace is found in keeping his memory alive, and carrying out his wishes so far as changed circumstances render it possible; the most comforting consolation that religion can offer is the hope of family reunion in a future life.

The ideal family is seldom completely realized, but all thoughtful men and women marry with the will to attain it. So far as they succeed, they accomplish what counts for most, whether estimated from the standards of welfare or happiness. The life of no man or woman who has been successful in the family is a complete failure. No one has led a successful life, if his or her home has gone to smash; achievements in other directions will not compensate a person for disaster in the most intimate personal relations. However unfortunate in later years, no one misses all in life who has been blest as a child with a good home. The memory of it will sustain and comfort him through the tribulations that may afterward come to him.

To make himself or herself worthy of marriage is an incentive that should prompt every young person to whole hearted effort in work and play. Every young man who has learned to appreciate what his own home may mean to him some day, will do his best to prepare himself for his future position as the head of a family. He will make the most of his opportunities in study, in social contacts, in college student activities, in business, and professional work.

To be worthy of marriage at its best is the strongest reason why a young man should be continent. He will desire to come to his bride with the same purity of mind and body that he expects of her. He will therefore train himself to think of sex in wholesome ways. He will avoid salacious books and plays. He will laugh off broad jokes when he is forced to hear them, and speedily forget them. Most of all, he will lead a life of strict continence. He will avoid prostitutes, because he will abhor participation in a traffic based upon the ruin of young girls doomed to shame, disease, and early death. He will not wish to run the risk of infectious diseases which may make marriage impossible for him, or may transmit disease and sterility to his wife, or blindness and even more distressing afflictions to his children. Even if methods of prophylaxis and contraception were ever to become both infallible for their purposes and also free from every danger to health—neither of which conditions is at all true at present—the desire to be worthy of marriage at its best would remain for the thoughtful a sufficient incentive to strict continence. The attention of those interested in this side of the matter may be called to the convincing words of Professor Durant Drake (*Problems of Conduct*, pages 210–216).

A young man who finds continence difficult will resolutely keep himself out of the way of temptation. In regular indoor and outdoor exercise, in concentration on intellectual efforts, business activities and æsthetic interests, and in the society of good women he will probably find effective means of sublimation. He should avoid alcoholic drinks of every kind, and places in which they are sold; for alcohol stimulates desire and removes inhibitions; most men who ruin themselves by sexual indiscretions do so under the influence of liquor. If with such precautions as have been suggested, he still finds self control a hard battle, he should seek the counsel of a physician, preferably a man of mature years and undoubted integrity. He will find such physicians wise and sympathetic; they are accustomed to giving advice on such matters to young men, suited to their particular needs.[16] He will think of the future when he himself will be a father with sons to advise; he will so conduct himself that he will be able to look his sons squarely in the eyes, and honestly to urge them to live as he has done himself. Many a father would gladly cut off his right hand, if he could undo his own reckless past and be able to talk in this way to his boys.

Young women are usually more thoughtful than young men when it comes to contemplation of marriage. They should prepare themselves at home and at school so that they will be competent home makers, wives, and mothers. They will be discriminating in accepting the attentions of young men, and seek the counsel of their mothers, fathers, and other older friends whose judgment is more mature, and who are not likely to be carried away by romantic sentimentality. They will appreciate that character, personal purity, and kindness are more important qualifications in a husband than wealth or social graces. A man who is devoted to his mother is likely to be a good husband and father.[17] There should be sexual attraction toward a future husband, but common tastes, interests, ideals, and purposes are equally important. True love has its romantic side, but it has these other aspects as well. A woman ought to be in full sympathy with and appreciation for her husband's vocation, and be willing to accept whatever scale of living his success in it will make possible. She ought not to permit him to sacrifice his choice of a vocation in order to be able to marry her sooner, or to provide her a more luxurious scale of living. At the same time romantic idealism ordinarily should not permit her to marry him before he can provide the necessities of a home.[18]

Both young men and women should avoid serious flirtations. Those who have many insincere love affairs are likely to become constitutionally incapable of the steadfast love and loyalty requisite for a happy marriage. A coquette is liable to end as a divorcee.

One born and brought up in the nineteenth century hesitates to express himself decidedly upon contemporary "petting" and neglect of chaperons. Customs change, and the openness and frankness of the present time have redeeming features. But many thoughtful observers believe that a partial though not complete return to the conventions of a generation ago is over due, and predict that it will take place within another decade. Even now the ordinary young man probably would not care to marry a girl whom he knew had experienced the caresses of most of his men acquaintances. A prudent young woman may doubt if a man who has the reputation of being a "fast worker" and "able to kiss any girl" would make a very good husband. People of refinement do not wish to select husbands or wives whose previous romantic history suggests bargain counters and second hand goods.

IV. DIVORCE, TRIAL MARRIAGES, ETC.

The ideal in marriage, as we have seen, is a lifelong union of husband and wife, in which each shares in the richer and fuller life which their union affords. The ethical problem is, by what laws and customs can society cause as many marriages as possible to approximate this ideal? In the light of this problem should be considered the ethics of divorce, trial marriages, and free love.

The objection to free love, and scarcely less to trial and companionate marriages[19] is that the relation would not be entered upon with the full expectation of a life long union. The ideal in marriage is not easily attained. Man is not instinctively monogamous; he only becomes so as a result of social training and individual virtue. Unless a man and woman were to set up their home with the confident expectation that they will love and cherish each other so long as they live, it would hardly be possible in most cases for their marriage to prove permanent. Each would be wondering if he or she could not have made a better match, and if it were yet too late. Each would be tortured by jealousy. There is always a little friction at times in every home, but people who expect to live together all their lives make up after each disagreement, and usually know that they are going to do so even while the dispute is on. It would be quite different in an order in which any quarrel could at once lead to a permanent separation and the formation of new alliances. Character and happiness are not to be found in that way; neither for man nor woman and certainly not for their children. Children who grow up in unhappy homes, or whose parents separate or become divorced, are not likely to develop as satisfactorily in either an intellectual or a moral way, as those who experience normal family relationships.[20]

There are those who maintain that divorce should be granted on the mutual consent of husband and wife. They reason in some such way as the following. If a marriage fails to secure its purpose, and if instead a home is a place of strife, jealousy, and ill will, neither husband nor wife can develop in character and happiness. Such a place is the worst possible for children to be brought up. Such a marriage ought certainly to be dissolved; and the man and woman ought to have the right to marry again. If they are not allowed to marry again, they will probably do worse. After their previous failure they will have learned by experience, and be wiser in their choice of mates.

Moreover, the parties directly concerned know best whether a marriage has become intolerable.   Courts should grant petitions for divorce signed by both husband and wife, merely taking precautions that proper financial provision is made for the wife and children.   Public scandal will thus be avoided, and unhappily married people will escape the cruel publicity that now often attends divorce suits.   These are typical arguments in favor of divorce by mutual consent.

On further thought, it will be seen that there are grave objections to legalizing divorce by mutual consent.   If this were to become law and custom, it would speedily degenerate into divorce at the desire of either spouse.   For neither could seem reasonable in holding the other to a marriage that he or she found disagreeable.   Painful as the situation would be, the husband or wife no longer loved would have to allow the other to depart in peace.   And if either spouse could at any time easily force the other to agree to a divorce, there would be little stability in the married relation.   Successful husbands would be the prey of charming adventuresses, whose youth and beauty would snare them away from wives who had grown old and physically unattractive from childbearing and from economic privation in the years of struggle while the husbands were getting started in their careers.   The heart of many a loving and faithful wife would be broken, and her children would lose their father's care, while the fickle man himself would become wretched and disillusioned in his second marriage.   Some men are more likely to become weak and foolish when they have attained prosperity at fifty than when they were struggling at twenty; laws and customs should protect them and their families so far as is possible.   Young wives, in other cases, would be disappointed that their husbands did not advance more rapidly, or because they devoted themselves too much to business.   They would look about to see if they might not marry wealthier or more chivalrous gentlemen.   Such affinities discovered, it would be easy to persuade their husbands to "give them their freedom".   Beautiful and ambitious but selfish young women would look on a present marriage as merely a temporary stepping-stone to a more advantageous one.

Husbands and wives under a system which allowed divorce by mutual consent would never feel secure of each other's love. There would be many crimes like Othello's, and far more of the intense human misery that prompts to them. Fewer men and women would persist in the effort to live in mutual love and devotion, and many more persons would miss the joys of marriage at its best. While permission of divorce by mutual consent would no doubt prove beneficial in some instances, there is every reason to believe that on the whole it would diminish rather than increase the total number of successful homes.

But how about the opposite extreme? Why not forbid divorce and remarriage altogether; only in the most aggravated cases permitting husband and wife to separate, and allowing neither to remarry? Those who favor this position base their arguments on theological doctrines rather than upon study of modern social experience. Few if any probate judges and physicians take this stand. In countries where divorce is forbidden altogether the double standard is more likely to mark the conduct of men; if a man's home life is unhappy and there is no legal escape from it, society is not very severe in judging him if he seeks consolation elsewhere in an irregular relation. In such countries illegitimacy is often frequent, and laws forbid courts to inquire into the paternity of illegitimate children. The latter grow up under a stigma, without the love and care of two parents in a normal home. Wives under a social system where divorce is forbidden absolutely are frequently taught that it is their duty to remain in homes where husbands are cruel, drunken, notoriously unfaithful, and even syphilitic. Children who grow up under such conditions have the years of childhood saddened, and at worst become mentally, morally, and physically abnormal. Very few free countries remain to-day in which divorce on the most serious grounds is not permitted.

The experience of the majority of modern free states has led them to authorize the courts to grant a divorce if a spouse is proved to have been guilty of such offenses as adultery, habitual drunkenness for several years, serious crime, desertion, or if impotent, or incurably insane. Other grave offenses are sometimes added to the list.[21] No wronged wife or husband is under any circumstances forced by law to ask for a divorce; he or she may forgive and endure as long as there seems hope that conditions may improve. But when a person appears in the courts and seeks relief from the marriage bond on such grounds as these, divorce should be granted. To allow divorce only on grave grounds is not open to the objections that we have seen to divorce by mutual consent.

Many are alarmed at the frequency of divorces in the United States. At the time of writing, one is granted to every six or seven marriages, taking the country as a whole; and for some decades past the ratio of divorces to marriages has been increasing. So far as this situation exists in some "states" because divorces are granted for trivial reasons or upon inconclusive evidence, reforms are urgent. Only grave grounds should be recognized; laws and methods of court procedure should be strict. In some way laws of marriage and divorce must be made more nearly uniform throughout the country. Many divorces are the result of hasty and ill-considered marriages. Laws might well require persons under twenty-one to obtain the consent of their parents or guardians before they marry. The application for a marriage license ought to be published two weeks in advance of the ceremony. A fortnight of deliberation before taking so momentous a step is a minimum which society might properly require. The interval between publication of the application for the license and the celebration of the ceremony would allow time for any to protest who know of reasons why the marriage should not take place. Men should be required by law to pass medical examinations showing that they are free from infectious diseases; no decent man could feel insulted at such a legal requirement, while without a law to that effect it often seems indelicate for a bride's father to suggest it.[22]

However, the frequency of divorce in the United States

is partly justified. Under present economic conditions it is easier than in former times or in other countries for a woman to find means to support herself and even one or two children; a woman is not forced to endure for herself and her children demoralizing domestic conditions because divorce would mean financial hardship or actual destitution. Countries where the legal grounds are substantially the same as in ours, but where divorces are fewer in number because the cost of a suit is excessive for the poor, or because little employment is available for a divorced woman, probably have fewer satisfactory homes than we. Our country has the reputation of being one in which home life on the average is unusually pure, in which women are respected, the single standard is generally observed by men, and prostitution is kept by law and public opinion somewhere near a minimum. Conditions are by no means perfect, and there is great room for improvement. But in these matters we can safely face comparison with most other free states, even those in which divorce is rare.

The ultimate solution of the divorce problem, apart from the remedies already suggested, is an elevation of the public moral conscience with regard to marriage itself. If the ethical ideal of marriage can be kept clearly before the minds of all of our people, if the significance of the marriage tie as an ethical sacrament can be constantly remembered, and all can be inspired with the will to lead pure lives in families bound together by ties of mutual love and common purposes, the divorce question will take care of itself. A divorce is not itself a disease; it is rather a surgical operation employed to remedy a disease. The cause of the disease is failure to appreciate the ethical values of the family itself. Clergymen and other moral leaders should attack the problem from this side; they can do much service if they can inspire the community with higher ideals regarding the ethical significance of marriage.

Young people are liable to be disturbed at the thought of marriage in these days, when fiction and the drama are largely concerned with triangular situations, and "realism" seems to consist of the depiction of unusual and morbid rather than typical, not to say morally ideal relations. They wonder whether marriages can ever be happy. This is to see marriage in a false perspective. Nearly all women and most men are pure. Only one marriage in seven proves so unsuccessful as to terminate in a divorce. The vast majority of married people find their highest satisfactions in their homes. Those who marry after careful thought, moved by mutual love and respect for each other and reverence for the married relation, are not likely to make a mistake in the most important decision of their lives. This is particularly true when young men and young women seek the advice of their fathers and mothers and other older friends *before* they become engaged to be married.[23]

V. Unsettled Questions Regarding the Position of Women

Women have gained, at least in principle, full civil and political rights. Such unjust restrictions upon their civic freedom as still remain in this country will be removed before many years, through the general sense of fair play and the efforts of such organizations as the women's clubs, the trade unions which have female members, the League of Women Voters, the National Women's Party, and the women's organizations in the regular political parties. However, many problems remain unsettled regarding the use that women should make of their freedom.

The old theory, coming down from father right, sometimes called the patriarchal or pseudo-domestic theory, of which the German Kaiser, Wilhelm II, was a famous exponent, maintains that "woman's place is in the home "; that her whole attention should be devoted to the four K's (*Kirche, Kleider, Küche and Kinder;* in English, four c's, church, clothes, cooking, and children). Before the industrial revolution there was much to be said for this theory. There was plenty for a woman to do in her home to occupy her time and render her efficient and happy. All the processes involved in making the garments which the family wore—from care for the unscoured wool and fresh flax through weaving, spinning, tailoring, and dressmaking, were carried on by women in the American colonial home. This was also true of all the lighter work in the curing and preservation of animal and vegetable food, and the manufacture of candles and soap. The average home was a dairy, a textile center, an illuminating plant, a cannery and meat packing establishment, a soap factory, laundry, cleaning and dyeing concern, and a manufactory of articles of clothing. A woman, if poor, could count upon the assistance of unmarried sisters or daughters, probably also of a female servant. Household servants were plentiful and not expensive, this being the chief form of employment for a girl outside of her own home. A wealthy woman would be a busy executive, directing the labor of numerous paid assistants, or, in the South, of slaves. A woman could well be as important a factor in economic production as her husband. Her activities could afford as much opportunity for self-realization and service as those of the virtuous woman described in the concluding chapter of the book of Proverbs.

To-day all this is changed. The home is no longer to the same extent an industrial center. The classes of women who in former days were employed as servants in these processes of production in homes are still weaving and spinning cloth and making it into garments, and are engaged in most of the other processes mentioned; but they are working in factories. Servants in most parts of America are now available only for the wealthy or decidedly well-to-do.

The result is that we now sometimes find two socially decadent types of women. (Of course the great majority of women do not belong to either of these unfortunate types.) There is the household drudge, worn out by the toil of unassisted housework without modern conveniences, and the care of children, with whom she often has no one to leave on the rare occasions when she might otherwise be able to snatch an hour for recreation. Then, almost equally pitiful, is what Professor W. I.

Thomas has called "the adventitious type of woman".[24] This
latter type of woman is found chiefly in the wealthier classes,
although she is discoverable at lower economic levels as the
spoiled child of an overworked mother. She has no economically productive tasks whatever. As a girl she devotes her most
concentrated thought to dressing herself to look pretty and capture a husband. Though this is a serious business in a way, it
is not one calculated to develop much force of character, or any
very solid qualities. After marriage, she does nothing at all except amuse herself by going into society, shopping, and possibly carrying on flirtations. At best she has no serious responsibilities,—no opportunity like her husband and brothers to
find happiness and self-realization in serious undertakings.

Some radical writers, mostly socialists, propose to remedy
the situation by drastic measures. The household drudge, they
say, can be eliminated through arrangements by which all families will live in apartment houses where food will be prepared,
clothes washed, rooms cleaned, and children cared for by professional workers who will attend to all these operations in a
wholesale way. They also wish to eliminate the adventitious
type of woman. They propose that every adult woman shall
be employed in some kind of work or business. The only exception will be mothers during pregnancy and lactation, who
will be financially supported by the state. No adult woman
shall be permitted to be financially dependent on a man for her
support. Women will have careers like men, with similar opportunities for productive work, self-realization, and happiness.[25]

The trouble is that such radical schemes would break up home
life. It is morally good for a man to support his own wife and
children; responsibility strengthens his character; he loves his
family better and he is more likely to be faithful to them. A
home is better for children, too. Home life and mothers really
count. Those who do not appreciate this, one suspects, are
either very thoughtless, or else have had unfortunate and un-
typical childhoods. Children are liable not to thrive either

physically or morally in public institutions, no matter how carefully supervised by nurses and physicians. Infectious children's diseases spread among them and the rate of mortality is high. Fond parents sometimes coddle their children over much, as the psychologists are pointing out to us; but while this is true, no child can gain the best spiritual development who does not have the personal care of natural or foster parents.

However, this much ought to be conceded to the radicals. When a father dies, or is an incurable invalid, or has disappeared and cannot be found and put to work to support his family, or is worthless and his wife has to divorce him so that she will have one less mouth to feed, a decent mother ought to receive state aid, so that she can stay at home and bring up her own children. That is the greatest service that she can render to society. Mothers' pensions are now provided in some of the United States, as well as in other lands, to meet such emergencies.[26] Mothers, if necessary, should be cared for at public expense when children are born. The right of every child to come into the world under favorable conditions should be safeguarded by the state at least to this extent. But a recreant father should be compelled to provide for his family whenever it is possible to make him do so, both for the good of his own soul, his family, and the public interest.

The lot of the household drudge can be mitigated to a large extent without resorting to radical measures. Among the classes of society who are likely to be included among the readers of this book the problem is fairly simple. Most housework in these days can be made easy by electrical appliances of various kinds,—stoves, washing machines, irons, vacuum cleaners, sewing machines, and the like—which are within the financial reach of the college graduate by the time that he is ready to marry. In building or renting a house or choosing an apartment, it should be remembered that from the point of view of the woman who has to do her own work the most important room is the kitchen. If this is convenient, not too large, and its furnishings so arranged as to save all needless steps, a healthy young woman

will not find her home work excessive.[27] For the laboring classes
the problem of the overworked housewife is not so easy of
solution.   Present movements for better housing with more
modern conveniences will, when completed, do something to
alleviate the situation.   Every city should have municipal
laundries where a woman at a nominal fee can do the family
washing with the use of modern machinery.[28]

It is unnecessary that any woman should belong to the adventitious type. Under modern conditions every healthy woman
ought to have a vocation. Every unmarried woman whose services are not needed in the home should, like her brothers, enter
a profession or business, as a matter of course. This is desirable
for the development of her own character and happiness. No
man or woman can gain the highest satisfactions in life who does
not have the opportunity for self-expression which creative work
alone affords. College women appreciate this, and most of them
who are not engaged to be married plan to enter vocations after
graduation.

The term vocation is identical in many minds with the law,
medicine, teaching, advertising, banking, commerce, engineering, pharmacy, library or secretarial work, social service, and
other occupations too numerous to mention. But why should
not home making also be reckoned as a vocation in this age
when modern machinery minimizes the time necessary for
routine tasks, and frees a woman for the larger activities of a
more intellectual and spiritual nature? It is a calling in which
there is opportunity for the cultivation of a wide variety of
interests and talents. No other vocation calls for such versa-
tility; for this reason it makes an appeal to women who are
adaptable and rightly deters those who are not. A housewife
who acquaints herself with the chemistry of foods can do much
to keep the family healthy and cheerful by properly balanced
meals. An understanding of simple rules of hygiene, as well
as some knowledge of medicines and nursing is found to prove
invaluable. An elementary understanding of accounting will
enable her to plan the family budget, and a wise husband will

be glad to give a capable wife the responsibilities of disbursing agent of the family.[29] In case the family income admits a margin for saving, an efficient home maker will make this possible. The wife should either assist in making investments or she should have an allowance of her own sufficiently large to enable her to accumulate savings to invest personally, after consultation with her banker. No woman should make her first acquaintance with the interior of a bank after she has been appointed administratrix of her husband's estate.

On the æsthetic side, no matter how large or how small the sum available for home decoration and furnishing, a woman with some knowledge of line, proportion, color, materials, and other principles of household art, will welcome the opportunity for the exercise of creative taste and ingenuity.

The vocation of home maker more than any other favors a woman's development in such of the more spiritual qualities, as tact, sympathy, patience, love, and understanding. A man's business or professional associates see only one side of him and that probably the best. Yet he at times tries their patience. A child's teacher usually sees him only as a pupil, and may often find him a sore trial. But the wife and mother has to deal with whole men and whole children, whether they are good-natured or irritable, ill or well, perverse and obstinate, or considerate and affectionate. And she must have an inexhaustible sense of humor, though at times she must not allow herself to give it outward expression. The ability to see and appreciate the inherent good in those about her, to invite and develop the free expression of each personality, to be a ready listener and a wise guide,—all this is not easy to do. Some knowledge of child psychology and educational theory and practice will be of great value to her, not only in training children in the home, but in planning the details of their education. The woman with intellectual interests will find in the problems of her home sufficient incitement to study literature treating of the various subjects mentioned, for she cannot draw from her reservoir of new ideas if the source has run dry.

However full this program appears, a married woman is not necessarily limited to her home for interests and activities. In time, keeping household accounts becomes a matter of routine; a properly balanced diet for the family is less difficult; system in the household is established. After children are old enough to be in school she often has free hours in the day which she can devote to economic activity of some kind, and so broaden her own life, increase the family income, and be of service to others. This becomes increasingly true as the children attain their maturity. There already are some kinds of remunerative work in which a married woman with hours of leisure can engage without neglecting her home. There will be more openings when business and industry realize that a woman trained in this school of experience has much to offer,—mature judgment, willingness to carry responsibility, an understanding of what is essential in the more fundamental matters of living.[30]

There are women, however, who need not consider financial returns for the free hours at their disposal, and this is well. Every city and town needs those interested in problems of community housekeeping, public health, the care of the aged, the delinquent, and the retarded. Such services may be undertaken individually or in groups. One has only to consult the list of suggestive constructive things accomplished by various women's clubs,[31] not to mention other organizations, to glimpse the possibilities for productive effort in these fields. Reclamation projects are quite as necessary in the social as in the industrial and engineering fields; all are intimately connected with one another.

There may be women in the home who do not feel particularly interested in such activities as those just mentioned. For them there is available the intellectual stimulus gained from the serious study of belles lettres, music, and the fine arts. European visitors occasionally remark that American women, although more often university graduates than their European sisters, devote less time to mental cultivation, with the result that their conversation is more trivial and commonplace. An

American college alumna too often sees no need in further studies. She has graduated and has her diploma. So she asks, why she may not forget her college subjects like her brothers who have gone into business. She is liable to limit her conversation to gossip, the weather, and housekeeping. Avoiding lectures, concerts, and thoughtful reading, in some cases she spends too much time at dances, bridge parties, and other frivolous social entertainment.

On the contrary, American matrons with leisure can do much to elevate the intellectual life of the country, not by giving superficial attention to a different topic every month, but by a serious consideration of the essential phases of some author's work, artist's composition, or historical movement. A successful man does not count his year worth much unless his balance sheet shows profits at the end of that period. May not a woman hold herself to standards quite as rigorously?

Better informed as a rule than men on the problems of the home and school, women should take active interest in local politics, serving on school boards and city councils. It seems to the author a proper division of duty for the wife to inform the family upon the merits of local candidates and issues, while the husband reports upon national parties, platforms, and candidates. Husband, wife, and adult children should exercise independent judgment in voting, but the opinions of Father and Mother will have weight in the provinces with which each is best acquainted. Churches, lodges, women's clubs, social settlements, and other organizations afford married women a wide variety of fields in which they can be useful.

The blame at the present time for the existence of women of the adventitious type therefore rests chiefly with themselves, or with the manner in which they were brought up. Nothing in the social situation makes it inevitable for any woman to belong in this category.

At present there probably is less difference between the activities of men and women than has been true at any time in previous social evolution, subsequent to the establishment of the paternal system in the relation of Kinship. And it seems probable that the differences between the sexes will continue to diminish during the coming generation. Women have virtually all of the civil and political rights of men. In America they are as well or better educated. Unmarried women are free to engage in practically all trades and professions. A large range of possible forms of self-expression and social usefulness are open to married women. Just as men began to wear their hair short, and left off silk, satin, and lace an hundred years ago, women to-day are adapting their dress to the requirements of an active life, and are preferring convenience and health to ornament. However, biological reasons and social convenience will always keep the sexes differentiated in their activities and interests to a certain extent. Most women will continue to be home makers, and only a minority will be engaged in business and the professions. The biologically greater eagerness of the male, to which Darwin called attention, will cause men to continue to take the initiative in courtship. Men will normally be the economic supporters of their families. The monogamous ethical system will remain essentially unchanged in theory. The ideal family will more often be realized in practice.[32]

REFERENCES

* J. Dewey and J. H. Tufts, *Ethics*, chap. XXVI.

* Durant Drake, *Problems of Conduct*, chap. XVII.

* H. Baker-Crothers and Ruth Hudnut, *Problems of Citizenship*, chaps. XII–XVI.

* J. H. Wigmore, editor, *Rational Basis of Legal Institutions*, chaps. XXXIX–XLVI.

* S. E. Mezes, *Ethics, Descriptive and Explanatory*, chap. XI.

* L. T. Hobhouse, *Morals in Evolution*, Part I, chaps. IV, V.

* A. Maude Royden, *Sex and Common Sense*.

* Ida M. Tarbell, *The Business of Being a Woman*.

* Robert Grant, *Law and the Family*, chaps. V–VII.

* R. C. Cabot, *What Men Live By*, chap. XIX.

* William McDougall, *Character and the Conduct of Life*, chaps. XVI–XX.

J. S. Mill, *The Subjection of Women.*
Helen Bosanquet, *The Family.*
Willystine Goodsell, *Problems of the Family.*
Edward Westermarck, *History of Human Marriage* (3 vols.).
G. E. Howard, *History of Matrimonial Institutions* (3 vols.).
Robert Briffault, *The Mothers* (3 vols.).

PART V

METAPHYSICS AND RELIGION

CHAPTER XIX

THE ETHICAL POSTULATES, AND THEIR SIGNIFI-CANCE FOR METAPHYSICS AND THE PHILOSOPHY OF RELIGION

I. Essential Postulates for any Possible System of Ethics

Investigators in any field are obliged to begin with certain assumptions which they do not endeavor to demonstrate at the outset. Mathematics starts with its well known axioms and postulates, which physics accepts, and with which it combines assumptions regarding space, time, energy, etc. Psychology implies all the postulates of the older natural sciences, and to these adds, or used to add, that of consciousness. With the progress of a science, its initial assumptions are revised from time to time in the light of new developments. In mathematics, for instance, the discovery of the geometries of non-Euclidean space has led to such a revision. The theories of Einstein and others are causing a restatement of the postulates of physics. Some psychologists think that they need no longer assume the existence of consciousness; the postulates essential to the conception of reflexes, conditioned and otherwise, they deem sufficient. If, in any science, to start with certain postulates results in a satisfactory explanation of known phenomena and the discovery of additional important facts not previously known, the postulates may be regarded as at least provisionally established.

There are certain essential postulates that must be made by any possible system of ethics, so far as one can judge at the present time. The future development of ethics may lead to their revision in ways that cannot be foreseen.

1. The first of these postulates is *the validity of the most simple and ultimate intuitions which form the predicates of our moral*

475

postulate does not need explanation.

judgments, such as "good", "bad", "evil", "better", "worse", "ought", and "ought not".[1] It may be possible to reduce "good" and "bad" to modes of "better" and "worse", or *vice versa.* "Good" and "right" may be taken to signify "what ought to be done"; and "bad" and "wrong", "what ought not to be done". However, such attempts at reduction are bound to terminate with a few intuitions that cannot be further reduced by logical analysis.

Psychologically, sociologically, and physiologically we can state the conditions that make moral judgments possible. Psychologically speaking, we are able to make moral judgments because we can reason, *i.e.,* think of possible consequences of an action, compare them with one another, and decide which we ought to prefer since in the long run they will most completely satisfy our desires, including those which we have for the welfare of other people. Physiologically interpreted, this process is a function of certain cells, located chiefly in the frontal lobes of the cortex of the cerebrum. Sociologically explained, as we have seen in previous chapters, the contents of the moral consciousness of any individual,—*i.e.,* the specific persons and actions to whom and to which he applies the moral predicates of "good", "bad", etc.—are chiefly due to the moral traditions of the social groups to which he belongs; although if he is reflective, he may make a few modifications on his own initiative. But to state the psychological, physiological, and sociological conditions of moral judgments is not to explain their unique character; any more than the characteristics of blue and red are accounted for by saying that each is the correlate of waves of light of certain lengths, or the characteristics of water by explaining that it is a combination in a certain proportion of elements of hydrogen and oxygen.

Ethics must assume, as a postulate, that there is a real distinction between "good" and "bad"; that the former "ought" to be done, and the latter "ought not" to be done. (This truth was conceded in Chapter XI to the advocates of abstract ethics.) Men often make mistakes in applying these moral predicates; they do not correctly distinguish between "good" and "bad", and they misinterpret their moral obligations. The ordinary man is right in applying moral judgments in the manner of his group. He does not know how to do otherwise; even if he did, the group would probably insist on his conformity. Yet the student of comparative ethics may discern that the moral judgments of a group are wrong in certain respects; somewhat different mores would promote their welfare and happiness more effectively, if only the group realized it. In coming to this affirmation, the student of comparative ethics pronounces his own moral judgments from the Eudæmonistic and Utilitarian standpoints of the twentieth century, which we believe to be the most adequate that ethical theory has as yet been able to obtain. Moral philosophers in future ages will doubtless have more accurate standards. No standards now known to man can be claimed to be absolute and eternal; all we can say is that our most carefully reasoned standards are objective for us.

2. Another essential ethical postulate is the *continuity of the ethical self*,—the "empirical me" of the first section of Chapter X. A man must in some sense be the same person who did the act for which he now rejoices or repents, and which his neighbors judge with moral favor or disapproval. If the self of any individual were merely a succession of mental states, or of conditioned reflexes, and did not know itself in some sense as a unity, it would be as absurd to pass moral judgments upon it as if it were a river or a steam engine.

3. Closely connected is the third ethical postulate, that of *moral responsibility and psychological freedom*. As we saw in the closing section of Chapter X, ethics assumes that a sane person in ordinary circumstances is responsible for his own acts, and that this responsibility implies freedom of choice.[3] How freedom is to be explained is a metaphysical question, on which determinists and indeterminists are not agreed; but each school accepts moral responsibility as a fact and tries to account for it.

4. *Any system of ethics must postulate a denial both of extreme optimism and of extreme pessimism*. This excludes any form of

optimism which declares that everything is absolutely perfect
as it is; that, despite anybody's actions, all is equally certain to
come out for the best. For on such a view it can hardly be affirmed that it really makes much difference what any one does
or what sort of person he is. It is doubtful whether any serious
philosopher has ever really intended to carry his optimism to
this extreme of moral indifferentism; but some philosophers and
poets who praise everything, find all good and deny the existence
of evil altogether, appear to their critics to come close to it.

Ethics would be rendered equally impossible by a pessimism
that affirmed that everything is already absolutely bad; that
nothing could possibly be made any worse no matter what
evils anybody were to do, nor better however hard everybody
might try to improve conditions. It is doubtful whether any
thinker has consciously intended to teach a philosophy of such
absolute despair. Schopenhauer, and thousands of years before him the early Buddhists, were pessimists. Both, however,
found means by which they believed that the suffering in the
world might be mitigated, and they indicated ways by which
the faithful might ultimately escape from evil altogether.
Most pessimists have been similar to other moral philosophers
in their moral precepts; the difference being that pessimists
believe all that can be done is to reduce evil to a minimum,
positive happiness and welfare being unattainable.

While, as has been said, neither optimism nor pessimism
has often consciously been carried to the extreme of moral indifferentism, it is justifiable to ask of any philosophy whether
its logical implications, if honestly thought out, would lead to
such an outcome. Whenever such can be shown to be the case,
the philosophy is demonstrably in conflict with the essential
postulates of ethics. And these postulates seem to be well established.

5. Closely related is a fifth ethical postulate, *the possibility
of moral progress*, both for individuals and for humanity. If
we could not believe that we were able to secure better organized characters for ourselves and for others, and so to advance in

pursuit of the values that constitute welfare and render happiness possible, the moral life would lose all meaning. Any system of philosophy that denies the possibility of moral progress to the extent of discouraging effort is a pernicious form of either pessimism or optimism. Equally opposed to ethics is any philosophy that goes to the opposite extreme and regards moral progress as certain, assured, automatic, so that human effort is superfluous. Most favorable to ethics is some form of *meliorism;*—the doctrine that the world is neither absolutely perfect nor hopelessly bad; that it is possible by united effort for each generation to leave it improved; that such improvement actually has been taking place in the history of moral evolution, and will continue in the future, not automatically, but because men concentrate their best efforts to that end.

Because a philosophical study like ethics, which has not yet become a special science, assumes certain postulates, it might not seem a necessary conclusion that these postulates are true. Even a science may sometimes be erected on false assumptions; think of alchemy, phrenology, palmistry, and many others! But ethics has been sufficiently successful in interpreting human conduct, and in proposing standards for its guidance, to render its postulates worthy of credence. To reject them would be to refuse to believe in the assumptions that underlie not only theoretical ethics, but also the practical morality of everyday life, upon which our social structure is based.

The author has expressed these five postulates in his own way. He believes, however, that all moral philosophers accept them in principle, and that all treatises in ethics assume them. Many students of ethics would prefer to express the postulates in different language, and to put a different emphasis on various details. Some would add other postulates to the list. Thus far in this chapter, however, the author believes that he has said nothing of a controversial character. The remainder of the chapter, on the other hand, will deal with topics on which the diversity of opinion among philosophers is as wide as that among thinking men in general.

II. Further Metaphysical Implications of Ethics

Metaphysics is the part of philosophy that attempts to discover the fundamental principles of reality,—the ultimate nature of the universe, and man's relation to it. Students who have taken a course in an American college styled "Introduction to Philosophy", or who have read a book with that or a similar title, have been studying metaphysics; for such courses and books usually devote little attention to the other branches of philosophy, such as ethics, logic, æsthetics, and the philosophy of religion. There are numerous schools of metaphysics to-day, and the adherents of each are hopeful that they are right and the others wrong; but long experience has taught metaphysicians to be mutually tolerant. All are willing to learn from one another, and none is entirely confident of his own position.

All contemporary schools of metaphysics accept the ordinary moral judgments of our time. All would assent, the author supposes, to the ethical postulates outlined in the preceding section. Ethics, of course, is only one of the fields of human investigation which metaphysicians must take into account in their endeavor to interpret the world as a whole. Those of a poetic or idealistic temper are likely to attach great significance to ethical and æsthetic judgments and aspirations, and to find in them keys to the nature of ultimate reality. Those of more realistic and scientific bent, on the other hand, are mindful that our galaxy of stars is so vast, that the evolution of man, a late arrival on a tiny planet, may not be momentous in the history of the universe; the moral judgments that make for human welfare and happiness do not necessarily reveal the ultimate nature of things so certainly as sciences like mathematics, physics, astronomy and chemistry, which deal with material more widely diffused in space.

There is at least one affirmation that the moral philosopher may make, which no system of metaphysics can reasonably exclude. However mechanical may be the operations of inorganic matter, and even of living beings other than man, the nature of the world does not entirely exclude man's initiative and freedom of choice. No fact, even in physics, is so certain as that of human moral responsibility. The latter has been verified by the experience of mankind in all nations and all ages. We know it to be a fact, because all social relationships have successfully assumed it. Human societies could not have endured if they had been built upon a fundamental assumption that was false. A man's conduct, perhaps, is conditioned by the operations of the cells in his nervous system; and the latter without doubt are subject to all the laws of mathematics, physics, chemistry, and physiology. Yet the cells of the human nervous system, when functioning normally, become a conscious personality which proceeds to pronounce some actions good and others bad, to recognize and act on moral obligations, and to pronounce judgments of moral approval and condemnation upon other persons. Ethics can produce sufficient evidence to refute any metaphysics of mechanistic materialism that might be carried to the point of denying the fact of human moral responsibility.

There are at least five prominent schools of metaphysics in the English speaking world at the present time. A brief mention of the significance attached by each to a few features of ethics will afford some idea of what metaphysical interpretations of ethics are possible.

Absolute Idealism, or Neo-Hegelianism, was the reigning philosophy in England and America at the opening of the present century; it still has numerous adherents. (See Chapter VII, section IV.) The proponents of this school put much emphasis on the organic unity of the self, and the interdependence of individuals in the social order. This is in accordance with their metaphysical theory of the organic nature of reality; everything is dependent on everything else, and the world as a whole is ultimately a complete æsthetic harmony. This school recognizes moral responsibility and explains it by the doctrine of self-determinism. (See pages 276–279.) Since for this school all evil is eternally turned to good in the Universe (conceived as an all inclusive Mind, the Absolute), critics claim that the reality of the moral life is reduced to a mere appearance, a phenomenon, and that the finite distinction between good and evil is rendered unimportant. It may be that this criticism is just, in the sense that the logical implications of Absolute Idealism would lead to such an outcome if they were rigorously thought out and accepted. The author has sometimes supposed so. As a matter of historical fact, however, Absolute Idealism has not rendered its adherents indifferent to practical moral issues. Their belief that in reality and to the Absolute the world is eternally and altogether good and lovely, and all evil turned to greater good acts on them as a stimulus to moral effort. Since they believe that all is perfect in eternity, absolute idealists set forth with zeal to put things right in time. Even some of the school, like T. H. Green, F. H. Bradley, and Bernard Bosanquet, who have held its characteristic doctrines in extreme forms, have made important contributions to systematic and applied ethics, and have been keenly alive to the social problems of their generation.[4]

Personal Idealism is a convenient general name by which to designate the views of numerous contemporary metaphysicians who differ from one another in many details, but who are united in opposition to Absolute Idealism in refusing to include all reality within a single Self or Absolute. On the contrary, personal idealists believe that the world consists of a plurality of distinct and independent persons; most of them are mentalists like Berkeley, and deny the existence of matter altogether. Personal idealists are indeterminists, so far as human freedom is concerned. Many of them believe that the so-called uniform laws of the natural sciences are in reality merely uniformities of averages, comparable to the statistics of the social sciences: this contingency in nature makes a place for human freedom of choice. Great emphasis is put on the unique significance and value of individuals, the genuine importance of the moral life and of its problems, the reality of evil, and the necessity of human effort to overcome it. Most personal idealists believe in the personal God of theism, who is supreme in the universe, but who allows men freedom of will and individualities of their own. The distinction between good and evil is real for Him; He will assist men to overcome evil and attain good. With a few exceptions, personal idealists are more orthodox from the standpoint of traditional religion than most other metaphysicians.[5]

Of all schools of contemporary philosophy, the proponents of Pragmatism are perhaps most interested in ethics. The derivation of the word Pragmatism (from *pragma*, action), suggests the spirit of the school. Truth, they believe, is discovered in action. Adopt an hypothesis tentatively, and see if it is possible to act as if it were true, without encountering facts that contradict it. The proof of an hypothesis, or its refutation, is found in such experimentation. Pragmatists are skeptical about the possibility of ascertaining the truth of propositions that cannot be tested in experience. For this reason, among others, they reject the doctrine of the Absolute. On the other hand, the real founder of Pragmatism, William James,[6] believed in a theistic God, because the facts of human religious experience seemed to him best explained in that way. Pragmatists insist that the world is plastic, constantly changing and evolving. This gives man the opportunity to advance. Through progress in the natural sciences man has learned to control his physical environment. Professor John Dewey has expressed the hope that comparable advances in the social sciences will be made in the present century so that men will learn to control their social relations. A higher order of general welfare and more equitable justice will thereby be achieved.[7]

Realism in its twentieth century forms can best be understood in contrast to Idealism, against which it has been a reaction.[8] Nearly all of us are idealists in the popular sense of the word; we believe in maintaining high ideals and endeavoring to realize them. But in contemporary metaphysics the term Idealism has a technical meaning; according to which, either everything in the universe is mental,—ideas and the minds that have them, the position of Personal Idealism; or else everything in the universe that is not mental is organically related to minds and dependent upon them and included with them in the Absolute—the position of Absolute Idealism. Both of these technical forms of contemporary Idealism assert that the ultimate character of reality can be discovered by the study of the characteristics of minds. In some mental process—thought, will, æsthetic feeling, or in all of them combined—is discoverable the key to the secrets of the universe. In opposition to all forms of technical Idealism, the various types of Realism are united in affirming a position claimed to be more in accordance with ordinary common sense: some realities, at least, exist whether any mind thinks about them or not. The character of physical objects is not affected by the mere fact that people are or are not looking at them or thinking about them. The contents of the lecture room remain between sessions of a class unaltered by their absence from all people's minds. Minds or consciousnesses are external relations that do not affect the physical objects that happen at times to be included within their perception or thought. Consequently the nature of ultimate reality is not discoverable by an analysis of thought or of other mental processes. Nor can we argue from a presumed analogy between ourselves and the world. Instead, the metaphysician must get his clues from mathematics and the natural sciences.[9]

All contemporary Realists, so far as the author is aware, are meliorists. They accept the facts of good and evil as they find them. An optimist or a pessimist is necessarily an Idealist in the sense that he interprets the good and evil events of life in accordance with some kind of transcendent pattern of a speculative character. If an optimist, his pattern is one of harmony and beauty, in which the facts that appear to us evil are transformed and given a new significance. If a pessimist, his pattern is of the opposite character; all experience is in reality frustration of every effort; what we ordinarily suppose to be good, when put into his world pattern turns out to be an illusion. The

Realist, like the Pragmatist, refuses to trust the capacity of thought to spin out such patterns of the universe, which cannot be tested by observation and experiment. So he is obliged to take events more at their face value; they are a mixture of good and bad, with the capacity for improvement by human effort; and that is meliorism.

All Realists agree that space, time, matter, and energy exist whether anyone thinks about them or not. Numbers and the other abstract principles of mathematics and logic are not *existing* things, lying about like physical objects; on the other hand, they are not mere ideas. They were valid before anybody ever happened to think about them. There are numbers that no one has ever counted, mathematical and logical laws that no one has ever discovered. Such principles have a certain kind of being, independent of minds; they may be said to *subsist*. Some realists affirm that "secondary qualities" (like colors, sounds, and odors, in contrast to the primary qualities of mass, number, motion, rest, time, space, and the other qualities of objects known to physics) exist independent of minds. Others believe that secondary qualities exist only when the objects to which they are attributed are in relation to organisms with specialized sense organs and nervous systems. A few Realists are willing to say that æsthetic values exist independent of persons. Is the flower that is born to blush unseen in the desert air beautiful? It is easiest to think that the atoms and molecules of the flower exist unperceived; it is harder, but still possible to think that its color and fragrance so exist; it is hardest of all, and only the most determined Realists find it possible to believe that the beauty of the flower is a quality that can exist independent of observation. It is easier for a Realist to believe that the secondary qualities and æsthetic values *subsist* as possibilities when they are not experienced, and that they only come into *existence* when perceived.

Moral obligations hold only for persons. Beings that were not at least conscious of themselves would not be persons at all. So it is impossible for a Realist to affirm that moral *facts* of any kind exist independent of minds. It is, however, possible for him to maintain that the *abstract principles* of morality have some kind of subsistence independent of minds. A few Realists believe that moral values somehow subsist like the Platonic Ideas; many of these values are as yet undiscovered, few are fully appreciated; but, like numbers, they do not owe their being or their validity to their recognition in minds: moral values are objective and eternal.[10]

The author is willing to admit the possibility that there may be absolute and eternal values; but as he pointed out in Chapter XIV, section V, no values at present known to man possess such characteristics. Human values constantly change, and ought to change with modifications in social organization and in the general character of civilization. To some minds it may be a comfort to believe that everything in the universe, including its most abstract values, is in constant growth. Nothing is so perfect that it will not yield to something better. Other thinkers prefer to believe that moral evolution is a gradual approximation in thought and life to a set of absolute and unchanging values that have their being or subsistence outside of time and place and all events. Two cautions are necessary. The man who talks constantly about "absolute and eternal values" must not confuse them with any of our poor human notions, none of which can endure forever; else he is likely to become a reactionary. On the other hand, it is even more dangerous to imagine, since no known values are absolute, that an individual is free to disregard the moral tradition and to do anything he pleases; that way lies moral anarchy. It is well to remember that change sometimes, but by no means always, is progress. Most of the moral judgments of our social order are just as binding on you and me as individuals as if they were absolute and eternal.

A very interesting modification of contemporary Realism has been advanced by the supporters of the doctrine of Emergent Evolution. According to this conception, first of all, primary and universal, are the points of space and instants of time.

From these somehow evolved the lowest and simplest forms of matter and energy. The latter, widely distributed in time and space, became integrated into stars and planets. Here on the earth, at least, and perhaps elsewhere, matter sometimes becomes organized with a certain complexity, and life *emerges*. An organism viewed one way is simply an aggregation of atoms and molecules; but in the organism this aggregation has many properties and modes of behavior peculiar to it. From lower forms of life emerge those with mind; more new characteristics appear. The most conspicuous levels of emergent evolution are those of matter, life, and mind; but there are innumerable substages. Each chemical compound is a unique emergent; its characteristics are not a mere sum of the elements contained in it. Every new living species has emerged from its ancestors. Each level involves those that precede it. For instance, man's capacity for reflection upon moral problems continues only so long as his brain and body function; the life of the latter is conditioned by physiological processes, which in turn imply the presence of chemical compounds whose integration is in accordance with the laws of mathematics and physics.

The doctrine of Emergent Evolution differs from materialism in the respect, among others, that no higher level is reducible to lower ones. Each level has novel characteristics. No one who merely had full knowledge of a lower level could predict the emergence of a higher one, with its unique qualities. If a person were to write out complete lists of the characteristics of hydrogen and oxygen, the two lists combined would not include all of the properties of water. If some celestial observer of the earth prior to the origin of life upon its surface had had a complete knowledge of the laws of inorganic chemistry, but had never seen a living being, he could not have predicted the appearance of organisms, nor the character of their functions. Organisms seek food and struggle for existence; they repair injured tissue and reproduce themselves; their various parts coöperate for the benefit of the whole; nothing of this kind is true of matter until it emerges upon the level of life. Since the character of a higher level could not be predicted in advance from a knowledge of lower levels, it is sometimes intimated that emergence is a matter of chance, indeterminism. This is not, as it seems to the author, a necessary feature of the doctrine of Emergent Evolution. Once a higher level has been carefully observed, and the manner noted in which the constituents of the prior level have been integrated and so have brought it into existence, the affirmation can be made that on all future occasions matter on the lower level will assume the character of the higher one whenever the same process of integration occurs. An omniscient mind would know in advance all the laws of emergent evolution on all possible levels.

It is obvious that on the earth morality has emerged only among men. The capacity to make moral judgments involves the development of the nervous system to the degree of complexity that marks off man from his nearest relatives. On the mental side, this involves reasoning powers superior to those of animals. It also implies life in families, care of children by their parents and the minimum of social organization that we find in the primitive horde. Given all these conditions, morality emerges. Reflective morality, as we saw in Chapter III, involves more, and emerges later. Before reflective morality can appear, men must be able to criticize their customs, and consider what changes they should make in them. The reflective stage probably implies some kind of a revolution in previous social organization,—the interaction of groups with different moral traditions, or some other radical change that forces people to think. Reflective morality, once it appears, as we saw in the cases of the Hebrews, and the Greeks, is very different from the customary morality that preceded it, and may properly be called a new level, or sublevel, of emergent evolution.

The emergent evolutionist may regard moral values as "tertiary qualities" that did not exist in any sense, until they first made their appearance. He will then confine the locus of moral values to man, and such other organisms with reasoning powers that may exist elsewhere in the universe. On the other hand, it is possible for an emergent evolutionist to believe that throughout the course of evolution there is an upward *nisus* or tendency toward "organization". To believe this last is to regard the world order as in some sense purposive, teleological. This "nisus" or tendency to "organization" may be conceived of as an intelligent Mind,—God. There are numerous other points, regarding which Emergent Evolutionists differ among themselves.[11]

III. ETHICAL IMPLICATIONS FOR THE PHILOSOPHY OF RELIGION

In Part I, we saw something of the function that religion has performed in relation to moral evolution in the earlier stages, among the Hebrews, Greeks, and Romans, and, in the form of Christianity, in medieval and modern moral development. Notice was taken of the moral significance of the religious sentiment and of the virtue of reverence (in Chapter IX). It was pointed out that the validity of morality does not depend on the acceptance of religious beliefs; our fellow citizens hold us in any case to the same civic, social, and personal obligations. The triumph of religious toleration during recent centuries does not lead to a lessened sense of the duties that we owe to ourselves and to one another to promote happiness and the realization of moral values in character and conduct.

We shall now consider whether human moral experience may throw light upon the probability of three articles of religious faith,—the validity of religious experiences, the existence and nature of God, and human personal immortality.

It is a well established fact in the psychology of religion, whatever the explanation may be, that men through both private and public devotions have what they call saving experiences, such as answered prayer, conversion, and mystical states. They gain increased wisdom and self-control, and more firmly integrated characters. They become truer to their ideals. They are more helpful to others. They obtain strength and support in overcoming temptations. They find comfort in times of sorrow and bereavement. They learn to love their enemies, and to return good for evil.

The immediate psychological explanation for such experiences is found in the subconscious, and its physiological correlates, the nerve cells. Stored up in the cells of our brains and nervous systems are reserve powers of energy of which we ordinarily are unaware. The practice of religion releases these powers and enables men to perform achievements of which they otherwise would be incapable. But is this all that is to be said upon the subject? Some undoubtedly would reply in the affirmative. Others would insist that the religious worshiper himself believes that his help has come from God, and that his belief should be taken into account in consideration of the problem. There are at least two hypotheses, in full accordance with scientific knowledge, which attempt to validate this belief.

According to one of these hypotheses, favored by William James and others, the subconscious energy breaking into the individual's consciousness comes from God, conceived theistically as a person, who in this manner gives aid to those who call upon Him. According to the other, more subtle hypothesis, God is conceived to be immanent in all things and in all events, but most of all in the mind of man, who is nearest like Himself. Without interference in any miraculous way with the normal processes of nature, man in his religious experiences becomes aware of and in some sense shares in the life of such a Power not himself that is operative throughout all the processes of evolution, and reaches His highest expression on this particular planet in the life of the good man at the moments when he feels himself closest to God.[12]

If it is possible to find sufficient evidence for the belief in God there will be reason for affirming that religious experiences are valid, and that the religious man is right in believing that they in some sense come from, or through, Him.

Let us consider for a moment the whole course of evolution. From tenuous inorganic matter in diffuse nebulæ, our earth gradually evolved into a planet, not yet with life upon it, but with the precise proportions of oxygen, hydrogen, and carbon in the stable compounds of water and carbonic acid that rendered the emergence of life possible under the most favorable conditions of which organic chemistry can conceive. This would hardly be a matter of luck; it has been calculated that there would, as a matter of mathematics, be only one chance in millions that such a combination would occur.[13] When an event takes place under such circumstances it seems reasonable to attribute it to a purpose. After life emerged upon the earth, probably from a favorable combination of inorganic elements, higher organisms evolved from more primitive ones, and man at last appeared with the capacity to reason and make moral judgments. From savage man in the life of the primitive horde, through slow and painful steps emerged civilized man, who has finally reached the relation of Citizenship, and is gradually attaining a better social order in which individuals are realizing values and achieving happiness.

As we look back over this whole course of emergent evolution on the only planet about whose history we know even a little, it would seem that an increasing purpose is gradually being consummated. What the course of evolution may be on other heavenly bodies, and whether it has any purpose at all, we can only guess; and we know that ours is by no means a large or conspicuous body in the heavens. But if the evolution of our earth has any purpose, it must be an ethical purpose,—the development of man and the attainment by him of moral values.

If now, we assume that terrestrial evolution has an ethical purpose, there remain before us two alternatives. First, we might suppose that moral values subsist somehow by themselves, like numbers, and that they would still have some sort of being even if no mind ever knew of them, or if no universe of matter and motion in space and time ever existed at all! We might then proceed to infer that somehow matter in its evolution on the earth followed a course that eventuated in the appearance for the first time of animals that could think of these moral values and endeavor consciously to realize them. Some philosophers have believed this to be a thinkable hypothesis, and one that can account for the facts with the fewest possible assumptions. There are, however, difficulties. Moral values, unlike numbers, refer always to persons; nothing could be thought to have moral value except as a person might be related to it in some way. A world devoid of persons could not even have instrumental value, much less could a system of abstract entities. Moreover, moral values always refer to persons in existing conditions, or conditions that conceivably might exist. It would be a contradiction in terms to speak of nonexistent moral values with reference to nonexistent persons, without the possibility that the latter might come into existence and realize the former. One could as well speak of round squares, or valleys without hills.[14]

The other alternative is to assume that the latent tendency in emergent evolution is personal, is God, or is directed by Him. It is certainly a great deal more difficult to suppose that values that were merely neutral entities, subsisting like numbers, could become directive of the course of evolution, than to believe that a personal Being, a Mind, has conscious purposes and directs the course of evolution, in order to effect the realization of moral values in the lives of human persons.

The hypothesis of God as immanent in evolution is strengthened by the facts of religious experience. If there were a God directive of terrestrial evolution, we should expect Him to reveal Himself to men as rapidly as they were capable of becoming aware of His presence. The gradual evolution from the crudest and most primitive notions of *mana*, through polytheism to monotheism, and to the Christian and Jewish religions of the present time, is precisely what we should expect on this hypothesis. God in the mind of each man would be the idealization of moral values to the furthest point that human ethical insight at the time would permit. With still further moral evolution we should expect advance in future man's conceptions of God, not because God is an imaginative projection of human experience, but because it will be possible for God to reveal Himself more adequately. We should expect each individual man in his private religious experience to become aware of the immanence of God to the extent that his moral and mental outlook renders possible. The facts in the history of religions and in present day religious experience are precisely what we should expect on such an hypothesis.

The nature of God is variously conceived by those who seek to draw religious implications from ethics. Least ambitious of all is the humanistic conception of God advanced by Auguste Comte in the last century, and more simply stated by some of our contemporaries. This notion of God can perhaps most simply be explained by an analogy. Think of a college or university. It has already endured for generations or for centuries. Its living members expect it to continue for ages to come. And of whom and of what does the college consist? Not simply and not chiefly of its material equipment. Much more does it include the persons who have studied and taught within its walls, and those who will be connected with it in future generations. All of these together constitute the college. Of most importance are the great alumni whom the college has inspired to brilliant achievements. The college seems, and in a sense is, more real and more enduring than any individual member. The college is personified as alma mater; songs are sung in her honor; statues and pictures are made of her; in the thoughts of those who love her, she becomes an incarnate being, a great dynamic force in their lives.

What is true of a college is true of a nation in a much larger sense. The nation endures. The nation is personified; her image appears on coins and stamps, in sculpture and painting; hymns are sung in her honor; men are proud to carry her flag and to fight in her behalf, laying down their lives if necessary with the conviction that they have devoted them to the best possible end.

Sublimer than any college or any nation is Humanity,—the whole human race conceived as a single personality enduring throughout all generations. Loyalty to Humanity is all embracing; it is something finer-than college spirit or even national patriotism, because it embraces all mankind in common devotion and loyalty. Think of God simply as the highest idealization of the common life of Humanity; God is Humanity personified! In the service of Humanity we have the unification of all ethical ideals. Let every man do all that he can to promote the common welfare and happiness of mankind; let every man worship Humanity and serve Her faithfully!

It has been claimed that a religion of Humanity would have a certain advantage from an ethical standpoint over all of the historic religions. It would be absolutely free from bigotry and intolerance. Every religion has at times gotten on somewhat of a tangent; it has regarded orthodoxy in creedal beliefs, fidelity in observance of ritual, or some other morally extraneous requirement as more important than the good life itself. That could never be true of the religion of Humanity; sacramental and doctrinal considerations could never usurp the supreme place that belongs to the moral values themselves.

For such reasons the religion of Humanity will ever be regarded with high respect by moral philosophers. Little demand on human faith is required for its acceptance. Simple, and yet sublime, not going beyond human knowledge yet capable of stimulating men to their highest moral efforts, it cannot fail to make a powerful appeal. But— Most of us would like to believe in a more cosmic God than Humanity. We hope that there is a Power friendly to us in control of the processes of physical nature. We wish to come into communion with such a cosmic God, and find in Him strength and support for our moral battles. Two arguments in favor of a cosmic God have already been briefly sketched, one based on cosmic evolution, and one on human religious experience.

There are at least two conceptions of a cosmic God current among contemporary students of the philosophy of religion. First, there is the conception of Absolute Idealism, that of an Infinite Mind transcending all space and time, a Universal Here, an Everlasting Now. To such an Absolute all the discords and evils in human finite experience are blended in an eternally complete harmony. This conception appeals to those who are temperamentally æsthetic and mystical rather than ethical and practical, and whose chief religious need is stability, assurance that all is and ever must be well with the world. To such persons the conviction that all is well with the Absolute, and that all will be well with us if we can completely identify ourselves with it, will be sufficient. Nor can it truly be said that all men who believe in such an Absolute content themselves with purely contemplative lives. The contrary has often been true. Many of them have been active workers in the service of their fellow men.

Intellectually, however, there are difficulties in the acceptance of God in the form of an infinite and all inclusive Absolute. It has been hard for some of the greatest Absolute Idealists to believe that the Absolute can be said to recognize moral values, to entertain purposes and endeavor to realize them, or even to reason and think at all. For moral values imply a conflict between good and evil, whereas to the Absolute all such conflicts are resolved in an eternal harmony. To have purposes is to be finite and limited, while to the Absolute all purposes are eternally fulfilled. To reason implies limited knowledge; by inferences from facts and premises that we know, we attempt to verify conclusions about which we are uncertain; but the Absolute experiences all reality in immediate sentience,—perceives all eternally at a glance. So certain—though not all—Absolute Idealists have denied that the Absolute should be identified with the God of religion. The latter is merely a very high order of appearance, a personal Being whom men anthropomorphically conceive of as coming to their aid in moral difficulties. The serene and ineffable Absolute is suprapersonal,— no human attributes apply to it. Some Absolute Idealists do not believe in human personal immortality.[15]

It undoubtedly is difficult to believe in a cosmic God who is infinite in all respects,—omnipotent, omniscient, absolutely good. How on such an hypothesis account for the evil that is in the world? It is often replied that the evil is inevitable in order that there may be good, that only through overcoming evil can men develop characters, that freedom of will is essential to character, therefore God was obliged to give men freedom of will; in so doing He foresaw that they would sometimes sin. But to argue in these ways is tacitly to abandon the doctrine of the omnipotence of God. For by such reasoning, God is limited in His choices, if not also in the material with which He has to work. He chose the best of possible worlds, but no perfect world was possible, even for Him to select.[16]

If we take the world as it presents itself to us, it appears full of imperfections, but it is gradually becoming better, as a result of human efforts guided by divine assistance. Evolution has by no means been a consistent progress in a straight line; most plants and animals diverged in tangent directions; most species long ago perished; many, like the amœba, appear to have made almost no progress at all.[17] Many branches of the human race, even, have made no great contribution to the advance of humanity. Think of the Byzantine empire which had as its heritage the glorious traditions of Greece and Rome, and which endured for a thousand years after the fall of Rome itself! What an opportunity, and how little was made of it! Is any book of history more dreary than Gibbon's account of that thousand years? To be sure the Byzantine empire preserved ancient culture rather imperfectly, passed it down to the western nations at the time of their Renaissance, and for a time acted as a buffer to protect them against the Arabs and Turks. But that is not a brilliant record for a thousand years of history. Yet it is more than most nations have contributed to the onward course of humanity. The author does not desire to press this type of objections further. The reader is doubtless familiar with the replies that defenders of orthodox traditions make.

The second conception of a cosmic God that has found support among contemporary philosophers of religion was perhaps first presented by John Stuart Mill[18] but came more into favor after being ardently championed by William James.[19] This is the conception of God as a Person, not infinite in power, although immeasurably more powerful than we. He is gradually bringing order into the world through the processes of evolution, and He calls on us for loyal coöperation. With His aid we can succeed, and He is always ready to come to our help when we seek Him in religious worship. Our relationship to Him, the author thinks, can be conceived in the orthodox tradition as that of children to a Father, who loves them, understands their difficulties, and does all possible to direct the course of cosmic evolution in their favor. God does not enjoy an ineffable vision of eternal harmony that is denied to us; but we now, or in the future shall, if we deserve to, share in the appreciation of all the achievements that He and we together can accomplish.[20]

This last view affords hope for the personal immortality of mankind. Supposedly we are in the world because God loves us as His children, and because we on this earth can aid Him in the realization of moral values. When a human being has come to the end of his earthly existence, he seems only to have begun to learn the worth of life, what moral values most to appreciate, and how to work to bring them into existence. It would seem that it will favor the progress of moral values in the universe, if human lives can continue to work with God elsewhere, bringing chaos into order, and realizing ethical ends. The work of God in the universe will be more completely triumphant if His children share in His victories, world without end. It might be asked,—cannot God bring other finite beings into the universe to carry out His purposes elsewhere? Has He need of us beyond this life? But if God is indeed a Father, would other children be a full compensation for those whom He loses here at their deaths? That would not be true of earthly parents, certainly. And we like to think of Him as loving us more, and not less, than our human parents. So we have reason to hope that endlessly in the ever evolving universe, as constellations and galaxies of stars pass out of existence and are replaced by others, in a mutual society of the redeemed we may share the love of our common Father.

But must not ethics posit rewards and punishments in a future state? Only the reformatory theory of punishment would seem to have a rightful place in a future life. The future existence may be like a school with different classes. Some at death may be ready to pass at once into higher grades. Some may have to take the work of a grade over again. But all will advance as rapidly as their efforts and achievements warrant; and all will finally arrive at the great Cosmic Commencement, followed by an eternity of joyful service and intimate communion with one another and with God.

Readers scarcely need to be told that the contents of this chapter have become increasingly speculative as we have gone on; nor that the implications of ethics for metaphysics and the philosophy of religion properly belong to those disciplines and not to ethics itself; nor that it has been impossible here to do more than to hint at them in a very fragmentary way. The account has been biased by a frank expression of the author's own inclinations and prejudices. It is hoped that all who care for these great problems will be interested to take up the study of metaphysics and of the philosophy of religion in treatises devoted to those subjects.

REFERENCES

* W. G. Everett, *Moral Values*, chap. XIII.
* M. W. Calkins, *The Good Man and the Good*, chap. XI.
* James Seth, *A Study of Ethical Principles*, Part III.
* J. A. Leighton, *The Individual and the Social Order*, chap. XLVII; *The Field of Philosophy*, Part III.
* G. W. T. Patrick, *Introduction to Philosophy*, chaps. IX, X, XXII, XXIII.
* R. W. Sellars, *Principles and Problems of Philosophy*, Part III.
* E. S. Brightman, *Introduction to Philosophy*, chaps. IX, X.
* G. P. Conger, *A Course in Philosophy*, chaps. XLV–XLIX, and pp. 532–543.
* W. K. Wright, *A Student's Philosophy of Religion*, Part III.
    William James, *Varieties of Religious Experience. The Will to Believe.*

Josiah Royce, *Spirit of Modern Philosophy*. *Religious Aspect of Philosophy*.

C. Lloyd Morgan, *Emergent Evolution*.

J. E. Boodin, *Cosmic Evolution*.

D. C. Macintosh, *Reasonableness of Christianity*.

W. R. Sorley, *Moral Values and the Idea of God*.

J. A. Leighton, *Man and the Cosmos*, Books IV, V.

Warner Fite, *Moral Philosophy*.

Hastings Rashdall, *Theory of Good and Evil*, Book III, chaps. I, II.

W. K. Wright, "The Relation Between Morality and Religion" in *Essays in Philosophy* (in honor of James H. Tufts, *et al.*), edited by T. V. Smith and W. K. Wright.

NOTES

NOTES

CHAPTER I

1. Herbert Spencer, *Data of Ethics*, page 6. (Edition published by Appleton & Co., New York.)
2. Aristotle, *Nicomachean Ethics*, Book I, chap. II. (Quoted from Welldon's translation, page 4, published by the Macmillan Company.)

CHAPTER II

This chapter in a general way follows Professor L. T. Hobhouse. *Morals in Evolution* (both first and third editions, Part I, chap. II). There are various details, however, in which the author has deviated from Hobhouse in favor of other authorities cited in the list of references at the end of the chapter, or in these notes.

1. It is true, of course, that all the savage tribes now in existence have had as long a line of human ancestors as we, and none of them are, strictly speaking, primitive men. But it is probably safe to assume that those features common to the most simply organized savage tribes in existence, scattered in many parts of the world, roughly correspond to what the social organization of primitive man must have been.

2. This is well brought out by W. H. R. Rivers in a brief article on "Mother Right" in Hastings' *Encyclopædia of Religion and Ethics*. Numerous illustrations will be found in his *History of Melanesian Society*.

The student of general ethics should read enough ethnographical literature to get some sense of the character of Kinship organization, and then he should stop, if he is going to do justice to other ethical topics. In addition to the works cited in the list of References at the end of the chapter, the author has found the following particularly helpful: B. Spencer and F. J. Gillen, *Northern Tribes of Central Australia;* A. W. Howitt, *Native Tribes of S. E. Australia;* C. Hose and W. McDougall, *The Native Tribes of Borneo;* Mary H. Kingsley, *West African Studies;* John Roscoe, *The Baganda;* J. G. Frazer, *Totemism and Exogamy;* W. R. Smith, *Kinship and Marriage in Early Arabia;* W. H. R. Rivers, *The Todas;* and *op. cit.;* various studies in the *Journal of the Anthropological Institute* and in the *Reports of the Bureau of Ethnology*.

3. The chief authorities on the Veddahs are F. and P. Sarasin, *Ergebnisse naturwissenschaftlicher Forschungen auf Ceylon in den Jahren 1884–1886*, and C. G. Seligmann, *The Veddas*.

4. Under the maternal system children of both sexes are likely to belong to their mother's totem. However there are many tribes among whom the totem passes through the father; and a few, like the Arunta of Central Australia, where children are likely to belong to different totems from both of their parents.

5. Lewis H. Morgan, *League of the Iroquois*, vol. I, p. 77.

6. *Idem*, vol. I, p. 87.

7. *Idem*, vol. II, p. 204.

8. *Idem*, vol. I, pp. 77 f.

9. Morgan's estimate was 25,000. *Op. cit.*, vol. I, p. 25. Lloyd thinks that there never were more than fifteen or sixteen thousand. *Idem*, vol. II, pp. 226–230.

10. *Absolute* communism, carried so far that individuals have no rights to private property, even in tools, clothes, and small personal effects, has probably never existed, except in certain religious orders that have appeared under civilization. But the Iroquois and many other Kinship tribes seem to have recognized no private rights in large game captured by the men, or in grain and vegetables raised by the women, much less in land or other large and enduring objects of value.

11. Traces of a prehistoric condition of mother right are found in early civilizations, but so far as the author is aware, no people has ever reached a civilization including knowledge and use of writing, permanent settlement on the land, and elementary commerce and industry, that had not passed beyond the maternal system.

12. Edward Westermarck, *Origin and Development of the Moral Ideas*, vol. I, pp. 161 f., and the authorities therein cited.

CHAPTER III

1. In this chapter, I have been most consciously influenced by Professor L. T. Hobhouse (*Morals in Evolution*, especially Part I, chap. I and Part II, chap. VIII), and by Professors John Dewey and J. H. Tufts (*Ethics*, chaps. I–V, IX). The advanced student should also

familiarize himself with the interpretations of moral evolution advanced by Professor Edward Westermarck (*Origin and Development of the Moral Ideas*), Alexander Sutherland (*Origin and Growth of the Moral Instinct*), and William McDougall (*Social Psychology, The Group Mind, Ethics and Some World Problems*). Much can still be learned from W. E. H. Lecky's *History of European Morals*. A convenient article, summarizing literature on the subject, entitled "Moral Evolution" was contributed by Professor J. H. Tufts to the *Harvard Theological Review* for 1912.

2. I do not here attempt to explain how men first began to make judgments, moral or unmoral. Some animals live in group relations that would inspire moral judgments if they were able to judge at all. The lowest men live in social relations not much superior, yet they pass moral judgments. What caused the change? The scope of this book does not permit an investigation of this interesting question further than a few general observations in Chapter VIII. (See pages 201 f., 207). All that I mean to insist upon at this point is, that the lowest known form of human social organization, the primitive horde, affords man sufficient experience for elementary moral judgments.

3. *Cf.* Professor J. M. Baldwin, *Mental Development*, chap. XII, and *Social and Ethical Interpretations*, chaps. VI–VIII.

4. E. Westermarck, *Origin and Development of the Moral Ideas*, vol. I, pp. 386–390, and the authorities there cited.

5. The contention here made, that the elements of morality developed in the primitive horde, prior to the appearance of the clan, is borne out by what is known of folk upon this level. There are, however, comparatively few such tribes in existence to-day, and less is certainly known of moral and social life on this level than we could wish. The claims of the text, therefore, must be conceded to rest more upon reasoning than direct empirical evidence. Westermarck's *History of Human Marriage* has shown that the animal ancestors of man probably mated in pairs and brought up their children together, and that the lowest human races lead a solitary life, except for pair marriage. Alexander Sutherland (*Origin and Growth of the Moral Instinct*) makes a strong case for the view that social sympathy has developed from parental care, and the higher moral relations from social sympathy. He does not recognize, as does Westermarck (in the *Origin and Development of Moral Ideas*) how important has been the rôle of resentment in moral evolution. But both sympathy and resentment arise in family

life, and are there first coördinated and controlled so that they serve a common good.

6. E. Westermarck, *Origin and Development of Moral Ideas*, vol. I, chap. II, esp. p. 35.

7. W. McDougall, *The Group Mind*, chap. IV, "The Group Spirit".

8. *Cf.* William James, "The Energies of Men" in *Memories and Studies;* J. B. Pratt, *The Religious Consciousness*, chap. III; W. K. Wright, *A Student's Philosophy of Religion*, pp. 215–218, 265–267; all on the influence of reserve powers of the organism in religious experiences. For the influence of group action in this connection, *cf.* E. Durkheim, *The Elementary Forms of the Religious Life*.

9. W. K. Wright, *A Student's Philosophy of Religion*, pp. 255 f.; 280–284; 341–343. *Cf.* Rudolf Otto, *Das Heilige*.

10. R. R. Marett, *The Threshold of Religion*. I. King, *Development of Religion*, chap. VI. A. H. Codrington, *The Melanesians*, esp. chap. VII, and articles on "manitu" and "mana" in Hastings' *Encyclopœdia of Religion and Ethics*. W. K. Wright, *op. cit.*, see Index under *mana.*

11. The terms "folkways" and "mores" originated with the late Professor W. G. Sumner *(Folkways).* The distinction as I give it I believe to be true, whether or not it is what Sumner intended.

12. L. T. Hobhouse, *Morals in Evolution*, 3d. ed., pp. 71–73, 88 ff.

13. Professor Lévy-Bruhl claims that they are prelogical; and he at least proves that a considerable part of the time they do not employ our methods of reasoning. He does not maintain that savages cannot reason at all, in our manner. *Les fonctions mentales dans les sociétés inférieures. La mentalité primitive* (English translation of the latter). Dr. Paul Radin *(Primitive Man as Philosopher)* who has attacked this position, makes it probable that a minority of individuals among a primitive tribe are both logical and independent thinkers.

14. Westermarck, *Origin and Development of Moral Ideas*, vol. I, pp. 195 f. *History of Human Marriage*, first ed., pp. 43 ff.

15. B. Spencer and F. J. Gillen, *Native Tribes of Central Australia*, p. 265. *Northern Tribes of Central Australia*, p. 330. J. Roscoe, *The Baganda.* Codrington in *Journal of the Anthropological Institute*, vol. XVIII, pp. 309–311.

16. Deuteronomy XXV. 5–10.

17. This is not natural selection in the sense of biology. What I mean is, that societies whose mores have greater survival value win

out in competition with other societies, and pass down their customs to their descendants by social tradition rather than biological heredity.

CHAPTER IV

1. In this chapter, I am largely indebted to Professor J. M. Powis Smith (*The Moral Life of the Hebrews* and *The Prophet and His Problems*) and to Professor Henry Preserved Smith (*The Religion of Israel*).

2. W. Robertson Smith (*Kinship and Marriage in Early Arabia, The Religion of the Semites,* and in journal articles) and G. A. Barton (*A Sketch of Semitic Origins*) find evidences of totemism and mother right in prehistoric Israel. A brief discussion and further references will be found in the *Jewish Cyclopædia* under "Totemism".

3. The best source authority on the moral conditions of this period is the book of Judges, if read with care to ascertain what the people actually thought and did, in distinction from the moralizing comments made by a Deuteronomic editor of a later century (who believed, for instance, that Yahweh expected them to worship him alone, and to exterminate all Canaanites without exception). Other sources are the opening chapters of I Samuel, Joshua (which exaggerates the amount of national unity that could then have existed) and Ruth (probably written after the return from the exile, and containing the inaccuracies inevitable in a work of historical fiction).

4. The sources for the history of this period are I and II Samuel, I Kings, II Kings (chaps. I–XII), and I Chronicles (chaps. I–XXV). Allowance must be made for theological interpretations and comments of editors of later centuries. Most of the laws in the early codes— Exodus XX. 23–XXIII. 33 and XXXIV probably were formulated during this period, though as here recorded they contain later additions and revisions.

5. The principal historical and prophetic sources for the period are the remainder of II Kings and II Chronicles (see preceding note), the books of Amos, Hosea, Micah, Isaiah (chaps. I–XXXIX), Nahum, Zephaniah, Habakkuk, and Jeremiah. The present book of Deuteronomy contains some later additions to the original code. The latter is often supposed to be the "book of the law", newly discovered, by which King Josiah was guided in his reforms (II Kings XXII, XXIII; II Chronicles XXXIV, XXXV).

6. Ezra, Nehemiah, and the books of the Maccabees are the chief historical books subsequent to the exile. Jeremiah and Ezekiel were prophets of the exile. Prophets subsequent to the exile were the contributors to Isaiah II (chaps. XL–end), Daniel, Haggai, Zechariah, Obadiah, Malachi, and perhaps Joel. The Psalms, of various dates, became "the hymn book of the second temple" (*i.e.*, the temple to Yahweh in Jerusalem built after the return from the exile). The "Wisdom" literature includes Proverbs, Ecclesiasticus (the Wisdom of Jesus the son of Sirach), Ecclesiastes, and the Wisdom of Solomon. Ruth, Jonah, and Esther were works of fiction written in the post-exilic period.

7. A typical illustration is Judges I. 3. Judah and Simeon are the names of tribes here personified and given the names of their traditional ancestors, two of the sons of Jacob,—a picturesque way of expressing the recognition of Kinship that frequently occurs in this book.

8. Other incidents of blood revenge are recounted in II Samuel III. 22–27; IV. 4–12; I Kings II. 5, 6, 28–34.

9. The Decalogue or "ten commandments", in the versions of Exodus XX. 1–17 and Deuteronomy V. 1–21, represents a still higher moral plane; but it is not certain that such markedly ethical versions of the Decalogue existed during this period.

10. *Cf.* A. O. Lovejoy, "The Origins of Ethical Inwardness in Jewish Thought" in *American Journal of Theology*, 1907.

11. *Cf.* H. P. Smith, *The Religion of Israel*, chap. XI.

CHAPTER V

1. In this sketch I have followed chiefly W. Warde Fowler, *The City-State of the Greeks and Romans;* J. B. Bury, *History of Greece;* and W. S. Ferguson, *Greek Imperialism*.

2. W. Warde Fowler, *op. cit.*, p. 96.

3. However, slaves were better treated at Athens than anywhere else in the world at that time. Racially not greatly different from their masters, they had more legal protection than negro slaves in the United States prior to the Civil War.

4. Fowler thinks that the adult male population of Athens in the age of Pericles was about 30,000, and that about 1900 different citizens held office of some kind every year. Offices were assigned by lot, so

that every citizen would serve about once in sixteen years. Those living in Athens and the Piræus probably attended meetings of the Assembly regularly, while the farmers in Attica came in on the more important occasions. Pericles introduced a small payment for attendance, so that the poor could afford to lose a day's work in order to be present. (Fowler, *op. cit.*, chap. VI.)

5. Thucydides, II, 37–41. (Jowett's translation; quoted by permission obtained through the publishers, the Oxford University Press.)

6. Summary discussions, containing the points of most concern to the student of comparative ethics will be found in W. Warde Fowler, *The City-State of the Greeks and Romans;* F. F. Abbott, *A History and Description of Roman Political Institutions;* Tenney Frank, *A History of Rome,* and *Roman Imperialism;* H. S. Jones, *The Roman Empire;* W. T. Arnold, *Studies in Roman Imperialism,* and *The Roman System of Provincial Administration;* C. W. L. Launspach, *State and Family in Early Rome;* James S. Reid, *The Municipalities of the Roman Empire;* G. W. Botsford, *Roman Assemblies;* L. Friedländer, *Roman Life and Manners under the Early Empire.* Among the fuller discussions the following are standard for the periods with which they deal: Th. Mommsen, *History of Rome;* G. Ferrero, *The Greatness and Decline of Rome;* Edward Gibbon (edited by Bury), *Decline and Fall of the Roman Empire.*

7. The Etruscans, probably of similar racial stock with the Latins, invaded Italy in ships, coming from Asia Minor. For about a century they were dominant in the region about Rome. They introduced a more advanced civilization, especially in the industrial arts and architecture.

8. Strictly speaking, only ten of the tables were formulated at this date, the other two being added a few years later.

9. The letters of Pliny the Younger, who was the personal representative of the emperor Trajan in Bythinia, show how wise and just Roman provincial administration could be.

10. This is true, although Caracalla's purpose seems to have been chiefly to increase the revenues by taxation.

11. The Earl of Cromer (*Ancient and Modern Imperialism*) calls attention to the fact that no modern imperialist nation has shown powers of assimilation at all comparable, despite the fact that British imperial rule is more just, humane, and efficient in its treatment of subject populations.

12. *Cf.* Matthew XX. 21; Romans XIII. 1–7; II Timothy II. 2; I Peter II. 13–17.

13. *Cf.* James Bryce, *The Holy Roman Empire.*

14. The Earl of Cromer, *op. cit.*

15. The Roman empire was by no means an unqualified success from a moral standpoint. However, its decline and fall seem to have been due to a variety of causes, partly moral but chiefly unmoral. The problem is too complex to deal with here, but all of the following were contributory causes. (1) The expansion of the empire beyond boundaries that were compact. (2) The failure of ancient scientists and philosophers to realize that pure science can be put to practical applications. Equipped with railways and rifles, the empire would have remained secure against barbarian attack. (3) The evils of the "melting pot": the fine old Roman stock was wasted in wars and settlement in colonies, and diluted by the influx into Rome of orientals and barbarians. (4) Slavery, excessive taxes, depreciated currency, exhaustion of the soil, and other economic causes. (5) The decline of the old religion, and the failure of any substitute, like Christianity, to become dominant and serve as an effective sanction for morality until too late. (6) The enervating effect of malaria and other diseases, which became widely spread, and which ancient medical science did not know how to check.

16. On Greek and Roman popular moral consciousness the elementary chapters by Paulsen, Dewey and Tufts, and Hobhouse, cited in the References to this chapter, are perhaps the best with which to begin. Fuller discussions will be found in the works by G. Lowes Dickinson, Matthew Arnold, Gomperz (especially opening chaps. of vol. II), De Coulanges, and R. W. Livingstone. *Cf.* also Gilbert Murray, *Four Stages of Greek Religion;* and L. R. Farnell, *The Higher Aspects of Greek Religion.*

17. Poets and philosophers vainly tried to moralize the popular conceptions of the gods. *Cf.* Th. Gomperz, *Greek Thinkers*, Book IV, chap. I.

18. Evidence for most of the statements in this and the previous paragraphs will be found in W. E. H. Lecky's *History of European Morals*, chap. II. For the position of women, *cf.* L. T. Hobhouse, *Morals in Evolution*, third edition, pp. 206–212. The earlier chapters of Edward Gibbon's *Decline and Fall of the Roman Empire* are still worthy of attention. *Cf.* also W. Warde Fowler, *Social Life at Rome in the Age*

of Cicero; Ludwig Friedländer, *Roman Life and Manners under the Early Empire;* Samuel Dill, *Roman Society from Nero to Marcus Aurelius,* and *Roman Society in the Last Century of the Western Empire.* A more unfavorable estimate will be found in W. R. Inge, *Society in Rome under the Cæsars,* especially chap. III.

19. The cultivation of the mystery religions shows that they did not entirely lack a yearning for the transcendent. A brief account of these will be found in G. F. Moore's *History of Religions,* and an enthusiastic eulogy of Orphism in Jane Ellen Harrison's *Prolegomena to Greek Religion.*

20. *Cf.* L. R. Farnell, *The Higher Aspects of Greek Religion,* pp. 56 ff.

21. Browning's beautiful poem "Pheidippides" does not exaggerate this attractive side of pagan morality.

22. This probably remained true of the majority of people, even during the Roman empire, which, though decadent in these respects, is now not thought to have been so depraved as historians used to represent it. *Cf.* S. Dill, *op. cit.*

23. The sentence of Socrates is the most notable exception, prior to the persecutions of the Christians. The latter are to be explained (although of course not justified) by what seemed to the pagan to be stubborn refusal to serve in the army, and a general lack of patriotic devotion to the empire because of absorption in their own religious rites and activities. After the Christians gained control of the imperial government they certainly were not more tolerant of paganism than the pagans of an earlier time had been of Christianity. Christian emperors went about the suppression of paganism very thoroughly, while Christian mobs massacred the pagans. On this whole subject, *cf.* E. Gibbon, *Decline and Fall of the Roman Empire,* and W. E. H. Lecky, *History of European Morals,* chap. II.

24. In attempting to characterize pagan morality, I have ignored the interpretation of Friedrich Nietzsche. Though a brilliant literary and classical scholar, he utterly lacked balanced judgment. His chief contribution to the interpretation of pagan moral values was to call attention, in an extremely distorted perspective, to certain ideals of courage and aristocracy that our utilitarian, humanitarian, and democratic age has in some measure overlooked. The undergraduate may profitably read his *Beyond Good and Evil* and *Genealogy of Morals* if he is shown by his instructor how to extract the truth sympathetically, without overlooking the hyperbole. As a matter of fact, Nietzsche was not so

extravagant as a hasty reading of the aphorisms has led many to suppose. A careful study of Professor W. M. Salter's *Nietzsche the Philosopher* is indispensable, if one would know what Nietzsche really meant.

25. A good though brief interpretation of ancient Chinese, Indian, and Persian moral philosophy will be found in Professor L. T. Hobhouse's *Morals in Evolution*, Part II, chaps. III and V. Henry Sidgwick (*Outlines of Ethics*, pp. 12–17) concisely indicates the extent to which Pythagoras and his followers, Heraclitus and Democritus, may be said to have foreshadowed the ethical standpoints of Socrates and later Greek thought.

26. Any good history of ancient philosophy will give an account of the Sophists. Those by Th. Gomperz (*op. cit.*, Book III, chaps. V–VII), H. Sidgwick (*op. cit.*, pp. 17–22), and Paul Monroe (*Text Book in the History of Education*) are excellent.

27. Xenophon, *Memorabilia*, Book IV, chap. II.

28. Plato, *Republic*, Book I. Probably it is safe to assume that this book is a fairly accurate picture of Socrates' method and opinions, although later books in the *Republic* advance many positions original with Plato.

29. "Moreover, Socrates lived ever in the open; for early in the morning he went to the public promenades and training grounds; in the afternoon he was seen in the market; and the rest of the day he passed just where most people were to be met; he was generally talking, and any one might listen." Xenophon, *Memorabilia*, I, i, 10 (translation by Marchant in the Loeb Classical Library).

30. For the method of Socrates, Plato is in general a more reliable guide than Xenophon. The first book of the *Republic* is a capital illustration of *irony;* the conversation with the slave boy in the *Meno* shows the rôle of leading questions in *maieutic*. The theory of the method is explained in the *Theaetetus*.

31. *Cf.* the characterization of Socrates by Alcibiades in Plato's *Symposium*.

32. Plato, *Apology*.

33. Plato, *Apology; cf.* Xenophon, *Memorabilia*, I, i, 17–19.

34. The account of the trial and death of Socrates in Plato's *Apology, Crito*, and *Phædo* (omitting the metaphysical arguments for immortality in the latter, which are not Socratic) may be profitably compared with the accounts of the trial and death of Jesus in the Gospels and with that of the death of Gautama Siddartha (the Buddha) in the

"Book of the Great Decease" (*Sacred Books of the East*, vol. XI). Early Christian apologists like Justin Martyr thought of Socrates as a forerunner of Christ in a sense similar to the Hebrew prophets. In some ways similar is the thought of the late Professor Gabriel Campbell in his essay entitled "Socrates, a Forerunner of Christ", *Bibliotheca Sacra*, LXXIV, pp. 194–222.

35. The emphasis certainly seems different in such dialogues as the *Protagoras, Republic, Phædrus, Phædo, Philebus*, and *Laws*. However, it must be conceded to Professor Paul Shorey (*The Unity of Plato's Thought*) that Plato's attitude on the hedonistic question was more consistent than has often been supposed.

36. The best authority on Plato's ethics is of course Plato himself. The writer most enjoys the ethical discussions in the *Protagoras, Gorgias, Republic, Phædrus, Phædo,* and *Philebus*. There are occasional brilliant passages in the otherwise heavy *Laws*. Besides Shorey (*op. cit.*), Gomperz (*Greek Thinkers*) and Zeller (*Plato and the Older Academy*) are particularly to be recommended. Some notice of Plato's ethics is taken by each of the various histories of ancient philosophy. Walter Pater's *Plato and Platonism* is attractive from a literary standpoint.

37. *Politics*, Book I, chap. III (Welldon's translation).

38. *Nicomachean Ethics*, Book II, chap. I; Book X, chap. VIII.

39. *Nicomachean Ethics*, Book IV, chaps. VII–IX, Welldon's translation, published by The Macmillan Company, New York.

40. On Epicureanism, Edward Zeller, *Stoics, Epicureans and Skeptics* is still a standard authority. *Cf.* also W. Wallace, *Epicureanism;* R. D. Hicks, *Stoic and Epicurean* (has bibliography); A. E. Taylor, *Epicurus;* W. E. H. Lecky, *History of European Morals*. Walter Pater's *Marius the Epicurean* is a modern classic. Lucretius, *De Rerum Natura* (translation by Monro) and Diogenes Lærtius, *Lives of the Philosophers* (trans.) state the technical positions clearly, while the poems of Horace show the Epicurean attitude toward life concretely. For a character sketch of an Epicurean, in contrast with those quoted in the text from Aristotle and Marcus Aurelius, the writer suggests the sketch of Horace by Theodore Martin, *Horace*, pp. 60–70.

41. On Stoicism, I have been chiefly influenced by E. Zeller, *Stoics, Epicureans and Skeptics*, and W. E. H. Lecky, *History of European Morals*. A good bibliography down to 1910 will be found in E. Vernon Arnold, *Roman Stoicism;* this is brought down to 1924 by R. M. Wenley, *Stoicism and its Influence*.

42. H. D. Sedgwick, *Marcus Aurelius*, pp. 17–24. This book contains original translations of the verses of Zeno and the hymn of Cleanthes.

43. Lecky, *op. cit.*, vol. I, pp. 193 f.

44. Zeno took his own life (in old age) because he had broken a finger, Cato because of the downfall of the Roman republic. The philosopher lays aside his body when it is no longer of service, as he would discard worn-out clothes. Zeller, *Stoics, Epicureans and Skeptics* (trans.), pp. 316–321.

45. *Meditations*, Book I, 16, translated by Rendall; published by The Macmillan Company, New York. Another sketch of Antoninus Pius is given in Book VI, 30.

46. *De Republica*, II, Barnham, trans.

47. *De Beneficiis. Cf.* Carlyle, *History of Medieval Political Theory in the West*, vol. I, chap. II.

48. Sir Henry Maine, *Ancient Law*, chap. IV.

49. On Cicero, Seneca, and the Roman lawyers, see A. J. Carlyle, *Medieval Political Theory in the West*, vol. I; Sir Henry Maine, *Ancient Law*, edited by Pollock; W. A. Dunning, *A History of Political Theories, Ancient and Medieval;* James Muirhead, *Historical Introduction* to the *Private Law of Rome* (edited by Goudy); Gaius, *Institutes* (with translation by Poste, revised by Whittuck, and introduction by Greenige, Oxford, 1904); *Institutes of Justinian* (with introduction, commentary, and translation by J. B. Moyle, Oxford, 1912).

CHAPTER VI

1. It is extremely difficult to state the influence of Christianity upon moral evolution with absolute fairness, and to avoid prejudice. Few writers on general ethics take it up at all, notwithstanding its importance. In view of the difficulty of the undertaking, the indulgence of readers is requested. No one can be more aware of the inadequacies of this chapter than its author. It has seemed unnecessary to go into the higher criticism of the synoptic gospels in an endeavor to discover how much of their ethical teaching originated with the historical Jesus himself. In any case, the actual influence of Jesus upon the moral evolution of Europe has been through the teachings attributed to him in the New Testament as it stands.

Besides the works listed in the References at the end of the chapter, the following are particularly valuable: Friedrich Jodl, *Geschichte der*

Ethik, vol. I, Book II; Theobald Ziegler, *Geschichte der christlichen Ethik*. C. E. Luthardt, *Geschichte der christlichen Ethik*, though an older authority, is still of value; the first volume has been translated.

2. See Chapter IV, pp. 83 f.

3. The following are among the New Testament passages on which these conflicting interpretations are based: Matthew V. 27–32; XIX. 3–12; XXII. 23–30. Mark X. 2–12; XII. 19–25. Luke XVI. 18; XX. 27–35. Romans VII. 1–4. I Corinthians VI. 12–20; VII; XI. 1–16. Ephesians V. 22–VI. 4. Colossians III. 18–21. I Timothy II. 9; III. 13; V. 1–16. Titus II. 5. I Peter III. 1–9. Galatians III. 28. Revelation XIV. 4.

4. For a summary account of the history of Christianity in its relations to war, with citations, see E. Westermarck, *Origin and Development of the Moral Ideas*, chap. XV.

5. Matthew XIX. 19–24. Mark X. 25. Luke I. 53; VI. 20; XVI. 19–31; XVIII. 24 f. James V. 1–6. Acts II. 44 f; IV. 32–35. *Cf.* Westermarck, *op. cit.*, vol. I, pp. 555 f; vol. II, pp. 280 f.

6. Matthew IV. 2; VI. 16–18; XVII. 21. Mark IX. 29. Luke V. 35. Acts XIII. 2. I Corinthians VII. 5. II Corinthians VI. 5.

7. See the scripture references in note 3, above. Westermarck, *op. cit.*, vol. I, pp. 653–655.

8. Romans XIII. 1–7. Titus III. 1, 2. I Peter II. 13–17.

9. The best authority on this subject is R. W. and A. J. Carlyle, *History of Medieval Political Theory in the West.*

10. Jude, II. Peter and the epistles of John contain the severest denunciations. Paul is constantly contending with factions that are introducing false views, especially in II Corinthians, Galatians, Colossians, and Philippians.

11. Matthew XXIV. 29–31. Acts I. 11. I and II Thessalonians (almost entire). Philippians II. 20; IV. 5. Romans XIII. 11 f. I Corinthians XV. 51. Revelation I. 1–3. The last chapter of the Fourth Gospel seems to be an appendix written by another hand after the author's death, to explain why, contrary to the expectation of many, the author had died before the second coming of Christ.

12. Hebrews and the Fourth Gospel are attempts of a very different character to accommodate the Jewish tradition to philosophy; II Peter, Jude, and the three epistles of John contend against heresies; I Peter is an epistle of encouragement in times of persecution, and such is the motive of Revelation.

13. Statistics are of course speculative. Perhaps these are near enough the truth to give a correct idea of the rapid expansion of Christianity, and the danger of its losing its identity in the Gentile inundation. The closing chapter of A. Harnack, *Expansion of Christianity* indicates the rapid growth of Christianity, and the uncertainty of numerical estimates.

14. *E.g., City of God*, Book XV. St. Augustine's *Confessions* is a striking revelation of the Catholic mores of his time in both their attractive and repellent features.

15. St. Thomas Aquinas is the basic authority in modern Roman Catholic ethics, other scholastics being studied more or less incidentally. The whole of the Second Part of the *Summa Theologica* (nine volumes in the English translation) deals with ethical subjects.

16. This philosophy underlies Dante's famous description of the "beatific vision" in the closing cantos of the *Paradiso*.

17. Duns Scotus († 1308) and his followers, the Scotists, on the contrary, maintained that ultimate moral principles are primarily *willed* by God; intellectual processes are secondary both for God and men. This makes the rational explanation of morality more restricted.

18. St. Thomas, *Summa Theologica*, First Part of Second Part (Prima Secundæ) question 94, article 2 (page 44 in English trans.). De Wulf, *Medieval Philosophy, etc.*, p. 110.

19. St. Thomas, *Summa, ibid.*, question 19, article 5; question 94, article 4; question 96, article 1, replies to Objections 2 and 3; question 100, article 1. Cardinal Mercier, et al., *Manual of Modern Scholastic Philosophy*, vol. II, pp. 250, 259. Maurice De Wulf, *op. cit.*, pp. 111–114. A. Sertillanges, *Philosophie morale de St. Thomas d'Aquin*, chap. XVI.

20. The discussion of political philosophy is chiefly in the *De Regimine Principium*. A good brief account will be found in W. A. Dunning, *History of Political Theories, Ancient and Medieval*, chap. VIII. The best authority on earlier medieval philosophers is Carlyle, *History of Medieval Political Theory in the West*.

21. Some explanation of the works on Roman Catholicism in the list of References at the end of the chapter may be necessary. The student ought by all means to begin by reading a little, at least, of St. Thomas himself. The short popular exposition in Ryan's *Introduction to Philosophy* will suffice to catch something of the spirit of con-

temporary Roman Catholic systematic ethics, while the more extended presentations by Father Rickaby and Cardinal Mercier will fill in the details. Ryan and Husslein's *The Church and Labor* contains official pronouncements by recent popes and bishops, papers by the authors, and a working bibliography of recent Roman Catholic literature on social and industrial problems. *Cf.* also *Justice First*, by Dr. John A. Lapp, president of the National Conference of Social Work, 1927.

22. Brief popular accounts of the Anglo-Catholic movement will be found in Williston Walker, *History of the Christian Church*, pp. 547–549; Wilfrid Ward, *The Oxford Movement*, and A. E. Manning Foster, *Anglo-Catholicism*, the latter two in the "People's Books". The spirit of contemporary American Anglo-Catholicism may be learned from such periodicals as *The Living Church* (a popular weekly) and the more scholarly *Anglican Theological Review* (published by the Columbia University Press).

23. *Cf.* T. B. Strong, *Christian Ethics*, chap. VII.

24. *Cf.* Luther's "Ninety-Five Theses" and the "Letter" accompanying them, in *Luther's Primary Works* trans. by Wace and Buckheim.

25. William James has indicated differences in Catholic and Protestant mental traits (*Varieties of Religious Experience*, pp. 81, 114, 227 ff., 244 ff., 330, and *passim*. How far blendings in different proportions of the three principal original European races or types, and how far more recent environmental influences have caused these differences is an interesting anthropological question into which it is impossible to enter here. *Cf.* William McDougall, *Is America Safe for Democracy?* pp. 100–102, 116; and *The Group Mind*, pp. 159–165; Ellsworth Huntington, *The Character of Races*, chap. XIV.

26. Such measures saved Protestant mores from the utter destruction with which they were threatened by misusers of newly discovered "Christian Liberty". Even Calvin's severe rule at Geneva was necessary. *Cf.* Th. Ziegler, *Gesch. der chris. Ethik*, pp. 481–486.

27. The classical work on this subject is Andrew D. White's *Warfare Between Science and Theology*.

28. For the general moral spirit of liberal Protestantism, in modern times, *cf.* Professor A. C. McGiffert's *The Rise of Modern Religious Ideas*, and in America since the Great War, Professor William Adams Brown, *The Church in America*.

Hints upon the distinctive moral influence of each of the more important types of Protestantism may be derived from the following: Ziegler, *op. cit.;* W. Walker, *op. cit.* L. H. Waring, *The Political Theories of Martin Luther;* T. C. Hall, *The Social Meaning of Modern Religious Movements in England;* J. S. Flynn, *The Influence of Puritanism on the Political and Religious Thought of the English;* Leighton Pullen, *Religion Since the Reformation.* On America, see Woodbridge Riley, *American Thought from Puritanism to Pragmatism,* and E. Huntington, *The Character of Races,* chap. XXI. Professor J. M. Mecklin has made interesting observations on the good and bad influences of Calvinism on American character in his *Introduction to Social Ethics.* Professor Rufus M. Jones (various books and studies) is a standard authority on the Quakers.

29. Expositions of systematic ethics by Christian clergymen containing little specific theology (like the works of Martineau, Harris, and Rashdall listed in the References to the chapter) really better represent contemporary Protestant ethical thought than do more markedly theological works on Christian Ethics.

CHAPTER VII

1. Extended References seem unnecessary in connection with this chapter. Its purpose is merely to complete the outline of moral evolution in Part II, and to afford a general impression of outstanding periods and tendencies. Beginners in philosophy who are taking a first course in ethics will do well to pass rapidly on to Part II.

2. He seems to think some slight restrictions necessary in the case of persons not likely to be bound by an oath of allegiance to the government. He apparently had in mind atheists, to whom he thought an oath would mean nothing, and Roman Catholics who desired the restoration of the Stuarts and might not think it necessary to keep oaths made to heretics.

3. Some writers on the history of education, actuated by the pedagogical desire to make some classical writer represent the modern theory of "formal discipline", choose Locke for this position, and thereby present him in a badly distorted perspective.

4. *Cf.* Sidgwick, *History of Ethics,* p. 189; E. A. Albee, *History of English Utilitarianism,* pp. 56, 62; W. K. Wright, *Ethical Significance of Feeling, Pleasure and Happiness in Modern non-Hedonistic Systems,* p. 34.

5. Professor Franklin H. Giddings acknowledges his indebtedness to Smith for the suggestion from which this conception grew in his mind. (*Principles of Sociology*, page x.)

6. I do not mean to affirm that all injustices to women have been absolutely eliminated everywhere. But those that now remain in most western countries are slight compared with those of former times. *Cf.* Chapter XVIII, below.

7. Down to the beginning of the nineteenth century most orthodox Christians believed that God created mankind with the foreknowledge that most of them would spend eternity in hell fire. The Universalist and Unitarian movements did much to force the acceptance of more humane views by the orthodox. Byron's *Cain* and Shelley's *Queen Mab* also helped to arouse the general moral consciousness. (*Cf.* G. Brandes, *Main Currents of Literature in the Nineteenth Century*, vol. IV, pp. 309–318.)

8. The phrase "equality of consideration" will be explained and defended in Chapter XVI.

9. "Rabbi Ben Ezra" and "Abt Vogler" are Neo-Hegelian in doctrine, while the "Ring and the Book" is Neo-Hegelian in both thought and manner of treatment. *Cf.* Sir Henry Jones, *Browning as a Philosophical and Religious Teacher*.

10. John and Edward Caird, T. H. Green, and Bernard Bosanquet were active in movements of social betterment, and even Bradley took as much interest in such matters as his health permitted.

11. Alexander Sutherland, *Origin and Growth of the Moral Instinct*. Edward Westermarck, *Origin and Development of Moral Ideas*. L. T. Hobhouse, *Morals in Evolution, Mind in Evolution, Social Evolution and Political Theory, Social Development*, etc. William McDougall, *Introduction to Social Psychology, The Group Mind, Outline of Psychology, Ethics and Some Modern World Problems, Character and the Conduct of Life*. John Dewey, *Human Nature and Conduct, Experience and Nature; The Public and Its Problems*. James H. Tufts (with Dewey), *Ethics*, Part I.

CHAPTER VIII

1. The general positions in this chapter follow Professor William McDougall, *Outline of Psychology*, and *Introduction to Social Psychology*, although they differ in a few details. The advanced student is also referred to Professor McDougall's *Group Mind, Is America Safe for*

Democracy? and *Ethics and World Problems*. Professor McDougall has defended his doctrine of instincts in "The Use and Abuse of Instincts in Social Psychology" (*Journal of Abnormal and Social Psychology*, 1922). I have defended these positions in "Conscience as Reason and Emotion" (*Philosophical Review*, 1916) and "McDougall's Social Psychology in the Light of Recent Discussion" (*Journal of Philosophy*, 1921).

The following are important alternative interpretations with which the advanced student should be acquainted: F. H. Allport, *Social Psychology*, (especially chap. III, with bibliography of the controversy on instincts on pp. 82 f.). Alexander F. Shand, *Foundations of Character*. E. L. Thorndike, *Educational Psychology*, vol. I. James Drever, *Instinct in Man*. J. R. Kantor, *Principles of Psychology*. C. C. Josey, *Social Philosophy of Instinct*. L. L. Bernard, *Instinct: A Study in Social Psychology*. R. S. Woodworth, *Dynamic Psychology*. W. E. Hocking, *Human Nature and its Remaking*. J. B. Watson, *Behavior, Psychology from the Standpoint of a Behaviorist*. H. C. Warren, *Human Psychology*. Robert H. Gault, *Social Psychology*.

2. Here and elsewhere in this and following chapters the language is at times that of interactionism. In an ethical treatise it is necessary to speak in popular language in places where a more technical discussion would be more guarded. I mean to assume no position in this book on the mind and body problem, and especially to be neutral between interactionism and parallelism. (My private preference is for the version of realism held by the emergent evolutionists, especially by Professor C. Lloyd Morgan in his *Emergent Evolution*. That is, consciousness is a relation of physical elements; it is neither an independent and interacting nor a parallel substance or series of processes. The relation of consciousness emerges when a mutual adjustment of organism and environment occurs in a certain manner; the action could not take place without this relation; consciousness "involves" the factors on lower levels, and they "depend" upon it. Professor Lloyd Morgan uses a somewhat different, and as I think, not so good terminology in his more recent *Life, Mind and Spirit*.)

3. The physical side of the emotion, consisting largely of organic disturbances, which, however, are often functionally useful, may be distinguished from the sensations and feelings that accompany it, and according to the James-Lange theory, are its conscious effects.

4. Possibly these illustrations involve the presence of the pugnacious instinct as well.

5. *Cf.* W. McDougall, *Outline of Psychology*, pp. 139–142; F. H. Allport, *Social Psychology*, pp. 58 f.; and above all, Wallace Craig, "Why Do Animals Fight?" (*International Journal of Ethics*, 1921).

6. Reliable semi-popular explanations will be found in such works as A. G. Tansley, *The New Psychology*, and Morton Prince, *The Unconscious*. The works of Freud, Jung, and Adler and their disciples contain important truth entangled with much imagination.

7. W. McDougall, *Outline of Psychology*, p. 353.

8. *Cf.* Th. Ribot, the *Psychology of the Emotions*, and the authorities therein cited.

9. W. McDougall, *Outline of Psychology*, p. 353.

10. John Locke, *Thoughts on Education.* John B. Watson, *Psychological Care of Infant and Child.*

11. I hope that these illustrations will not appear exaggerated. Most of them have been suggested to me in conversations by those disposed to take the position that instincts have no existence at all, or at least do not play enough of a rôle in human conduct to be taken into account in ethics. However, some who are willing to concede that instincts exist and play their part in the moral life of men, may yet think them fewer and more plastic than I do. An instructor who takes such a stand will have no difficulty in giving his classes milder illustrations that will serve to differentiate his position from the two extreme positions here contrasted.

12. See Chapter XVI.

13. In this account of the principal primary impulses, it will be observed that I have endeavored to avoid controversial positions as much as possible. While I have unreservedly proclaimed my belief that the principal primary impulses are instincts, I hope that most of what I have said in this section will be acceptable to those who believe them to be habits, and to those who regard them as simply class names for a variety of modes of behavior. Nothing that has been said here is dependent on the acceptance in biology of either Darwinism or Lamarckism, mechanism or vitalism. No theory regarding the origin of instincts has been assumed.

14. See pages 63, 69 f. above. *Cf. A Student's Philosophy of Religion*, pp. 223–230; W. McDougall, *Social Psychology*, chaps. IV, XV; *Outline of Psychology*, pp. 155 f.; 170–176.

On crowd psychology G. Tarde's *Laws of Imitation*, Le Bon's *The Crowd*, and E. A. Ross' *Social Psychology* are classical. I suppose, following McDougall, that imitation, sympathy, and suggestion in at least some of their forms are inherited tendencies. However, I think I have said nothing here that would not hold if Professor F. H. Allport is right in calling them "conditioned emotional responses" (*Social Psychology*, chap. X).

15. *Theodore Roosevelt's Letters to His Children*, edited by J. B. Bishop, pp. 60–64.

On play in relation to morality and social psychology, *cf*. W. Mc-Dougall, *Social Psychology*, chaps. IV and XV, and *Outline of Psychology*, pp. 170–173. The classical works are Karl Groos, *The Play of Animals*, and *The Play of Man*.

On the moral value of athletics in colleges, *cf*. Alexander Meiklejohn "What Are College Games For?" *Atlantic Monthly*, Nov. 1922; Walter Camp, "The Frankenstein of College Athletics", *World's Work*, November, 1923; in secondary schools, R. H. Jordan, *Extra-Classroom Activities*, New York, 1928.

16. In the *Poetics*. The translation and notes by Lane Cooper make this classic interesting and intelligible to the undergraduate. S. H. Butcher's translation and commentary (under the title *Aristotle's Theory of Poetry and Fine Art*) are better for the advanced student. A short but extremely wise and illuminating discussion of the relationship between moral and æsthetic judgments will be found in H. Rashdall's *Theory of Good and Evil*, vol. I., pp. 148–151, 177–183.

17. *Cf*. W. McDougall, *Outline of Psychology*, pp. 417 f.; and Alexander F. Shand, in *British Journal of Psychology* (*General Section*) XIII, p. 125.

18. *Outline of Psychology*, pp. 421 f.

19. *Nicomachean Ethics*, Book VIII, chaps. III, IV.

20. *Outline of Psychology*, pp. 425 f.

21. E. D. Starbuck, *Psychology of Religion*, pp. 85–89; W. K. Wright, *A Student's Philosophy of Religion*, pp. 242 f.

22. W. McDougall, *Social Psychology* (fourteenth edition), chap. V, supplementary chap. III. Alexander F. Shand, *Foundations of Character*, in almost every chapter.

23. Alexander F. Shand, *Foundations of Character*, p. 106.

24. A. F. Shand, *op. cit.*, Book I; chap. XI.

CHAPTER IX

1. The conception of virtues as habits, cultivated rationally in response to social demands, was advanced by Aristotle.

The doctrine of sentiments employed in this chapter follows William McDougall, *Social Psychology*. (*Cf.* also his *Group Mind*, and *Outline of Psychology*, chap. XVII.) The chief difference is, that here the question is left open whether sentiments are organizations of native instincts or of very early formed habits, the noncommittal term "primary impulses" being employed instead of "instincts". A conception of sentiments in some respects similar will be found in A. F. Shand's *Foundations of Character*.

The identification of virtues with rationally organized sentiments is possibly original with the author, who has set it forth and made applications of it in the following articles: "Ethical Objectivity in the Light of Social Psychology", *Philosophical Review*, July, 1913; "The Evolution of Values from Instincts", *idem*, March, 1915; "Private Property and Social Justice", *International Journal of Ethics*, July, 1915; "Ethical Aspects of Internationalism", *idem*, April, 1918; "On Certain Aspects of the Religious Sentiment", *Journal of Religion*, Sept, 1924. *Cf.* also *A Student's Philosophy of Religion*, chaps. XIV, XV.

2. The argument advanced in this section will be found at greater length and with more technical considerations in the first of the author's articles cited in the preceding note.

3. Professor William McDougall believes that the essential defect in such a man as Gladstone or Wilson is a certain *naïveté*—a failure to understand and appreciate his own motives, so that he has a whole-hearted uncritical confidence in the rightness of his opinions and purposes, and believes himself to be always on the Lord's side. *Character and the Conduct of Life*, pp. 80–82.

4. Aristotle, *Nicomachean Ethics*, Book III, chap. X (quoted from Welldon's translation, published by The Macmillan Company).

5. Though he does not state it in exactly this way, this seems to be a logical inference from the observations of workingmen reported by Mr. Whiting Williams, *Mainsprings of Men*.

6. Thomas Mott Osborne, *Society and Prisons*, *Within Prison Walls*, etc.

7. The facts in regard to the evil effects of alcohol and references

to the more reliable literature are given by Professor Durant Drake, *Problems of Conduct*, chap. XVI. On several interpretative points in this section, the author is indebted to President S. E. Mezes, *Ethics, Descriptive and Explanatory*, chap. XI. The argument that, while the state cannot make people virtuous by legislation, it can endeavor to make social conditions favorable for the growth of morality, with applications to drink and other evils, was advanced by Thomas Hill Green, *Philosophical Works*, vol. III, pp. 382–386. *Cf.* Green's *Principles of Political Obligation*, "The right of the state to promote morality".

8. W. K. Wright, "The Psychology of Punitive Justice", *Philosophical Review*, September, 1908.

9. The best single chapters on Justice of which the author knows are those by President S. E. Mezes, *Ethics, Descriptive and Explanatory*, chap. XIII, and the late Dean Hastings Rashdall, *Theory of Good and Evil*, vol. I, chap. VIII.

10. Aristotle, *Nicomachean Ethics*, Books VIII, IX.

11. On this point, Herbert Spencer's chapters in the *Data of Ethics* on Egoism and Altruism and their reconciliation are classic.

12. *Cf.* F. Paulsen, *System of Ethics*, trans. by Thilly, pp. 227–231.

13. Theoretically, Justice and Love ought to become identical.

14. Josiah Royce's *Philosophy of Loyalty* finely sets forth the implications of this virtue. Galsworthy's play, *Loyalties*, is an impressive portrayal of the difficulty in our imperfect society of reconciling sentiments of loyalty to diverse groups.

15. Hugo Münsterberg was perhaps the first of recent moral philosophers to call attention in a striking way to the ethical importance of Economy, in his *Eternal Values*.

16. In the ethical thought of Kant, respect plays a particularly prominent rôle. See Chapter XII.

17. It will of course be understood that the terms "respect" and "reverence", here employed to designate specific virtues, have been more or less arbitrarily appropriated by the author for the purpose. The words are popularly employed in many different ways. Plato sometimes included "reverence" among the chief virtues.

18. The greatest danger for religion is that of getting on a tangent, and emphasizing something else (like orthodox beliefs or conformity to ritual) more than goodness itself. For instances in which Christian-

ity has thus sometimes erred in the past, see L. T. Hobhouse, *Morals in Evolution*, Part II, chap. IV, esp. pp. 499–515 (third, one-volume edition).

CHAPTER X

1. The ethical student may well begin the psychological study of the self with the chapters on this and related topics in James' *Principles of Psychology*. Next to this work, the author is most indebted to William McDougall, *Social Psychology*, chaps. VII–IX, and J. R. Angell, *Psychology*, chaps. XX–XXII.

2. Kant's rather technical exposition will be found in the "Transcendental Deduction of the Categories" in the second edition of the *Critique of Pure Reason* (trans. by Max Müller), with which a good commentary should be read. Among those available in English, Edward Caird's *Critical Philosophy of Kant*, F. Paulsen's *Immanuel Kant* (trans.), and Norman Kemp Smith's *A Commentary to Kant's Critique of Pure Reason* may be recommended.

A less difficult treatment will be found in T. H. Green's *Prolegomena to Ethics*, Book II, chap. II. *Cf.* also the "self psychology" of Professor M. W. Calkins, *First Book in Psychology*, especially chaps. I, II, and XII, together with the references given in the appendices to these chapters.

3. *Troilus and Cressida*, act III, sc. iii, lines 103–123. *Cf.* E. Caird, *Critical Philosophy of Kant*, vol. II, p. 26.

4. David Hume, *Treatise of Human Nature*, Book I, Part IV, p. vi. Immanuel Kant, *Critique of Pure Reason*, on the "Paralogisms of Pure Reason".

5. E. A. Schäfer, *The Endocrine Glands*.

6. That a man's sentiments constitute what we mean by his personality can be seen with reference to the problem of personal immortality. Does man continue, himself, to live after death? When this question is asked, reference is not to the pure ego, nor to the soul as a simple substance, but to whether a soul whose character and personality, made up of sentiments, persists in another life, knowing itself to be continuous with the man whose "empirical me" became separated from his mortal body at death.

7. The literature on this is quite extensive. Most general works on psychology and psychiatry give expositions and references. A recent book with articles by eminent psychiatrists is *Problems of Personality*,

edited by Dr. MacFie Campbell and others in honor of Dr. Morton Prince.

8. *Cf.* C. H. Cooley, *Human Nature and the Social Order.*

9. *Cf.* J. S. Mackenzie, *Manual of Ethics*, third edition, pp. 97 f.

10. Gabriel Tarde, *Laws of Imitation* (trans.); Gustav Le Bon, *The Crowd* (trans.); E. A. Ross, *Social Psychology;* W. Trotter, *Instincts of the Herd in Peace and War;* W. M. Conway, *The Crowd in Peace and War.*

11. William McDougall, *Social Psychology*, see "sympathy, active" in Index.

12. Perhaps Adam Smith and Schopenhauer did not fully realize this, although the former came close to doing so. An entire ethical system cannot be erected on sympathy. On the other hand, it is even more impossible to dispense with all feeling and emotion, and derive ethics from abstract reasoning. Reason in ethics must be a *synthesis* of emotions and sentiments so as to form a unified self; reason cannot be a *substitute* for them.

13. The general doctrine of pleasure and unpleasantness advanced in this section has been adapted from Professor G. F. Stout, *Analytic Psychology*, chap. XII (from which most of the illustrations have been taken); and from Professor William McDougall, *Social Psychology*, Supplementary chap. I, and *passim. Cf.* also his *Outline of Psychology*, pp. 191–193, 268–271.

14. These four sanctions are given by Jeremy Bentham. (See Chapter XIII, below.) As mentioned here, the statement of each sanction has been modified, in some respects, *e.g.*, the hedonism is eliminated.

15. On duty and conscience, *cf.* Herbert Spencer, *Data of Ethics*, chap. VII, for a famous empirical interpretation. Kant's position will be found in his *Fundamental Principles of the Metaphysic of Morals* (trans. by Abbott). For St. Thomas Aquinas, on conscience, see pp. 151–153 above. Other conceptions are summarized in Hastings' *Encyclopædia of Religion and Ethics*, under "Duty" and "Conscience".

16. *Cf.* William McDougall, *Social Psychology*, chap. IX. On the place of reason in the moral life a popular statement will be found in Dewey and Tufts' *Ethics*, chap. XVI; and a fuller treatment in L. T. Hobhouse, *The Rational Good.*

17. A. K. Rogers, *Theory of Ethics*, p. 148.

18. Ethical writers who profess to reject the "freedom of the will"

are usually determinists who use the expression to designate indeterminism; they do not deny psychological freedom and moral responsibility as defined here.

19. Good popular expositions and defenses of determinism by W. G. Everett, *Moral Values*, chap. XII; and H. Rashdall, *Theory of Good and Evil*, Book III, chap. III. In defense of indeterminism, the best popular work is William James' *The Will to Believe* (especially the essay entitled "The Dilemma of Determinism"). *Cf.* also F. C. S. Schiller, *Riddles of the Sphinx*, and *Studies in Humanism*, chap. XVIII. More technical defenses of indeterminism will be found in James Ward's *Realm of Ends*, and Henri Bergson's *Time and Free Will* (trans.). A neutral popular treatment will be found in G. W. T. Patrick's *Introduction to Philosophy*, chap. XIX. *Cf.* W. K. Wright, *A Student's Philosophy of Religion*, chap. XXI. On the psychology of volition, the chapters in James' *Principles of Psychology* on Attention, Habit, and Will should first be read, and then McDougall's *Social Psychology*, chap. IX.

CHAPTER XI

1. It is often said that Intuitionism disregards consequences altogether. It would be hard to find many ethical systems that could be unqualifiedly classified as Intuitional to this extent, however. The tendency among writers usually called Intuitionists is to put chief emphasis on implicit acceptance of moral principles, on conscience, and upon motives. As compared with systems classified as teleological, little account is taken of consequences.

2. Henry Sidgwick, *Methods of Ethics*, Book III, chap. XIII.

3. L. Fison and A. W. Howitt, *Kamilaroi and Kurnai*, pp. 256 f; cited by E. Westermarck, *Origin and Development of the Moral Ideas*, vol. I, p. 118.

4. It would be difficult to cite contemporary writers who unqualifiedly advocate what has here been called "Abstract Ethics". However, a tendency in this direction exists in some quarters. The doctrine that "good" is intuitive and unanalyzable will be found in Dr. G. E. Moore's *Principia Ethica*. *Cf.* also Mr. Thomas Whitaker, *The Theory of Abstract Ethics*. Professor A. P. Brogan believes that moral judgments are always comparisons between alternatives, so that "better" is the ultimate intuition, in terms of which "good" and "bad" can be defined. (*Journal of Philosophy*, XVI, pp. 96–104; XVIII, pp. 197–209.) This general form of intuitionism has been effec-

tively criticized by Professor R. B. Perry, *General Theory of Value*, pp. 34–40, 131–134, and *passim*.

5. James Martineau, *Types of Ethical Theory*, vol. II, pp. 266, 270. *Cf.* Sidgwick's criticisms of Martineau's table in his *Methods of Ethics*, to which I am indebted.

CHAPTER XII

1. Quotations from Kant have usually been taken from the translations by T. K. Abbott in his *Kant's Theory of Ethics*.

2. It seems to be generally agreed in the United States that legal attempts to prohibit liquor saloons, houses of prostitution, and gambling dens are morally justifiable; these are instances in which external conditions unfavorable to welfare are removed. Laws making individual drinking, gambling and fornication criminal would probably be regarded by most American moral philosophers as improper attempts to make people virtuous by legislation. Whether the legal prohibition of the liquor traffic in all of its forms is or is not beyond the proper sphere of legislation is as much debated at the present time among moral philosophers as other citizens.

3. It is surprising in how many respects Kant, living in Prussia at the close of the eighteenth century, had the ideals of his contemporaries in America. He also foresaw the desirability of some kind of federal union of all the nations of the world, in order to assure permanent peace; and he predicted that a league of nations would probably be realized before a complete federation could be brought about. A comparison of his essay on *Everlasting Peace* with Woodrow Wilson's celebrated Fourteen Points is instructive. *Cf.* E. Caird, *Critical Philosophy of Kant*, vol. II, pp. 335–350; and F. Paulsen, *Immanuel Kant* (trans.), pp. 343–361.

4. A short essay, published in a Berlin periodical in 1797 and translated by Abbott (*op. cit.*, pp. 361–365).

5. Kant's position regarding the murderer on the island might be defensible on teleological grounds, *e.g.*, to protect mankind against him by making it impossible for him ever to return to civilization and commit further crimes. This is not Kant's thought, however. His argument is purely formalistic; the murderer should be executed in conformity to the universal law of retribution. *Cf.* Caird, *op. cit.*, vol. II, pp. 343–345, and the passages in Kant's works therein cited.

6. *Cf.* H. Rashdall, *Theory of Good and Evil*, vol. I, pp. 116 f.

7. Josiah Royce's otherwise excellent *Philosophy of Loyalty* is perhaps the most important American ethical treatise of the present century that contains conspicuous elements of formalism. These are justly criticized by Professor W. G. Everett, *Moral Values*, pp. 45–49.

CHAPTER XIII

1. Besides *intensity* and *duration*, Bentham mentions the *certainty* of the pleasant and unpleasant consequences occurring, *fruitfulness* in producing further pleasant or unpleasant effects, and *purity* (freedom from mixture with its opposite). These considerations, however, are all quantitative, and reducible to intensity and duration.

2. *Cf.* J. S. Mackenzie, *Manual of Ethics* (third edition), Book II, chap. IV, § 6.

3. J. S. Mill, *Utilitarianism*, chap. II (pp. 8 f., in the Everyman edition). As a result, Mill's view is more like Eudæmonism than is Bentham's.

4. These illustrations have been taken from James MacKaye's *Logic of Conduct*, sessions 25 and 37. This book is the best defense of Utilitarianism advanced in our generation, so far as the author is aware. Professor MacKaye avoids the fallacies of the classical Utilitarians, and presents the case with cogency and clearness. *Cf.* also his *Economy of Happiness, Happiness of Nations*, and *Americanized Socialism*.

5. Professor James MacKaye (*op. cit.*) does not base his defense of Utilitarianism on psychological hedonism. Neither does Professor Ralph Mason Blake in several contributions to the *International Journal of Ethics*, 1926–1928.

6. Herbert Spencer, *Data of Ethics*, chaps. XI–XIV.

7. Mr. MacKaye affirms, apparently on intuitional grounds, that pleasure is good, and happiness is pleasure, meaning that each term is identical with the others. This seems to me to be an instance of the "naturalistic fallacy" pointed out by Mr. G. E. Moore in *Principia Ethica*. Mr. MacKaye, however, is completely satisfied with the identification. He thinks it logically follows that the accumulation of the greatest possible amount of happiness is of "maximum interest to mankind". To define the good in any other way, he thinks is "convictionism", and involves circular reasoning. (*Logic of Conduct*.)

8. Professor A. K. Rogers thinks it fatal to choose one's vocation from hedonistic considerations, and not from interest in the work itself and a sense of its value. Pleasure affords no principle for the intelligent direction of work. On the other hand, hedonism is a better guide in the selection of avocations and amusements. (*Theory of Ethics*, pp. 157 ff.)

9. For the casuistical illustrations discussed in this section, showing the comparative laxity of Utilitarianism, the author is chiefly indebted to Hastings Rashdall's *Theory of Good and Evil*, vol. I, chap. VII.

10. Perhaps the emancipation of the American negro slaves could be regarded as such. Everybody is now agreed that slavery was wrong. It has been argued that it is impossible to prove this by Utilitarian tests. Yet, even though negroes were happier while slaves than after they became free they lacked self-respect; they were mere means and not ends in themselves.

Christianity might be instanced as furnishing an argument for Eudæmonism rather than Utilitarianism. On Utilitarian grounds it could no doubt be shown that Christianity has in the long run made human life "happier" in the hedonistic sense. But few defenders of Christianity would claim that its principal service to mankind has been, or ought to have been, to increase the bulk of human pleasure. More important is the fact that Christianity has taught men to appreciate more and loftier virtues (such as "love" or charity in the Christian sense), and to strive more earnestly to attain them. Christianity makes divine grace available to men, and so enables them to lead more virtuous lives. Christianity has made men morally better. To make men morally better is more important than to make them happier.

CHAPTER XIV

1. A Utilitarian like John Stuart Mill who recognizes qualitative differences in pleasures differs less from Eudæmonism than the stricter hedonists who do not recognize them. Professor Durant Drake, although more orthodox than Mill in his hedonism (*Problems of Conduct*, pp. 139–144), calls his own position "eudæmonism" (*op. cit.*, p. 88). On the whole Professor Drake's position seems more like Utilitarianism than what is called Eudæmonism in the present volume.

2. We may suppose that the whole evolution of the Earth has been purposive or teleological. This, the author thinks, is the strongest argument for the existence of God. (*Cf. A Student's Philosophy of Religion*, chaps. XVIII, XIX.)

3. W. G. Everett, *Moral Values*, chap. VII. The comments in this section have been suggested in a general way by Professor Everett's discussion, although they differ in various details. *Cf.* also Hugo Münsterberg, *The Eternal Values*.

4. John Ruskin, *Unto this Last*, etc. *Cf.* F. W. Roe, *The Social Philosophy of Carlyle and Ruskin*, chap. VI, and J. A. Hobson, *John Ruskin, Social Reformer*, chap. II, and any of the biographies of Ruskin. John Dewey, *Experience and Nature*, chap. IX.

5. This seems to be part of Professor R. B. Perry's thesis that a value is "any object of any interest". (*General Theory of Value*, chap. V.)

6. William James, *Principles of Psychology*, vol. I, p. 311; *Briefer Course*, p. 187.

7. James Melvin Lee, *Business Ethics*, chap. VI, "Truth and Untruth in Business".

8. The undergraduate who is interested in the further study of values might be referred to chapters in Professor Everett's *Moral Values*, and Professor Bouglé's *Evolution of Values* (English translation by Mrs. Sellars). The more advanced student should take up Professor R. B. Perry's *General Theory of Value*, and the studies by Professor W. M. Urban in the *Journal of Philosophy*, vols. XIII, XIV, and the *Philosophical Review*, vols. XXXII, XXXIII.

CHAPTER XV

1. A famous phrase employed by Professor F. H. Giddings (*Principles of Sociology*, etc.).

2. Psychologists and anthropologists are not yet certain whether the native intelligence of some backward races will admit of much education. They should be given every opportunity to advance which they are capable of using, and which the taxable resources of the country can provide. Such books as Miss Katherine Mayo's *Mother India* and *The Isles of Fear*, while perhaps overdrawn, do not appear to have been successfully disputed so far as essential facts go; they abundantly establish the impossibility of full native self government in India and the Philippines in our time. *Cf.* Sir Valentine Chirol's authoritative work on *India* (London, 1926); Dean C. Worcester, *The Philippines, Past and Present* (New York, 1914); and Robert Watson Hart, *The Philippines To-day* (New York, 1928). Professor Walter Phelps Hall

in his *Empire to Commonwealth* shows the progress toward self government that has been made in the various portions of the British empire during the past thirty years.

3. The Mormons were compelled to abandon polygamy. Slavery and the liquor traffic were abolished by constitutional amendment without compensation to vested interests. Books and plays believed by public opinion to be indecent are forbidden. Revolutionists are not permitted to agitate for the overthrow of the government by violence. Labor leaders cannot publicly advocate violence in strikes, nor sabotage. Pacifists during war time have not been permitted to circulate propaganda whose effect would be liable to induce soldiers to desert, or otherwise to break down morale and make it more difficult for the nation to win. Other instances will occur to the reader, but they are all extreme cases.

4. The problem of sovereignty cannot be studied thoroughly except in connection with the general philosophy of the state. The advanced student may well begin with T. H. Green's *Principles of Political Obligation*, reading in connection with it the works of Hobbes, Spinoza, Locke, Rousseau, and Austin therein cited. This would give an excellent foundation without troubling with Kant and Hegel, who have said little of merit that has not been better said by Green. Next might be taken up Bernard Bosanquet's *Philosophical Theory of the State* and L. T. Hobhouse's *Metaphysical Theory of the State*. After getting the background of works like these, the student will be ready to consider the case for pluralism in Duguit's *Law in the Modern State* and one of H. J. Laski's books (*Studies in the Problem of Sovereignty, Authority in the Modern State, Grammar of Politics*). The most satisfactory solution of the problem of sovereignty, in the author's opinion, has been worked out by Professor R. M. MacIver (*The Modern State, Community,* etc.). *Cf.* also Norman Wilde, *Ethical Basis of the State;* H. Krabbe, *The Modern Idea of the State* (with an excellent introduction by the translators, G. H. Sabine and W. J. Shepard); W. A. Dunning, a series of volumes on the *History of Political Theories,* supplemented by the *Dunning Memorial Volume* edited by Merriam, especially Chap. III by F. W. Coker, giving a convenient account of recent pluralistic views. W. W. Willoughby in *An Examination of the Nature of the State* and *Fundamental Concepts of Public Law*, advances an important juristic theory of the state, which is ably criticized by his pupil, Johannes Mattern, in *State Sovereignty and International Law.*

5. The true philosophical view of natural rights seems to me best put by T. H. Green, *Principles of Political Obligation*. The various rights are treated in detail by Herbert Spencer, *Justice*. D. G. Ritchie (*Natural Rights*) shows the limitations of the doctrine.

6. Citizens have ground for complaint at the excessive length of ballots in some states, and in the frequency of minor elections. In rural New England too much time is demanded by town, precinct, and school meetings. After all, there is a limit to the amount of the citizen's time that the state has a moral right to claim for the performance of his political duties.

7. The duties of the citizen with reference to political parties are wisely discussed by Professor H. R. Bruce, *American Parties and Politics*, chap. XIX.

8. Dewey and Tufts, *Ethics*, see Index under "Freedom, formal and real."

9. A good summary will be found in L. T. Hobhouse's *Morals in Evolution*, Part I, chap. VI.

10. *Cf.* Robert H. Elder, "Trial by Jury; Is it Passing?" in *Harper's Magazine*, April, 1928.

11. Unless of course he is a member of a professional criminal organization, with financial resources and political influence.

12. Sturdy individualist as he was, Herbert Spencer thought that it should be the duty of the state to administer justice without cost in civil cases. (*Principles of Ethics*, vol. I, pp. 210 f.)

13. George Clarke Cox, *The Public Conscience*.

14. (*Cf.* chap. VIII, note 5, page 521 above.) Professor William McDougall says that the condition of the excitement of pugnacity is an obstruction to the activity of any of the other instincts; that its excitement is dependent upon or secondary to the excitement of other impulses. (*Social Psychology*, American revised edition, p. 62; older editions, pp. 59 f.)

15. Professor Edward Westermarck has established the fact that resentment is the psychological motive of punishment (*Origin and Development of Moral Ideas*, opening chapters). That moral judgments of college students regarding retributive punishment rest ultimately on resentment seems to be clearly indicated in a series of investigations by Professors F. C. Sharp and M. C. Otto, although these investigations were made with a different problem in mind. (*International Journal of Ethics*, vol. XX, pp. 341–357, 438–453. *Cf.* also Sharp's

A Study of the Influence of Custom on the Moral Judgment, and his recent text on *Ethics*.) Several points in this section have been developed at fuller length by the author in "The Psychology of Punitive Justice" (*Philosophical Review*, Nov. 1911).

16. W. R. George, *Citizens Made and Remade: an Interpretation of the Significance and Influence of the George Junior Republic*.

17. Thomas Mott Osborne, *Society and Prisons, Within Prison Walls*, etc.

18. Examples are Alfred E. Smith, Governor of New York and Democratic presidential candidate in 1928; Patrick Joseph Hayes and George William Mundelein, American Roman Catholic Cardinals.

19. Dewey and Tufts, *Ethics*, pp. 42, 44, 66.

20. *Cf.* Benjamin Kidd, *Principles of Western Civilization*, p. 156, and William McDougall, *Social Psychology*, revised ed., p. 296, older editions, p. 290.

21. William James, "The Moral Equivalent of War" in *Memories and Studies*.

22. The distinctions between virtuous nationalism, cosmopolitanism, and chauvinism are well brought out by Professor William McDougall in *Social and International Ideals*. Other phases of nationalism are also discussed by him in *The Indestructible Union, Is America Safe for Democracy?* and more profoundly in *The Group Mind*. The following works on nationalism represent various points of view:—W. B. Pillsbury, *Psychology of Nationality and Internationalism*. G. P. Gooch, *Nationalism*, and Ramsay Muir, *Nationalism and Internationalism*, two good brief historical sketches, the latter showing that nationalism has led to internationalism, and that opposition to the former has accompanied hostility to the latter. Rabindranath Tagore, *Nationalism*. C. C. Josey, *Race and National Solidarity*. John Oakesmith, *Race and Nationality*. C. J. Hayes, *Essays on Nationalism* (last chapter the best).

23. Professor Warner Fite's profound and eloquent *Moral Philosophy* pronounces all morality to consist chiefly in mutual understanding. Immorality is due to lack of understanding. This general doctrine seems very clearly applicable to relations between nations.

24. Some of the ideas in this section were advanced by the author more confidently in "Ethical Aspects of Internationalism", a paper published in the *International Journal of Ethics* in July, 1918.

CHAPTER XVI

1. Plato did this in the *Republic*, and More in *Utopia*.

2. The moral philosopher is ordinarily competent to consider only the very general aspects of the economic process. Many economic problems are too technical on the economic side for him to discuss at all intelligently; *e.g.*, the tariff, the banking system, regulation of the issue and sale of stocks and bonds, the settlement of international debts. Once the economic consequences of each policy proposed for the solution of such problems can be certainly forecast, the ethically preferable policy is likely to become obvious.

3. The National Bureau of Economic Research estimated the *per capita* income in the United States at $586 in 1918. It has been claimed that between 1 and 2% of the people in the United States own $\frac{1}{2}$ of the property and receive about 15% of the income. Over 85% of the population gainfully employed have incomes less than $2,000 per year. On the other hand, from $\frac{2}{3}$ to $\frac{3}{4}$ of the total national income goes to wages and salaries, while only $\frac{1}{3}$ to $\frac{1}{4}$ is paid to property (rent, interest, profits from risk). *Cf.* L. D. Edie, *The New Economics*, pp. 185 ff., and the references therein cited. Wesley C. Mitchell, et al., *Income in the United States*, Its Amount and Distribution, 1909–1918, vol. I (National Bureau of Economic Research). The more recent report of the Federal Trade Commission (69th Congress, first session, Senate Document No. 126) entitled *National Wealth and Income*, shows that the national income has been increasing; this study allots a smaller fraction of the national income to labor, because it reckons the entire income of a farmer, shopkeeper, or manufacturer, who works himself, as the product of capital.

4. This saying is credited to Simonides by Plato (*Republic*, Book I, 331). It appears in the introductory chapter of the *Institutes of Justinian*, where it is supposed to be quoted from Ulpian. (*Cf.* S. E. Mezes, *Ethics, Descriptive and Explanatory*, pp. 327 f.)

5. That there may be emergencies in which a person would be morally justified in taking the property of another will be conceded by most persons, only in extreme or in seemingly trivial cases. (*Cf.* F. C. Sharp, *Ethics*, pp. 24–29.)

6. John Locke, *Treatises of Government*, Book II, chap. V. (In vol. V of Locke's *Works*, edition of 1823.)

7. The right of bequest is limited. American laws assure a widow

some portion of her husband's estate regardless of his testament, usually by homestead and dower rights. French law does not permit a man to disinherit any of his children except for grave reasons. In all countries the state has the power to take a considerable portion of an estate in inheritance taxes.

8. The ethics of the "unearned increment" is not so simple as it seems at first glance. The general public is not an abiding corporate personality of such a nature that it can claim a right to increments in land values on the ground that it has exercised prudence, self-denial, or risk with reference to them. So far as anyone has a claim for these reasons, it is the holder of the land himself. If a city were to buy a tract of land, lay a boulevard through it, and sell the adjoining lots at a profit, the city would have a clear right to the increment; but unless cities are willing to run the risks of real estate speculation, have they a right to the profits? And how about the losses of those whose property declines in value through no fault of their own, as often happens in a large city? Should they receive compensation at public expense for the decrement? Can the community claim a share in all the profits in real estate investment, and yet expect individuals to bear all the losses? Henry George's doctrine is ably discussed from the ethical standpoint by Professor J. A. Ryan, *Distributive Justice*.

9. This phrase, as well as the general doctrine for which it stands, I owe to Hastings Rashdall, *Theory of Good and Evil*, vol. I, chap. VIII. I have applied the doctrine in my own way, not following Rashdall closely.

10. Few moral philosophers have ever defended aristocracy in this unqualified sense. Plato favored a privileged class of guardians because he believed that everybody in the state would benefit by their leadership. Nietzsche condemned Christianity and Utilitarianism because he thought that their influence, in preserving the weak, was resulting in the degeneration of Europe, in other words, in multiplying upon the planet an inferior type of human beings. He thought preference should be given to prototypes of supermen in order that the whole earth in the long run might be inhabited by a superior type of beings.

11. It is only when parents are vicious or totally incompetent that their children should be separated from them. Extreme poverty is not now regarded as a sufficient reason for breaking up a home. Social workers try to set a poor family on its feet economically, and not to disband it.

12. A collectivistic society would in some way have to provide special privileges to a class chosen in infancy to take the place of the present inheritors of property, and perform the functions of a leisure class.

13. Professor H. R. Seager says that of the 30 largest trusts organized prior to 1904, only half have proved successful. Trusts have many merits as well as defects. Government regulation is a policy preferable either to prohibition or government ownership. (*Principles of Economics*, third edition, chap. XXV.)

14. *Cf.* Mr. Whiting Williams, *Mainsprings of Men, What's on the Worker's Mind*, etc.

15. The officers of the Railway Brotherhoods and the American Federation of Labor are taking this stand. It has been well expressed by Mr. W. N. Doak, senior vice-president of the Brotherhood of Railway Trainmen, in "The Worker's Point of View of the Present Industrial Situation", published in the report of the Sixth Annual Y. M. C. A. Conference on Human Relations in Industry, at Estes Park, Colorado; July, 1926, pp. 35–74. See also references cited in note 24, below.

16. *Cf.* Mr. Whiting Williams, *Mainsprings of Men*, chap. III.

17. A good concise account of the Communist movement will be found in Mr. H. J. Laski's *Communism*. The classical works are Karl Marx' *Communist Manifesto* and *Capital;* these constitute the Bible of the movement. Among the authoritative Russian works are N. Lenin, *The State and Revolution*, N. Lenin and L. Trotzky, *The Proletarian Revolution*, and L. Trotzky, *Terrorism and Communism, Defence of Terrorism*, etc. A sympathetic characterization of the atmosphere of Russia under Communism is given by Miss Anna Louise Strong, *The First Time in History;* a scholarly economic interpretation has been furnished by Professor James Mavor, *The Russian Revolution*. On the Communistic movement in America, *cf.* James Oneal, *American Communism* (New York, 1927, Rand Book Store).

18. The stronger and more successful American labor unions have always had little sympathy with Socialism, and have found this agitation by a small but noisy Socialist minority a great deal of a nuisance. *Cf.* the autobiography of Samuel Gompers.

19. The literature of Socialism is voluminous. The following are representative of the best of it. I. B. Cross, *Essentials of Socialism*. H. W. Laidler, *Socialism in Thought and Action, A History of Socialist Thought*. J. Ramsay Macdonald, *The Socialist Movement*. H. G. Wells,

New Worlds for Old, The Open Conspiracy. Sidney and Beatrice Webb, *A Constitution for the Socialist Commonwealth of Great Britain, The Decay of Capitalist Civilization.* Graham Wallas, *The Great Society.* R. H. Tawney, *The Acquisitive Society.* Bertrand Russell, *Principles of Social Reconstruction, Proposed Roads to Freedom.* J. A. Hobson, *Work and Wealth.* W. H. Mallock, *A Critical Examination of Socialism.*

20. Alexander M. Bing, "The Wreck of the British Guilds" in *The Survey,* January, 1925, pp. 348 ff.

21. The best book on Guild Socialism is by Professor Niles Carpenter, *Guild Socialism,* a full exposition and fair criticism. The chief proponent of the movement is Mr. G. D. H. Cole, *Guild Socialism, Social Theory,* etc. The following treat of Syndicalism:—J. A. Estey, *Revolutionary Syndicalism.* L. Levine, *Syndicalism in France.* G. Sorel, *Reflections on Violence.* F. Brissenden, *The I. W. W., a Study of American Syndicalism.* J. G. Brooks, *American Syndicalism: the I. W. W.*

22. Mr. James Peter Warbasse, author of *Co-operative Democracy.* As a corrective, some more critical estimate of coöperation should be read with this book,—*e.g.,* F. W. Taussig, *Principles of Economics,* third edition, chap. 61. *Cf.* also Sidney and Beatrice Webb, *The Consumers' Co-operative Movement.*

23. Messrs. John Spargo, W. E. Walling, and other famous American proponents of Socialism before the war, seem to have forsaken the movement. *Cf.* "Where are the pre-War Radicals?" in the *Survey,* vol. 55, pp. 556 ff.

24. Professor T. N. Carver, *The Present Economic Revolution in the United States. Cf.* Mr. David F. Houston, "Every Worker a Capitalist" in *World's Work,* January, 1925. Mr. Warren N. Stone, president of the Brotherhood of Locomotive Engineers, agrees with Professor Carver that the American labor movement is advancing toward a system of coöperation rather than war, and that it is far in advance of that in any other country ("Labor's Chain of Banks", in *World's Work,* November, 1924). Mr. Ramsay Muir, a British observer who has recently visited America seems to agree with this point of view, in his *America the Golden.*

25. *Cf.* W. K. Wright, "Private Property and Social Justice", in the *International Journal of Ethics,* July, 1915, reprinted in part by J. H. Wigmore, *Rational Basis of Legal Institutions,* chap. XXIX.

26. My attention was first called to this comparison by Professor James H. Tufts.

CHAPTER XVII

1. C. F. Tauesch, *Professional and Business Ethics*, pp. 78–83. Professor Tauesch has in recent years also contributed several articles on various phases of professional ethics to the *International Journal of Ethics*.

2. Rev. S. Z. Batten, D. D., in "The Ethics of the Ministry", in C. L. King's *Ethics of the Professions and Business*, p. 147.

3. *Cf.* the "Code of Ethics" of the Pennsylvania State Education Association, 1920, in King, *op. cit.*, p. 272, § V (c).

4. C. T. Taeusch, *op. cit.*, pp. 54 f.; 64–66.

5. The works by Heermance, King, and Lee (given in the list of References at the end of the chapter), contain some of these codes, and give references to sources where others can be found.

6. "Principles of Medical Ethics" of the American Medical Association, adopted in 1912; given by C. L. King, *op. cit.*, pp. 260 ff.

7. "Canons of Ethics for Lawyers", adopted by the American Bar Association in 1908. In C. L. King, *op. cit.*, pp. 254 ff.

8. Given by C. L. King, *op. cit.*, pp. 223–228.

9. E. L. Heermance, *The Ethics of Business*, chaps. I, II.

10. Daniel Starch, *Principles of Advertising*, pp. 56 ff.

11. Heermance, *op. cit.*, pp. 51–55.

12. *Cf.* F. C. Sharp, "The Ethics of the Competitive System" in Wigmore's *Rational Basis of Legal Institutions*, p. 71, which was originally published under the title "Some Problems of Fair Competition" in the *International Journal of Ethics*, Jan., 1921.

13. Vocational psychology is still in its infancy, and has a long way to travel before it will be a science whose conclusions are not subject to a considerable margin of probable error.

CHAPTER XVIII

1. It is true that the ideal of monogamic marriage is not rooted in biological functions, but is a social product, as Mr. Robert Briffault says. (*The Mothers*, especially chaps. X, XXX.) But my statements here, I think, are also true.

2. John Fiske, *Outlines of Cosmic Philosophy*, see Index under "Infants".

3. Edward Westermarck, *History of Human Marriage*, fifth ed., vol. I, pp. 31–36. Not all apes mate in pairs, some are polygamous.

4. Westermarck, *op. cit.*, chaps. III, IV.

5. Westermarck, *op. cit.*, chap. XXXI. B. Spencer and F. J. Gillen, *The Native Tribes of Central Australia. The Northern Tribes of Central Australia.*

6. In this section I have been influenced mostly by the convenient and reliable summary by Professor L. T. Hobhouse, *Morals in Evolution*, Part I, chaps. IV, V. The chief standard authorities are Westermarck, *op. cit.* (best on origins and primitive peoples), and G. E. Howard, *History of Matrimonial Institutions* (best on marriage under civilization). A more recent authority is Robert Briffault, *The Mothers* (3 vols., Macmillan, 1927). For the Romans, see James Bryce, *Essays in History and Jurisprudence.* For the period from Augustus to Charlemagne, W. E. H. Lecky's *History of European Morals* is still a standard authority.

7. Except possibly in Egypt and Babylonia in early periods.

8. There was no legal and little moral condemnation of abortion, infanticide, and acts of sexual perversion. Men felt little moral obligation to be continent outside the marriage relation. The excavations at Pompeii reveal much obscenity and prostitution. There was a great deal of legislation during the early Roman empire against adultery; *prima facie* evidence that there was need of it, and also that the moral consciousness was sufficiently sound to enact it.

9. Hobhouse cites evidence for this statement; *op. cit.*, pp. 211 f.

10. In fact, the churches seem to have favored this development. They took St. Paul literally. (See chap. VI above, pages 141 f.)

11. *Cf.* Hobhouse, *op. cit.*, one volume edition, pp. 219 ff., containing the frequently quoted statement of Blackstone.

12. Mary Wollstonecraft, *Vindication of the Rights of Woman.* John Stuart Mill, *The Subjection of Women.* W. R. Waterman, *Frances Wright.* Other early advocates of the rights of women are mentioned by G. E. Howard, *History of Matrimonial Institutions*, vol. III, pp. 237 ff.

13. For an account of these, see H. Baker-Crothers and Ruth Hudnut, *Problems of Citizenship*, chaps. XIII–XV.

14. Helen Bradford Thompson, *Psychological Norms in Men and Women*, republished as *The Mental Traits of Sex.*

15. An expression employed by Professor Hobhouse, *op. cit.*, one vol. ed., pp. 231 f.

16. Some physicians advise occasional auto-erotism in such cases.

Cf. W. F. Robie, *Rational Sex Ethics*, chaps. III, IV; and *Sex and Life*, pp. 231–237, 259–270.

17. The Freudian psychology and the Œdipus complex need be heeded only as they may serve as a warning against the son whose mother is too devoted to him and consequently has spoiled him.

18. There are cases in which it would be expedient for a young couple to marry with the understanding that the wife will continue to support herself at her own vocation for a year or two, if there is reasonable certainty that it will not be necessary indefinitely. But marriages so planned are more or less hazardous; a girl should not enter one without taking the advice of her parents and more mature friends.

19. "Trial marriages" are advocated by Mrs. E. C. Parsons (*The Family*, and articles in the *International Journal of Ethics*, vol. XXIV, XXV—the latter republished, with omissions, by J. H. Wigmore, *Rational Basis of Legal Institutions*). Companionate marriages are proposed by Judge Ben B. Lindsey and Wainwright Evans in *Companionate Marriage*, who insist that upon their plan marriages would be entered with the expectation of permanence, but their arguments do not appear convincing to the critical reader.

20. Such novels as Mrs. Humphry Ward's *Daphne, or Marriage à la Mode* and Mrs. Edith Wharton's *The Children* show how the privilege of divorce can be abused under present conditions. Such abuses would be the rule rather than the exception under a system of free love, trial or companionate marriages, or divorce by mutual consent.

21. In a few American "states" divorces are granted on rather slight grounds, although not so trivial as newspaper reports might lead readers to suppose. A convenient summary of the grounds on which divorce is permitted, together with marriage laws, etc., in most of the countries of the world, as well as the American "states", will be found in *An International Year Book of Child Care and Protection*. The edition of 1924, which is before me, is edited by Edward Fuller, and published by Longmans, Green & Co., London.

22. Eighty per cent of American divorce suits are uncontested. In these the courts ordinarily have only the evidence submitted by the applicant. It is therefore difficult for them to prevent collusion between plaintiff and defendant, which, when it occurs, almost amounts to divorce by mutual consent. A few American "states" grant divorces on grounds that seem notoriously insufficient to the rest of the country. In Nevada in a recent year out of 613 divorces granted all but 88 were

to persons who had come to the "state" for the purpose. There is great lack of uniformity between the divorce laws of different "states". An enterprising man, not adverse to travel, could accumulate seven different wives in as many different "states" without breach of law so as to subject himself to criminal process. That is not likely to happen. But it is a grave injustice that families moving from one "state" to another may find marriages illegal and children illegitimate. Attempts have been made to try to secure uniform legislation by the different "states"; but it is practically impossible to induce 48 different legislatures to pass identical statutes. An amendment to the federal constitution was introduced by Senator Capper in 1924 at the instance of the General Federation of Women's Clubs, which would enable Congress to pass uniform laws for the whole country on marriage, divorce, the legitimation of children, and the care and custody of children when affected by divorce. The Women's Clubs also prepared a bill providing for the legislation that they would advocate, should such a constitutional amendment make it possible. *Cf.* Judge Robert Grant, "Marriage and Divorce" in the *Yale Review*, Jan., 1925. On the constitutional amendment and bill referred to, *cf.* Willystine Goodsell, *Problems of the Family*, pp. 391 ff., and the *Journal of Social Hygiene*, vol. 9, March, 1923, pp. 170–173.

23. When a person announces his or her engagement to friends, the latter out of courtesy often feel bound to offer congratulations or felicitations. Deterrent advice at that time would probably be resented, and in any event would not be likely to have much weight.

24. W. I. Thomas, *Sex and Society*, pp. 223–247.

25. A comparatively mild presentation of the radical point of view is given by H. Baker-Crothers and Ruth Hudnut, *Problems of Citizenship*, chap. XVI.

26. Accounts of such legislation will be found in the publications of the Children's Bureau of the United States Department of Labor.

27. Birth control, by methods advised by the family physician, will keep children from coming too fast for her to give them proper care, or becoming a burden to her.

28. Counsel regarding birth control should be given by physicians in personal interviews at free clinics, every precaution being taken to see that the advice is understood, and that it is suited to the particular case. At least this much must be conceded to Mrs. Margaret Sanger (*Motherhood in Bondage*).

29. There are a few girls whose training before marriage has not given them a sufficient sense of responsibility to be trusted in this way, as instanced in H. G. Wells' novel, *Marriage;* but such girls are, I think, rare in America.

30. Once in a long while there may be a family in which the wife is the proper wage earner, and the husband a born home maker, as imagined in Mrs. Dorothy Canfield Fisher's novel, *The Home Maker.*

31. *Cf.* Alice Ames Winter, *The Business of Being a Club Woman*, who enumerates "a partial list of suggestive constructive things accomplished by various women's clubs", pp. 147–151. There are 125 items in the list, and all of them must have been of substantial service to the individuals and communities in whose behalf they were undertaken.

32. Notwithstanding all that has been said in this chapter, the author is willing to concede that women are at a disadvantage in some ways as compared with men, in that as a rule it is impossible for them to marry and continue to give as undivided attention to vocations outside of the home as men can do. But the responsibility for this does not rest with the male sex, nor with human institutions and customs. Injustices due to the latter causes in past ages have now mostly been removed in free countries. The physiological relation of a mother to her child necessitates her presence in the home if the child is to have proper nurture and care. Married women whose first duties are to their homes cannot usually be so efficient in business and industry as their brothers and unmarried sisters; employers are not to blame for this inevitable fact. For the other side of the argument, *cf.* Willystine Goodsell, *Problems of the Family*, chap. XVI–XVIII.

CHAPTER XIX

1. *Cf.* G. E. Moore, *Principia Ethica*, and chap. XI, section I, above.

2. Professor A. P. Brogan believes that the other intuitions can be reduced to "better", which is therefore the "fundamental value universal". See note 4, chap. XI, above. He has put his theory to work in numerous empirical investigations reported in the *International Journal of Ethics*, beginning with the issue of January, 1923.

3. This statement is subject to the further qualifications suggested by the comments regarding punishment of the partially insane in Chapter XV (page 380).

4. There never has been a satisfactory elementary presentation of Absolute Idealism. Perhaps the closest approximation is Professor R. F. Hoernlé's *Idealism as a Philosophy*. Classical presentations of a semi-popular character are Josiah Royce's *Spirit of Modern Philosophy* and *Religious Aspect of Philosophy*. Among the more technical works are: T. H. Green, *Prolegomena to Ethics*. F. H. Bradley, *Appearance and Reality, Ethical Studies*. Bernard Bosanquet, *Principle of Individuality and Value*, and *Value and Destiny of the Individual*. A. E. Taylor, *Elements of Metaphysics*, and *Problem of Conduct*.

5. The most eminent recent representatives of this general standpoint have perhaps been the late Professor James Ward (*The Realm of Ends*), and Professor W. R. Sorley (*Moral Values and the Idea of God*). American exponents are Professors Mary W. Calkins ("The Personalistic Conception of Nature" in the *Philosophical Review*, vol. XXVIII, 1919), and Warner Fite (*Moral Philosophy, Individualism*). The late Professor Borden P. Bowne (*Personalism*, etc.), founded a school of Personalism, in which Professors E. S. Brightman (*Religious Values, A Philosophy of Ideals*, etc.), A. C. Knudson (*Philosophy of Personalism*), and R. T. Flewelling (*Reason in Faith*) are eminent. The last named is editor of the *Personalist*, a journal devoted to the interests of the school.

6. James gave the credit for the origin of Pragmatism to Charles Pierce from whom he borrowed the word. But Pierce repudiated the type of philosophy which James made famous as Pragmatism, and renamed his own position "Pragmaticism".

7. Professor John Dewey is the most eminent living American Pragmatist. Technically his type of Pragmatism is known as Instrumentalism. Among his popular works are *Reconstruction in Philosophy*, and *Human Nature and Conduct*. His chief work dealing with metaphysics is *Experience and Nature*. Dr. F. C. S. Schiller's *Riddle of the Sphinx* is the most comprehensive semi-popular discussion of metaphysics by a Pragmatist. Other of his works are *Humanism, New Studies in Humanism*, and *Formal Logic*. Professor A. W. Moore has defended Pragmatism in *Pragmatism and its Critics*. Professor E. S. Ames has defended religion, from the standpoint of Pragmatism (*Psychology of Religious Experience, The New Orthodoxy*, etc.); while Professor M. C. Otto has attacked it (*Things and Ideals*). William James' *Pragmatism* and *Meaning of Truth* are good volumes with which to begin on Pragmatism, but the student will not get far unless he

reads some of the above works also. The best critical history of Pragmatism is by Professor Emmanuel Leroux, *Le Pragmatisme Américain et Anglais* (Paris, Alcan, 1923).

8. Practically every European philosopher prior to Berkeley († 1752) was in some sense or other a realist. Idealism in the technical sense is chiefly a nineteenth century product, beginning in Germany shortly after the death of Kant in 1804.

9. The best popular introduction to contemporary Realism of which the author knows is Professor R. W. Sellars' *Principles and Problems of Philosophy*. More technical but clear discussions are Professor W. P. Montague's *Ways of Knowing*, and Professor E. G. Spaulding's *The New Rationalism*. On the ethical side, noteworthy are Mr. G. E. Moore's *Principia Ethica* and his briefer but not less technical *Ethics;* as well as Professor R. B. Perry's popular *Moral Economy*, and technical *General Theory of Value*. *Cf.* also Professor E. B. Holt's *The Freudian Wish*. The Critical New Realists a few years ago issued a series of *Essays in Critical Realism*, edited by Professor Durant Drake. More recently Professors Drake, A. K. Rogers, J. B. Pratt, and G. Santayana have elaborated their own positions in independent volumes.

10. Although altogether inadequate, I hope this will not appear a misleading characterization of the subtle position of Professor E. G. Spaulding (*The New Rationalism*).

11. The most important work on Emergent Evolution is Professor S. Alexander's *Space, Time and Deity*. Professor C. Lloyd Morgan makes the *nisus* God, and is in general favorable to the ordinary conceptions of religion (*Emergent Evolution; Life, Mind and Spirit*). Among American Emergent Evolutionists attention should be called to Professors R. W. Sellars (*Evolutionary Naturalism*), and J. E. Boodin (*Cosmic Evolution*).

12. *Cf.* W. K. Wright, *A Student's Philosophy of Religion*, pp. 255 f., 280–284, 304, 340–344, 388–390, 402–410.

13. Professor L. J. Henderson, *The Fitness of the Environment, The Order of Nature*, and an article in the *Philosophical Review*, vol. XXVII.

14. *Cf.* Professor W. R. Sorley, *Moral Values and the Idea of God*, pp. 76–79, 116–129.

15. *Cf.* Professor R. F. A. Hoernlé, *Idealism as a Philosophy*, pp. 312–316. Attempts to bring this type of philosophy more into harmony with ordinary religious and ethical aspirations have been made by Professor A. S. Pringle-Pattison (*The Idea of God in the Light of Recent*

Philosophy), and still more, by Professor Clement C. J. Webb (*God and Personality, Divine Personality and Human Life*, "Outline of a Philosophy of Religion" in *Contemporary British Philosophy*, second series, edited by Muirhead).

16. It is sometimes said, as by Professor Sorley (*op. cit.*), that though the earth is not perfectly adapted for human happiness it is admirably suited to develop character and fortitude. But it would be hard to show that there is complete correlation between terrestrial arrangements and the perfecting of human character. The most that could be argued would be that the general arrangement of things gives the majority of people a favorable environment in which to develop their characters. Granting this, for the sake of argument, it would imply a limited God, who with the material at hand—matter and energy—developed as favorable a world as conditions made practicable.

17. I owe this illustration to a paper, which I think has not been published, by Professor W. H. Sheldon.

18. Chiefly in his posthumous *Three Essays on Religion*, and *Autobiography*.

19. *The Will to Believe*, p. 61; *The Varieties of Religious Experience*, p. 519; *Pragmatism*, pp. 72, 80; *A Pluralistic Universe*, pp. 310 f., 318.

20. The doctrine has been defended in diverse forms by Professor L. T. Hobhouse (closing pages of *Development and Purpose*), and the late Dean Hastings Rashdall (*Theory of Good and Evil*, pp. 211–246, 286–294, 335–356; and "Personality, Human and Divine" in *Personal Idealism*, edited by Henry Sturt). Mr. H. G. Wells has made it widely known but without doing it justice, in his well intended but philosophically crude *God the Invisible King*. Still more crude are the naïve forms of the conception justly attacked by Professor M. C. Otto, in his *Things and Ideals*. My own version will be found in various sections with the caption "The Author's Opinions" in Part III of *A Student's Philosophy of Religion*.

INDEX

INDEX

Abbott, F. F., 509
Absolute, the, 188, 482
Academy of Plato, 113 f.
Acquisitive impulse, 203.
Adler, A., 521
Æsthetics, 211 f., 340, 344 f., 348 f.
Affection, 261 f.
Agape, 139
Agriculture, 369, 410
Albee, E. A., 194, 333, 518
Alexander, A. B. D., 164
Alexander, S., 545
Alexander the Great, 73, 98, 105, 116
Allport, F. H., 520 f., 522
America, United States of. See United States of America.
Anger, 201
Anglo-Catholics, 155, 163
Alter, 257
Altruism, 151, 238, 322. See Benevolence, Charity, Love.
Ames, E. S., viii, 544
Amos, 72, 79, 80
Angell, J. R., viii, 525
Animals, 331
Antisthenes, 113, 125
Antoninus, Marcus Aurelius, 102, 126 f.
Antoninus Pius, 126 ff.
Apatheia, 125
Appetites, 199
Aquinas. See Thomas Aquinas.
Aristippus, 113
Aristocracy, 93 f., 100, 121
Aristotle, 8, 116–122, 151
Arnold, E. V., 513
Arnold, Matthew, 134, 510
Arnold, W. T., 509
Art, 39, 52, 66, 69, 93, 96, 212, 344 f., 348 f.

Athens, 94 ff., 108
Athletics, 211, 339
Ataraxia, 123
Augustine of Hippo, 151, 342, 384
Augustus Cæsar, 101
Aurelius, Marcus. See Antoninus, Marcus Aurelius.
Australia, aborigines of, 27 f., 51
Authority, relation of, 33–40, 59 ff., 67, 69, 77 ff., 92, 98 f., 101, 383
Autonomy, Kant's doctrine of, 308–311
Axioms, ethical, 291 f.

Baals, 72, 76
Bacon, B. W., 163
Bacon, Francis, 169
Baker-Crothers. See Crothers.
Baldwin, J. M., 505
Baptism, 147
Barbarians, 105, 121, 129 ff., 139
Batten, S. Z., 539
Bayet, A., 163
Beauty, 348 f.
Benevolence, 121, 238, 240. See Love, Charity.
Benjamites, 75
Bentham, J., 131, 185, 318, 328, 332, 526, 529
Bergson, H., 527
Berkeley, G., 482
Bernard, L. L., 520
Bernays, E. L., 444
Binder, R. M., 444
Bing, A. M., 538
Birth control, 542
Bizzell, W. B., 87
Boodin, J. E., 545
Bosanquet, B., 189, 471, 482, 519, 532
Botsford, G. W., 509

549